THE PLANNERS GUIDE TO
COMMUNITYVIZ

THE ESSENTIAL TOOL FOR A NEW GENERATION OF PLANNING

Also by Tom Daniels:

Small Town Planning Handbook, 3rd edition (Tom Daniels, senior author)
When City and Country Collide: Managing Growth in the Metropolitan Fringe
Environmental Planning Handbook: For Sustainable Communities and Regions, with Katherine Daniels
Holding Our Ground: Protecting America's Farms and Farmlands, with Deborah Bowers

THE PLANNERS GUIDE TO
COMMUNITY VIZ

THE ESSENTIAL TOOL FOR A NEW GENERATION OF PLANNING

Doug Walker and
Tom Daniels

An Orton Family Foundation Book

American Planning Association
Planners Press

Making Great Communities Happen

Chicago | Washington, D.C.

© 2011 the Orton Family Foundation

Published by the American Planning Association

205 N. Michigan Ave., Suite 1200, Chicago, IL 60601-5927
1030 15th St., NW, Suite 750 West, Washington, DC 20005-1503

www.planning.org/plannerspress

CommunityViz is a product of Placeways LLC, which developed it with the support of the Orton Family Foundation. The American Planning Association (APA) is not affiliated with the Orton Family Foundation or Placeways LLC. APA does not explicitly or implicitly endorse or otherwise support CommunityViz above or instead of any other planning-related software or tools.

ISBN: 978-1-932364-93-4 (pbk.)

Library of Congress Control Number 2010919603

Printed in the United States of America

All rights reserved

If you are new to CommunityViz, we encourage you to visit the website for video demos and other interactive educational materials.

http://placeways.com/communityviz

Photo Credits

Chapter 1 Section opener courtesy of MAPSUP™ Digital Interactive Map Support

CONTENTS

Preface: The New Generation of Planning	xiii
Introduction: Communities, Planning, and CommunityViz	xvi
Computers and Planning	xvi
A New Generation of Planning	xvii
What CommunityViz Does	xvii
CommunityViz Roots and Development	xviii
CommunityViz and All Kinds of Planning	xviii
The Orton Family Foundation's Heart & Soul Planning Philosophy	xxi
Practical Benefits of New Generation Planning	xxi
How to Use This Book	xxii
Special Terms	xxiv
CommunityViz: An Overview	**xxv**
Scenario 360	xxv
Common Applications	xxvii
Integration with ArcGIS	xxvii
3-D Visualization within Scenario 360	xxvii
Scenario 3D	xxvii
Scenario 3D Exporter and Viewer	xxvii

I. FOUNDATIONS — 1

Chapter 1: Getting Started	**4**
Define Your Study Area	4
Create an Area Profile	5
Identify Problems and Forces of Change	6
Identify Key People and Organizations	7
Describe Decisions That Need to Be Made and Questions to Answer	8
The CommunityViz Project Framework for Decision Making	8
The Difference Between Decisions and Information	10
Describe Goals	10
Chapter 2: Technical Needs and Data Resources for CommunityViz	**11**
Computing Resources and Technical Staff	11
Data Resources	12
Data Best Practices and Ethics	12
Experts, Specialized Models, and Crowds	13
Chapter 3: Planning Study Design Guidelines	**15**
About Scenario Planning	15
How Scenario Planning Principles Influence Project Design	18
Geodesign and Making Decisions without Scenarios	18
Project Practicalities	19
Time and Budget	19
Trade-Offs and Limitation of Feasible Planning Projects	20
Analysis Design	21
Iterative Design	23
Design for Transparency	23

Multimedia Design	24
Visualization Priorities	25
Technology Selection	26
Communication Design	26
Design for a Living Comprehensive Plan	26

Chapter 4: Custom Impact Models and Analysis — 28

Why and When	28
Types of Impact Models and How to Create Them	28
Rate-Based Impact Models	29
Coefficient-Based Impact Models	30
Spatially Dependent Impact Models	31
External Models	31
How to Choose a Model	31
Creating a Custom Analysis	32
Technical Section: Dynamic Analysis in Scenario 360	32
Dynamic Attributes	32
Indicators	33
Assumptions	34
Scenarios	34
Setup Tools	35

Chapter 5: Three-Dimensional Scenes — 36

Why and When	36
Choosing a 3-D Platform	36
How 3-D Works	37
Partly Transparent Textures	38
Shadows and Lighting	38
Active Materials	39
How a 3-D Scene Is Built	39
Creating a 3-D Scene	40
Get Data	41
Create a Base Model	42
Model Development Proposals or Scenarios	43
Create Presentation Aids	44
Special Considerations for Metro and Regional Models	44
Teaching Example	45

Chapter 6: Getting the Most from 3-D — 50

The Art of Making Effective 3-D Scenes	50
Providing Good Information	50
Making the Computer-to-Real-World Connection	50
Enhancing Subjective Feel	51
Solutions to Common Challenges	52
Soft Features	52
Numerous Features	52
Large Areas	53
Uneven Terrain	54
Choosing Accessories	54
Conclusion	54
CASE STUDIES: Klamath River, California and Oregon;	55
Manchester, Vermont	57

II. COMMUNITY VISIONING, VALUES, AND GROWTH PROJECTIONS   61

Chapter 7: Visioning   63
Why and When   63
Beginning the Visioning Project   64
Assessing the Current Situation   64
Scenario Building   65
    Low-Tech Visioning   65
    Scenarios Created by the Public   66
    Scenarios Created Internally   67
    Best Practices for Creating Scenarios   67
Selecting a Preferred Scenario   67
Implementation Plan   68
Teaching Example   68

CASE STUDY: Metropolitan Boston, Massachusetts   72

Chapter 8: Growth Projections   75
Land Use Designer   75
Build-Out Wizard   76
    Build-Out Steps   78
    Density Rules   79
    Commercial Buildings   79
    Keeping Perspective   79
TimeScope   80
Allocator   81
External Models   81
Combining Growth-Planning Decision Tools   82
Data Needs and Sources   82
Teaching Example   83

CASE STUDY: Middlebury, Vermont   87

Chapter 9: Value Mapping and Special Places   90
Value Mapping   90
    Why and When   90
    Articulating Core Values   90
    Value Mapping Steps   90
    Making a Value Tree   91
    Value Elements   92
    Value Drivers   92
    Physical Form   93
    CommunityViz Value Indexes   93
    Using Value Mapping   94
Mapping Special Places   94

CASE STUDIES: Allegheny County, Pennsylvania;   95
                    Exeter, Rhode Island   98

III. MAKING PLANS — 101

Chapter 10: Local Comprehensive Plans — 104
Why and When — 104
Data Needs — 104
Describing Current Conditions — 106
Creating Scenarios — 106
Modeling Impacts — 107
Engaging the Public — 108
Teaching Example — 109

CASE STUDIES: Durango, Colorado; — 115
Mooresville, North Carolina — 118

Chapter 11: Regional Land-Use and Transportation Plans — 121
Why and When — 121
Data Needs — 121
CommunityViz Tools — 123
  Analysis Templates — 123
  Scale-Changing Formula Functions — 123
  Sketch Tools — 125
  Linking to External Models — 125
  Analysis Grids — 125
Teaching Example — 127

CASE STUDIES: Greater Nashville, Tennessee; — 131
Washington County, Utah — 133

Chapter 12: Site Selection and Assessment — 135
Why and When — 135
Suitability Concepts — 136
CommunityViz Tools for Suitability Analysis — 137
  Suitability Wizard — 137
  Nested Suitability — 138
  Categories — 138
  Alerts — 138
  Assumptions and Charts — 138
  Symbology Tools — 139
Scoring Systems for Centers and Neighborhoods — 139
Teaching Example — 141

CASE STUDIES: Squamish, British Columbia, Canada; — 144
Calumet County, Wisconsin — 147

Chapter 13: Resource Plans — 149
Data Needs and Sources — 149
  Working with Raster Data — 150
Valuing Resources — 151
Conditions and Targets — 151
  Assessing Implementation Strategies — 152

CommunityViz Tools		152
Scientific Modeling		152
Evaluation of BMPs		153
Optimizer		153
LandFrag Wizard		154
Teaching Example		154
CASE STUDIES:	Topsham, Maine;	158
	Delmarva Peninsula, Delaware, Maryland, and Virginia	160

IV. REVIEWING REGULATIONS AND DEVELOPMENT PROPOSALS — 163

Chapter 14: Analyzing Zoning Regulations — 166
Why and When — 166
Data Needs — 166
Zoning Development Capacity Analysis Using the Build-Out Wizard — 166
Zoning Development Capacity Calculations Outside the Build-Out Wizard — 170
Estimating Capacity Utilization — 171
Teaching Example — 171

Chapter 15: Cost-of-Services Analyses, Capital Improvements, and Pro Formas — 176
Data Needs and Sources — 177
Setting up a Cost-of-Services Analysis — 177
Using a Cost-of-Services Analysis — 179
Analyzing Subdivision and Land-Development Regulations — 179
Pro Forma Analyses — 180
Teaching Example — 180

Chapter 16: Design Review and Form-Based Codes — 185
About 3-D Modeling for Design Reviews and Form-Based Codes — 185
Using 3-D for Design Review — 187
    Modeling Proposals for Design Review — 187
    Displaying the Scene — 187
Using 3-D for Drafting and Applying Form-Based Codes — 188
Indicators for Design Review and Form-Based Codes — 189
    Site-Specific Indicators — 189
    Comparative Community Indicators — 189
Teaching Example — 190

CASE STUDY: Westminster, Colorado — 194

V. COMMUNICATING AND INTERACTING 197

Chapter 17: Public Meetings, Presentations, and Charrettes 198

Why and When	198
Public Meetings	199
Charrettes	199
Presentation Techniques and Best Practices	202
Designing the Analysis	202
Understanding the Audience	202
Designing the Display	203
Speaking with CommunityViz	204
Venue and Logistics	205
Presenting 3-D Scenes	206
Keypads and Online Polling	207
CommunityViz in Workgroups	209
Workgroup Learning Curves	209
Introducing Interactive Capabilities to Workgroups	210
Best Practices for Using CommunityViz with Workgroups	210
CASE STUDIES: Fort Lupton, Colorado;	212
Northern Rocky Mountains, Idaho, Montana, Wyoming, and Alberta and British Columbia, Canada	214

Chapter 18: Reports, Displays, and Websites 216

Reporting and Display Features	216
Reporting and Display Best Practices	216
Images of 3-D Scenes	218
Project Website	218
Web-Ready Reports	218
Website Images and Data	218
WebShots Wizard	220
3-D Scenes on the Web	220
Sharing a Complete Analysis on the Web	221
More Web Options	222

Chapter 19: Beyond Planning Projects 223

Anticipating Planning Problems	223
Connecting Plans to Day-to-Day Processes	224
Supporting Other Departments	225

APPENDICES — 228

Appendix 1: When and How to Get Help — 228
Readiness Self-Assessment — 228
- CommunityViz Skills — 228
- Technical Environment — 228
- Organizational Readiness — 228
- Partners and Collaborators — 228
- Modeling Skills and Resources — 229

Staffing for CommunityViz — 229
Working with Consultants — 229
CommunityViz Resources — 230

Appendix 2: Data Management — 231
Data Management Best Practices for Analysis — 231
Data Management Best Practices for 3-D Visualization — 232
Using Data from Multiple Sources — 232

Appendix 3: Performance — 234
Analysis Performance — 234
3-D Performance — 235

Appendix 4: Data Sources — 238

Appendix 5: CommunityViz Features — 243
Scenario 360 Features — 243
- Integration with ArcGIS — 243
- 3-D Visualization — 243
- Dynamic Charts — 243
- Scenarios — 243
- Decision Tools — 244
- Interactive Analysis and Modeling — 245
- Communication and Engagement — 247

Scenario 3D Features — 248
- Scenario 3D Exporter — 249
- Scenario 3D Viewer — 250

Contacts — 251

References — 253

Glossary — 254

Acknowledgments — 263

Index — 264

PREFACE: THE NEW GENERATION OF PLANNING

An exciting approach to community planning is emerging thanks to advances in computer software and a greater emphasis on public participation in the planning process. Planners can now blend information about a community with public values to create more effective plans and elected officials can make better, more informed decisions to shape change in their community. The combination of high-tech tools with more collaboration among community residents, planners, and elected officials is the new generation of planning.

CommunityViz and Geographic Information Systems (GIS) have become essential tools for planning and design in the 21st century. CommunityViz is a GIS-based software program with a remarkably wide variety of planning applications. For instance, CommunityViz allows planners to compile, analyze, and understand large amounts of data in order to draft "living" comprehensive plans that communities will actually implement. Planners can also use CommunityViz to conduct build-out and growth studies to estimate the pace and location of new development over time. CommunityViz's powerful visualization tools can depict proposed developments so that planners, elected officials, and the public understand neighborhood contexts and visual impacts, and suggest changes before developments are built. In short, CommunityViz allows planners to organize, analyze, and display a large amount of information; planners, citizens, and elected officials can use this information to make more effective comprehensive plans and more informed day-to-day decisions about the type, style, density, and location of new development.

CommunityViz embodies two important beliefs about planning: 1) greater public involvement in planning leads to better decisions about land-use patterns, development design, and the retention of the community's heart-and-soul assets—those special characteristics and places that local residents hold dear; and 2) more transparency in the planning process builds community trust and leads to more durable plans, effective land-use controls, and wise infrastructure investment.

There are two general kinds of community planning: technical and political. Technical planning involves gathering, analyzing, and presenting information about a site, neighborhood, city, or region. Technical planning appears to be straightforward: either the information exists or it doesn't. Yet, understanding and conveying what the information means requires knowledge about planning as well as communication skills. CommunityViz helps planners, residents, and elected officials to marshal facts about the existing conditions in the community and to present those facts in readily understandable charts, graphs, maps, and 3-D scenarios.

Another aspect of technical planning is identifying and projecting trends into the future. If it appears that the trends will not produce desirable outcomes, then a new comprehensive plan implemented through updated land-use regulations, new infrastructure investment, revised design guidelines, or financial incentives can influence the trends to produce better outcomes. The analysis of trends naturally leads to visioning: what changes would the residents of the community like to see over the next 20 years? What would further the town's heart and soul assets? Planners can use CommunityViz to illustrate likely development build-outs over time and to create alternative future scenarios based on different assumptions. Ultimately, community residents will select a preferred scenario, which will then become the basis for the goals and objectives of the comprehensive plan. In turn, the comprehensive plan will set the legal foundation for the zoning ordinance and subdivision regulations, and provide guidance for public infrastructure investment.

Community planning is also a political process. Elected town boards, county commissioners, and city councils have the authority to make legally binding decisions about whether to approve new developments and whether to adopt a comprehensive plan, zoning and subdivision regulations, and capital improvements programs. A major obstacle with the political side of planning is the challenge of "selling" planning to skeptical elected officials and residents. Public distrust of government is common, and elected officials are often reluctant to spend money on drafting a new comprehensive plan and land-use regulations or making major infrastructure investments. CommunityViz, with its strong visualization and analytical abilities, gives planners a powerful new way to engage the public and officials by making information come alive. CommunityViz can make the planning process more transparent, thus promoting trust and collaboration between citizens and officials. Done well, CommunityViz can attract more people to the planning process.

THE OLD GENERATION OF PLANNING

The old generation of planning, which dominated the second half of the 20th century, featured technical data about a community's population, economic base, and housing, as typified by the 701 plans funded by the U.S. Department of Housing and Urban Development (HUD) beginning in 1954. But the analysis of information in these plans was cursory and perfunctory. There was no visioning process or sense of place-making. Few communities considered or analyzed information on historic resources or the natural environment. The purpose of the old type of planning was to qualify for state and federal grants and to plan for development that would expand the local tax base and provide more jobs. Virtually any kind of development was viewed as positive for the community. Single-use cookie-cutter zoning ordinances promoted sprawl and dependence on the automobile. The standards for development design were minimal. Planners and elected officials saw only an architect's or artist's drawings of a proposed development, not how the development would fit in with its surroundings. Cost-of-services studies were few and far between. And, especially in the 1950s and 1960s, it was common for a local government to pick up most, if not all, of the infrastructure costs associated with a new private development.

The old generation of planning was wholly inadequate to respond to a near doubling of America's population from 1950 (150 million) to 2000 (282 million). During that era, several cities lost more than 30 percent of their population as growth in the suburbs exploded. Air and water quality declined until the federal government enacted national standards in the 1970s. Sprawling developments and reliance on the automobile increased America's dependence on oil. New developments replaced the historic and natural heart-and-soul assets of many communities.

The old generation of planning was often carried out in backroom deals between developers and elected officials, and planning consultants paid only lip service to public participation while carrying out the desires of the elected officials. Consultants frequently produced boilerplate comprehensive plans that could be used by any community. Public participation in the planning process was not encouraged, and the public was largely apathetic. Often, elected officials did not want the public to know what was happening in the community. The bottom line was: If local taxes were not rising too fast, the local officials would have a good chance of being reelected.

Today, thanks to CommunityViz and GIS, the primary challenges in community planning are not so much technical as political. A major political hurdle to effective planning is a lack of leadership and political will on the part of elected officials, which results in weak, outdated comprehensive plans that sit on the shelf collecting dust. Their "if it ain't broke, don't fix it" attitude neither anticipates change nor tries to shape it. This do-nothing mentality has been prevalent in the thousands of small towns that have been swallowed up by expanding metropolitan areas, and in more remote places that have failed to attract new economic activity. CommunityViz can help elected officials find political will by providing good information about the design of proposed developments and by gauging public values and support for plans and development projects.

COMMUNITY PLANNING IN 21ST-CENTURY AMERICA

Community planning in 21st-century America will have to balance development with preservation in order to retain heart-and-soul resources and environmental quality while accommodating more people and development. The choices and decisions communities face will be difficult. Good data, careful analysis, and visualization through CommunityViz will be essential for involving the public and for wise decision making by planners and officials.

Over the next 40 years, community planning in America will be driven by three powerful trends: 1) population growth, 2) environmental concerns, and 3) the cost of community services. In 2010, America's population reached 310 million. The U.S. Census Bureau is projecting that by 2050 there probably will be 440 million Americans. Where are another 130 million Americans going to live and work? This surge in population has the potential to change the face of communities all across America. There will be pressure to build on greenfields, as well as a need to redevelop cities and inner suburbs. CommunityViz will help planners in design review to promote well-designed developments and re-developments, as well as in regional visioning, growth projections, and build-out analyses. CommunityViz will help communities understand the environmental impacts of new development and infrastructure and enable a community or region to rate and rank the suitability of natural areas, farmland, and forestland for preservation. In addition, it can be used in natural resources management to achieve a variety of goals.

Cities and towns will need to pay more attention to the cost of services as their populations grow and new developments are built. CommunityViz can assist with cost-of-services studies, which will allow communities to better manage their finances. CommunityViz can aid in mixing land uses through the analysis of zoning capacity. It can show a range of compact building design scenarios with a range of housing types where growth is directed to existing settlements and places with adequate public services. CommunityViz users can promote distinctive neighborhoods and communities with a strong sense of place by identifying heart-and-soul resources and the development preferences of the local residents.

In day-to-day decisions about development proposals, CommunityViz will help predict how a development will look and the likely cost of services to the community. Because CommunityViz is an engaging technology built on the principle of transparency, it will encourage citizens and stakeholders to collaborate in development decisions.

Finally, regional planning will become the new community planning. Many of us live in one jurisdiction, work in another jurisdiction, and shop in a third jurisdiction. We may think locally, but we act regionally. CommunityViz can help with the drafting of regional plans and the blending together of local plans.

The new generation of planning is rapidly emerging. CommunityViz and GIS give a community the technical capacity to gather, analyze, and display information and to involve citizens in envisioning the future. As a result, a community's comprehensive plan can be based not only on technical knowledge and numbers but also on residents' values—those heart-and-soul assets they hold dear about the community. On the political side, CommunityViz helps promote a more transparent planning process thus increasing trust between elected officials and the public. Consequently, communities, landowners, developers, and elected officials will make better, more informed decisions and create more effective plans, land-use regulations, and infrastructure investments that enhance the quality of life for residents now and for years to come.

INTRODUCTION: COMMUNITIES, PLANNING, AND COMMUNITYVIZ

Attractive cities, towns, and counties have three ingredients in common: The residents care about their community; there is strong leadership; and people make informed decisions about growth and change. Residents value their community's character—those special places and customs that make their community a good place to live and work. Forces of change, including population growth, infrastructure projects, residential and commercial development, and the global economy, affect the futures of all communities. But we believe that communities and regions can make choices that shape their own futures.

Planning is about anticipating change and organizing resources to accomplish specific goals. People plan for major financial events, such as retirement or sending children to college. Communities plan where to locate future commercial and residential development; where to expand and repair transportation systems, sewer and water facilities, and schools; how to maintain the natural environment and recreation opportunities; and how to design their buildings and public spaces. Community planning does not replace the real estate market, but it can complement market forces in ways that accommodate both private and public needs. Developers and landowners can make business decisions and earn profits from development projects, but planning ensures that the location, type, and style of projects are consistent with the public interest in health, safety, and general well-being.

Communities can plan for their future character. Planners can think not just about the mechanics of accommodating growth but also about what the people in the community value: their heart-and-soul resources. A community that cares about itself lets its character drive development, not the other way around.

Community planning occurs at many scales: from single-building sites to metropolitan regions and multi-state watersheds; from open landscapes to urban neighborhoods; from 30-year plans to daily permit approvals. Community planning involves fundamental questions, such as:

- Where should new houses, apartments, and commercial buildings be located?
- What roads, schools, water, and other infrastructure will we need in the future?
- Will our tax revenues be enough to pay for services?
- What will our traffic be like, and can it be reduced?
- What will happen to our natural environment?
- What will become of our local way of life and those places we hold dear—the heart and soul of the community?
- What can be done to improve the quality of life in our community?

Communities have long used the comprehensive planning process to create master plans and to implement those plans through zoning, subdivision regulations, and capital improvements programs, as well as day-to-day decisions about individual development proposals. This process, from its broadest strategies to the cumulative effects of its smallest details, helps to guide what communities become. Community planning shapes the physical spaces we live in, the services we depend upon, and the overall character of the community. Good planning increases the likelihood of achieving the future the community wants.

COMPUTERS AND PLANNING

Effective planning also depends on good information. A generation ago, records were kept on paper and calculations were done by hand. It was often hard to find accurate data on such basic topics as landownership, soils, and water quality. Daily planning administration was overwhelmingly the primary focus, and projections of future development and its impacts were rarely accurate. Gradually, advances in computer technology enabled advances in planning. Maps and ownership data migrated from filing cabinets to databases, so access to basic information not only improved, but also became more accessible to more people. Computer programs made specifically for map-based information—geographic information systems, or GIS—made it possible for planners to organize data and create custom maps, so data became easier to analyze and understand. Routine planning administration became more efficient and reliable. Many planning departments have put their comprehensive plans, zoning ordinances, and meeting agendas and minutes on the Internet. This wealth of information has enabled the public to gain a better understanding of their community's growth management framework, individual development proposals, and specific planning decisions.

A NEW GENERATION OF PLANNING

GIS software has brought about a new generation of planning. A computer no longer just stores data, crunches numbers, or processes words: it is a sophisticated tool that enables planners to solve problems, anticipate change, picture alternatives, and engage broad audiences in the process of shaping the community's future. A future development forecast no longer means little numbers on large spreadsheets; now it means interactive digital maps and automatic calculations performed in an instant. Such computing power allows you to make more specific and clearly defined choices. You can try out a choice, such as a particular residential zoning density, and see how much development it can accommodate. You can test different assumptions about growth rates. You can ask more questions, and think more comprehensively about the environmental and fiscal impacts of a development proposal or a new comprehensive plan. Picturing a proposed development is no longer a matter of viewing the architect's rendering on a sheet of paper; now you can take a self-guided tour through an interactive, 3-D world where you can see the project from any angle and in the full context of its surroundings. Planning is better in this new generation because information is more complete and transparent, analysis is far more thorough, communication is more open and interactive, and planners, developers, and elected officials can make more informed decisions.

Computer technology is a powerful tool for the *technical* aspects of planning; but this technology also supports the *human* and *political* aspects of planning. Although residents, community leaders, and landowners may care how their neighborhood or community will look and function, it is unlikely they are professional planners. The best way for them to understand proposed changes to the built environment or landscape is to *see* them: to look at 3-D models and interactive maps that show alternative designs or plans for development. Visualization and interactive computer technology draw residents into the planning process and thus strengthen political support for community planning. Technology aids in the creation of plans, ordinances, and infrastructure investment programs that make sense to people.

WHAT COMMUNITYVIZ DOES

Just as GIS gives computers special abilities for working with maps, CommunityViz is a software package that extends general-purpose GIS with special capabilities for community planning. CommunityViz offers a wide array of tools for visualization, analysis, and communication about planning alternatives and their impacts. The CommunityViz way of working with maps, information, and plans is called *scenario planning* or *geodesign*.

CommunityViz offers realistic and interactive 3-D visuals, intelligent maps, and dynamic analysis tools for understanding potential or proposed changes to a community or region. CommunityViz helps illustrate alternative futures, capturing and conveying facts as well as the values of the residents. As a result, CommunityViz gives people a better way to foresee, understand, and communicate the implications of their decisions.

CommunityViz can help planners create growth models, evaluate neighborhood design, draft regional plans, set land-use priorities, or identify land for preservation from an individual site to a regional study.

COMMUNITYVIZ ROOTS AND DEVELOPMENT

The CommunityViz software program was created by the Orton Family Foundation—based in Middlebury, Vermont, and Denver, Colorado—and had its initial public release in 2001. The Orton Family Foundation was formed in 1995 to help citizens in small cities and towns meet the challenges of planning for the future. CommunityViz has two underlying planning philosophies: 1) Greater public involvement in planning leads to better decisions about land use patterns, development design, and the retention of the community's heart-and-soul resources; and 2) More transparency in the planning process builds community trust and leads to more durable plans and effective land-use controls and infrastructure investment. Every part of the software's design is meant to promote these fundamental ideas. In 2005, the Orton Family Foundation spun off a for-profit company called Placeways LLC—based in Boulder, Colorado—to take over development and marketing of CommunityViz throughout the United States and across the globe. Placeways shares the foundation's philosophies for the software and maintains the same principles in its work.

Thousands of companies, nonprofit groups, landowners, and all levels of government now use CommunityViz. Placeways maintains a vigorous research-and-development program and regularly issues new releases. The current generation, CommunityViz 4.x, represents more than 10 years of continuous enhancements and improvements. CommunityViz is used by local government planners and planning consultants at public meetings, by private planners exploring different development scenarios, and by GIS professionals integrating specialized models and other tools. As we shall see, local and regional government planners use CommunityViz for a wide range of land use planning projects. And colleges and universities use CommunityViz to instruct students in land use planning and development design.

COMMUNITYVIZ AND ALL KINDS OF PLANNING

This book focuses primarily on how CommunityViz can improve public land use planning to produce orderly growth and change. Land use planning is a political process of deciding the pattern of land development in a city, town, county, or region. A major part of land use planning is the process of updating and implementing a comprehensive plan. Land use planning emerges from a public consensus indicated in a comprehensive plan and implemented through zoning and subdivision ordinances and public investment in infrastructure. Through day-to-day decision making about land development proposals, the community expresses what changes it either will or will not accept. The book also explains how to use CommunityViz for transportation planning, managing natural resources, community value mapping, visualization and design review, public participation in the planning process, and what we have termed "Heart & Soul Community Planning" (see sidebar on page xx).

It takes a wide variety of information to reach a public consensus or shared vision for the community and to draft a comprehensive plan, a set of implementing ordinances, and an infrastructure investment strategy. CommunityViz enables planners to create, organize, and present the information that people need to reach a consensus. CommunityViz has tools to produce and present data on geographic features, economic activity, environmental quality, public opinions, and 3-D visuals.

CommunityViz offers powerful tools for assessing the visual, fiscal, environmental, and social impacts of a proposed plan. Impact assessment can be done on any scale, from an individual site to an entire region. In reviewing a site proposal, for example, a design review board can examine an interactive 3-D model of a building that clearly illustrates how it will appear and how it will affect the appearance of the neighborhood. The board can also make use of easy-to-understand displays that indicate how the proposal will affect the city's budget, utility demands, parking, schools, and other infrastructure needs. In other words, CommunityViz can help provide elected officials, planning commission members, planning staff, and the general public with a complete picture of how a proposed development would change the community. What a difference from the past, when it was not uncommon for a planning commission to require the developer to float balloons to show the proposed building height!

CommunityViz supports many stages of the conventional comprehensive planning process, which is driven by projections of future population and the need for a variety of land uses, including housing, commercial and industrial firms, schools, and recreation (see Figure A). But this standard numbers-driven approach overlooks how people feel about their community and what features make that community special. These features form what can be called the community's *heart and soul*, which may include the Main Street shopping district, the farmers market, older residential neighborhoods, scenic vistas, and river corridors, as well as community customs and events. These features are part of the reason why people live in a certain community, and they give a community its identity and distinctive feel. CommunityViz can also support planning that incorporates heart-and-soul features, as well as population projections and land use needs. But the goal of Heart & Soul Community Planning is to avoid planning decisions that would harm or disrupt the community's cherished features.

Figure A *The traditional planning process*

1.	The governing body recognizes the necessity for local planning.
2.	The governing body commits people and money to the planning process and the drafting of a comprehensive plan.
3.	The governing body designates the planning commission, planning staff, and a consultant, if necessary, to draft the comprehensive plan.
4.	The planning commission prepares a work schedule, gives notice of meetings with the public to work on the comprehensive plan, and appoints a comprehensive plan advisory committee.
5.	Planners gather information and conduct public information and needs surveys.
6.	The public participates in the planning process through community and neighborhood meetings and visioning.
7.	The planning commission drafts a statement of planning goals and objectives.
8.	The governing body approves or modifies the goals and objectives.
9.	Planners draft the comprehensive plan elements including: existing conditions, economic base, housing, land use, transportation, and community facilities.
10.	The planning commission reviews, amends, and then recommends the draft comprehensive plan to the governing body. The governing body formally adopts the community comprehensive plan.
11.	The planning commission and planning staff draft the zoning ordinance, subdivision, and land development regulations, and a capital improvements program to implement the comprehensive plan. The governing body formally adopts the zoning ordinance, subdivision regulations, and capital improvements program.
12.	The planning commission uses the comprehensive plan, zoning and subdivision ordinances, and capital improvements program in making day-to-day decisions about proposed development projects. The governing body has the final say and makes the legally binding decisions about proposed development projects.

The following Declaration of Community Heart & Soul Beliefs *was drafted at the 2007 CommunityMatters Conference in Burlington, Vermont. More than 40 people who attended a special meeting to define the rights and responsibilities of community residents signed it.*

DECLARATION OF COMMUNITY HEART & SOUL BELIEFS

We the undersigned believe that every community must explore and express what makes it special—its Heart & Soul elements—and describe those tangible and intangible elements that if lost would fundamentally change the character of their place. Once articulated and acknowledged, community Heart & Soul serves as the "Bill of Rights and Responsibilities" for citizens as they make decisions about the future.

We believe that when a community takes the time to get to know itself and its Heart & Soul elements, it will gain a sense of identity and purpose that will empower its citizens to make strong, enduring decisions and take action to protect and strengthen who they are.

We believe in a direct democratic process. There is no place in this process for "inclusion as usual." Traditional gestures toward inclusion are bankrupt; they engender neither trust nor common purpose. Only by going to, listening to, and learning from everyone—the influential and the forgotten, old timers and newcomers, young and old, rich and poor, business owners and workers, professionals and tradesmen, the noisy and the quiet, the caregivers and the gatekeepers—can shared purpose and identity live in and guide a community.

We believe in the strength of connection. Through connection, Heart & Soul communities can define their place in the world and contribute to a broader region of ideas, people, economies and natural systems. This connectedness gives communities an evolving understanding of themselves to steer their futures in a world of change.

We believe in the necessity of reciprocating citizens' trust and participation with results: actionable plans and visions for a future that are grounded by the reality of each community's circumstances.

We believe that community planning steered by Heart & Soul will tap into sources of creativity within communities. Decisions and actions relating to development, planning and policy must reflect and reinforce the community's self-identity. This approach must guide planning, zoning, public investment, development, design, budgeting and management.

We believe that Heart & Soul elements must be monitored as closely as any economic indicator. Heart & Soul must be so deeply enmeshed in the community's identity that making a decision without reference to it will be as unthinkable as making a decision without reference to its economic effects.

We believe in the importance of celebrating successes, in measuring Heart & Soul results as yardsticks for accountability, and in asking citizens how to do better. We care about sharing success and validating progress to influence the wider world.

THE ORTON FAMILY FOUNDATION'S HEART & SOUL PLANNING PHILOSOPHY

The Orton Family Foundation is convinced that people need ways to connect with one another, ways to share what they know and feel, and ways to nurture the heart-and-soul features of their communities. In addition, the greater the number of people who become involved in planning their communities, the more effective the plans, ordinances, and decisions about change are likely to be. CommunityViz can be particularly useful when a community or planning consultant follows a planning process that respects and protects the local heart-and-soul features. The Heart & Soul Community Planning approach is especially helpful in steps five and six of the traditional planning process listed in Table A: information gathering, and public participation and visioning. Residents are their own experts when it comes to knowing where the special places are and why they are important to the community; they hold those places dear and do not want to lose or alter them. CommunityViz can help planners capture this knowledge and take it into account when drafting a comprehensive plan. The result is a plan that residents are more likely to embrace as their own.

Community planning in America has often been done in back rooms or near-empty public meeting rooms. All too rarely has the community planning process successfully engaged a broad base of local citizens. Simply put, greater citizen participation results in better decisions. The broader the participation of residents in the planning process, the more buy-in and sense of ownership of the comprehensive plan they are likely to feel, and the better the planning outcomes are likely to be. CommunityViz is an excellent tool for increasing participation in the planning process, and can even make the planning process fun! Ideally, residents and elected officials will work together to articulate a shared vision for the community that will serve as the foundation for its comprehensive plan.

CommunityViz can help a community adapt to change while maintaining or enhancing those places and features that residents value most. In this way, a community can grow and evolve without becoming "Anywhere, USA." One of the strengths of CommunityViz is the ability to monitor how a community is changing incrementally over time through the ongoing process of permitting and development. Communities that identify clear goals and limits for their heart-and-soul resources can ensure that they are not gradually eroded.

PRACTICAL BENEFITS OF NEW GENERATION PLANNING

Cities, towns, counties, and regions face many challenges. Population growth in fast-growing areas can bring changes seemingly overnight in the form of new residential and commercial development. In other places, population loss and economic decline offer little hope for the future. Finances may be tight, and the need for urgent action may seem to outweigh the wisdom of planning for that future. In the face of challenges such as these, it is easy for residents to lose faith in the planning process and disengage. Elected officials may lose their taste for public participation, and planners may lose patience with long-range planning.

The new combination of computer technology, planning to protect heart-and-soul resources, and promoting public participation leads to better planning outcomes in the long run. Public participation that elicits community values and identifies special places can result in plans that stand the test of time and day-to-day decisions that protect special places. A planning process that engages audiences early on builds buy-in and support. Broad public engagement produces greater understanding of problems and opportunities, and better planning decisions about the location and type of development. And the interactive visualization and data analysis that CommunityViz provides means that the process of revising a comprehensive plan is often short, satisfying, and highly productive, rather than a series of meetings drawn out over several months.

Communities need to decide how to deal with many economic, environmental, and social considerations to create vibrant places in which to live now and in the years to come. These decisions are important and complex. Making wise, informed decisions requires combining environmental science, economic data, and many points of view—the task for which CommunityViz was designed. CommunityViz is a valuable and effective tool in the hands of planners like you. This book describes how you can work with CommunityViz in a new generation of planning practice.

HOW TO USE THIS BOOK

We wrote this book to enable you to use CommunityViz to its fullest. It contains: descriptions of CommunityViz features and tools; explanations of recommended techniques for designing planning projects and using CommunityViz to address a variety of planning tasks at the site, neighborhood, community, and regional levels; and chapters on particular planning applications such as drafting a comprehensive plan and conducting a zoning analysis.

This book is not a CommunityViz instruction manual. For details about operating the software, refer to the technical guides; help system, tutorials, and other resources available within the software or online.[1] This book is intended to help you learn how to use CommunityViz for planning.

Figure B presents the order of the chapters and their contents. Chapters are generally self-contained, so you can read them in any order or skip to the section you need.

If you are new to CommunityViz, we recommend you read An Overview (page xxv) and chapters 1 to 3 to get started. Those chapters explain how to use CommunityViz in a planning project, beginning with the selection of a study area to analyze, the assessment of data needs, the application of scenario planning and geodesign, and finally, the creation of a "living" comprehensive plan, which can be continually updated. Chapters 4 to 6 introduce CommunityViz technology, including dynamic analysis, impact models, and 3-D. Move on to the chapters in sections 2, 3, and 4 that address your particular kind of planning project. Review the chapters in Section 5 that cover the communication you will need to carry out your project.

Each chapter begins with an introduction to the topic, and then goes on to provide information and advice. Several chapters contain a teaching example that illustrates key points and adds practical suggestions for working in the real world. Many chapters conclude with case studies of actual projects in which the tools or techniques described in the chapter were applied.

Sections 2, 3, and 4 explore the comprehensive planning process, starting from visioning and proceeding through the drafting of plans, to plan implementation and design review of proposed developments.

In Section 2, Community Visioning, Values, and Growth Projections, we describe how to use CommunityViz to get a community to articulate a vision at the beginning of the comprehensive planning process. That process often involves analyzing growth trends, for instance through a build-out analysis, so a community can understand where it is likely to be heading. This initial stage of the planning process is the best time for a community to clarify its values, and we describe how CommunityViz can produce values maps of the important heart-and-soul features of the community.

In Section 3, Making Plans, we discuss how you can use CommunityViz in drafting town and city plans, regional plans, and natural resource plans. This section also includes a chapter on using CommunityViz to select project sites and set land-use priorities.

Section 4, Reviewing Regulations and Development Proposals, explains how a community can use CommunityViz to implement a comprehensive plan. It covers how CommunityViz can help you analyze the zoning ordinance and subdivision and land development regulations, perform cost-of-services analyses, and conduct a design review of development proposals.

In Section 5, Communicating and Interacting, we focus on how to use CommunityViz to engage the public at meetings, support workgroups, and create reports and interactive websites.

The appendices provide additional information that you may need in your work with CommunityViz. Appendices 1 to 4 focus on best practices and technical tuning, and Appendix 5 provides a tour of CommunityViz features and capabilities.

---

1. Online CommunityViz resources are available at http://placeways.com/communityviz.

Figure B Chapter layout and content

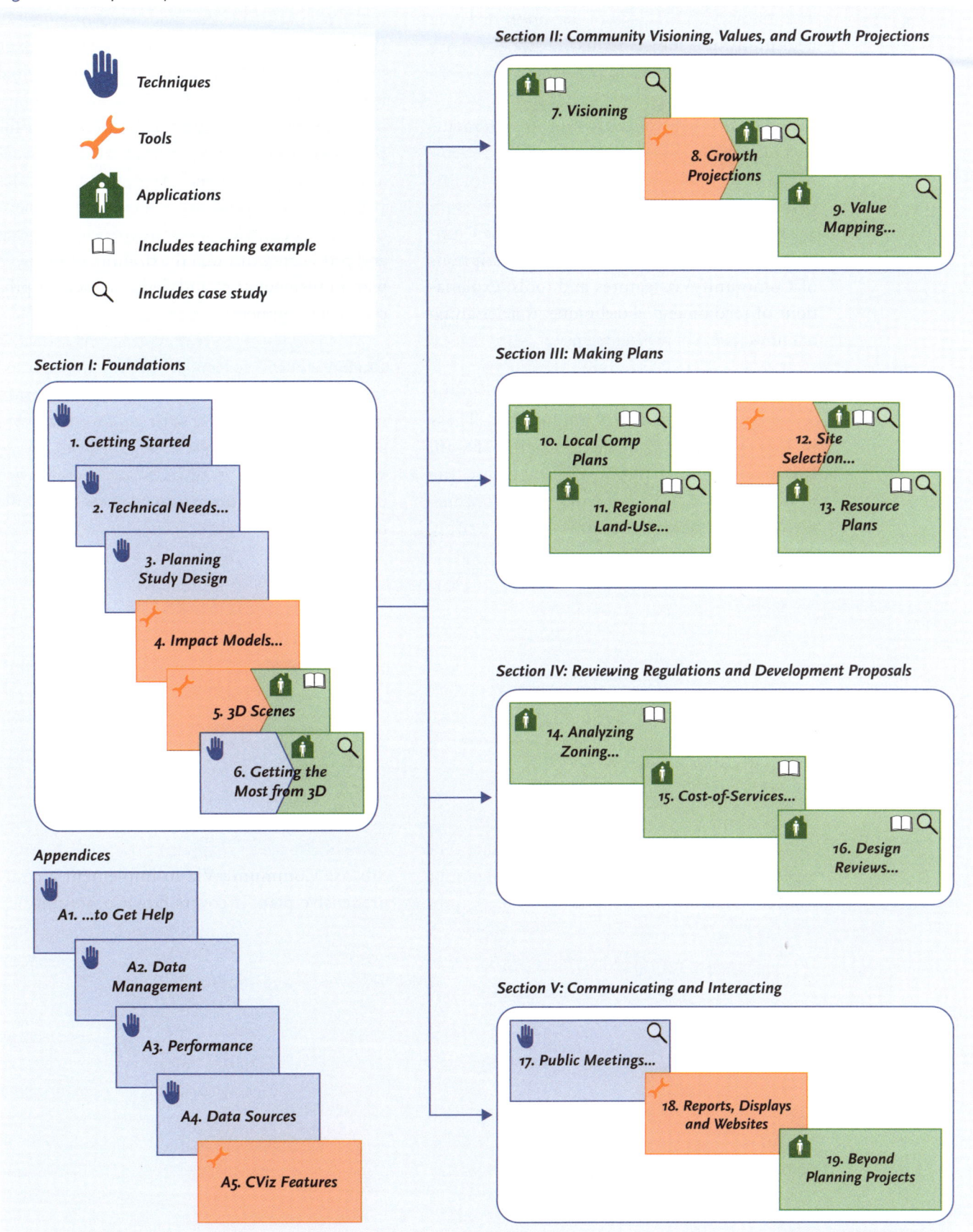

SPECIAL TERMS

The glossary at the back of the book provides definitions of technical terms, but we also use a few nontechnical terms in particular ways.

We: *We* means the authors, but in statements such as "We find *x* to be true" or "We recommend," the authors are also drawing on the collective experience of CommunityViz staff, experts at Placeways, and other longtime CommunityViz practitioners with whom we work.

You: *You* means the reader, either as an individual or as part of a project team.

Project: We use the term *project* to refer to the set of tasks involved in a planning study. These include: the organizing and managing of staff, the promotion of public participation, the undertaking of technical work with CommunityViz analysis and visualization, the writing of reports, and more.

Analysis: Narrowly, a CommunityViz *analysis* is the related set of files that one component of the software—Scenario 360—uses for a given project, analogous to a Microsoft Word document. We usually include 3-D and other multimedia as part of the term. In keeping with the practice of CommunityViz users everywhere, we also use the term *analysis* to describe the work you do with CommunityViz during a project; in other words, you can both *create* a decision-making framework called an analysis and *work* with the framework to conduct an analysis of a site, neighborhood, city, or region.

Engagement: *Engagement* means the process through which people other than the CommunityViz operator work with a CommunityViz analysis. CommunityViz is designed not just to present information but also to interact with people by responding immediately to public input or inquiries.

COMMUNITYVIZ: AN OVERVIEW

community*viz*® If you are new to the world of CommunityViz® planning software, welcome![1] This section provides a quick introductory tour of the features and capabilities of CommunityViz. The rest of the book will take you on a richer, deeper journey through how to use CommunityViz for a wide variety of planning projects. For demos, tutorials, and live resources, visit the CommunityViz website, or read more about CommunityViz's features in Appendix 5.[2]

CommunityViz plugs into and extends the capabilities of the leading GIS software, ArcGIS® Desktop, which is produced by the Environmental Systems Research Institute, Inc. (Esri).[3]

Planners, natural resource managers, local governments, Metropolitan Planning Organizations, for-profit businesses, and many others use CommunityViz to help them make decisions about the future of their communities and regions. CommunityViz gives you ways to create plans or development proposals, and then it shows you their impacts on the economic, environmental, and social systems of the planning area. By learning about those impacts and comparing alternatives, people can make better, more informed public and private decisions.

The general term for what CommunityViz does is *decision support*. Some of the techniques you can use in decision making include scenario planning, geodesign, sketch planning, 3-D visualization, suitability analysis, impact assessment, and growth modeling. In short, CommunityViz has a wide range of applications that aid in decisions about the location, type, and design of development.

Almost anyone can use or benefit from CommunityViz, in the same way that almost anyone can benefit from a piano: If you don't know how to play piano, you can listen. Similarly, members of the public who never actually touch CommunityViz can benefit from its interactive visual displays during a public meeting or on a website. If you are a beginning piano player, you can play simple tunes that sound nice; and the longer you practice, the more sophisticated your playing can become. CommunityViz is the same way: It provides some easy-to-use tools that almost anyone can apply to produce basic analysis and visualization. As you gain experience, you can do increasingly complicated projects. Finally, if you are a piano composer, you write music that others can play and enjoy. CommunityViz analysts, such as planners and GIS professionals, use this software to create the studies that private clients, public officials, and general audiences use.

There are two primary components of CommunityViz: Scenario 360™, which provides interactive analysis tools and a decision-making framework, and Scenario 3D™, which offers one of several ways to create information-rich, interactive 3-D scenes.[4]

SCENARIO 360

CommunityViz Scenario 360 is designed to help people make informed decisions about the future of their neighborhoods, communities, and regions. With Scenario 360, you can:

- Easily create and experiment with hypothetical "What if?" scenarios

- Assess economic, environmental, social, and visual impacts of proposed developments, plans, land-use regulations, and infrastructure investments

---

1. CommunityViz is a registered trademark of the Orton Family Foundation.
2. Online resources for CommunityViz are available at http://placeways.com/communityviz.
3. ArcGIS is a registered trademark of the Environmental Systems Research Institute, Inc.
4. Scenario 360 is a trademark of the Orton Family Foundation. Scenario 3D is a trademark of Placeways LLC.

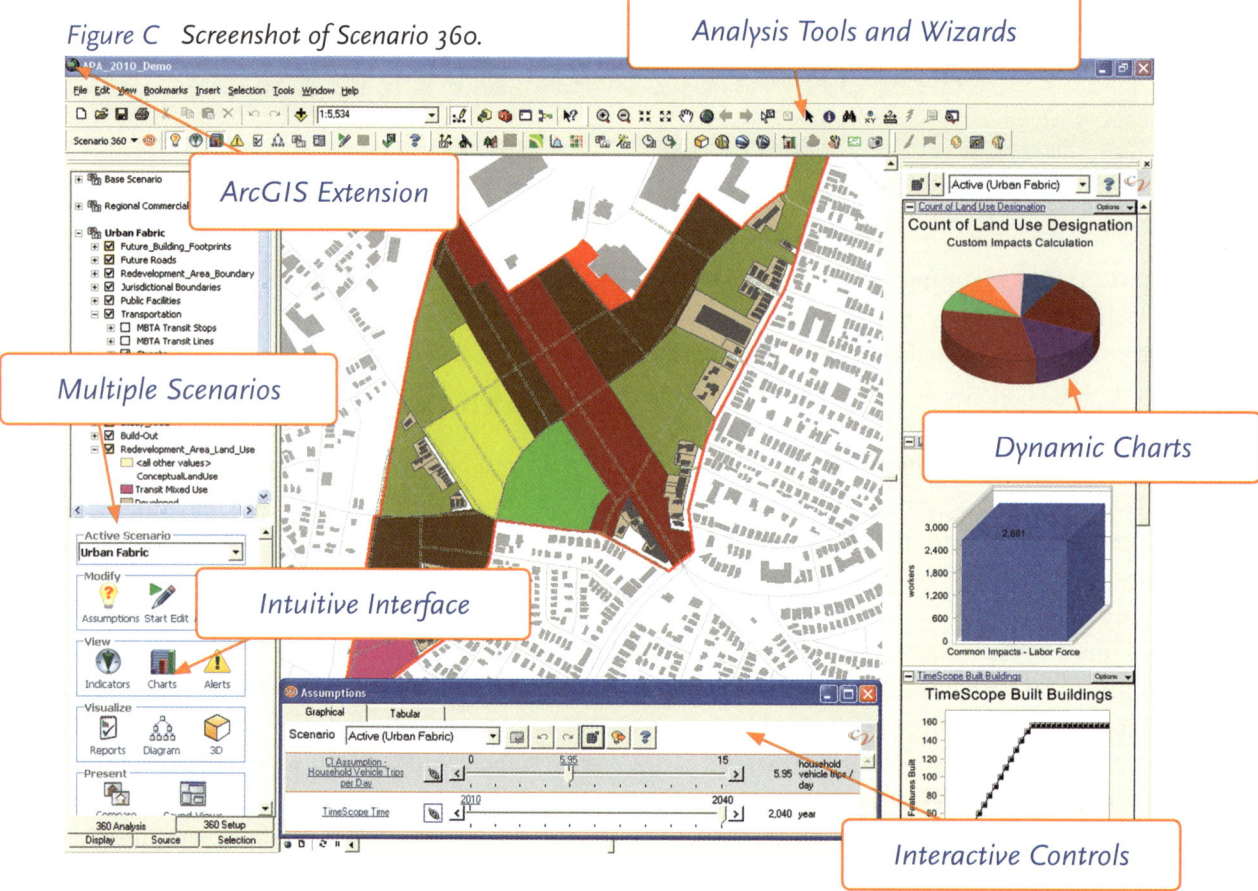

Figure C Screenshot of Scenario 360.

- Make assumptions and quickly change assumptions
- View impacts of proposed changes to a site, neighborhood, city, or region
- Make comprehensive, informed decisions
- Connect to 3-D visualization tools.

Scenario 360 (see Figure C) makes the community planning process more visual, more collaborative in a public setting, and ultimately more effective. Some of the key features include:

- **Land Use Designer**, which lets you "paint" land-use types on a map and instantly see associated social, economic, and environmental impacts. You can use predefined land-use models or create your own.
- **Build-Out Wizard**, which calculates the development capacity of your land, numerically, spatially, and in 3-D visuals. In addition, the Allocator lets you project where development will occur over time.
- **Suitability Wizard,** which automatically scores different locations according to suitability factors you specify and lets you apply variable weightings to each factor. The suitability wizard is most often used to rate land according to its suitability for development.
- **TimeScope™**, which lets you look at changes in development impacts year-to-year simply by moving a slider bar
- **Tools for viewing multiple scenarios** side by side in one analysis
- **Tools for easily creating web-ready illustrations** of an analysis for viewing interactively in 2-D or in 3-D through Google Earth®[5]
- **Dynamic charts, alerts, and other displays** updated in real time as you explore alternative plans and actions.

---

5. *Google Earth* is a trademark of Google.

COMMON APPLICATIONS

Here are some of the most common applications of Scenario 360:

- Comprehensive planning
- Site selection and evaluation
- Build-out analysis
- Development proposal analysis
- Public participation
- Estimating infrastructure costs
- Visual impact analysis
- Land evaluation and sustainability analysis
- Drafting of environmental impact statements
- Forest management planning
- Wildfire risk assessment
- Habitat fragmentation evaluation
- Water quality management

INTEGRATION WITH ArcGIS

Scenario 360 runs as an extension to ArcMap and integrates smoothly with the rest of ArcGIS Desktop. This means that you can use all your existing GIS data and plans, as well as the full capabilities of ArcGIS, together with CommunityViz.

3-D VISUALIZATION WITHIN SCENARIO 360

Scenario 360 allows you to connect to 3-D visualization tools, giving you new ways to see your community as it is and as it could be:

- For viewing your analysis in its global 3-D context, Scenario 360 can export your scenarios, layers, charts, extruded buildings, and Google SketchUp® objects into KMZ format for immediate viewing in Google Earth, ArcGIS Explorer, or other tools that can use KMZ format files.[6]

- Scenario 360 also works within ArcScene, a component of the ArcGIS 3D Analyst extension. Used together, Scenario 360 and ArcScene provide an integrated 3-D environment to perform visual analyses and make decisions about the location, type, and design of development.

- Scenario 3D, included as part of the CommunityViz package, enables you to create realistic, interactive 3-D scenes.

SCENARIO 3D

Scenario 3D is a companion to Scenario 360 in the CommunityViz suite and works as its own ArcGIS Desktop extension. Scenario 3D brings maps to life by helping you create realistic, interactive, and sharable 3-D scenes (see Figure D). You make Scenario 3D scenes by starting with an ArcGIS map and then specifying how the 2-D features on the map will be represented in the 3-D scene. When viewing a scene, you can move through the scene as if you were there, walking, flying, and looking around. You can also click on objects to read more about them or hear them "talk." Buildings, trees, and roads all appear in photo-realistic detail, and terrain rises and falls underfoot. Shadows, lighting, and fog effects lend a tangible sense of place. The idea is to help you get a feel for the place you are seeing. You make scenes using the built-in models and resources of Scenario 3D or models in standard formats including Google SketchUp and Computer Aided Design (CAD).

SCENARIO 3D EXPORTER AND VIEWER

Scenario 3D comes in two parts, Scenario 3D Exporter and Scenario 3D Viewer. Scenario 3D Exporter (see Figure E) is an ArcGIS extension for creating 3-D scenes.

Here are a few key points about the exporter:

- It is a toolbar extension for ArcMap; no other software is required.

- It sets up scenes from ArcMap features, layers, and scenarios.

---

6. SketchUp is a registered trademark of Google.

- A variety of methods to convert 2-D to 3-D are available, ranging from the use of simple symbols to the use of templates.

- Three-dimensional terrain can be created from contour lines or digital elevation models (DEMs).

Figure D A screenshot from an interactive 3-D scene in Scenario 3D

Figure E A Scenario 3D Exporter screen

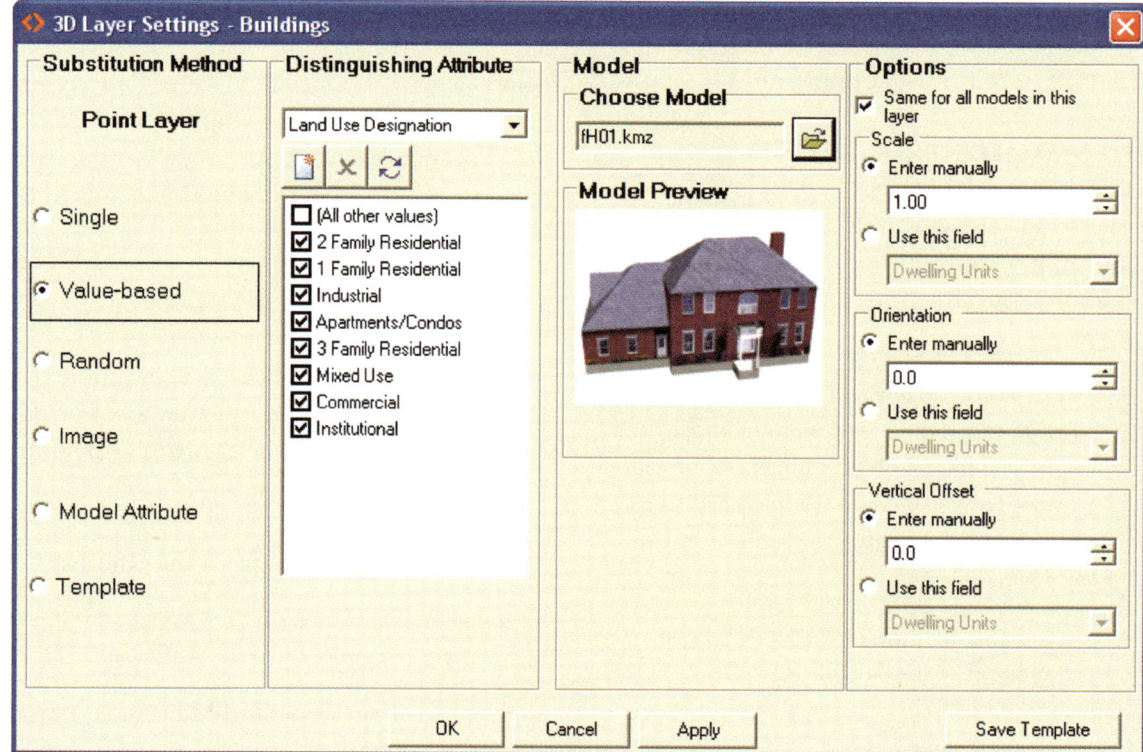

- The software includes a library of hundreds of 3-D models and textures, or you can add your own photos or 3-D models in SketchUp KMZ, 3ds, and COLLADA formats.[7]

The Scenario 3D Viewer (see Figure F) is a stand-alone viewer that lets you explore scenes created by Scenario 3D Exporter.

Here are a few key points about the viewer:

- There is a free download available, so anyone can view Scenario 3D scenes.[8] It has six modes of navigation, including flying, walking, and maneuvering.

- Environmental effects can be created, including fog, shadows, and lighting.

- Bookmarks, saved fly-through paths, and built-in movie recording are provided.

- Multiple scenarios can be contained in one file.

---

7. 3ds Max and Maya are registered trademarks of Autodesk. 3ds Max (formerly 3D Studio MAX) and Maya are popular 3D rendering and animation packages from Autodesk.

8. Download is available at http://placeways.com/communityviz.

Figure F A screenshot from the Scenario 3D Viewer

This is the end of the quick tour of CommunityViz and its components, Scenario 360 and Scenario 3D. Now you are ready to learn about how you can use all of the features and capabilities of CommunityViz for better planning.

SECTION 1: FOUNDATIONS

NAVIGATING THIS SECTION

Section 1 provides information, tools, and techniques that apply to almost any CommunityViz project. This section introduces the core CommunityViz concepts of scenario planning, geodesign, dynamic analysis, and 3-D. It also describes how to organize a CommunityViz project and design an analysis. The first three chapters in this section are a good place for most readers to start in order to understand the basics of how to use CommunityViz for community planning.

Chapter 1, Getting Started, recommends that you begin by establishing a broad understanding of the place where you will be working. It describes steps for defining the study area, creating an area profile, understanding forces of change, and identifying stakeholders in the planning process. Chapter 1 also introduces important aspects of the CommunityViz approach to decision making, starting with defining the questions you want to answer, knowing the difference between decisions and information, and understanding the importance of transparency in your work.

Chapter 2, Technical Needs and Data Resources for CommunityViz, explains the appropriate computing resources you need, including equipment, data, and expertise. These needs are not daunting, but you ought to be aware of them. This chapter also includes a section on best practices and ethics for working with data.

Chapter 3, Planning Study Design Guidelines, starts with two of the central concepts of using CommunityViz for planning projects: scenario planning and geodesign. From there, it describes how to plan your project and design the approach you will use. CommunityViz imposes very little structure. You can design your study to meet the particular needs of a planning problem, based on the people you will be working with, the resources you have available, and your budget. We encourage you to design for a living plan, which may be a comprehensive plan, a site plan, a transportation plan, or a natural resources plan. A living plan can easily be updated and stays useful as a guide for decision making.

Not all readers will need to go through chapters 4, 5, and 6 at first. Chapter 4, Custom Impact Models and Analysis, describes the essentials of CommunityViz formulas and dynamic analysis, which lay the foundation for the technical parts in the rest of the book. Chapter 4 also covers impact models and how to create them. The latter part of the chapter explains CommunityViz analysis calculations and how to create dynamic attributes, assumptions, indicators, scenarios, and other components to answer planning questions.

Chapter 5, Three-Dimensional Scenes, presents the fundamentals of 3-D scenes, including the Google Earth Exporter, Scenario 3D, SketchUp, and other tools. This chapter describes how 3-D works, the 3-D data you need, and the basic procedures for creating a 3-D scene.

Chapter 6, Getting the Most from 3-D, goes into more detail on how to use 3-D for maximum effectiveness. There is also a section on solutions to common challenges of working in 3-D.

BACKGROUND PLANNING CONCEPTS FOR THIS SECTION

The first step in planning for a community, a region, or a specific project is to get organized. A poorly organized planning effort has a much lower likelihood of success than a well-structured and systematic one.

To begin, you must define the geographic area for which you are planning. This may be a political jurisdiction, such as a city, town, or county; or it may be an area that has no fixed political boundaries, such as a neighborhood, region, or watershed. Next, look at the history of the area and the changes it has gone through over time. Then, conduct an inventory of the major features of the area: the population, land uses, economic base, transportation systems, natural resources, housing, public infrastructure, and historic buildings and sites. Collect the data from your inventory into a GIS database. Now you are ready to explore current issues of concern to the area residents and the forces of change they are facing. You will need to identify the key stakeholders and organizations that have an interest in the future of the area. You can use the data you have gathered to analyze the planning area and identify strengths, weaknesses, opportunities, and threats (SWOT analysis). Working with the stakeholders and organizations will enable you to identify the area's heart and soul: those features and characteristics that the area residents would not want to lose. You will also determine what decisions need to be made about the planning area, as well as forge a consensus on general goals and specific objectives for its future. For example, in planning for a neighborhood, decisions will need to be made about the mix of residential and commercial uses, and the mix of single-family and multifamily housing. A goal for the neighborhood might be to promote affordable housing, and a specific objective might be to build more housing on smaller lots.

To conduct the inventory of the planning area, you will need: 1) adequate computing resources, 2) trained staff, and 3) readily available data sources. Computer capacity has expanded considerably in recent years, so even laptops have enough memory to use GIS and CommunityViz.

To produce technically sound information, create accurate maps, ask "What if?" questions in scenario planning, and respond to questions from the public and elected officials, a project team needs to include staff trained in GIS and CommunityViz. If a local government does not have staff trained in GIS and CommunityViz, one or more experts can be hired on a contractual basis (see Appendix 1).

CommunityViz and GIS should not be used with a black box approach to planning, in which technical staff controls the process. Transparency, which leads to public understanding, is very important when using GIS and CommunityViz. While no one expects the public to become proficient in GIS and CommunityViz, citizens should have a basic understanding of the data and models being used, and how GIS and CommunityViz produce useful information for planning. The more transparent the data, the more the public will tend to trust that data and become involved in the process of creating plans and ordinances, and in the review of development projects. More important, the greater the number of residents who become involved in the planning process, the better the resulting plans, ordinances, infrastructure investment programs, and decisions about development proposals are likely to be. As you will see in Section 5, CommunityViz has several tools for engaging and interacting with the public.

Data are important for informed planning, but don't let an apparent lack of data discourage you. Many data resources may already exist for the planning area, especially if it is a city or county. For instance, the U.S. Census Bureau has a wealth of data on population, housing, and economic activity. Soils maps are available in digitized form from the Natural Resources Conservation Service, and the U.S. Geological Survey has topographic quad maps. State departments of the environment and natural resources have data on air and water quality, water supply, wildlife habitat, wetlands, and natural hazards. The U.S. Environmental Protection Agency has maps of hazardous waste sites, especially in low-income areas. Although it can be expensive to create an initial GIS database for a planning area, the database is relatively inexpensive to maintain and update. Because planning is a continual process, a GIS database is a valuable tool both in the short run and over time.

One of the most frequently neglected steps in the planning process is the understanding of alternative solutions to a problem. By considering alternative solutions, you can gain insights into the strengths and weaknesses of each alternative and then select the best solution. You can think of each alternative solution as a scenario with a different amount, type, pattern, and location of development that will have a different appearance on the landscape and different impacts on local environmental, social, and economic systems. CommunityViz is particularly useful in scenario planning because it can compare alternatives side by side within a single analysis. It can show 3-D layouts of alternative proposed development proposals, a community or parcel build-out under various zoning densities, and the fiscal impacts of a variety of land uses and development densities. Also, CommunityViz can illustrate the potential effects of different development designs on the community's heart and soul resources.

In short, CommunityViz provides good information about the appearance and quantitative impacts of proposed developments, plans, and land-use regulations. This information helps to produce better public decisions about where and how a community should grow and develop. CommunityViz is a tool, not an oracle of future events or a provider of conclusive evidence. People, not computers, make decisions. Planning is a political process, not simply a technical one. Often, decision makers have to weigh a variety of issues and residents' concerns. This human element makes planning as much an art as a science.

With any planning effort, you need to be aware of the limitations of time and budget. We strongly recommend that you use proven project management and scheduling tools to maintain control of the work. Delivering a planning project on time and under budget is another way to gain support for the project.

Strive to create a living comprehensive plan that the public, landowners, developers, and elected officials can use as they make decisions about the future of the place they live or invest in. A good practice is to make the plan available online at the community's website. Interactive features can further illustrate planning concepts and goals.

Visualization is still new enough in the planning world that standards and practices are not yet well established. More than 300 urban and suburban communities in the United States have adopted form-based codes to regulate the appearance of new buildings and building renovations. A number of communities have adopted design review standards for new buildings and renovations, mainly in historic districts. But for new developments on greenfield sites, few communities have visual assessment guidelines or regulations. In the late 1990s and early 2000s, developers could wow their audiences with computer-generated 3-D visuals of proposed projects. Unfortunately, the wow factor could also mask the realities of a project, and the finished results were sometimes an unpleasant surprise. Tools such as CommunityViz and SketchUp are making visualization accessible enough for it to become a normal part of the comprehensive planning and development review process. We expect that the same standards of transparency and fairness that now apply to fiscal and environmental impact assessments will also apply to the visualization of development proposals, comprehensive plans, zoning, and subdivision regulations.

1 GETTING STARTED

KEY CONCEPTS AND TERMS IN THIS CHAPTER

- Area profile
- Decisions versus information and enough good information
- Forces of change
- Stakeholders
- Study area
- Transparency and black box models
- Using models and data

Planning the future of a community and its land uses is a bold undertaking. Public plans, regulations, infrastructure investment, and private development choices will affect many lives and produce broad and long-lasting consequences. Whether the planning area is a 1-acre site, a small community, or a metro region, your planning decisions need to be based on good information and careful analysis of available options.

There are many ways to use CommunityViz. In growth planning, for example, you can project the population 20 years from now and enter different development densities to produce an array of scenarios with different impacts on land consumption, water quality, traffic, and public finances. You choose the data, variables, and scenarios to use. CommunityViz is also an effective tool for analyzing the suitability of sites for development or conservation, conducting zoning capacity analyses, undertaking design reviews, and for many other planning applications. Its analytical and visual tools will give you insights about current planning challenges and the future opportunities in the planning area that will help you draft land-use plans and regulations, identify infrastructure investment needs, and make day-to-day decisions about development proposals.

In this book, we do not prescribe a recipe that is just right for every particular planning project, but we do provide many ideas and examples. You need to determine how best to use CommunityViz in your planning process and how it can help to involve and inform the general public and elected decision makers.

This chapter and the next two chapters will guide you through how to design a CommunityViz analysis in a planning project. To use CommunityViz effectively, you should approach a planning project with a step-by-step work plan and time schedule. As part of the work plan, it is important to balance the high-tech of computer software analysis and visualization with the personal touch of human interaction. Your audience and clients need to get a feel for CommunityViz in order to understand how it produces results and how those results embody the needs and desires of the residents of the planning area.

DEFINE YOUR STUDY AREA

Start your planning project by defining the place where you are working and where you will apply CommunityViz. You may first think of the place in terms of political jurisdictions and borders, but these are not the only kinds of boundaries. For example, planning projects often focus on watersheds, ecological regions, and Metropolitan Statistical Areas. Think about your place as the sum of all the natural and human systems in the *study area*. Although your plan may be implemented in a limited area, your plan must be drafted with an awareness of how your study area fits into larger ecological or economic regions. For instance, a land-use plan for a city that ignores land-use activity in the suburbs will likely miss important economic and transportation influences.

The art is to choose a study area that is large enough to capture the important characteristics of the natural and human systems you will be considering but small enough to be manageable. Define the study area early in your project, because much of the subsequent work will depend on that definition.

Although there is no formula for choosing the proper size of a study area, our experience suggests the following guidelines:

- For a large or multijurisdictional region such as a county or metro area, use exact political boundaries. The influences of the natural and human systems outside the boundary are usually small enough that they can be ignored.

- For a rural town or small city surrounded by mostly undeveloped land, use a larger area, such as an impact area, county, watershed, or other natural boundary that captures the homes of most of the people who use the town or city as their commercial and social center.

- For a small- to medium-sized city or town in a suburban area, adjacent to similar cities and towns, use a larger area that captures any key commercial centers, natural amenities, or transit hubs. It may not be necessary to gather detailed data outside the primary jurisdiction, but the location of key features will often help you identify major land-use influences coming from outside your planning area.

- For a neighborhood smaller than a city or town, use the entire city or town if possible.

- For a single site in an urban area, use the neighborhood; and for a single site in a town or suburb, use the entire town or suburb.

- For an undeveloped natural area such as a park or preserve, use the encompassing watershed boundary or a boundary large enough to incorporate prime habitats of key plant and animal species.

Once you have identified the study area, use it as a guide for gathering data. In most cases, you will want GIS layers that cover the entire study area; clip out and discard data that extends beyond the study area. You will also want statistics, measurements, and other data that correspond as closely as possible to the entire study area.

CREATE AN AREA PROFILE

The more you know about your study area, the better your planning effort with CommunityViz is likely to be. We recommend that you gather available, relevant information to create an *area profile*. An area profile is a broad overview of the place where your planning project will occur. The information you need to gather is similar to that used for a comprehensive plan, so you may be able to draw from existing sources, or conversely, your work may contribute to other planning efforts, such as an update of a comprehensive plan.

There are two primary goals in compiling and analyzing information for the area profile. The first is to understand the present day situation: population, geography, economy, environment, community character and values, heart-and-soul resources, and so on.

The second main goal is to understand trends, both from the recent past and projected 20 years or more into the future. The history of a community or region over the past 20 years tells the story of how and why the community or region has evolved in terms of population, economic base, character, and land-use patterns. Expected future trends may illustrate opportunities or threats in the study area involving, for example, water quality and water supplies, the economic base, housing, and transportation networks.

Don't try to create new data or build an encyclopedia at this stage. As the project progresses, you will identify more specific data needs for particular plans, models, or analyses. A theme that recurs throughout the CommunityViz process is the principle of using *enough good information* for the analysis. As you assemble the area profile, gather information that gives you a general understanding about the place and its natural and human systems. Summaries are better than details; coarse scale is better than fine. For more on data collection, see Chapter 2.

Below are several types of data that are often useful for a planning project. This list is meant as a starting point; you can modify it to suit the particulars of your planning project, and you will not necessarily need all of the information in this list. For data sources, see Appendix 4.

Useful planning data include:

- Population data
- Geographic base layers, or base maps showing information such as roads, buildings, waterways, and special places
- Photos, including aerial photos; photos of iconic buildings and places, local events, and street scenes; and photos from the past
- Economic data, including data about tax revenues, employment, and assessed property values
- Transportation data
- Housing data
- Environmental and natural resource data
- Planning data, such as maps of zoning districts and land uses.

If you are studying the heart-and-soul resources of a community, the area profile should include elements such as these:

- Articulated core values of the community
- Favorite or special places
- Landmarks
- Gathering places
- Informal social networks and events
- Informal boundaries.

IDENTIFY PROBLEMS AND FORCES OF CHANGE

Both for yourself and for audiences that you will eventually work with, you will need to identify, articulate, and to the extent that it is possible, quantify the problems and forces of change affecting the study area. Doing this helps to give you a broad and realistic context for your study area.

You may discover problems through looking at statistical trends or forecasts for population growth, housing needs, or water use. Other problems may be tied to specific recent or anticipated events, such as the opening or closing of a large local business or the planned development of a new transportation project. Some problems may be linked to longer-term challenges such as chronic underemployment.

Forces of change can be either concrete, such as a new zoning ordinance, or abstract, such as the public's desire for less traffic on a particular road.

The more deeply you think about the problems and forces of change, the more you will begin to understand the natural and human systems affecting your study area. CommunityViz can model conventional systems, such as the local economy or the transportation network, as well as unconventional systems, such as the local volunteer network. You will rapidly find that the natural and human systems of every place are interconnected. And forces of change that affect one system influence others as well. Putting together an area profile is a good exercise for making sure you are considering the most important elements of each system in your planning project.

For each problem or force of change, try to specify the following (see Figure 1.1 for an example):

- Name
- Brief description
- How it is manifested
- How it is measured
- Direct effects, desirable or undesirable
- Important indirect effects, desirable or undesirable
- Direct causes, if known
- Important indirect causes, if known
- Current state or condition, if known
- Satisfaction with current state or condition
- Desired future, if known

Figure 1.1 Problem or force of change worksheet example

ISSUE or FORCE of CHANGE WORKSHEET	SAMPLE
Name	Residential population growth
Description	Increase in the number of people living here
How manifested	More residents each year
How measured	Annual % change, incl. births, deaths, move-ins, move-outs
Direct effects	Scarce housing, busier downtown, crowded schools, more traffic...
Indirect effects	Higher house prices, healthier local retail, higher percentage of newcomers...
Direct causes	Regional/national trends, good quality of life, new employers...
Indirect causes	Recreation opportunities, local university, not sure what else?
Current state	Growth rate was 1.3% over last 10 years
Current satisfaction	Some think too high; some think too low
Desired future	Not clear; advantages and disadvantages

Later, you will come back to these problems and influences as you build a CommunityViz analysis that will help you forge a planning response. To start, though, you can create an outline or set of worksheets and then fill in and refine the problems and outside forces as your information and understanding grow.

IDENTIFY KEY PEOPLE AND ORGANIZATIONS

Planners and designers use the term *stakeholders* to refer to the people, businesses, government agencies, and nonprofit organizations that can influence or be affected by the outcome of a group decision. Early in your planning project, you will want to identify the stakeholders in your study area. Cast a wide net. A basic tenet of CommunityViz is that *you can learn from everyone*. The more perspectives you consider, the more robust your results will be, even if you ultimately make a decision that is contrary to the interests of particular stakeholders. Here are some potential stakeholders to consider:

- Developers and landowners who are proposing developments or changes to the local comprehensive plan, or zoning or subdivision regulations
- Elected and appointed officials who make decisions about the city, town, township, or county
- Business leaders
- Local government employees who will implement decisions
- The public, which usually means people who live or work in the planning area
- Formal and informal advocacy groups and social networks
- Experts and data providers on important planning topics
- Residents who understand the heart and soul of the community
- Those people who may not normally participate in the process, such as low-income residents and ethnic minorities.

As you identify each stakeholder, try to understand what their stake is: how they might influence decisions, how they might be affected by decisions, and what their desired outcomes might be. Later, you will begin to quantify these interests to use in your CommunityViz analysis.

DESCRIBE DECISIONS THAT NEED TO BE MADE AND QUESTIONS TO ANSWER

A key step in starting a CommunityViz project is articulating the decisions that need to be made and the questions you want to answer. This exercise gets to the heart of the way CommunityViz works.

THE COMMUNITYVIZ PROJECT FRAMEWORK FOR DECISION MAKING

Newcomers to CommunityViz often ask, "What will it tell me?" The short answer is, "What do you want to know?" A longer explanation is in order, though.

If you have been working with traditional computer modeling programs, "What will it tell me?" is a natural question because many software programs are designed to give specific answers based on specific data inputs. These are called closed models—or more familiarly, black box models, because their operations take place hidden from view, as if in a sealed, opaque box.

There are data inputs, there is a repeatable but unknown computing procedure, and then there are data outputs (see Figure 1.2).

When you use a black box model in a project, the main question is which model to use. The choice often depends on the answer to a subsequent question: "What will it tell me?" If the model's specified outputs give you the information you need, then, as shown in Figure 1.3, you simply gather the required input data, run the model, and receive your answers. This is a simplification, perhaps, but it describes the essence of the black box approach.

CommunityViz takes a very different approach. It is designed to help people make informed choices, and therefore it tries to operate from the *person's* point of view. A typical flow chart for using CommunityViz is illustrated in Figure 1.4.

Figure 1.3 Using black box model for projects

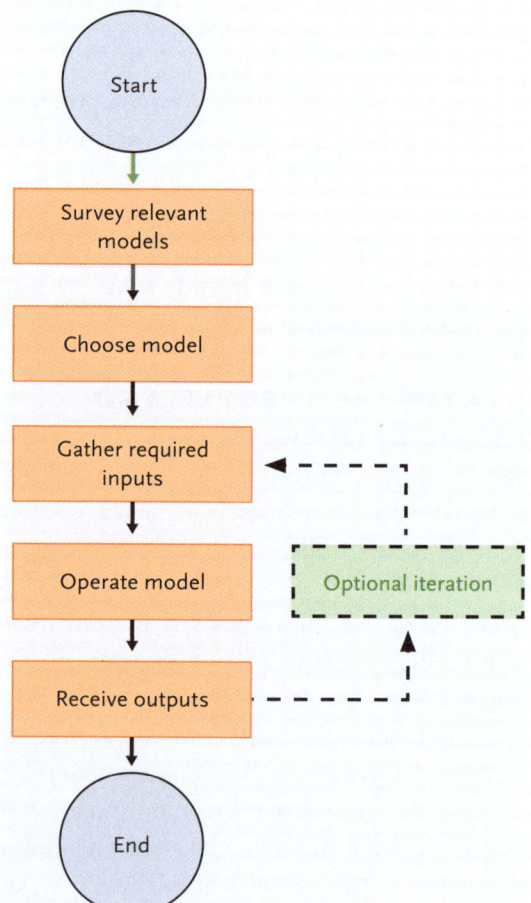

Figure 1.2 Black box model

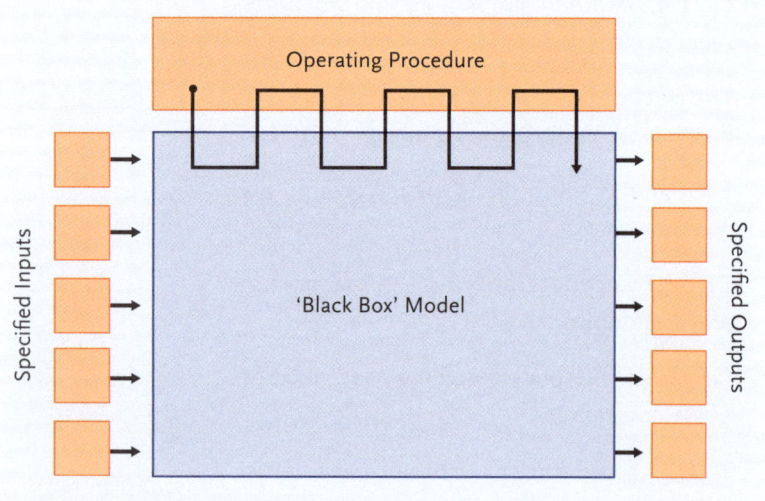

Getting Started

Figure 1.4 Using CommunityViz for projects

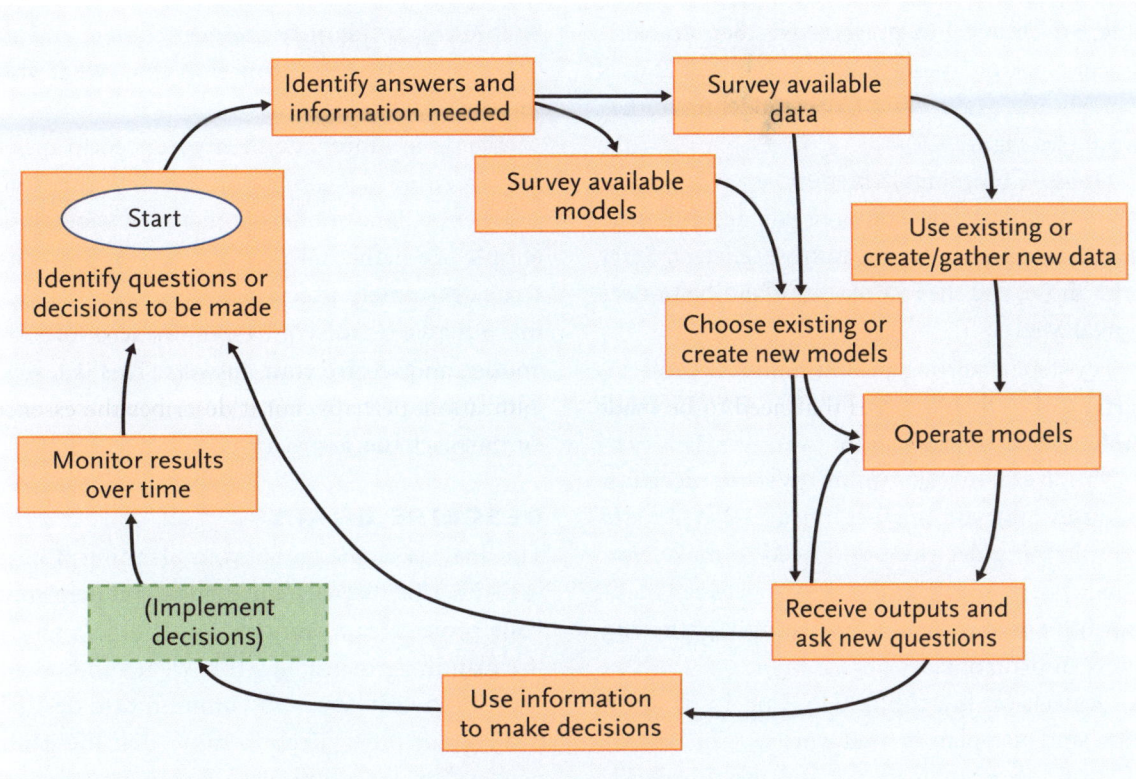

Figure 1.5 CommunityViz modeling framework

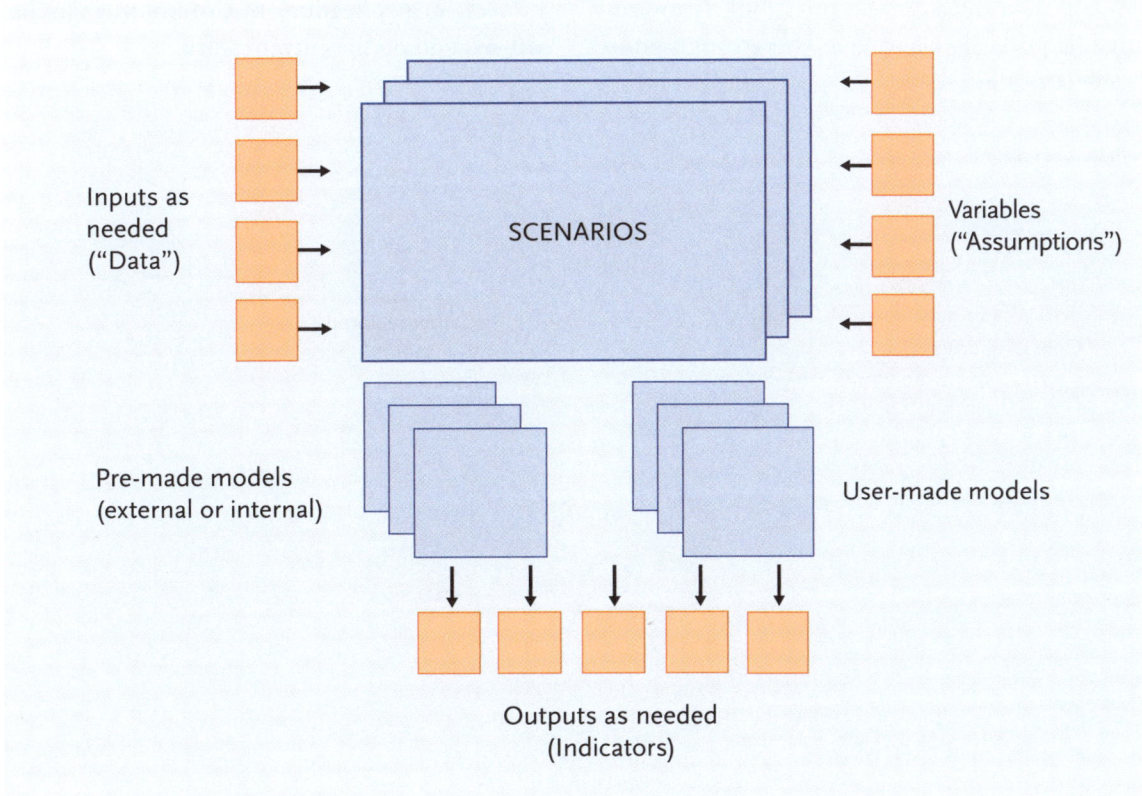

This process is more interactive, more flexible, and much less prescriptive than conventional black box modeling. CommunityViz uses models, but as part of a larger modeling framework (see Figure 1.5).

To use CommunityViz effectively you need to know what planning decisions you need to make and what questions you want to answer. Start with those, and the rest of your planning project will follow.

THE DIFFERENCE BETWEEN DECISIONS AND INFORMATION

If you are using CommunityViz for decision making and you are beginning to articulate the planning decisions you need to make, you should be aware of the distinction between making informed decisions and simply gathering more information.

A decision is a choice: Do A or do B; adopt this land-use plan or that one; use this site or that site; approve or do not approve this development proposal. In order to choose wisely, you want information about the impacts, consequences, trade-offs, and costs of a potential action. As a decision-support tool, CommunityViz is designed to give you enough good information about each choice of action to enable you to identify the best choice, and to give you no more information than what you require.

Using no more data than you need to make an informed decision can save considerable time, effort, and money. Sometimes people are tempted to gather all possible data and to construct extremely precise models, but you can make better use of your time and resources by determining the necessary amount and detail of data to produce effective plans, ordinances, and development decisions.

DESCRIBE GOALS

The final task at the start of your planning project is to describe its goals. Clear goals will help you, your project team, and the stakeholders guide the planning process, identify when and how to use CommunityViz, and communicate desired project outcomes. Keep in mind that the goals need not be just technical, such as mapmaking or a build-out analysis. One goal, for example, may be to build trust among different stakeholders. Another goal may be to discover new planning projects or applications of CommunityViz that will expand on the current work.

2 TECHNICAL NEEDS AND DATA RESOURCES FOR COMMUNITYVIZ

KEY CONCEPTS AND TERMS IN THIS CHAPTER

- Best practices and ethics for data
- Computing resources
- Data needs
- Experts
- Technical staff

Computer technology is advancing quickly. Each year the speed of computation, the clarity of visualization, and the capabilities of the GIS platforms underlying CommunityViz improve. The accessibility of data and the portability of software applications are also increasing. This rapid progress is good news, but it means that if we give recommendations regarding file sizes or computing requirements, they may soon be obsolete. Therefore, in this chapter, we focus on practices for finding data and computing with GIS and CommunityViz that we think will hold true for at least a few more years.

COMPUTING RESOURCES AND TECHNICAL STAFF

Before you begin using CommunityViz on a planning project, take an inventory of your computing resources and compare them to the requirements of the current version of CommunityViz and its underlying GIS platform. Keep in mind that there are many ways to use CommunityViz that do not require the combination of a full GIS platform and CommunityViz. These activities include creating portable graphics and reports, using portable viewers, setting up partly interactive websites, and more. Also consider the computing resources that the people assisting you or using the results of your planning project will need.

Chances are good that you will find adequate computing resources for CommunityViz, even if it means you need to share computing resources with other partners, such as a university, council of governments, or regional planning commission.

In addition to GIS-capable computers, take an inventory of your supporting equipment. If you will be presenting CommunityViz in public, you should have a high-quality digital projector and a laptop computer. To make large paper maps for displays or workshop exercises, access to a plotter is helpful; as an alternative, a commercial print shop may be able to produce large maps. Creating and maintaining an interactive website for your planning project allows you to reach and involve a large audience at their convenience. A good way to engage large, in-person audiences in a CommunityViz analysis is to rent or buy polling keypads, also known as clickers. They enable an audience to vote at the same time on alternative development scenarios and can help a group reach consensus in a short amount of time (see Chapter 17).

To undertake a CommunityViz analysis, you do not need to have computer science skills but you do need to be comfortable with numbers and math at about the level required to use an Excel spreadsheet. If you do not have experience with GIS, we recommend you include in your team a GIS professional who can manage the more technical aspects of CommunityViz for the planning project. CommunityViz analysis also favors a user who is familiar with planning and zoning concepts and is comfortable with advising on public planning decisions. In our experience, a planner and a GIS professional often make a good two-person team, though many CommunityViz practitioners work well on their own or in larger teams. Appendix 1 provides additional suggestions.

DATA RESOURCES

Our optimism about the advancement of computer technology in planning is more restrained when it comes to data. CommunityViz depends on a variety of data, both geospatial and otherwise, and the better the data, the better the analysis. But accessing good data has long been a challenge for GIS professionals and planners. Data can be hard to find, difficult to acquire from others, expensive, inaccurate, hard to understand, and difficult to manage. Data collection and analysis can be one of the most time-consuming and frustrating parts of a planning project. We are sympathetic to the complaint we frequently hear that a planning project simply cannot be done because of problems with data.

Fortunately, there are two major reasons not to despair about data when working with CommunityViz. First, data availability has progressed immensely over the past 20 years, particularly in the United States. Federal agencies have led the way by setting up online repositories of geospatial data, census data, and aerial imagery; and state and local governments are following the trend. Meanwhile, nonprofit organizations and for-profit businesses have set up their own databases, and the practice of data hoarding is gradually giving way to free and open data sharing. At the start of any planning project, we recommend that you do a survey of data available online for your study area.

Second, CommunityViz is flexible. In almost all cases, you can work with what you have, make approximations, or otherwise get by in even the most barren or chaotic of data environments. Your results may be less precise, and more work may be required than ideal, but you will probably be able to provide useful information for decision makers.

Data strategies for particular types of analyses are covered in Chapters 7 through 16. Appendices 2, 3, and 4 address general topics on performance and data management. Figure 2.1 provides a checklist to help you organize your computing and technical resources.

DATA BEST PRACTICES AND ETHICS

Because data are the lifeblood of planning analysis, you want to be careful how you collect, use, and present data to be as clear and accurate as possible in your analysis. A few best practices for working with data are worth noting:

- Process. Do not attempt to work with data that you do not understand; look for expert advice if needed. Use a transparent, repeatable, documented process for gathering data. Keep notes on sources and any changes you make to the data.

- Quality. Use only reliable data from qualified sources. Avoid hearsay or data provided by advocates for a particular point of view. Be sure that data sets are complete enough that they do not leave out potentially important information, and that they are as precise as they claim to be.

- Impartiality. Be fair in collecting, processing, and presenting data. Beware of your own biases, particularly when choosing which data to collect and report.

- Presentation. CommunityViz is meant to inform people and promote understanding. While fidelity to the original sources is important, a good presentation almost always calls for a certain amount of data processing and interpretation. Present data as clearly and visually as you can, emphasizing charts and maps, and minimizing large tables of numbers and information that is too complex. Let the audience know your sources, and any limitations and uncertainty in the data.

- Context. Think through how to set the context for certain types of data. Is it helpful to show how a town's population growth compares to that of the region or state? Is it helpful to discuss whether a particular trend, such as a growing scarcity of affordable housing, is local or national?

Figure 2.1 Computing and technical resource checklist

RESOURCES	ITEM	NEEDED?	SOURCE (SELF, PARTNERS)
CommunityViz System Requirements			
	CommunityViz licenses		
	ArcGIS licenses		
	Operating system		
	System drivers, frameworks		
	Companion software (e.g., SketchUp)		
Online/Offline Platforms			
	Project website		
	Online polling		
	Online video		
	Kiosks		
	Downloadable content		
Supporting Equipment			
	Projector		
	Plotter		
	Keypads (clickers)		
Personnel			
	Planning expertise		
	GIS expertise		
	CommunityViz expertise		
Data			
	GIS data		
	Nonspatial data		
	Online data services		

EXPERTS, SPECIALIZED MODELS, AND CROWDS

Not all data reside in databases. Much of the information you need may be in the heads of experts, in the code of a specialized software tool, or in the wisdom of a crowd. At the start of your planning project, you will want to identify as many of these potential sources as you can. Estimate how much time and expense might be required to get the information you need, and develop strategies for collecting it.

Experts in a particular field often know more than appears in any document or online source. The more critical a particular natural or human system is to your study area and planning effort, the more useful it is to seek out expert advice. There is an art to using this advice, however. Be aware that the knowledge and data provided by experts is valuable, particularly to them. If you freely share or distribute that expert information, it may not be fair to the experts. Respect an expert's position, and his or her expectation of financial compensation, as you discuss ways to incorporate their knowledge into your planning project.

Information about a particular study area or natural system may be easiest to create by using a specialized software tool. The software program NatureServe Vista, for example, provides an excellent platform for storing and using information about the impact of development on biodiversity. Regional planning agencies often have sophisticated models of their transportation networks. If such data or models are relevant and available, you will want to identify them at the beginning of your planning project. In most cases, CommunityViz can exchange data electronically with local and regional planning agencies, saving you the effort of collecting data, models, and information.

Drawing out the information available from a crowd—such as local residents or particular stakeholder groups—is an art and science. This book discusses how to use CommunityViz in public settings to encourage audience participation and elicit responses to planning and development alternatives. For instance, if there is a question you would like answered about housing options in a particular neighborhood, you can show the audience a range of housing mixes in different scenarios using CommunityViz and measure the responses. But also consider how you might use CommunityViz in an online community survey or an interactive website to gather information from the public about a comprehensive plan update.

3 PLANNING STUDY DESIGN GUIDELINES

KEY CONCEPTS AND TERMS IN THIS CHAPTER

- Change models
- Design for a living comprehensive plan
- Designing studies, analyses, and 3-D scenes
- Geodesign
- Impact models
- Indicators
- Project planning
- Scenario planning
- Technology selection and limits of technology
- Uncertainty

A planning study should include the goals of the study, questions to ask, data needs, public participation activities, and a schedule for completing an analysis of the study area. The planning study should also note when and how CommunityViz can help to produce results that you, your client, the public, or elected officials can use to make informed planning decisions. This chapter provides advice for the design of many types of planning studies, such as scenario planning and project planning. But the details of any planning study will depend on your particular topic, budget, schedule, and the characteristics of the study area. Sections 2 through 5 provide more detailed information about particular types of planning projects and analyses.

ABOUT SCENARIO PLANNING

Scenario planning, one of the primary strengths of CommunityViz, is a powerful decision-making approach that has been widely used for at least 100 years. In this chapter, we will describe how scenario planning works within CommunityViz and highlight the practical applications of scenario planning in real-world projects.

Figure 3.1 illustrates how scenario planning is typically used in the decision-making process.

Figure 3.1 Scenario planning in the decision-making process

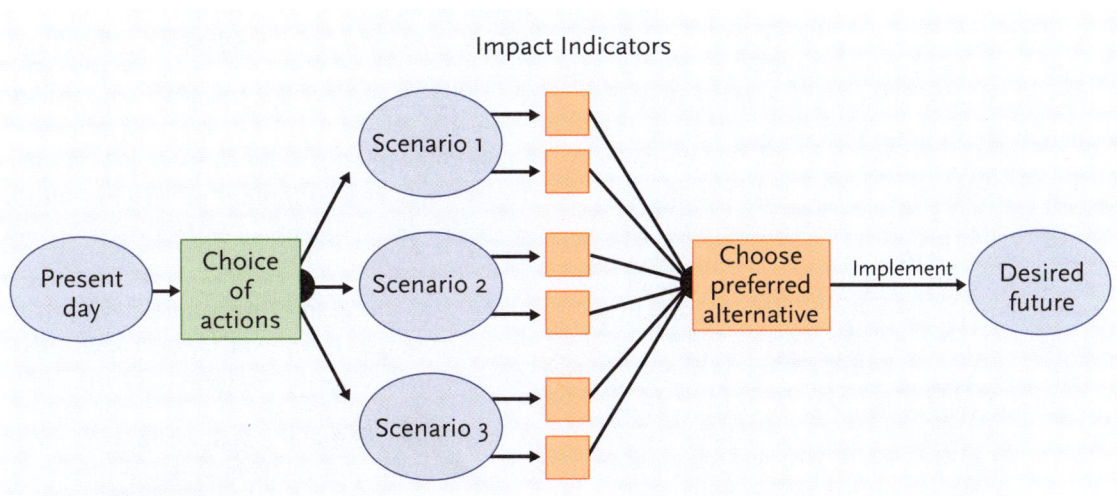

Scenarios describe possible alternative futures that might result from actions taken today. A scenario can incorporate visual changes, as well as changes in population, fiscal conditions, environmental quality, and heart-and-soul resources. The actions can be as simple as building or not building a structure, or as complex as overhauling the zoning ordinance. Usually, the purpose of creating scenarios is to combine a large number of variables into a small representative set of alternatives that illustrate major differences in outcome. For example, you don't need to compare all possible population growth rates; you can look at one low, one medium, and one high growth rate. You might also look at one land-use policy that encourages downtown density and another one that allows more growth in suburbs. Particular combinations of growth rates and policy options produce scenarios: say, a high growth/downtown density scenario, and a low growth/suburban scenario.

In CommunityViz, the characteristics of each future scenario are calculated based on computerized *sketches* of development proposals or on mathematical *growth models* or *change models* that can estimate future development, population, or fiscal impacts resulting from present-day actions.[1] For example, CommunityViz might help you calculate the number of new residential buildings that will be built in the suburbs in the future based on the land-use policy assumptions of each scenario.

The second step in scenario planning involves using quantitative metrics called impact indicators, or more simply *indicators*, to measure the results of each scenario. Indicators measure the characteristics of future scenarios that are important to decision makers and stakeholders (see Chapter 1). Traditional indicators are numbers such as property tax revenues, acres of land conserved, or the amount of vehicle traffic. Nontraditional indicators, such as a happiness index, can be useful as well. Indicators are generally calculated using *impact models*, which can range from simple to very sophisticated. Decision makers sometimes set *targets* for particular indicators, such as a minimum acceptable size of wildlife habitat or a maximum acceptable budget.

The third step in scenario planning is a comparison of the indicator results for the various scenarios. The comparison provides a general understanding of how different natural and man-made systems respond to planning or development actions, and to one another. In practice, CommunityViz users often create new or modified scenarios for further comparison. Eventually their comparisons lead to the selection of a preferred scenario.

Finally, the decision makers document and implement planning actions that they expect will produce the desired future outcome.

There are several important points to note about scenario planning:

- Scenario planning is an excellent way to study complex and interdependent natural and man-made systems. It is usually too complicated and expensive to look at all possible alternative scenarios, so you should choose a few scenarios that best fit the possible or desired outcomes. Explore a few scenarios at a time to learn about important elements and system interactions, such as the impact of population growth on water supplies. There is no simple procedure for determining which scenarios to create. Instead, most practitioners use their own judgment and some rules of thumb (detailed below) to create the first few scenarios. In subsequent scenarios, increasingly insightful information usually emerges from an exploration of possible changes to the natural and man-made systems.

- Scenarios are imperfect and incomplete models of future outcomes, and that is okay. Their

---

1. Another method of projecting future results is simulation, in which virtual systems act and interact with one another through thousands of cycles of virtual time. A simulation, for example, might specify a number of rules by which thousands of virtual people are born, age, buy real estate, commute to work, and so on, during a simulated passage of time. After many repetitions, their behavior is statistically analyzed to derive likely future results. Although this technique was present in early versions of CommunityViz through a module called Policy Simulator, simulation is not offered in current versions of CommunityViz. However, simulation results can still be used as models through links between CommunityViz and an external application running in parallel.

purpose is to inform present-day decisions, not to precisely predict an uncertain future. Scenario planning is most effective when it is updated every few years to adjust to new conditions.

- Indicators are crucial because they measure the comparative success of alternative scenarios. Characteristics of a scenario that do not have indicators will tend to be overlooked. Thus, it is important to have a comprehensive set of indicators that includes all the important characteristics of each scenario, not just the easily quantified ones.

- Indicator values need to produce a correct ranking of scenarios. The primary goal of scenario planning is to correctly rank the scenarios by each indicator score. But an indicator score does not have to be perfectly accurate, just accurate enough to produce a correct ranking.

  This point is often lost on public audiences who are seeing scenarios for the first time. If the model says that Scenario A costs $100 and Scenario B costs $80, it may be tempting to delve into whether A actually costs $97 or $102. But for the purpose of deciding between Scenario A or B, determining an exact cost of A doesn't matter as long as the rankings of A and B are correct. The only caveat is the uncertainty of the model used to create the indicator, which is the next point.

- Rarely is a model perfectly accurate. Virtually every model has a degree of uncertainty in its results, meaning that the particular number (or indicator) the model produces is within a range of values that may be correct. Uncertainty is usually a result of limitations in the model rather than carelessness on the part of the people using the model. Unfortunately, people who use models often overlook uncertainty, sometimes with negative consequences.

The example in the bullet point above is illustrated in Figure 3.2. If Scenario A costs $100 with an uncertainty of ±$5 and B costs $80 with an uncertainty of ±$5, then you can be confident that A costs more than B. But if the uncertainty in the model is ±$15 for both scenarios, then it is possible that A actually costs $85 and B costs $95—in other words, that A costs less than B. It is important that you as the analyst take care to illustrate this point to audiences if there is significant uncertainty in your models.

Figure 3.2 Examples of the effects of uncertainty

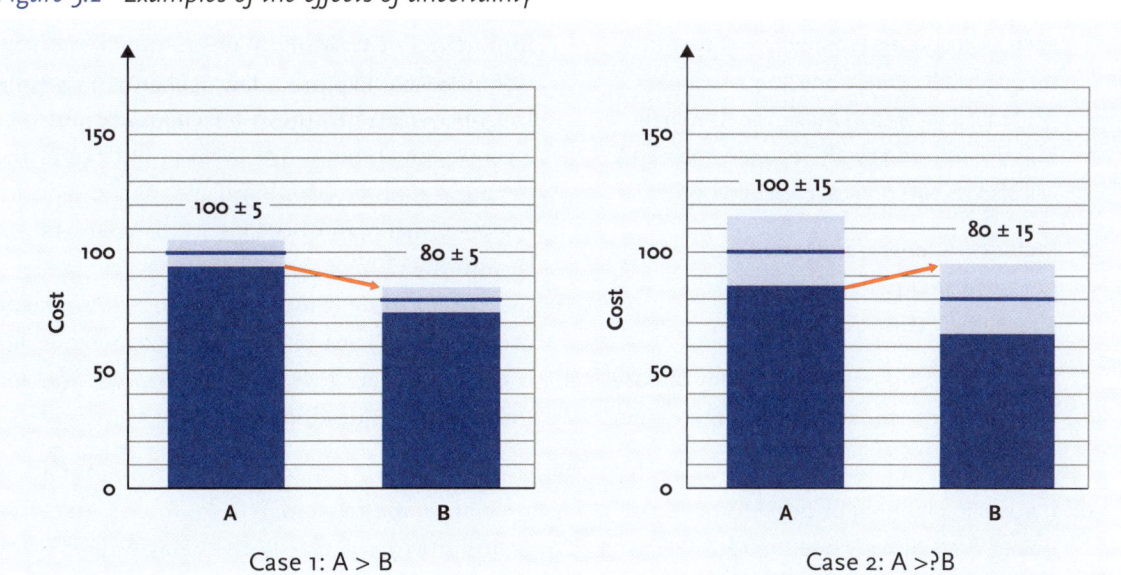

HOW SCENARIO PLANNING PRINCIPLES INFLUENCE PROJECT DESIGN

To include the scenario planning principles in the design of your project:

- Determine the natural and man-made systems that affect your planning area, and which ones you will model and include in your scenarios.

- Determine the indicators on which comparisons between scenarios will be based. Think comprehensively about what to measure, and include at least one indicator representing the interests of each stakeholder and at least one indicator for each important system. If your list lacks balance—for example, it contains 500 economic indicators and two environmental ones—determine appropriate summary indicators to use. Focus on *what* you want to measure; you will begin to determine *how* to measure it in the next stage.

- Determine the change models you will use for studying the natural and man-made systems, and the impact models you will use for generating indicators. The ability to select models requires a good understanding of CommunityViz capabilities and the particular models and their inherent uncertainties.

- Determine the starting scenarios you will create. Here are some rules of thumb:

    a. If you have several broad, independent goals, such as economic prosperity and environmental health, create one scenario for each goal that attempts to maximize its benefit. This will help you clarify separate goals and will also reveal conflicts with other goals.

    b. Include a scenario representing a business-as-usual policy, for comparison with alternative future scenarios.

    c. Consider including a present-day or base scenario for comparison with alternative future scenarios.

    d. If specific planning or development proposals have already been made, give each one a scenario.

    e. Start with five or fewer scenarios. In some cases, you may need only one scenario, as the next sections explain.

GEODESIGN AND MAKING DECISIONS WITHOUT SCENARIOS

Although scenario planning is a well-established and proven technique, you do not always need to compare alternative scenarios. You can instead set up a simpler, more flexible analysis that contains only a single map. You will still create indicators and run models as described previously, but with a focus on measuring and improving a single scenario design.

People sometimes use the term *geodesign* to describe this combination of geography and development design. In general, geodesign is a process for creating a plan or development design that includes the following steps:

1. Sketching one or more development proposals that include geographic information

2. Getting fast feedback about the implications of the proposal(s)

3. Making modifications

4. Deciding on a final plan or development design.

You can employ the sketching aspect of geodesign by using CommunityViz Scenario Sketch tools or any other method of drawing, importing, or creating maps and data that represent potential plans or development designs. In CommunityViz, the fast-feedback response to a geodesign comes in the form of indicators and dynamic analysis. Modifying a design and deciding on a final plan or design are also parts of any CommunityViz process.

To determine whether scenario planning with multiple scenarios or single-scenario geodesign is most appropriate for your project, ask yourself the following questions:

- Am I studying many interrelated natural and man-made systems? If so, multiple scenarios may help clarify the relationships and trade-offs.

- Do I have a broad range of options? If so, multiple scenarios can illustrate the diversity of choices. If not, a single scenario may be more appropriate.

- Am I making fundamental choices or simply refining small points of an existing development design or plan? Using multiple scenarios makes more sense when you are making fundamental choices. Geodesign is usually geared more toward improving an existing development proposal or site plan.

- Am I making a decision or taking measurements? If you are simply evaluating the effects or dimensions of a plan that has already been made, you do not need either scenario planning or geodesign, because their purpose is to change plans or designs. You will still use impact models, indicators, and dynamic analysis to take measurements, but you will need to work with only a single fixed scenario.

CommunityViz provides powerful tools for analyzing information and making decisions regardless of whether your approach is scenario planning, geodesign, or measurement of a static plan, or you are working toward your own solution to a particular problem. As you design your planning project, remember to focus first on the questions you are trying to answer or the problem you are trying to solve. With those goals in mind, the proper study approach will probably become clear.

PROJECT PRACTICALITIES

There is never enough time and money to do everything you would like to do with CommunityViz in a planning project. We recommend you survey the project ahead, weigh goals against resources, and design the planning study with priorities in mind.

TIME AND BUDGET

Estimating the time and effort required for using CommunityViz in a planning project is not always straightforward. It is not like preparing for a hike up a mountain where the path is known and many others have gone before. Using CommunityViz in a planning project might be closer to boating on a lake where the route is not fixed and weather conditions may vary. Even so, some guidelines are useful.

We recommend that you use a Gantt chart indicating the timeline for the planning project, when each part of it should be completed, and who is responsible for completing each part. This simple organizational tool will help you avoid confusion over who is supposed to do what and when. A planning project that drags on well beyond its proposed end date will tend to lose public interest and incur increased costs, both of which do not bode well for a planning effort.

The main purpose of Figure 3.3 is to help you understand and review the major tasks in your project for purposes of time and budget planning. It shows some elements common to most CommunityViz projects, but specific elements will certainly differ from project to project.

In Figure 3.3, we have highlighted the tasks in lighter green that, in our experience, require the greatest amount of time and effort on the part of the CommunityViz analyst. Perhaps the only surprising highlighted task is "interaction design/creation," by which we mean using CommunityViz to create an effective presentation and then deliver it to an audience. This task includes deciding what to show, assembling a coherent story line, knowing what questions to ask, deciding whether and how to use 3-D and multimedia, and much more. These topics are covered in detail in Section 5, Communicating and Interacting. For now, it is sufficient to note that this is a significant task in project planning.

The longest CommunityViz project featured in this book took about three years and the shortest about two months. A time frame of three to six months is typical for the CommunityViz phase of a public community planning project. For smaller private-sector projects, a complete CommunityViz analysis can be done in a matter of days or even hours given specific objectives.

We have found that data collection and processing takes anywhere from essentially no time if a working geodatabase is already in place, to perhaps two or three weeks if little or no data is available to begin with and you are seeking a sophisticated analysis. If completely new data must be created, such as an original trails map or results from a community values survey, then several weeks will be needed. Building the analysis normally takes a few weeks, though the time varies greatly depending on the study's complexity and novelty, and on the analyst's level of experience.

TRADE-OFFS AND LIMITATIONS OF FEASIBLE PLANNING PROJECTS

A wise manager will design a planning project in which the goals, data needs, and scenarios are reasonably matched with the financial and personnel resources and technology available. The graphs in Figure 3.4 illustrate two of the most important project trade-offs: complexity of anal-

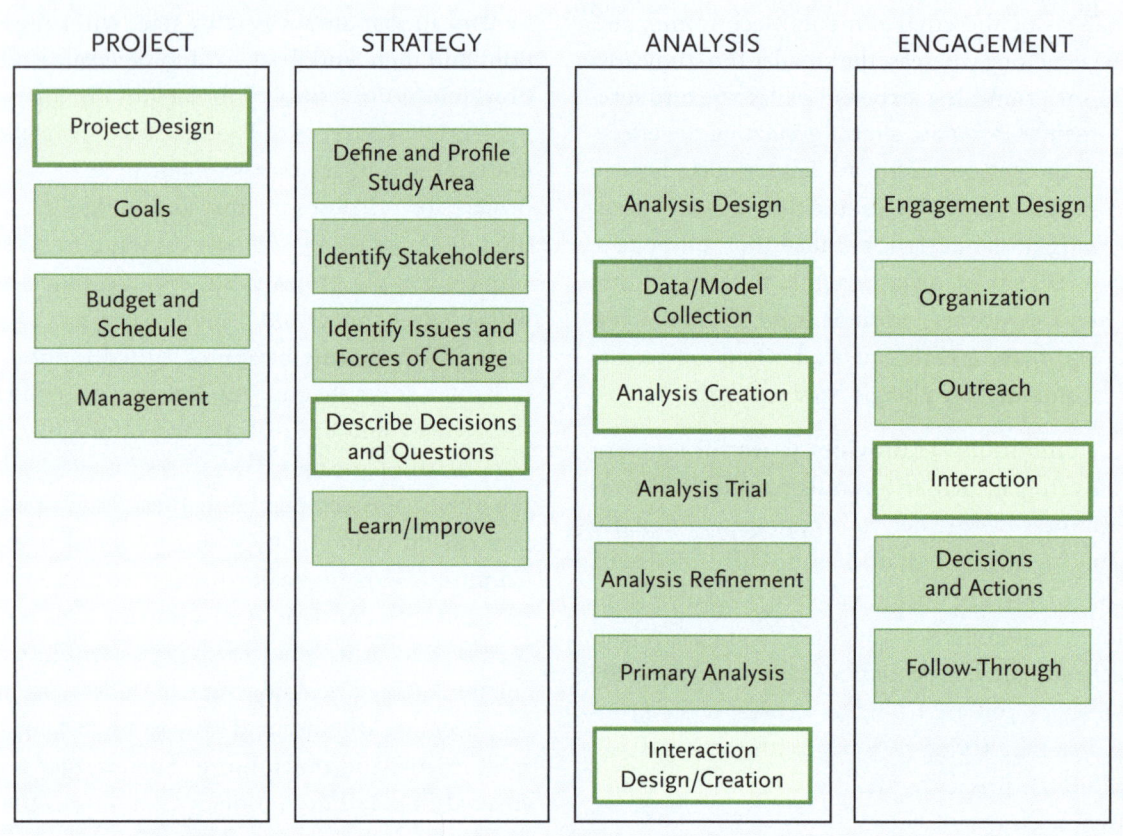

Figure 3.3 Common project tasks

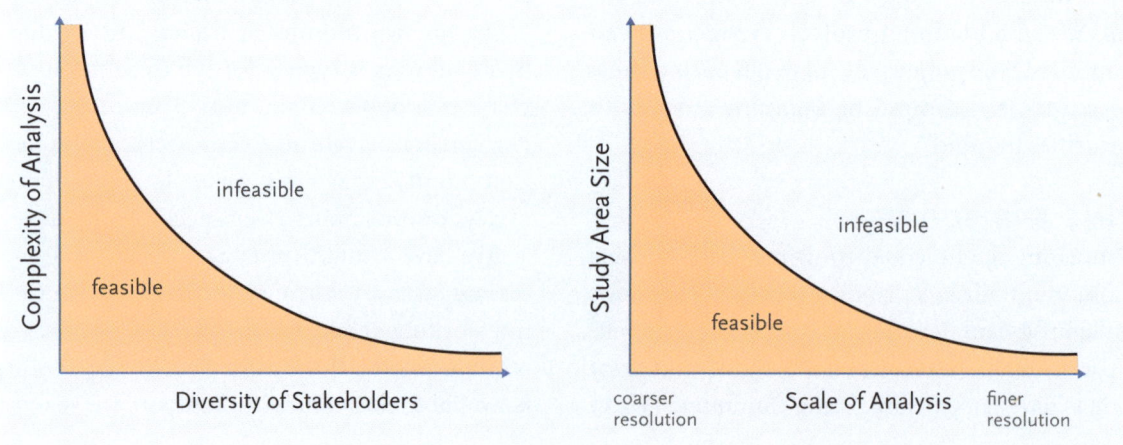

Figure 3.4 Technology capacity limits

ysis versus diversity of stakeholders, and study area size versus analysis scale. The more diverse the stakeholders, the less complex the technical analysis, because of the need to consider so many different points of view. Conversely, with fewer stakeholders and fewer points of view, the technical analysis can be more complex, focusing on environmental and economic features, rather than social aspects. The larger the study area, the more expensive it is to do a fine-grained, detailed analysis of the environmental, economic, and social factors; whereas, the smaller the study area the easier and less expensive it is to conduct a fine grained analysis and hence the more useful the computer technology.

Other trade-offs and limits may exist. Overzealous project managers sometimes overlook such limits, but understanding them is important for identifying feasible and infeasible planning projects.

If a planning project appears at the outset to hold technical risks and press the limits of feasibility, our best advice is to: a) recheck the analysis and project design to see if you can still derive good answers from a slightly simpler or more step-by-step approach, and b) try some small-scale experiments before scaling up to a full-blown analysis.

ANALYSIS DESIGN

In the general sense of the term, a CommunityViz *analysis* is the evaluation components you set up when using the software. It is analogous to the set of files in a folder. Technically, an analysis includes: data, maps, charts, 3-D and multimedia, and so on. In some cases, though, the term *analysis* is used more narrowly to mean just the computational parts of the project, such as models and formulas, not the 3-D scenes. Here we are using *analysis* in the more general sense.

Designing an analysis means creating a work plan that you can illustrate in a work outline or flowchart. The design tells you what you will need to do, how you will support the decision-making process, approximately which models and data you will use, and what your initial priorities will be. In other words, it is a way to think about and plan the work ahead.

Designing the analysis is a subset of the overall design of the planning project. You should recognize that there is a continual interplay between how people will use the analysis and what the computer will do. You usually start designing the analysis after you have compiled the area profile and identified the technical resources, as described in Chapters 1 and 2.

It is almost always best to start with questions and then work backward to determine the CommunityViz analysis you need to do. Figure 3.5 shows an overview of a typical approach to analysis design using CommunityViz.

Figure 3.6 shows a CommunityViz analysis in greater detail, illustrating how the models and data consist of a number of choices. In this flowchart, you first imagine how the analysis will guide a choice of actions during a public

Figure 3.5 Designing an analysis

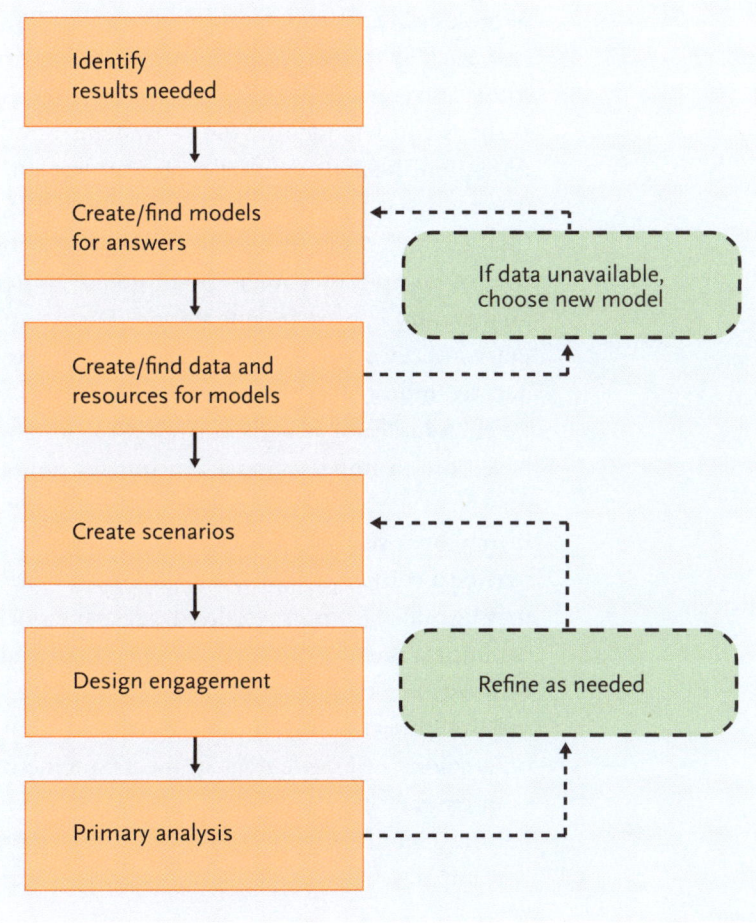

Figure 3.6 Designing an analysis (modeling details)

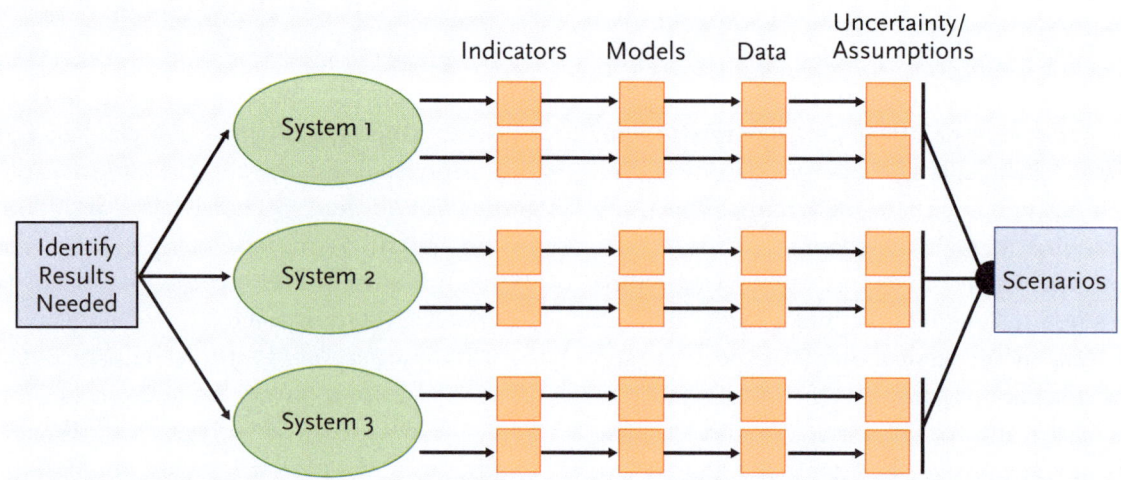

presentation. What choices will the audience face, and how will they learn more about them? What maps, charts, data, and other information will they need to see?

The potential scenarios will affect economic, environmental, and social systems. Although all those systems interact, it is more practical to start by looking at each one separately. For a given system, such as the natural environment, what are some convenient ways to break out subsystems? Perhaps you will identify the subsystems of air, water, and habitats. Within each of those subsystems, what are the key measures—the indicators—of success or failure of a given scenario? In this example, they might be air quality, water quality, and habitat fragmentation. Each summary indicator may be broken down into more-detailed indicators as well.

Each indicator is derived from a calculation based on an impact model. An impact model may be as simple as a number or an assumption, it may be a single CommunityViz formula, it may be a complex CommunityViz analysis, or it may be pulled from a specialized external model. An impact model may even be a collection of all of those. For example, imagine you are modeling the impact of a new housing development on a colony of prairie dogs in the area. One of your impact indicators might be "prairie dog habitat viability," measured from 100 percent (no impact) to 0 percent (no prairie dogs can survive). A simple model might be based on the amount of habitat area covered by buildings or pavement. If half the colony is covered, your indicator is 50 percent. A more sophisticated model might take into account the size of the colony, its proximity to houses, and other data that could be included in a CommunityViz formula. The next level up might involve a detailed statistical analysis based on field data of prairie dog habitats collected from similar developments, for which you would connect CommunityViz to an external database. Finally, you might decide to do a complete ecosystem assessment that takes into account not just prairie dogs and houses but also other animals, vegetation, groundwater, and other factors. For a model such as this, you would use several tools and models, all tied into your CommunityViz scenarios.

In some ways, your selection or construction of a model drives the analysis, but a model is of no use without data and the rest of the analysis framework.

The next step is to gather and apply data to the model. Data gathering usually begins earlier than model building because it takes more time. Often, the data required for a particular model are not immediately available. At this point, CommunityViz provides you with three choices: 1) obtain the data, 2) approximate the data or consider a data range or scenario, or 3) choose a new model. Any of these options can work well, depending on your circumstances.

Once you have assembled the indicators, impact models, and data, you will see in what ways they are interdependent, and the characteristics of the natural and human systems will become clearer. At this point in the analysis design, you will create scenarios. Keep in mind that scenarios represent only variations in planning or development *proposals*, not variations in the planning area itself or the systems that affect it. With CommunityViz, it is easier to create a single scenario first and then add alternative scenarios later.

In the final step of the analysis, you need to think about how you want audiences to interact with the analysis, and then create an engaging presentation. This step often involves creating maps, charts, scenes, and multimedia. A CommunityViz presentation is not like a slide show. Instead, it is a dynamic system for communicating information and responding to audience participation. In creating the presentation, you may also see a need to include additional analysis so that you can make certain points more clearly, such as: additional indicators, for example, vehicle miles traveled; easier ways to make changes to scenarios for example, more sketching options for adjusting residential density; or easier ways to ask "what if?" questions, for instance, changing assumptions about infrastructure costs.

ITERATIVE DESIGN

The design of any CommunityViz analysis is never completely correct the first time, and you should expect to improve your analysis over time. We recommend that you test your initial analysis on yourself or with a small, safe audience. Find out which parts make sense, which parts do not, what questions arise, and anything else that will help you increase clarity. These lessons will allow you to refine the analysis prior to sharing it with larger audiences.

DESIGN FOR TRANSPARENCY

Transparency is a core tenet of the philosophy of CommunityViz. To us, transparency means that nothing is hidden: Any audience member or client can look into the analysis and see how it was done and where the answers came from, unlike the results of a black box model. CommunityViz software is designed to support transparency, but the transparency of any given analysis is up to you.

Transparency is important for both practical and ethical reasons. We believe that people have a right to understand decisions that affect them. Decision makers use the results of a CommunityViz analysis to make choices that affect the lives of the people who live and work in the study area; those people have a fundamental democratic right to know about and to participate in those decisions. In addition, we think that a group review of a plan or development proposal generally leads to better outcomes than a closed-door review by planners or a planning consultant. If the logic, assumptions, and design of the CommunityViz analysis are open to inspection and comments, it is easier to make changes or correct mistakes and thus improve the analysis.

A transparent design lets you address questions and comments from the public quickly and directly, which adds credibility to your analysis and saves time. Finally, by focusing on transparency from the beginning, you will have an easier time writing up reports and documents at the end of the planning project.

Transparency does not mean that all parts of the analysis must be evident to all audiences. CommunityViz analysis is often complex, and for most audiences a summary of the assumptions, data, models, and analysis results is both welcome and appropriate. A well-designed analysis makes it easy for audiences to start from a summary presentation, ask questions, and receive more details if desired.

The following fictional dialogue provides an example of how transparency shows up in a well-designed CommunityViz analysis.

> ***Presenter:*** You can see from this chart that Scenario A costs less than Scenario B.
>
> ***Audience member:*** What costs are you including?
>
> ***Presenter:*** By clicking these controls, I can quickly show that the calculation includes

the initial building costs, transaction costs, and maintenance costs over time.

Audience member: Do your maintenance costs include staff salaries?

Presenter (clicking): Yes, you can see that here.

Audience member: How much are you assuming the salaries are?

Presenter: Right now salaries are set for an average value of ten thousand, but that is easy to change because I have used a variable assumption, which you can see on this slider.

Audience member: Ten thousand seems high to me. You should try eight thousand.

Presenter: Okay, here goes. (*Moves the slider and waits for the analysis to be updated.*) You're right: That change made Scenario A cost *more* than Scenario B. It looks as if staff salaries make a big difference. Maybe we should do more research to refine that number. Can you help us with that?

To allow this kind of dialogue to occur, you need to take just a little extra care as you set up your CommunityViz analysis:

- Be clear about assumptions, and if there is any doubt, set them up as assumptions that can be changed in the analysis.

- Use a modular or component-based design. In this example, it was useful that the cost model was constructed with distinct components rather than as one single complex formula.

- Wherever possible, label analysis components—for example, salaries—clearly using plain English rather than technical abbreviations. Include descriptions in the description fields provided.

MULTIMEDIA DESIGN

Multimedia in CommunityViz includes 3-D scenes and videos, animated maps, interactive websites, and other presentation and visualization formats that go beyond fixed maps, charts, and reports. These multimedia tools can play a range of roles in your planning project, from none at all to being the dominant feature.

The first two questions to ask yourself are: "Is multimedia needed?" and "For what purpose?"

Start by considering the potential benefits of using multimedia. A large body of behavioral and physiological research tells us that the decision-making process relies far more on emotion than on reason. Even after learning all the pros and cons about a plan or development project, people need to *feel* that a decision is right before they will commit to it. Our experience with CommunityViz is that audiences want the ability to make an emotional connection with future scenarios as part of their decision-making process. Multimedia, particularly 3-D scenes, can help make this happen.

We also know that models and complicated information presented through CommunityViz are not always easy for a nontechnical audience to understand. It may be unrealistic to expect people who have never seen your analysis before to understand the questions the analysis is attempting to answer, absorb the key information the analysis is providing, ask perceptive questions about the analysis, and make firm decisions about a proposed plan or development—all within the space of an hour or two. Such an exercise is challenging to experts and nonexperts alike. CommunityViz does not cause decision making to be complex; the complexity arises from the conflicting interests of stakeholders and the interdependent natural and human systems that need to be considered in making decisions about the future of a site, neighborhood, community, or region.

A picture really is worth a thousand words, and a 3-D multimedia representation is probably worth a thousand pictures. A well-rendered 3-D scene instantly conveys huge amounts of rich information in a way that almost everyone can understand. Add to that a judicious use of statistics and data and you have a powerful tool to facilitate group decision making.

Another benefit of CommunityViz multimedia is the "gee whiz" factor—the excitement and interest generated by a novel, effective technology that most audiences have not seen in action. In our experience, a presentation that promises 3-D and other multimedia will attract a larger audience than one that does not. We find that once the audience—whether a large public group or a smaller working team—has been drawn into the planning project by the visuals, they are more prepared to discuss the analysis of the planning area and the decisions that need to be made.

On the other hand, multimedia is not always necessary or even desirable. Multimedia has a tendency to steal the show during public presentations, taking up too much time and attention before the audience has had a chance to analyze the information and move on to making decisions. Multimedia also has a tendency to consume project resources. At Placeways, there is a saying, "The 3-D is never done." In a project utilizing 3-D, team members require constant reminders to focus on the project deadline and stay under budget. And finally, you should be aware that multimedia requires specific skills and technical resources.

If you decide to use multimedia in your planning project, your project design will follow a pattern similar to the design of a CommunityViz analysis. Most of the complexity of multimedia in CommunityViz is in the 3-D. The structure of the typical multimedia design flow in Figure 3.7 is only slightly different from that of the analysis design shown in Figure 3.5, with 3-D resources and 3-D models replacing map data and impact models. The main difference is that in 3-D, data gathering precedes modeling: You start with photos, maps, and data about the study area, and then you decide how to make 3-D models of the area.

VISUALIZATION PRIORITIES

You have to take extra care if you use multimedia in your planning project. The visual and emotional power of multimedia can greatly influence audiences and decision makers. In particular, you have to guard against misleading people with visualization. But sticking to a few best

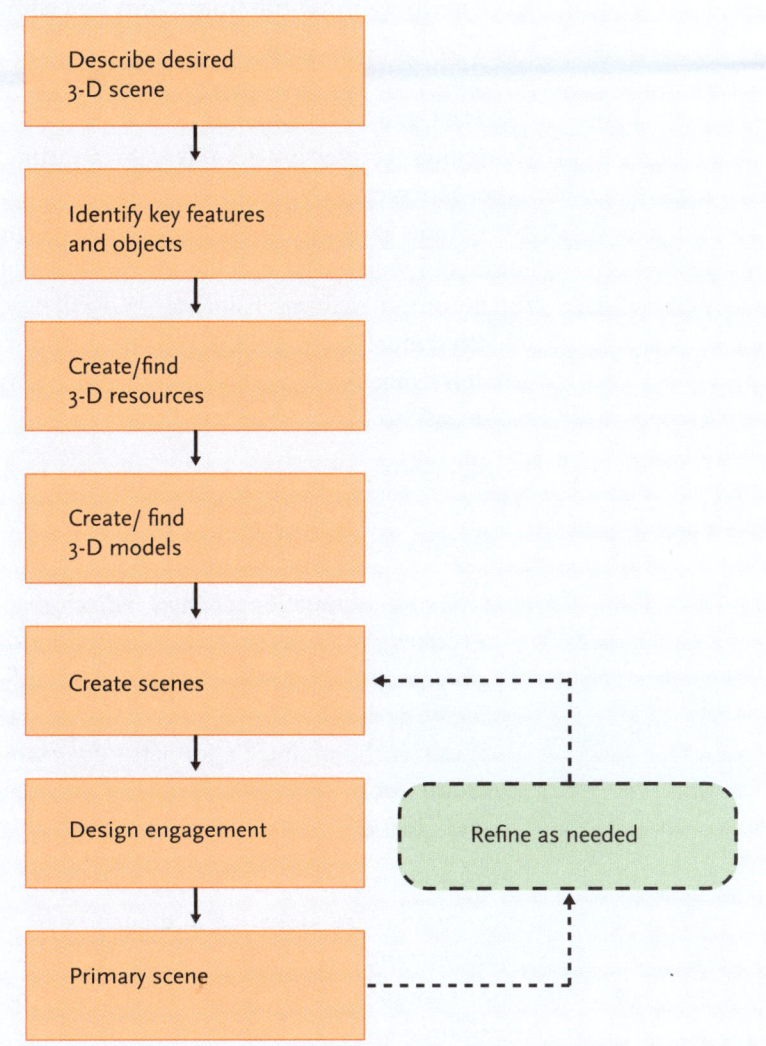

Figure 3.7 3-D project design

practices throughout the visualization process will help ensure fair and honest results. Chapter 6 provides details.

The primary consideration for using visualization in the project design is choosing what to show with CommunityViz. It is very tempting to dedicate most of your resources to a single visual scenario, usually the one you prefer or are proposing. But when you present this one scenario to the public or to a client, you will tend to limit the conversation to a yes/no debate that does not consider alternative scenarios. Furthermore, the scenario that receives the most attention in an analysis will tend to look the best, possibly adding a bias. Ideally, all scenarios should be represented fairly and equally. However, in practice you will have limited time and resources, so you will have to prioritize how much time and effort you spend on each scenario.

TECHNOLOGY SELECTION

CommunityViz Version 4.x offers three distinct options for creating 3-D scenes, plus a large selection of tools for creating web content, embedding audio and video clips, making animated maps, and more. In designing an analysis, you will need to determine which tools and techniques to use. The following questions may help you identify multimedia needs and opportunities.

1. Who is the audience? This question may have several answers, such as stakeholder teams, the general public, and elected officials.

2. What new information, such as indicator values, does the audience need to understand? Can you convey this information efficiently, clearly, and accurately without multimedia? If not, which multimedia formats—for example, an interactive website—would meet the need most efficiently?

3. What spatial information, such as dwelling units per acre, does the audience need to understand? Which multimedia formats—for example, 3-D scenes—would present this information most effectively?

4. What new impressions about the project is the audience likely to form in the absence of multimedia? Would multimedia change audience impressions or improve their understanding?

5. What subjective information, such as personal stories, do you want to convey? Could multimedia help?

6. How and in what settings—public meeting, private company, or community-wide web site—will the multimedia be used? Based on technical requirements and cost constraints, which technology is best suited to that setting?

7. How much time and money do different technology choices require relative to the project deadline and budget? What is the priority of the multimedia technology compared to other project needs?

COMMUNICATION DESIGN

Sometimes, CommunityViz is not the centerpiece of a planning project, but rather an accessory tool for providing additional visualization and clarity. At other times, the CommunityViz analysis is central, but organizers surround it with a public outreach and communication effort designed to reach larger audiences. In both cases, you as the CommunityViz analyst will want to pay extra attention to communication formats such as websites, public meeting materials, and broadcast and print media. CommunityViz offers a wide array of communication-oriented outputs, ranging from very easy-to-produce reports to more time-consuming 3-D scenes. You will want to select the communications that work best within your budget.

DESIGN FOR A LIVING COMPREHENSIVE PLAN

Local government comprehensive plans are all too often put on the shelf, their findings forgotten and their recommendations unheeded. While some people might argue that just going through the comprehensive planning process benefits the community, we believe that the shelf is not the intended destination of a comprehensive plan.

We recommend that you create a living comprehensive plan that will lead to changes in implementing ordinances and public infrastructure investment, carefully considered day-to-day planning decisions over time, and long-term monitoring of the performance of the plan and necessary adjustments to the plan to keep it up to date. Here are several recommendations for creating a living comprehensive plan:

- Throughout the planning process and particularly during meetings with the public, distinguish between the desirable and the possible. There is nothing wrong with creating a community vision for what is desirable. As described in Chapter 7, visioning can provide direction, focus, and momentum for drafting a comprehensive plan. The real world, however, imposes financial and physical constraints, which means you need to set priorities and make trade-offs. A comprehensive plan that fails to confront these realities will be impossible to implement and will quickly land on the shelf. On the other hand, a well-designed CommunityViz analysis that models key natural and man-made systems, presents realistic scenarios, and clarifies choices that need to be made will help you to incorporate into the comprehensive plan pragmatic choices of action that will increase your chance of achieving a desired future.

- Think in terms of time spans, annual cycles, and continuous monitoring of changes in the community compared to the goals and objectives of the comprehensive plan. Through TimeScope and other tools, CommunityViz is well equipped to help you model a succession of land-use changes through time. When you design your analysis, consider including a detailed timeline, or perhaps two or three milestone dates 10 or 20 years in the future. Your analysis can project what will or should be happening at each future date. Those results may help inform your comprehensive plan objectives, and very importantly, you may use those results to compare your expected progress according to the plan with your actual progress. If you begin to see a departure from expectations a few years down the road, you can revisit and refine the comprehensive plan.

- If possible, set targets, indicator values, and other measurements of the progress of your comprehensive plan. One popular format for doing so is called a dashboard, which is essentially a collection of targets and indicators covering a variety of topic areas, such as acres of parkland or units of affordable housing. You can set up dashboards through CommunityViz, and then update the measurements and report on progress each year. This process, known as benchmarking, keeps the comprehensive plan "alive" and noticeable to the public and elected officials.

- The concept of a living plan can also be used with other plans that guide public or private decisions that affect the community. These include transportation, open space, resource, and site plans. The idea is to have the planning commission and elected officials refer to these plans when making decisions about infrastructure investment, land-use regulations, and development proposals. Also, the public should be able to gauge the progress toward achieving the goals and objectives of the plans over time; and private landowners and developers should understand how their proposed developments fit into these plans.

- Use and re-use your analysis. One of the strengths of CommunityViz is that the logic of its analysis persists. You can use CommunityViz again and again, on different places and on different data sets, or in the case of a living comprehensive plan, on incremental changes over time. If you have set up an analysis to choose a location for, say, a new elementary school, you can use many parts of the same analysis again two years later when it is time to locate a new library. You can also use the analysis to track new building permits, the square footage of infill development, and other changes in your community year by year.

4 CUSTOM IMPACT MODELS AND ANALYSIS

KEY CONCEPTS AND TERMS IN THIS CHAPTER

- Analysis setup
- Assumptions
- Attributes, dynamic attributes, and attribute tables
- Dynamic analysis
- External models
- Formulas, Formula Editor, and Formula Wizard
- Impact models and custom impact models
- Indicators
- Lookup tables

CommunityViz has many levels, which build on one another. At the base level are tools for: writing formulas; creating charts, indicators, alerts, and maps; and working with external models. This chapter describes these basic elements of CommunityViz.

The next levels contain wizards and tools for setting up analyses, with the emphasis on common planning studies, such as site suitability and build-out. The highest levels involve presenting scenarios and exploring analyses that have already been created. If you are more interested in planning applications than in technical setup, you can safely skip ahead to Section 2.

Basic CommunityViz building blocks, such as formulas, enable you to tailor an analysis to the special needs of your project. A custom analysis is not rare or difficult; almost every real-world CommunityViz project contains at least some custom-made components. This chapter explains how to create your own indicators, models, and analysis framework using the setup features of CommunityViz.

Our emphasis here is on the process, not on the details of operating CommunityViz. For operational details, refer to the online tutorials, on-screen directions, and built-in help that comes with the software.

WHY AND WHEN

CommunityViz distinguishes between creating the decision-making framework and working with it. The creation part is called *setup* and is usually done by a CommunityViz analyst. Once the decision-making framework has been built, you can work with it by sketching scenarios, changing assumptions, viewing results, and so on. The decision-making framework is called an *analysis*, and working with the framework is called the *analysis process* or *geodesign*.

CommunityViz decision tools provide a starting point for many types of analyses, including land-use design, build-out, site suitability analysis, and more. A custom analysis allows you to supplement decision tools and create new kinds of analyses that decision tools do not provide. An exception is the Custom Impacts Wizard, which is a hybrid of decision tools and custom analysis. It will be described later in the chapter.

TYPES OF IMPACT MODELS AND HOW TO CREATE THEM

CommunityViz analysis provides decision makers with indicators so they can compare scenarios or perform geodesign and make informed decisions (see Chapter 1). Indicators are often displayed in charts and give information about the important natural and man-made systems in the study area. The indicator values come from impact models that you have built into your analysis. Examples of indicator values include tax revenues, water requirements, or more-abstract measurements, such as a happiness index associated with a particular development. An impact model is a combination of data and calculations about the scenarios you are studying.

To understand how CommunityViz calculates indicator values using impact models, you need to understand how the Scenario 360 analysis engine works. Figure 4.1 presents an overview of a Scenario 360 analysis, and the technical section at the end of this chapter provides more details.

You have several options for creating impact models. In this section of the chapter, we use the example of modeling the amount of water consumption that will result from future residential growth to describe the range of impact models, available from very simple ones to more sophisticated ones.

RATE-BASED IMPACT MODELS

The very simplest model sets a *rate*, or multiplier assumption. This method is often used by the Common Impacts Wizard. In the water-use modeling example, you make an assumption about the average amount of water use by a household, such as 300 gallons per day. Then you multiply the 300 gallons per day by the number of households in your scenario to estimate the total daily water use:

Total daily water use = (Number of households) × (Average rate of use per household per day)

To add a little more sophistication to this model, you might decide to make two different rate assumptions: one for single-family homes (350 gallons per day) and one for multifamily dwelling units (250 gallons per day):

Total daily water use = (Number of single-family households × Average rate of use per single-family household per day) + (Number of multifamily households × Average rate of use per multifamily household per day)

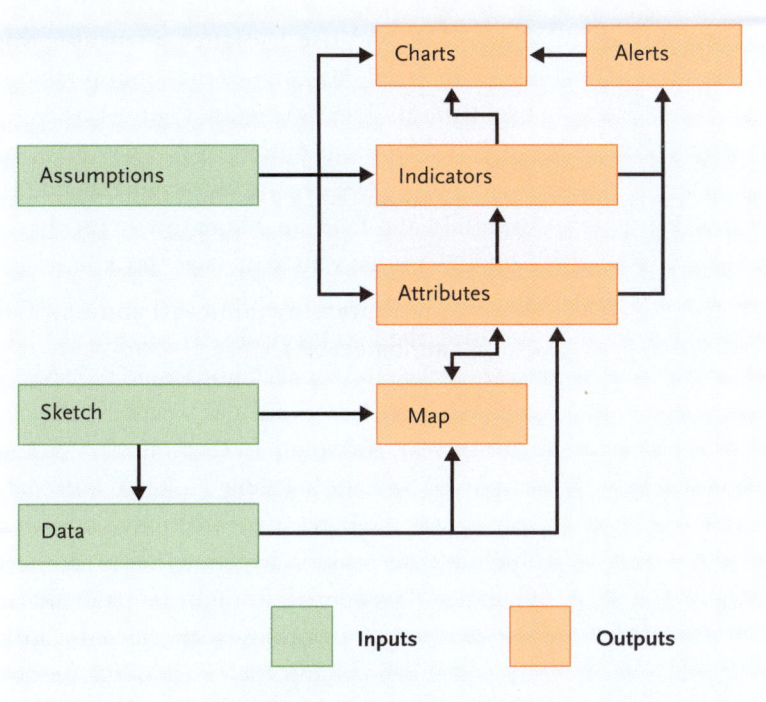

Figure 4.1 Simplified diagram of Scenario 360 components and their primary relationships

Note: Data tables, diagrams, reports, and scenarios not shown

If you needed even finer resolution, you could keep adding assumptions for different types of homes. If the analysis became too complicated, you might switch to using a simple *lookup table*, which is a way to summarize data by categories and link it to indicator formulas within your analysis. In this case, the lookup table summarizes the rates of daily water use by household type (Figure 4.2). The indicator formula associated with Figure 4.2 would multiply the number of households of each of the five household types by their respective water usage rates to find total daily water consumption.

Figure 4.2 An example of a simple lookup table

HOUSEHOLD TYPE	WATER USAGE RATE
Rural single family	350
Large-lot single family	350
Medium-density single family	280
Townhome	250
Apartment	225

You can easily create a lookup table from scratch in CommunityViz, or you can point to an existing table anywhere in your GIS data. The Land Use Designer often uses this approach, and you can see the lookup table it uses from its Table View (see Figure 4.3).

If your lookup table grows very large, or if it changes frequently, you might decide to maintain the table in Microsoft Excel. Excel provides an easy way to manage the data, and it allows you to make additional calculations. For instance, the Excel spreadsheet might calculate water usage rates for each household type based on additional factors such as weather patterns, time of year, and so on. In CommunityViz, you can set up an External Table Link that automatically reads the Excel-generated usage rates and updates your analysis any time the spreadsheet changes. This approach might be particularly handy if you are working with the water utility and they maintain their own usage models based on household information. Rather than creating all of your own estimates, you could simply link to their tables.

COEFFICIENT-BASED IMPACT MODELS

Impacts often depend on a combination of factors, not just a single factor such as the household type we have been using so far. For example, public policies that encourage best practices—such as Leadership in Energy and Environmental Design (LEED) building design, low-flow toilets and showerheads, and gray-water recycling—can help reduce residential water use. The effects of these practices are usually quantified in terms of percentage changes, called *coefficients*. For example, building codes that require the use of efficient plumbing fixtures reduce water usage by x percent, gray-water recycling saves y percent, and so on.

Including coefficient-based formulas that are more complex than straight percentages is also possible. For example, you can add assumptions or calculations giving the expected rate of adoption of new technologies and then use that information to refine your estimates of household water consumption. Coefficients can also depend on spatial relationships, which is the next level of sophistication.

Figure 4.3 *Screenshot of the Land Use Designer's Table View, displaying the values it uses for land-use designations*

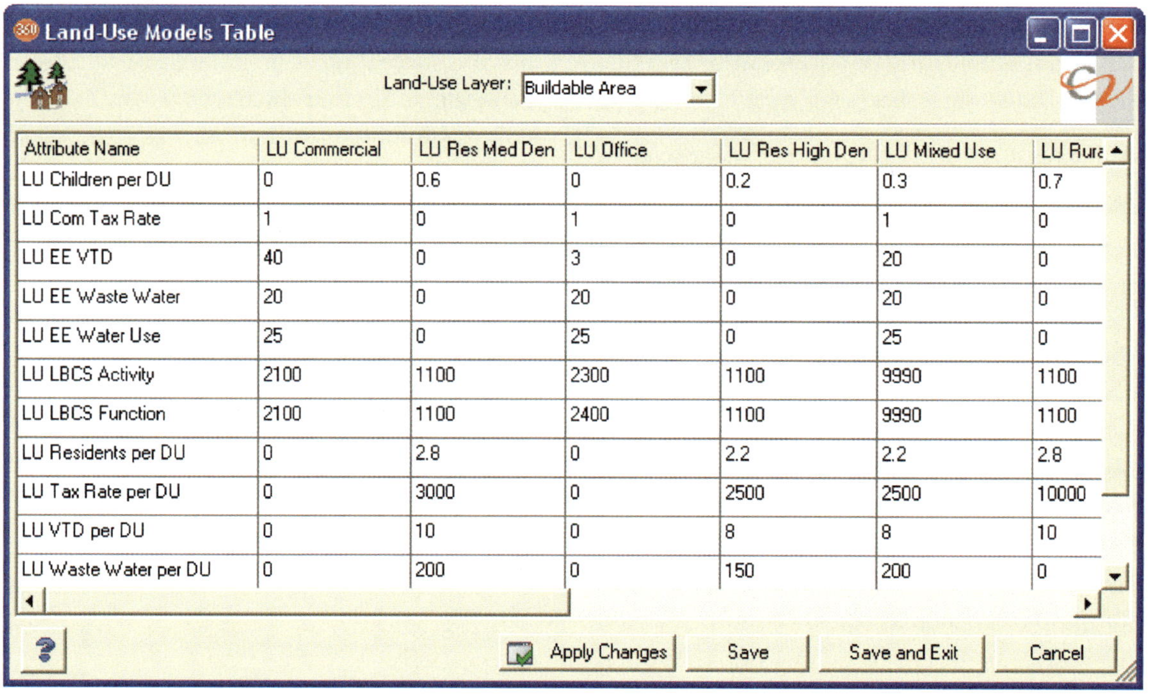

Attribute Name	LU Commercial	LU Res Med Den	LU Office	LU Res High Den	LU Mixed Use	LU Rural
LU Children per DU	0	0.6	0	0.2	0.3	0.7
LU Com Tax Rate	1	0	1	0	1	0
LU EE VTD	40	0	3	0	20	0
LU EE Waste Water	20	0	20	0	20	0
LU EE Water Use	25	0	25	0	25	0
LU LBCS Activity	2100	1100	2300	1100	9990	1100
LU LBCS Function	2100	1100	2400	1100	9990	1100
LU Residents per DU	0	2.8	0	2.2	2.2	2.8
LU Tax Rate per DU	0	3000	0	2500	2500	10000
LU VTD per DU	0	10	0	8	8	10
LU Waste Water per DU	0	200	0	150	200	0

SPATIALLY DEPENDENT IMPACT MODELS

Many impacts depend on spatial factors. For example, in your residential water use analysis, you may want to take into account outdoor water use, such as the watering of lawns: The larger the lawn, the more water is used. The example is a little stretched here, but you could calculate the lawn area of every parcel in a scenario by subtracting the area of the building footprint, driveway, and sidewalk.

A similar calculation is sometimes used to determine the area of impervious surface in a development proposal. More common examples of spatially dependent impacts are travel demand estimates based on the "4 Ds": density, diversity, design, and destinations. Each "D" is a number you can calculate using standard CommunityViz spatial functions. Once you know the D values for a scenario, you can use them in formulas to generate an estimate for the number of trips generated.

EXTERNAL MODELS

You do not have to do all of your modeling within the CommunityViz analysis engine. CommunityViz can work in concert with a variety of external tools and models.

We already mentioned the option of linking CommunityViz to external spreadsheets. You can connect to number-intensive models such as cost-of-service calculators, real estate pro forma models, and spreadsheet-based growth projections. Often, you need to consolidate an external spreadsheet's results into a simple column format suitable for the database structure used in GIS and CommunityViz, but the process is not difficult. External Table Links are updated automatically but in only one direction: from the spreadsheet *into* CommunityViz. To send CommunityViz data such as house counts or road miles *out* to the spreadsheet, you must go through a manual step.

Simply by exchanging tables, you can exchange CommunityViz data not only with spreadsheets but also with almost any software tool that uses tables or databases.[1] Updates are not necessarily

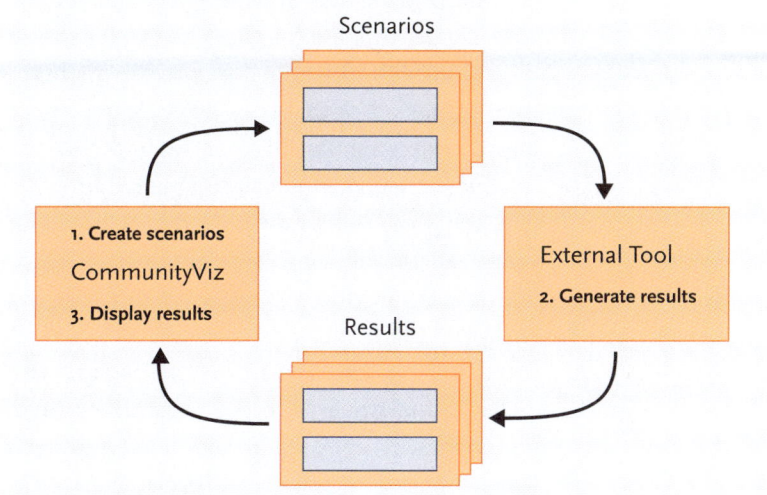

Figure 4.4 Linking to external software tools

automatic, but the amount and type of data sent back and forth is virtually unlimited.[2]

Finally, you can use CommunityViz in parallel with other software applications (see Figure 4.4). To do this, you use CommunityViz as the framework for the project and as the tool for creating and managing scenarios. You send data layers and tables to the external software tool in batches, one scenario to a batch. Then you operate the external tool and finally put its results—new layers, new indicator results, and so on—back into your CommunityViz analysis for display and possible further processing. The charts in CommunityViz provide a particularly good way to display the findings of the external software tools side by side with the rest of your analysis. We find this method works well when your project spans several disciplines, such as natural resource management, energy infrastructure, and land use planning.

HOW TO CHOOSE A MODEL

The rule of thumb for choosing a model is to use the simplest one that works. The goal is to

---

1. The databases need to be in an ArcGIS-compatible format.

2. Another, more technically advanced, way to link to external models is by using custom scripts. Custom scripts are small pieces of software code—usually in VBA or Python—that run outside of CommunityViz and can do whatever you program them to do. The most common reason to use them is to perform an iterative calculation—that is, a calculation that requires looping through a particular procedure many consecutive times. To do so, you include a Custom Script function in a CommunityViz formula and include all the input parameters the script requires.

give yourself enough good information that you can make informed decisions (see Chapter 1). In practice, this means that the model should correctly tell you whether Scenario A is better than Scenario B with a reasonable degree of certainty. If you find that all scenarios look the same for the particular impact you are studying, it is probably time to refine your model. Conversely, if A is always better than B regardless of how many more details you include, then you can stick with the model you have.

Another consideration is the weight that decision makers give to the particular impact you are studying, such as water consumption. If the impact is central to the decision, focus on making a more precise model. If the impact is being included only for context or background, a less precise model will do.

CREATING A CUSTOM ANALYSIS

Designing the details of a custom analysis calls for the same perspective as designing the project as a whole: Start with objectives to achieve in your charts, alerts, and indicators and design from the top down (see Figure 4.5). Think about what information you would like to see and how you would like to see it presented—for example, as charts, indicators, sketches, and color-coded maps. To create those, you will need impact models that include specific assumptions. Finally, think about how a client or audience will interact with the analysis, such as changing assumptions, sketching maps, and comparing scenarios.

Once you have thought through these needs, you will have a good idea of the components required for your analysis. Create those components, starting with data and dynamic attribute formulas, and gradually aggregate your results into user-friendly indicators and charts. In other words, build the setup from the bottom up. This procedure will give you a basic setup, but expect to make further changes as you work with the analysis, learn more, and discover new questions to ask.

TECHNICAL SECTION: DYNAMIC ANALYSIS IN SCENARIO 360

This section of the chapter gives an overview of dynamic analysis in Scenario 360. Technically minded readers should refer to CommunityViz documentation for a more rigorous description.

DYNAMIC ATTRIBUTES

The analysis processing step starts with the data stored in your ArcGIS system in a *geodatabase*. If you are unfamiliar with the concept of a geodatabase, you can think of it as something like an Excel workbook containing many pages of spreadsheets. In addition to numbers and words, the geodatabase also contains geospatial information such as shapes and locations.

In a GIS system, the items you see on the map are called *features*, and they are stored in collections called feature classes, or *layers*. For example, a Parcels layer might contain all the parcel features on the map, and a Trees layer might contain all the trees.

The geodatabase can hold more information about each layer than what you see on the map. For example, the geodatabase can store not only the shape and location of each parcel, but also its size, zoning, owner, and so on. Those characteristics of a feature are called *attributes*. Each layer in the geodatabase has an associated table, called an *attribute table*, like the one shown in Figure 4.6. In the table, each row represents an individual feature, and the columns contain the values of the various attributes.

Figure 4.5 Design and setup sequences

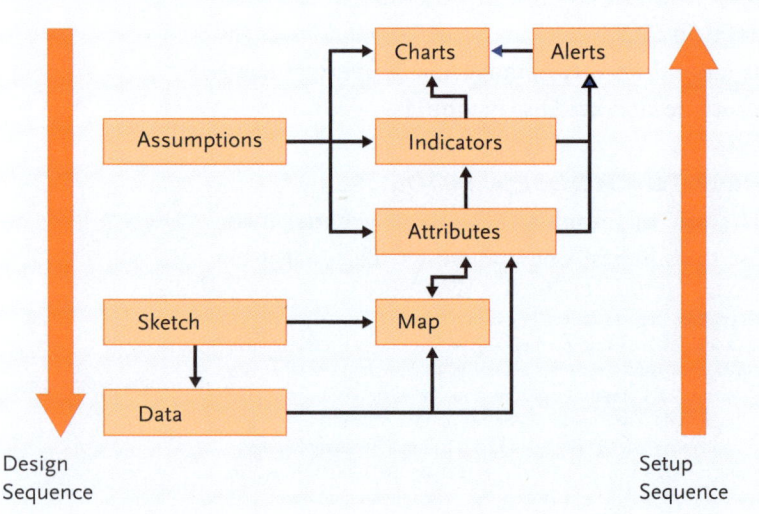

Figure 4.6 Attribute table

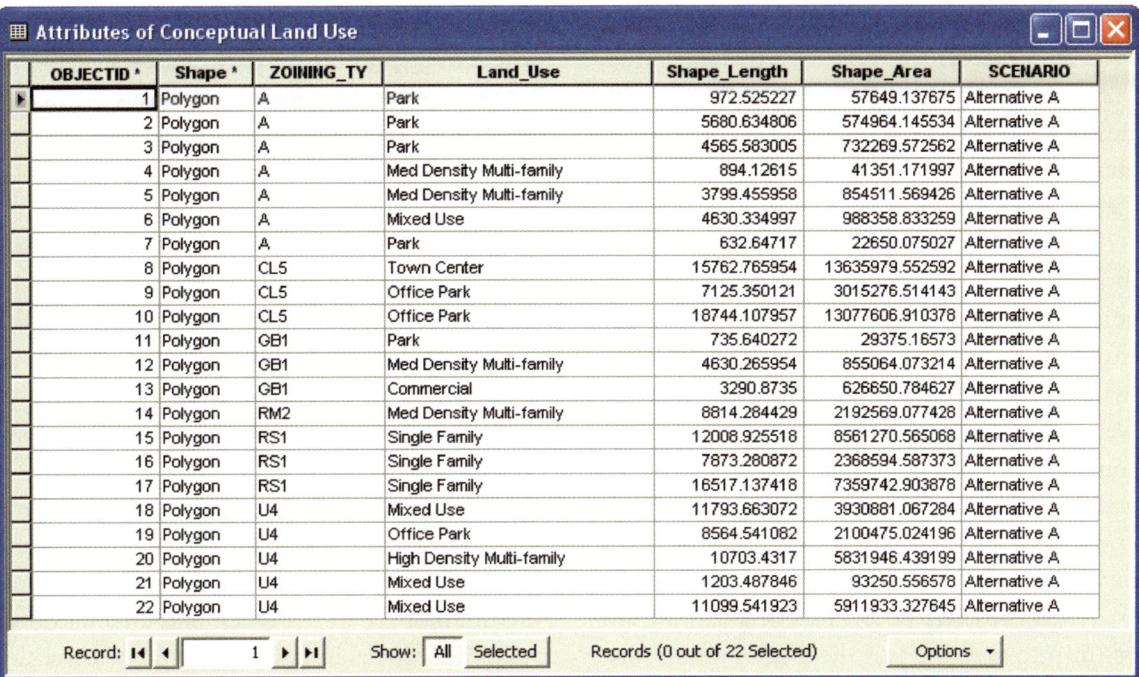

The Scenario 360 analysis engine manages attribute tables much as Excel uses spreadsheets. Both software programs employ formulas to determine and change some of the values in the table. As you work with your analysis or do geodesign—for instance, sketching new features on the map or changing assumptions—the analysis engine detects the changes and uses its formulas to calculate new values. A change in a single feature or number may set off a cascade of changes in many other features and their layers as well, in the same way that changing the value of a single cell in Excel may cause many other cell values to change. This unique ability of Scenario 360 transforms a GIS from a static data repository to a dynamic data analysis tool. That is why the attributes that have formulas attached to them are called *dynamic attributes* and their formulas are called *dynamic attribute formulas.*

The formulas can do many kinds of calculations. The simplest calculations are numeric, such as adding two numbers or calculating a percentage. Other calculations may be spatial, such as determining distances between features on the map. When you write a formula, you can include not just plus and minus signs, but also more than 70 other functions that handle counts of particular features, distances between features, physical overlaps of different features, and much more. As a result, within a Scenario 360 analysis, features on the map contain dynamically updated information about themselves and their relationships with everything else on the map. The features on the map are part of a system, just like real objects in a real study area. When you create system models in Scenario 360, you do it in part by writing dynamic attribute formulas that describe how your economic, environmental, or social systems work.

INDICATORS

Formulas can also drive indicator values. Many indicators are simply sums or averages of attribute values. For example, you could calculate an indicator that shows the amount of parkland in your study area by summing the acreage of every parcel with the land use attribute equal to "Park." If you were to use Scenario Sketch tools to simulate purchasing certain parcels to make more parks, the indicator value would update automatically to show more parkland.

Indicator formulas can also be more complex, taking advantage of most of the same functions found in dynamic attribute formulas.

ASSUMPTIONS

Assumptions in Scenario 360 are variable inputs used by indicator formulas and dynamic attribute formulas. It is easiest to think of assumptions in terms of the *slider bar* controls, which you can use to set the values of your assumptions (see Figure 4.7).

Unlike indicators and dynamic attributes, assumptions are not driven by formulas. Instead, you as the analyst specify a name for the assumption and a range of allowed values, and that range is displayed on the slider bar controls. You set the particular value of an assumption at any time during the analysis, and the Scenario 360 analysis engine uses the value of the assumption as an *input*. Indicator values and dynamic attribute values are *outputs*.

When you create a formula, you can include assumptions as part of the equation. Following the park example above, you could create another indicator giving the estimated annual maintenance cost of your parks. The formula would multiply the total park area by an assumption you set up for the annual maintenance cost per acre of parkland. If you changed the cost per acre assumption the indicator showing the total maintenance cost would change as well; or if you increased the total area of parkland through sketching on the map, the total maintenance cost would increase. Thus, the indicator value for the cost of park maintenance could be affected by assumption changes or sketching on the map.

SCENARIOS

Scenarios in a CommunityViz analysis mimic scenarios in real life. They represent the same place (the study area) with the same natural and human systems (models and formulas) but with differences in key choices or possibilities (sketches and assumptions). (See Figure 4.8.)

Figure 4.7 Assumptions slider bars

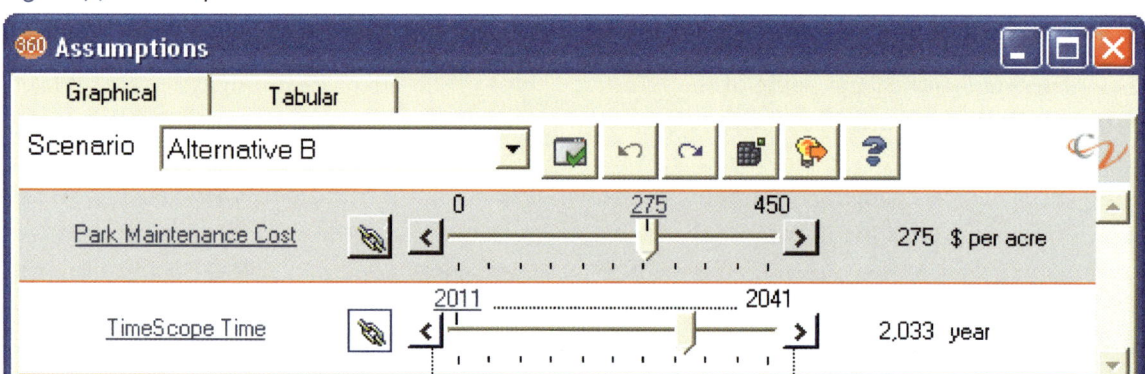

Figure 4.8 Similarities and differences between scenarios within an analysis

SCENARIOS WITHIN AN ANALYSIS HAVE THE **SAME:**	...BUT THEY MAY HAVE **DIFFERENT:**
map layers	map features within layers
symbols for each map layer	
designation for each layer as dynamic or not	
attributes for non-dynamic layers	dynamic attribute values
formulas for dynamic attributes	
charts created	chart values
	chart elements
alerts created	alerts currently triggered
indicator formulas	indicator values
assumptions created	assumption values

If you are doing simple geodesign, you might use only one scenario. If you are doing more structured scenario planning, you will have more than one scenario.

When you set up an analysis, it is often best to start with a single scenario. Create all the components—dynamic attributes, assumptions, indicators, charts, alerts, and so on—you need, and then create additional scenarios if desired. Most of your work will be copied automatically, and the only changes you make will be the ones that are specific to a particular scenario, such as map features or assumption settings.

SETUP TOOLS

Setup begins with processing data, for which you can use standard ArcMap tools such as Add Data and geoprocessing tools such as Define Projection. ArcGIS sketch tools can create new layers as you perform geodesign, and Scenario 360 also provides its own Add Data tool, which makes it easy to create new data layers if you need them.

If you use any decision tools, they will set up a number of components for you. However, for custom modeling you will want to create your own formulas for dynamic attributes and indicators. We recommend you work on one system or impact model at a time. In most cases, you will use the Formula Wizard or the Formula Editor to create formulas. The editor is more flexible, but some people find the wizard easier to use. As you work, remember to follow best practices for transparency

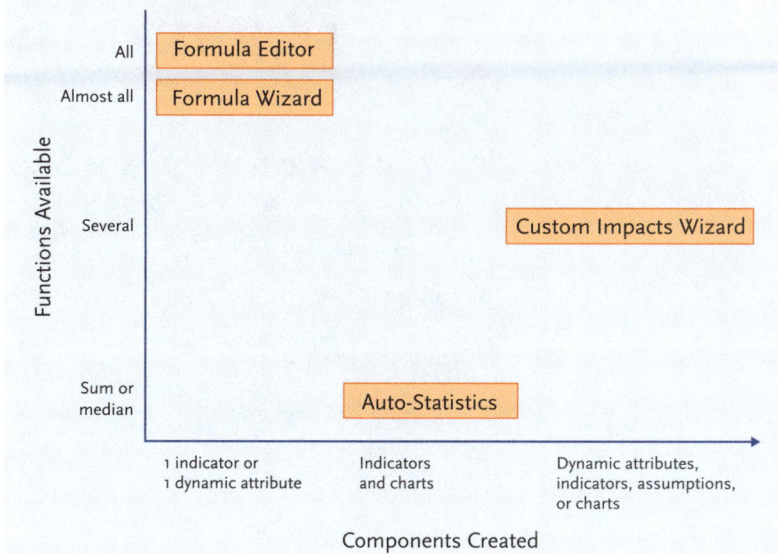

Figure 4.9 Selected formula creation tools

(see Chapter 3) by clearly labeling components and maintaining an organized, modular design.

Purists believe that assumptions should be designed and created ahead of time, but pragmatic analysts simply make assumptions as they need them. The formula tools usually provide a way to jump out of a formula in the middle of writing it, create an assumption you need for that formula, and then jump back in. You make alerts and charts in the final stage of your setup.

You may be able to save time by using Auto-Statistics buttons or the Custom Impacts Wizard. These tools make several components at once, as illustrated in Figure 4.9.

5 THREE-DIMENSIONAL SCENES

KEY CONCEPTS AND TERMS IN THIS CHAPTER

- Data sources for 3-D
- ArcGIS 3-D tools
- How 3-D works
- Creating 3-D scenes
- Google Earth Exporter
- Metro and regional models in 3-D
- Scenario 3D
- SketchUp models, KMZ, and CAD

The ability to create interactive 3-D representations of plans and development proposals is a tremendous asset for any planning project. Three-dimensional images form a common language that everyone can understand. Three-dimensional visualization provides you, public audiences, and diverse workgroups with a vivid way to examine land-use planning scenarios, geodesign sketches, development proposals, and site design. At the regional and metro scale, visualization gives people a good sense of locations and distances, and an overview of land-use patterns and environmental systems across the landscape. At the building and neighborhood scale, visualization illustrates development form, massing, density, design, and even subjective characteristics such as the feel of a place.

Three-dimensional visualization is a fundamental part of both the technology and the philosophy of CommunityViz, and the software provides an array of capabilities for creating 3-D scenes from your 2-D maps and analysis. If you decide to make a 3-D scene, you can choose from a range of options, such as a five-minute export of basic layers and shapes, or a sophisticated, highly realistic scene. This chapter provides advice on choosing a 3-D platform and the mechanics of creating a 3-D scene.

WHY AND WHEN

CommunityViz 3-D scenes are designed to support informed, collaborative decision making about land use plans, development proposals, and neighborhood design. They can convey objective and subjective information, attract public participation, deepen discussions, and support visual analysis and assessment. But CommunityViz 3-D has limits, so you will need to use other software tools if you are doing engineering-level analysis, building scenes meant only for 2-D displays, designing individual buildings, or doing architectural design.

CommunityViz 3-D can play a role throughout the planning process. In the early phases, you can make 3-D models of existing conditions to provide a visual setting and context. As proposals or scenarios begin to emerge, you can show them in sketchy form, and as the proposals become more specific, you can add detail to the 3-D scene. Three-dimensional visualization works at the site, neighborhood, city, or regional scale, though you may need to adjust your 3-D platform according to the size of your data files.

CHOOSING A 3-D PLATFORM

CommunityViz offers several methods for creating 3-D scenes. The Google Earth Exporter is built into Scenario 360 and provides a fast, easy way to make Google Earth-compatible KMZ files.[1] You can also view KMZ files with ArcGIS Explorer and other tools. Scenario 3D has its

---

1. A KMZ file is a zipped (compressed) version of a KML file, both of which are used by Google Earth. The name *KML* stands for "Keyhole Markup Language."

own ArcGIS extension, and it can work with or without Scenario 360. Scenario 3D is more sophisticated than the Google Earth Exporter and gives you the ability to make richer, more detailed scenes that you view in the Scenario 3D Viewer. Google Earth exports are so easy that it often makes sense to make both a Google Earth scene and a Scenario 3D scene (see Figure 5.1 for more details). You can also use Scenario 360 analysis tools within the ArcGIS 3-D tool called ArcScene for an effective, highly integrated 2-D or 3-D experience. This chapter focuses on the Google Earth Exporter and Scenario 3D.

HOW 3-D WORKS

A 3-D scene starts with a flexible mesh of interconnected lines called the *wireframe*. The mesh corresponds to the surfaces in the scene. Each line segment in the mesh is always perfectly straight, and the spaces between line segments are flat triangles. There are no truly curved surfaces in the scene, only many small, flat triangles. The triangles in a scene have different sizes and dimensions; the computer calculates the optimal arrangement to cover any given surface. A square, for example, consists of two triangles. A circle is composed of many triangles (see Figure 5.2).

You might think of each triangle as a piece of clear, hard plastic that has paint on it. The paint is a solid color, a pattern, or an image; we call this a *texture*. Figure 5.3 shows a car model and its wireframe. Notice how the textures give a greater impression of shape.

Also, notice how many more triangles are used for the wheels than for the rest of the car, which has mostly straight edges. In general, curved surfaces and edges are more difficult to render in 3-D because they require many more triangles. Each triangle requires computer processing, and scenes with too many triangles will overburden even the fastest processors. A scene that is too large or detailed for the computer will take a long time to load, and as you navigate through it, your motion will be jerky, slow, and

Figure 5.1 Some considerations for selecting a CommunityViz 3-D platform

CHARACTERISTIC/CONSIDERATION	GOOGLE EARTH EXPORTER	SCENARIO 3D
Setup	Wizard in Scenario 360	Scenario 3D Exporter (stand-alone or accessible from Scenario 360)
File format	KMZ	SCENE
Viewer	Google Earth, free from Google	Scenario 3D Viewer, free from Placeways
Minimum setup time	Minutes	Minutes
Typical setup time	Minutes	Hours
Typical users of shared file	General public; KMZs are widely recognized	Project participants
Suitability for public meetings	Excellent	Excellent
Suitable study area size	Region or city (bigger and smaller are possible)	Neighborhood or site (bigger and smaller are possible)
Level of detail	Low–medium	Medium–high
Ability to represent multiple scenarios	Yes	Yes
Existing buildings	Some available in viewer, or add your own SketchUp models	Add your own SketchUp models
3-D model types	SketchUp/KMZ or COLLADA	SketchUp/KMZ, COLLADA, or 3ds (compatible with most CAD tools)
Terrain	None, or use terrain built into viewer	None, or provide your own
Lighting, fog, etc.	No	Yes
Near-ground navigation	Acceptable	Excellent
High-altitude navigation/zoom	Excellent	Acceptable

Figure 5.2 How squares and circles are represented in the 3-D scene

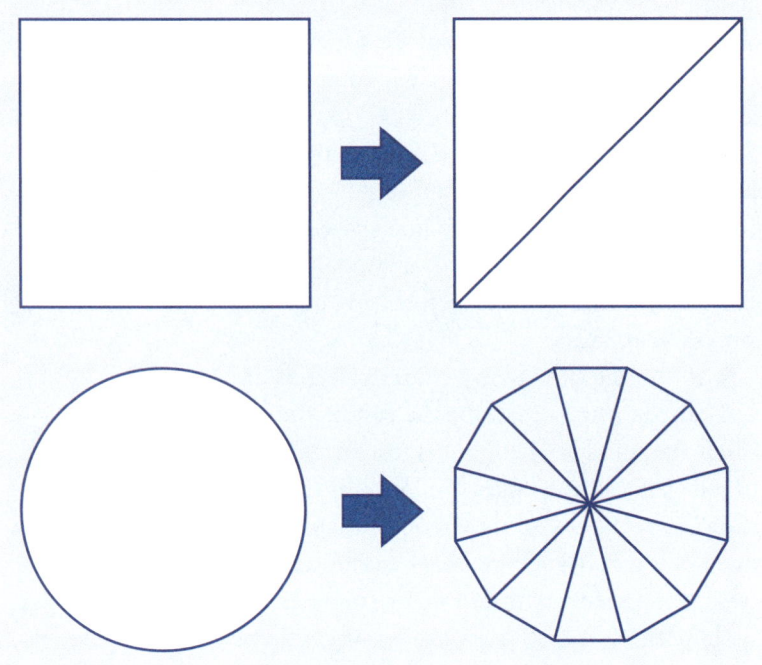

Figure 5.3 A car model and its wireframe

unpredictable. Therefore, software designers must perform a balancing act: In CAD systems, where high fidelity is very important but the focus is on a single building or object, designers tune their 3-D models to use thousands of very small triangles that give the impression of smooth curves. They use up their triangle "budget" in a small area. In GIS, where context is important, designers spread their triangles over a larger scene, so triangles are generally larger and curves are not as smooth. Geographic information systems also enable you to move around the scene quickly and easily, which requires fewer total triangles.

PARTLY TRANSPARENT TEXTURES

Parts of a texture can be transparent, which provides a very useful way to model curves and irregular shapes in a 3-D scene without creating too many triangles. Figure 5.4 shows a classic example, the so-called X-tree model. The model gives the impression of a tree with thousands of leaves, but it uses only four to eight triangles. The triangles form two rectangles that cross at right angles along the trunk of the tree. The texture is a photo of the tree from the side, and the background of the photo is transparent. The visual effect is convincing, particularly at a distance. In 3-D parlance, the transparent part of a texture is called the *alpha channel*.

The technique of including transparent areas in image textures works well for rendering many other complex shapes, such as people, plants, and animals, and soft edges. However, this technique tends to be less effective when the surfaces are viewed edge-on, such as the tree in the center of Figure 5.4, and it is hard to render asymmetrical shapes this way.

SHADOWS AND LIGHTING

Some 3-D tools, such as Scenario 3D and SketchUp, include shadows and lighting. The Google Earth viewer does not. Lighting properties are part of the 3-D model itself, and they specify darker or lighter textures on the sides of objects when they are facing away from or toward the scene's virtual light source or virtual sun. Lighting can enhance the 3-D visual

Figure 5.4 Two views of an X-tree model and its underlying triangles

effect. Shadows do what you expect them to do: They darken textures on nearby surfaces that are blocked from the virtual sun. In Scenario 3D, shadows darken only ground textures, not other objects. Shadows also enhance the visual effect, and they can provide additional useful information when you are studying urban gardens or solar access for solar panels.

ACTIVE MATERIALS

Another type of texture is called an *active material*, *material*, or *shader*. A small software program that makes constant adjustments governs the appearance of the texture in an active material. For example, the ocean texture in Scenario 3D has constantly moving ripples on its surface, and it accurately reflects the clouds in the sky from any given angle (see Figure 5.5). Google Earth does not support active materials.

HOW A 3-D SCENE IS BUILT

A scene is built literally from the ground up. It starts with a wireframe of the ground, known as the terrain (see Figure 5.6).

The wireframe terrain itself is not visible in the scene, but it serves as the base for all the data

Figure 5.5 Water, an example of an active material (screenshot from an interactive 3-D scene)

Figure 5.6 Wireframe of the terrain underlying a 3-D scene

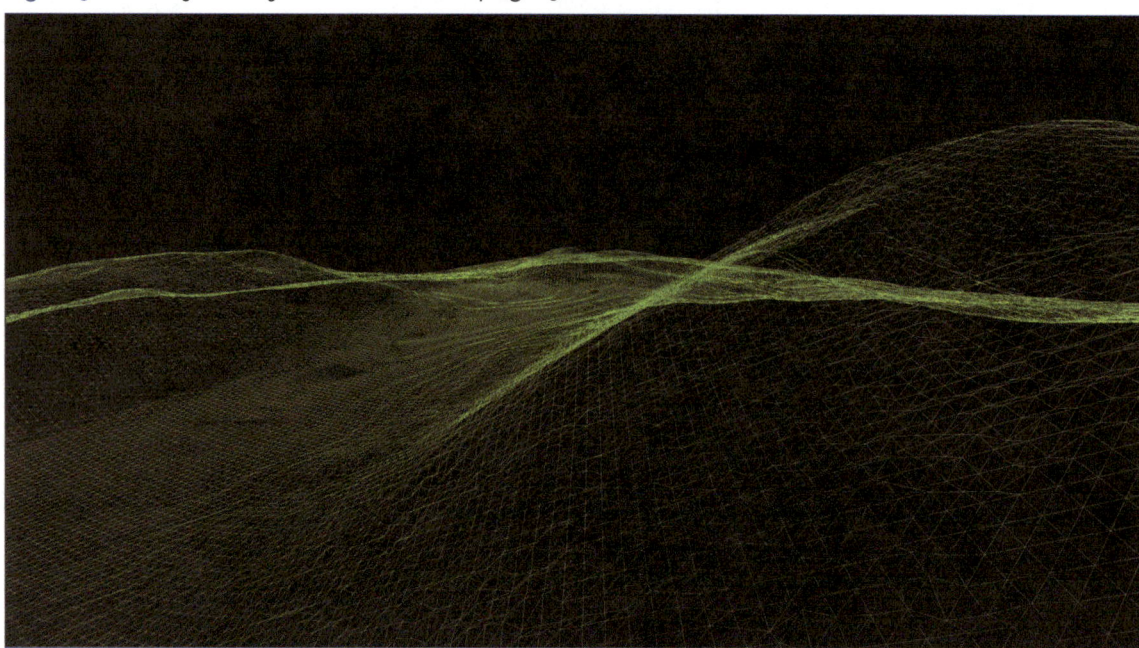

Figure 5.7 Anatomy of a 3-D scene

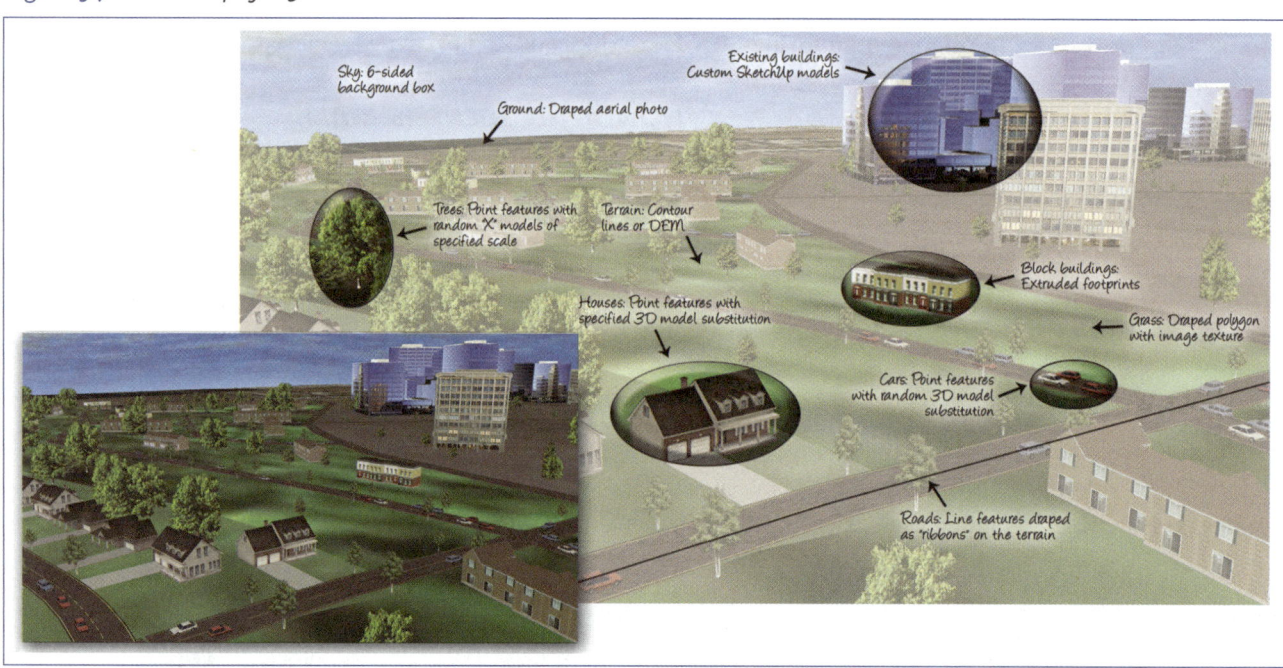

layers and features that make up the scene. A ground cover layer, such as an aerial photo, is draped on the terrain like a blanket. In Google Earth and other 3-D map services, the ground is provided for you. In Scenario 3D, you make it yourself. The rest of the scene consists of layers from your GIS map. Just as you can choose symbols for features in 2-D, you can choose symbols, models, and other substitution methods for features in 3-D. Figure 5.7 illustrates some of the more common substitution techniques.

CREATING A 3-D SCENE

Here are the basic steps for creating a CommunityViz 3-D scene using Scenario 3D or the Google Earth Exporter.

GET DATA

You may need or be able to use the following data:

- Baseline GIS data, including roads, trails, cities, natural features, and so on. You will normally already have this data in ArcMap. If you use the Google Earth Exporter, much of this data will already exist in the Google Earth viewer.

- Terrain. Terrain is not always required, because you can use flat ground in Scenario 3D, and Google Earth provides its own terrain. However, if you are using Scenario 3D, a terrain layer is often desirable. Typical data types are contour lines, triangulated irregular networks (TINs), and digital elevation models (DEMs) in raster format, available online from government sources such as the U.S. Geological Survey. If you have higher-resolution data, such as Lidar imagery, you can usually use it after converting it to a GIS-compatible format. Most of the time, you should select the highest resolution terrain you can find, although resolution of less than 6 inches is unnecessary and may lead to problems with file size. In some cases, you'll need to reduce the study area of the scene to keep file sizes down, but the trade-off is typically worthwhile.

- Analysis layers, such as a parcel map or a suitability map. These will come from your Scenario 360 analysis.

- Landscape and hardscape maps giving the location of sidewalks, driveways, trees, plantings, grassy areas, retaining walls, signs, and other features that are visually important. These are frequently used in Scenario 3D, but less so in Google Earth. Often, landscape and hardscape maps are available from CAD or SketchUp models provided by landscape designers. Another source is artists' sketches, which you can import into ArcMap as images and then georeference. If these sources are not available, you can sketch the features by hand.

- Aerial imagery. If high-quality aerial imagery is available, using it to replace features and groundcover you would otherwise model yourself can save you time. It can also help you to position existing objects. Aerial imagery usually comes from free or low-cost online services or from specialty providers. Use the highest-quality imagery available for your main study areas, and lower-resolution imagery in outlying areas to minimize file size. Google Earth provides its own aerial imagery, but you can overlay higher-resolution imagery if you need to.

- Building and context photos. You can use photos of the sides of existing buildings as a quick way to make a good-quality model; you paste them onto simple block structures as textures. In addition, photos of a site, neighborhood, or study area are useful for reference as you construct the scene. Two good sources in addition to local residents' photos are Google Maps Street View and Bing Maps. Sometimes you will find that existing buildings are already modeled within Google Earth.

- Roadway dimensions and striping. It is sometimes important to show the exact widths of roadways, lanes, and parking spaces in the scene. These data should be available from the local engineering, public works, or highway department. As with landscaping, you can use CAD or SketchUp files, designers' drawings, or your own sketches.

- Building points, or footprints and heights. Including the building footprints makes it very easy for you to create a scene with proper building bulk and massing, because you can simply extrude the footprints into three dimensions. If you don't know the correct heights, you can approximate them. Building footprint points allows you to place 3-D models of buildings in the correct locations, even if the models are not exactly the same as existing or proposed buildings. A large collection of generic building models that work in Scenario 3D or Google Earth is available online from the Google SketchUp 3D Warehouse, and Scenario 3D also provides a built-in library.

- Tree data. You can generate your own tree location points by using the Build-Out Wizard or sketching tools. For visually important trees, such as those along a road, you can sometimes get points by looking at an aerial image. Trace the tree's shadow in the image to find its base. For species and heights, it is generally acceptable to use a random mix that is similar to the mix of actual trees.

- Custom 3-D models. Use custom-made SketchUp or CAD models for the most important buildings, landmarks, and objects in the scene. Often these come from the developer; but you can also make them yourself using SketchUp, which is free and easy to learn. However, it can take several hours to make a single model.

- Accessory 3-D models. Scenes often include accessory elements such as cars, pedestrians, additional trees, and outdoor furniture. In most cases, you can add accessory elements by sketching locations on the map and using generic 3-D models from Scenario 3D's library, the Google SketchUp 3D Warehouse, or other convenient free sources.

- Other data. The list above is not exhaustive, and other data needs may arise in special circumstances.

CREATE A BASE MODEL

The base model contains elements of the scene that will not change from scenario to scenario. The size of the base model corresponds to the analysis study area, and in most cases it shows existing conditions. Creating the base model is often the most time-consuming phase of the project, but once you have made the model, you can use it again for future projects.

Your goal is to create a scene that effectively represents the place you are modeling. It should contain good information and allow the viewer to picture and feel the real place. It is a representation, not a replica: You do not need to recreate every detail, and you must choose your priorities, because you have a finite amount of technical computing capacity. (Refer to Chapter 6 for specific information on creating effective scenes that balance visual quality and technical performance.)

Start from the ground up (see Figure 5.8). Create a terrain and a ground image (if needed), then add roads, and if you have them, parcels, lots, or other area-covering polygons. Often, you can use grass or pavement textures to represent these polygons to create realistic ground cover (see Figure 5.9). Sometimes, you may want to retain the symbolic colors you were using on the 2-D map so that you can convey particular information such as zoning designations or suitability scores. If you want to be able to switch between different representations while displaying the

Figure 5.8 A 3-D scene, beginning with a ground image (screenshot of an interactive 3-D scene)

Figure 5.9 A 3-D scene with extruded building footprints and road polygons added (screenshot of an interactive 3-D scene)

scene, it's best to make two copies of the layer in the 3-D scene and choose which one to turn on.

Next, add existing buildings, which may come in many forms. If you have building points, represent them with 3-D models of buildings oriented to face the nearest road. You can use custom 3-D models if you have them, or else generic 3-D models matched as closely as possible to the actual styles and sizes of existing buildings. If you have building footprints, you can extrude them with simple colored sides and tops, or with more-complex textures such as images of real buildings. For urban streets, use online image services such as Google Maps Street View or Bing Maps to capture photos of the building fronts, and then paste those onto your 3-D models (see Figure 5.10).

Landmarks, well-known buildings, and other important objects should be modeled carefully and placed accurately in the scene.

Add trees. Start with any data you have on existing trees, but also be prepared to sketch in additional trees as you work on the scene.

Add more layers. You don't need to put every layer from your 2-D data into the 3-D scene, but do review your emerging scene and consider whether it would benefit from additions.

Sketch in additional features. At this scale, it's likely that you will want to add layers solely for the purpose of improving the visual appearance of the 3-D scene (see Figure 5.10). You do so by sketching or editing features in 2-D and then exporting them into 3-D. You may find it useful to place all the 3-D-only layers into a single layer group in ArcMap for easy management.

Review the scene with other people. In addition to simply asking for their suggestions, try to gauge the effectiveness of the scene in conveying good information and helping them picture and feel the study area. Make improvements as needed so that the scene is clearly recognizable as a representation of the study area (see Chapter 6 for details).

MODEL DEVELOPMENT PROPOSALS OR SCENARIOS

This section of the chapter focuses on modeling development proposals and scenarios for sites and neighborhoods; Chapter 6 addresses larger areas. For each scenario in your decision-making process, make a scenario in the 3-D scene.

If the proposed development project will replace an existing development, you may need to modify the existing scene so you can turn off features that show the existing development. For example, if you are looking at a redevelopment site, you might split the Existing Buildings layer into two layers: one for existing buildings on the site, and another for existing buildings surrounding the site.

Next, add the proposed ground layers, including roads and ground cover. Make sure that the ground cover of the proposal obscures any existing ground cover shown in aerial photos.

Figure 5.10   A 3-D scene with 3-D building models added (screenshot of an interactive 3-D scene)

Figure 5.11   A 3-D scene with accessories added: trees, cars, bicyclist, and pedestrians (screenshot of an interactive 3-D scene)

Add proposed buildings. If the project is small, models of particular buildings often come from the developer's CAD or SketchUp files. If those are not available, make your own or use similar models from a library of generic models. If the project is larger, you may need to run the Build-Out Wizard with spatial build-out to generate building points or footprints. If you use spatial build-out with commercial buildings, be sure to specify building sizes in the wizard to get the correct number of buildings in the scene.

Add any landscaping and hardscaping features specified in the development proposal. It is important to keep these separate from accessory features that are not specified in the proposal.

Next, you can add accessory features, but keep them in separate layers so that you can turn them on and off.

Again, review the emerging scene with other people to verify its accuracy and effectiveness, and to solicit suggestions for improvement.

CREATE PRESENTATION AIDS

Once the scene is nearly complete, think about how you will present it. Make bookmarks and paths that allow you to move quickly to places you want to show. Adjust the transparency of layers if needed, and think about environmental effects such as lighting and fog. You may want to develop and rehearse a particular sequence for the presentation. Also, consider how you will share the scene with others using images, videos, and sharable viewer files.

SPECIAL CONSIDERATIONS FOR METRO AND REGIONAL MODELS

As the size of the study area of the 3-D scene increases, its role in decision making changes as well. At the scale of a medium-sized city or larger, it is neither helpful nor necessary to model particular sites or neighborhoods in fine detail. Instead, use the 3-D scene to illustrate context, locations, growth patterns, density, and analytical data such as site suitability (see Figure 5.12).

The CommunityViz technology of choice at the metro or regional scale is usually the Google Earth Exporter, which produces files that you can also view in ArcGIS Explorer. You can also use Scenario 3D, but you will need to make more tradeoffs in detail to achieve satisfactory performance.

Figure 5.12 *Regional-scale 3-D model in Google Earth (screenshot from an interactive 3-D scene)*

Figure 5.13 Two scenarios for future development around a highway interchange

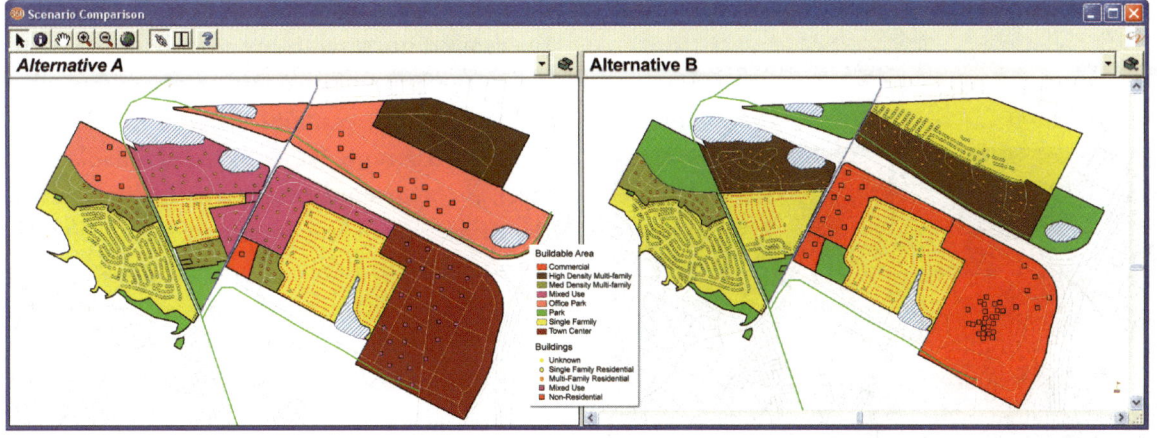

Google Earth and ArcGIS Explorer provide good aerial imagery in most locations. If you need to overlay higher-quality images for your study area, you can simply add them to your analysis and then export them. In most cases, the aerial images or the road maps provided by the online service will meet your needs for illustrating existing roads.

You will need to export your own Roads layer for proposed new roads, and sometimes for existing roads. You can set up road symbols in ArcMap and then export the layer as an image to Google Earth. Making a road image slightly transparent in the Google Earth viewer improves its appearance.

For proposed new ground cover, make polygon layers in ArcMap and export them. Experiment with colors, because Google Earth and ArcMap may render colors differently. If you are illustrating new buildings in a forested area, create clearings or lawns around building points so that the new development will appropriately clear some land. One good way to make lawns is to buffer building points by a certain distance, such as 40 feet. However, ArcMap's buffer tool creates circles made of geometric arcs, which Google Earth does not support. To resolve this problem, use ArcMap's Generalize tool to transform the circles into polygons with six or eight sides.

Be selective when adding proposed new buildings, because you will not be able to show large numbers of buildings in fine detail. (Chapter 6 provides some suggestions on how to display many buildings.) Consider using abstract representations of land-use polygons, such as 3-D extrusions whose height corresponds to density.

You will also need to be selective with trees, accessories, and custom models, because of file size. A rule of thumb is to stay above 1,000 feet when displaying visuals of a regional scene. This means that small features will not be particularly visible and are usually not needed.

TEACHING EXAMPLE

The following example illustrates a variety of visualization techniques used to create a Scenario 3D scene of a fictional mixed use development surrounding a highway interchange. Two alternative developments were created in Scenario 360 (see Figure 5.13). We used the Build-Out Wizard to generate the building points based on sketches of the conceptual land-use plan for the study area.

To create a 3-D scene, we started from the ground up. The terrain in the area was level, so we decided to forego a terrain layer. For the ground image, we wanted to use a higher-resolution image in the 3-D scene than the medium-resolution image we had been using for reference during 2-D analysis. The overall study area was 10 square miles, but we focused on the conceptual land-use plan, which covered only five square miles. We captured several high-resolution *tiles* from our online image service and then used simple photo editing to combine them into a single large image called a *mosaic*. We used this mosaic as the base ground image for the scene (see Figure 5.14).

Figure 5.14 Ground image in 3-D

Figure 5.15 Section of ground cover in the 3-D scene. Note the existing houses (lower left), new lawns (center), and new pavement (top).

Figure 5.16 Existing buildings represented as extruded, semitransparent footprints

In the area of the proposed development, we wanted to overlay existing conditions shown in the ground image with appropriate new ground cover. The Build-Out Wizard creates a "Buildable Area" layer that contains an attribute describing land-use type. We used the Buildable Area layer as the ground cover layer, to show where the development was proposed. We specified a pavement texture for commercial areas, a lawn texture for residential areas, a grassland texture for parks, and so on. Where there was existing development, we did not include features in the Buildable Area layer, so existing houses and roads remained uncovered. A close-up of the result appears in Figure 5.15.

Although the existing houses looked good from above, they were flat and therefore not visible when you moved around the scene at ground level. We wanted to show their bulk and massing in 3-D, but we did not want to distract the viewer's attention from the new development proposal. We decided to use extruded footprints to provide a simple representation of the existing buildings in 3-D. We made the extrusions partly transparent to enhance the effect. Figure 5.16 shows the result. In some parts of the study area, we lacked footprints for existing buildings. Instead, we used existing building points and substituted Monopoly® house models, which gave a similar effect, although the sizes were not quite as accurate.

For streets, we used a simple texture substitution for each line segment in the Streets layer. If streets had been an important part of our study, we could have refined this technique by using different textures and widths for each class of street or road. We extruded the shapes by several inches to mimic the thickness of pavement.

Intersections where line segments in the same layer cross pose a challenge, because the 3-D platform has no way of merging intersections into a single road segment or deciding which one to lay on top of the others. This problem is illustrated in the top image of Figure 5.17. Our response was to create a new polygon layer and sketch in intersection *caps*, or covers, at key intersections. This was a fast, simple solution to the intersection problem.

If particular intersections had been more important to us, we would have made custom caps for each one, paying closer attention to alignment, striping, crosswalks, and other details.

There was a barn in the study area, and we had noticed that local residents often mentioned it when describing the area. In addition, both of our scenarios showed a park around the barn. We wanted to show the well-known barn and knew that we could not use a generic model, so we created the barn in SketchUp (see Figure 5.18). The model we created was not particularly detailed, but we based it on photos of the actual barn so that the textures and colors were accurate and the building would be instantly recognizable within the scene.

For new buildings, we used 3-D building models in KMZ format from the Scenario 3D model library and the Google SketchUp 3D Warehouse. There were several ways we could have related particular building models to different building types in the 2-D analysis. The Build-Out Wizard's visual build-out module provides one straightforward method. Alternatively, we could have used standard ArcMap tools to give each building a text attribute with the location of the file containing the 3-D model we wanted to use. In this case, we wanted flexibility and fine control over the models, so we wrote our own custom formula in the Buildings layer that assigned a code number to each building. For example, part of the formula gave houses in the low-density residential section a random number between 15 and 19. Then, in the Scenario 3D Exporter, we associated 3-D building models with each code number. This arrangement made it easy for us to change code numbers or 3-D models, one at a time or in bulk, as we created the scene. To orient each building so that it faced its nearest road, we wrote a simple Angle To formula in Scenario 360.

Driveways were another consideration for residential buildings (see Figure 5.19). Driveways are visually important in suburban developments. However, the length and placement of each driveway depends on the house model, and we wanted to be able to change house mod-

els easily. Our solution was to use 3-D building models that included driveways, either in their original form or after we performed a simple edit in SketchUp. This is a small example of

Figure 5.17 A street intersection before and after the application of an intersection cap

Figure 5.18 Model of the well-known barn

Figure 5.19   Building models and driveways in the 3-D scene

Figure 5.20   The 3-D scene prior to adding accessories

a more general technique, which is to create building-specific landscaping within the building model itself, rather than as separate GIS layers. It works easily on flat terrain, but on hilly terrain you may need to add extra basements and footings to make the landscaping contact the ground in all places. Hilly terrain also makes it difficult to use just one SketchUp model for an area larger than a single lot.

We now had a 3-D model that showed most of the analysis layers we had been using (see Figure 5.20). It included two scenarios. Creating the second scenario was easy, because it used most of the same 3-D substitution rules as the first scenario, so the Scenario 3D Exporter could create it automatically.

The final phase was to add trees and other accessories. We did trees in two parts: area trees and street trees. For area trees, we sketched about 2,500 tree points on the 2-D map. The sketching process was easy, because we were not worried about exact placement and we could copy and paste most of the points. Using Scenario 360 formulas, we gave each tree point a random value for height, species, and orientation, and then we instructed Scenario 3D to use those values for the tree points. For street trees, we needed to place points carefully in order to space the trees evenly and accurately along the roads. To do this, we made a separate Street Trees layer. We could have used ArcSketch tools or other utilities to create tree points, but it was just as easy to use the Build-Out Wizard's Follow Roads feature to place a series of points in the proper locations. The wizard works just as well for tree points as for building points. We used a similar technique for cars, adding an orientation attribute so that the cars would be aligned parallel to the roads' centerlines. Finally, we added ponds, additional vegetation, and other accessory layers.

After creating a first draft of the scene, we asked colleagues and local residents to review it. Based on their suggestions, we made some changes to the residential house models to better reflect local styles. From the residents, we also learned how people usually reached the area—by going north on the interstate rather than south—and which perspectives of the area they were most familiar with, such as looking northeast from the entrance to the existing subdivision. We used this information to create some paths and bookmarks in the scene for public presentations later on.

The final scene (see Figure 5.21) provided a clear, credible, information-rich illustration of the 2-D proposals we started with.

Although we used time-saving shortcuts and left out many details, the scene served its purpose well: It made the 2-D concept plan for the proposed development come alive for general audiences and supported better decision making. By prioritizing our work and taking advantage of the tools available to us, we were able to create a useful scene in two days. Had our needs and constraints been different, a similar project

Figure 5.21 The final 3-D scene

might have taken anywhere from a couple of hours for a simple scene to a couple of weeks for a very sophisticated scene. Overall, the 3-D scene provides a greater amount of information than the 2-D representation and brings a new level of understanding about development proposals to the decision-making process.

6 GETTING THE MOST FROM 3-D

KEY CONCEPTS AND TERMS IN THIS CHAPTER

- The art of making effective 3-D scenes
- Best practices for making 3-D scenes
- Solutions to common 3-D challenges
- Triangles, TINs, and X-tree models

This chapter contains advice on how to optimize the visual effectiveness and performance of 3-D scenes, whose fundamentals were described in Chapter 5. The focus here is on CommunityViz Scenario 3D, though most of the same principles apply to the CommunityViz Google Earth Exporter, ArcGIS Explorer, and other GIS-based 3-D tools.

THE ART OF MAKING EFFECTIVE 3-D SCENES

Although 3-D technology is advancing rapidly, it is still impossible to make a perfect 3-D scene. The art involves making the 3-D scene as effective as possible given technical constraints. A well-rendered 3-D scene gives your audience: a) good objective information, b) the ability to make a mental connection between the computer display and the real world, and c) a good subjective feel for the place you are modeling. Against these goals, you must balance technical constraints: the number of triangles and other limits on processing capacity, the time and effort required of the 3-D artist, and the availability of graphic and visual resources.

PROVIDING GOOD INFORMATION

A 3-D scene makes land-use plans, development proposals, and GIS data much easier to understand. But unlike a well-written plan or most GIS maps, a 3-D scene reflects the artist's interpretations of a site, neighborhood, city, or region. When you make a 3-D scene, you are playing the roles of analyst and artist, and it's important to make sure you play both roles well. Here are some best practices for the analytical aspects of a 3-D scene:

- Use the information you have. If your 2-D data includes road widths, house styles, tree heights, or other information about the appearance of objects, use them in the 3-D scene if you can. If you are using Scenario 3D, take advantage of its ability to identify features and display a table of all their attributes in a geodatabase.

- Distinguish between material and accessory forms. Material forms will have a significant effect on the decisions people make based on viewing the scene. Examples might include development density, lines of sight, and building dimensions. It is important to make these as accurate as you can. Accessory forms, such as people and trees, are still important, but you can allow yourself more leeway in their size and location.

- Provide fair, unbiased representations. The goal of your 3-D scene is to provide an objective picture of the project, not one that makes it look either better or worse than it would in reality.

MAKING THE COMPUTER-TO-REAL-WORLD CONNECTION

People looking at a 3-D scene for the first time sometimes perceive it as a video game or a fictional place. But if you have built the scene well, viewers will soon recognize it as a place they know. They will connect the computer display to the image of the location they have in their mind's eye, so that when you show proposed changes on the screen they can vividly imagine those same changes in real life. This transition to a focus on the proposed changes is important, because otherwise people will respond to the scene, not to the planning proposal you are modeling. The transition usually happens with time, but there are a few things you can do to speed it up:

- Include iconic features. Iconic features are ones that residents see frequently and associate with a particular location. Examples include old trees, landmark buildings, favorite restaurants, and statues, among others (see Figure 6.1).

- Include navigational cues. These are the signs, traffic signals, and street names that people use to help them find their way when they drive or walk to the location. It's often helpful to zoom from a maplike aerial view down to the ground-level scene. "Welcome to _____" signs are effective (see Figure 6.2).

- Show recent changes. If a highly visible tree was recently cut down or a new building just finished, showing those changes can help tie the scene to the present.

ENHANCING SUBJECTIVE FEEL

No one can be certain what makes a 3-D scene feel like the real place, but here are some suggestions for enhancing subjective feel:

- Pay attention to ground-level details. A big part of creating a 3-D scene is getting the buildings right, but do not ignore the surroundings. Plantings, sidewalks, parking lot striping, driveway curb cuts, and even pavement texture might make important differences.

- Navigate carefully. Three-dimensional viewers provide many capabilities for moving around the scene. When you are ready to share the feel of the place, it's best to walk or move slowly through the scene at about 5 to 10 feet high, looking slightly upward.

- Avoid artistic extremes. It is possible to make a very *attractive* scene using visible brushstrokes, watercolor textures, and interpretive patterns. We have seen, for example, a scene that looked like an Impressionist painting but was actually illustrating a new parking lot. It's also possible to make a very *impressive* scene by using the latest computer software, lots of special effects,

Figure 6.1 Nondescript location (top) made "real" by the addition of an iconic building (bottom) (screenshots from an interactive 3-D scene)

Figure 6.2 "Welcome to Victor, Idaho" sign (screenshot from an interactive 3-D scene)

Figure 6.3 Plantings along the stream give the waterline a softer feel (screenshot from an interactive 3-D scene).

and other technical fireworks. However, these and other methods that emphasize the scene itself detract from the audience's ability to develop an accurate feeling for the study area.

- Choose your priorities. Our brains are accustomed to focusing on a small part of the visual field, and they also routinely "fill in" missing visual information. So long as the main area of focus is carefully rendered, people tend to make a mental connection to the real world even when there are details missing or small inaccuracies in the periphery of the scene. If you have limited resources, concentrate your efforts on the most visually important components and use basic sketches for the rest.

- Use accessories carefully. People, cars, and other moving objects have a lot to do with the feel of a place. Use them, but do not exaggerate their number or size.

SOLUTIONS TO COMMON CHALLENGES

Here are suggestions for keeping the file size of a scene small while maintaining good visual quality, particularly in challenging situations.

SOFT FEATURES

Soft features are those that do not have straight edges, such as plants, people, water, fabric, wheels, and balls. Three-dimensional modeling tools of all kinds, including Scenario 3D and SketchUp, have trouble with soft features because present-day technology is based on triangles. Here are some techniques to deal with soft features:

- Use transparent textures and active materials (described in Chapter 5) to embed soft 2-D edges into the 3-D scene.

- Use the viewer's Layer Transparency tools to make objects slightly transparent. This blurs the sharp edges that make a soft feature look hard.

- Place small plantings along hard edges that are supposed to be soft, such as shorelines or the edges of lawns (see Figure 6.3).

- Use Photoshop or a similar tool to add a color gradient to an image texture that fades out near the edges.

- Pay attention to file sizes and triangle counts on 3-D models of soft objects. Sometimes a single model of a person, for example, can consume a significant fraction of your 3-D computing resources.

- Use billboards, which are flat poster-like objects, together with image textures and transparent backgrounds. A billboard is like half of an X-tree model (see Figure 6.4).

Figure 6.4 Example of "billboard"

NUMEROUS FEATURES

A city contains thousands of buildings, and a forest contains millions of trees. Your 3-D platform will not support modeling each of these individually, so you will need to find compromise techniques:

- Use high-resolution aerial photos, and view them from above. The photos do

Figure 6.5 Tree fences from the side (left) and from overhead (right) (screenshots from an interactive 3-D scene)

not necessarily have to represent existing conditions; you can use photos of similar building or vegetation patterns as ground cover textures for new proposals. To add a stronger 3-D effect, try making the layer slightly transparent and setting it about 20 feet off the ground.

- Use *fences,* which are vertical surfaces covered with image textures and transparent backgrounds. Fences are like long billboards following the terrain. From a distance at ground level, they act like the backdrop on a stage, giving the impression of faraway forests, mountains, or skylines. Figure 6.5 provides an example.

- For forests, try patterns of tree fences. For example, you can extrude contour lines to make a series of fences running along the side of a mountain. It sometimes helps to make a series of crossing fences, like a mesh or grid.

- Use Monopoly® buildings, which are very simple six-surface building models with four sides, an angled roof, and solid colors. Each one consumes very few computing resources, and when viewed from afar in large quantities, they can give a good sense of scale and mass (see Figure 6.6).

- Use many copies of a few models. If you reuse the same house model 100 times in a particular scene, the 3-D viewer needs to save it only once. You still display 100 times as many triangles as a single model, but the memory savings are often worthwhile.

LARGE AREAS

A large study area has many thousands of features and a large file size, but there are actions you can take to control the file size:

- Trade the level of detail for a bigger study area by using coarser terrain, simpler building models, and so on.

- View small parts of the study area at a time. Even if the overall scene is complex, the viewer only needs to process those parts that are visible at any given time. If you focus on small areas and avoid panoramic views, you will be able to move through the scene more smoothly.

- Make more than one scene. For example, make one large overview scene with details, and then make two or three close-up scenes focusing on particular areas of interest.

- Use more than one tool. Sometimes it works nicely to set context with a globe viewer such as Google Earth, then zoom in and switch to a more detailed scene in Scenario 3D.

Figure 6.6 A Monopoly house

UNEVEN TERRAIN

Steep hills, road cuts, building pads, curbs, berms, swales, mounds, and other small variations in terrain are hard to model for two reasons. One is that they use a lot of triangles; both the fine detail and the curved, organic shapes add triangles to the terrain's wireframe. The other is that data are scarce. Except for Lidar or perhaps landscape design models, most sources of terrain data do not include such fine detail. This is a particular problem for Google Earth and similar online services. Here are some things you can do:

- Make or modify your own terrain. Using ArcGIS 3D Analyst, SketchUp, or other 3-D modeling tools, you can edit your initial terrain model to add areas of higher detail. This technique is particularly useful in places where the natural ground line has been lowered, such as with a road cut or site grading. Note that terrain does not change between scenarios.

- Make your own objects. You can make 3-D mounds and then place them on the ground. This technique only works for places where the natural ground line has been raised. If you place any objects on top of the mounds, you will need to adjust the height of the objects manually so they sit above the mounds.

- Use thick ground-cover polygons. Scenario 3D provides tools for lifting ground-conforming layers such as lawns, sidewalks, or roads above the ground and filling in the sides. This works well for curbs, for example. Thick ground cover can also be useful for hiding sharp edges in the terrain caused by a low triangle count.

CHOOSING ACCESSORIES

Accessories are objects in the scene that are not integral to the plan or development proposal under consideration but add a sense of liveliness and context. Examples include people, cars, bicyclists, additional vegetation, street furniture, bus stops, signs, banners, mailboxes, landscaping features, and wildlife. These objects tend to improve the look of a scene, but they use up computing resources and take time to create; and if they are overused, they can distract from the development proposals, land-use plans, or land-use controls you are trying to illustrate. Here are some suggestions for how to choose accessories:

- Model typical use, not peak use. This applies to traffic density, pedestrian density, park visitors, and so on.

- Try to use as few accessories as you can while still achieving a realistic feel to the scene. Your tendency will almost always be to add just a few more, but keep your focus on the planning issues at hand.

- Favor images and billboards over solid models. Accessories are not the focus of the model, so it is less important that they be visible from all angles. For example, it may be better to Photoshop an image of a window flower box onto your building texture, than to create a true 3-D model of the flower box.

- Use plenty of trees. Novice modelers are often surprised at how many trees there are in the real world. If you are using X-tree models, the technology can tolerate hundreds of them.

- Use plantings, street furniture, and other accessories to break up long uninterrupted lines in the scene such as roads, the sides of large buildings, large parking lots, or mowed fields. This will make the scene look better, and it will also improve the viewer's depth perception.

- Use accessories to show scale. Placing a familiar object such as a person or a car next to an unfamiliar object such as a new building or a wind tower is a useful, unobtrusive way to give a sense of size.

CONCLUSION

CommunityViz provides a wide array of tools for making 3-D scenes. This chapter provided suggestions for using these tools to make the most effective scenes possible. Keep in mind that even simple, quickly constructed 3-D scenes can be useful. It is rare to use all the tricks and techniques we have described in a single project; use them judiciously as particular needs arise.

The creation of 3-D scenes is still partly an art form, and we encourage you to use your own original ideas and visual communication skills to create the best scenes you can.

CASE STUDY
DAM REMOVAL VISUALIZATION

Location: Klamath River, California and Oregon
Partners: American Rivers; TerraCognito GIS Services, Inc.

The Klamath River rises in a high basin ringed by Oregon's Cascade Mountains and flows more than 250 miles to the Pacific Ocean at Klamath, California. Its watershed includes tribal trust lands, parts of Crater Lake National Park, six national wildlife refuges, and three reaches designated "wild and scenic river." Along the Oregon–California border, PacifiCorp operates the Klamath Hydropower Project, a series of five mainstream dams. In 2001, PacifiCorp began a dam relicensing process with the Federal Energy Regulatory Commission (FERC), which included a series of studies about the future of the dams and the possibility of removing them.

The relicensing studies examined social, environmental, and economic issues. Economic studies showed that it would be less expensive for PacifiCorp to remove the dams and generate or purchase power from another source than to bring the dams into compliance with the environmental and operational standards. According to American Rivers, an active participant in the relicensing process, "removal of four dams on the Klamath would put the river's legendary salmon and steelhead runs on the road to recovery, and would help end decades-long disputes over river management in the basin."[1]

Project Description American Rivers played a lead role in communications and in negotiations between PacifiCorp and federal and state government agencies. In addition, American Rivers coordinated the development of much of the scientific and technical information related to the removal of the dams.

American Rivers retained TerraCognito GIS to develop detailed visualizations of the removal of the two largest dams—the Copco and Iron Gate. The first visual models showed the existing conditions. Next, visual models were created to depict the stages of dam removal, including the drawdown of reservoirs and subsequent riverbed restoration and revegetation. These interactive visual models allowed people to "fly" up the river, to float down it, or to view it from their own vantage points and virtually see the effects of the dam removal. According to American Rivers's California field office director, Steve Rothert, "the visualizations may not have changed any opponents' minds about whether the dams should be removed, but they went a long way to inform nearby landowners about the visual impacts, to help them understand the extensive restoration and revegetation process, and to have the whole process seem less threatening."

Technology and Tools TerraCognito employed CommunityViz 3.0, SiteBuilder 3D, ModelBuilder 3D, Spatial Analyst, and Photoshop to develop the visualizations. To model existing

> *The [CommunityViz] visualizations allayed many fears, filled in gaps, and also served to inspire many people about how soon a free-flowing Klamath River could become a functional, aesthetic resource that could benefit the environment and community.*
>
> —Steve Rothert
> Field Office Director, California
> American Rivers

---

1. American Rivers factsheet, www.americanrivers.org/assets/pdfs/Klamath_Fact_Sheet8394.pdf, accessed April 30, 2010.

Figure 6.7 Klamath River under existing conditions and after drawdown

Screenshot courtesy TerraCognito GIS

Figure 6.8 Projected future conditions, several years after drawdown

Screenshot courtesy TerraCognito GIS

conditions, TerraCognito fused satellite imagery with aerial photography and U.S. Geological Survey digital elevation models (DEMs). Recent bathymetric data and historic maps provided the basis for creating the post-removal valley floor and river course, while historic photos, U.S. Forest Service forest data, and 3-D spatial analysis were all used to model other post-removal conditions (see Figure 6.7).

Useful details in the models included landscape features such as cliffs, sandbars, sediment rings, and accurately located vegetation for each stage of drawdown and removal. The visualizations were made available in multiple forms: as a slide show of still images, as time-lapse animations over 10 years from dam removal to full restoration, and as animated movie clips of fly-throughs following the course of the river (see Figure 6.8).

Outcomes In 2006, FERC issued a draft environmental impact study that extensively described the ecological and economic benefits of decommissioning and removing the dams. In November 2008, PacifiCorp, the federal government, and the states of California and Oregon signed an agreement in principle stating that "the benefits of dam removal outweigh the potential costs and impacts." A final dam removal settlement agreement was signed in early 2010, which required the Secretary of the Interior to make a final determination of the public interest in the removal of the dams. After an expected positive determination in 2012, more detailed design work and permitting will follow, with actual dam removal expected by 2020.

CASE STUDY
WIND FARM VISUALIZATION

Location: Manchester, Vermont
Partners: Town of Manchester; Village of Manchester; Orton Family Foundation; Consensus Building Institute; Placeways LLC

Residents of the Town of Manchester, Vermont, love their Little Equinox Mountain (Figure 6.9). It's no surprise, then, that Manchester's town plan calls for keeping maintaining the ridgetop as open space. But the plan also supports renewable energy projects. When a Maine-based wind energy company proposed to build five modern wind turbines atop Little Equinox Mountain, spirited debate was sure to follow. In order to channel residents' passions into an informed and fair decision-making process, the town worked with a handful of partners to design the Little Equinox Wind Forum to engage citizens over a period of five months prior to the annual town meeting.

The forum addressed many issues—site planning, ecology, energy, and economics—but from the outset, it was clear that visual impact would be a key concern to residents who were accustomed to an uncluttered view of their mountain. Project partners engaged Placeways LLC to create a detailed visual model of the proposed wind energy project so that residents could see for themselves how the proposed turbines would look (see Figures 6.10 and 6.11).

Project Description The forum held five informational meetings culminating in an all-day wind summit. At each meeting, information from panels of experts and written summaries of peer-reviewed studies were made available. Presentations were followed by ample time for questions and answers. Between meetings, residents could add their questions and concerns to a rolling list so that they could be addressed

Figure 6.9 Little and Big Equinox mountains seen from Manchester, Vermont

Courtesy Lee Krohn

Figure 6.10 *Wind turbines seen from downtown Manchester (screenshot from an interactive 3-D scene)*

Figure 6.11 *Wind turbines seen from above*

in order. Information boxes were available at the town office and the library, and information was posted on the town website. The local newspaper and community access television station reported on the wind energy issues and debate.

One meeting was devoted exclusively to aesthetics. Using a partly customized version of CommunityViz, Placeways developed a detailed 3-D model of the project site and the surrounding area. The model served as an objective tool that let residents "fly" around helicopter style and see the wind turbines from anywhere, including their own neighborhoods and favorite gathering places in the community. The scene contained photo-realistic models of iconic downtown buildings and historic sites as well as technically accurate models of the proposed turbines, with rotating blades and night lighting. A free, fully navigable scene was made available online and on DVD. The visualizations were an important part of the final wind summit, at which participants voiced their opinions during facilitated table discussions and via keypad polling.

Technology and Tools Placeways used CommunityViz SiteBuilder 3D to develop the 3-D scene, and ModelBuilder 3D and Creator to craft the wind turbines and other important objects. Other tools and processes used in the wind forum process included a series of informational meetings, panels of experts, facilitated table discussions, summaries of peer-reviewed studies, a rolling list of issues, the town website, weekly meetings of a core project planning committee, keypad polling at the final wind summit, and active participation by local print and television media.

Outcomes The process was successful in improving residents' knowledge of the wind farm proposal and related impacts. It was also successful in creating an atmosphere of civil discourse, although no clear "yea" or "nay" consensus resulted. The wind developer elected not to pursue state approval for the project. However, when a new wind energy proposal is made, the developer, elected officials, and the community will be much better equipped to consider the kinds of concerns that should be addressed in project design and in any approval process.

> *The [CommunityViz] visualization software was especially helpful... Its real value was in taking a 'tour' of the town so people could see the impacts for themselves.*
>
> —Harley Lee
> Endless Energy Corporation

An important result of combining citizen engagement with CommunityViz was that participants felt they gained a realistic sense of how the proposed wind farm would look. Regardless of whether they liked or disliked the sight of five wind turbines, participants uniformly reported that they understood the visual impact. During keypad polling at the wind summit, 94 percent of participants indicated they had enough information on visual impacts, while 80 percent felt they had enough information about impacts on property values, and the potential energy and financial benefits to the community.

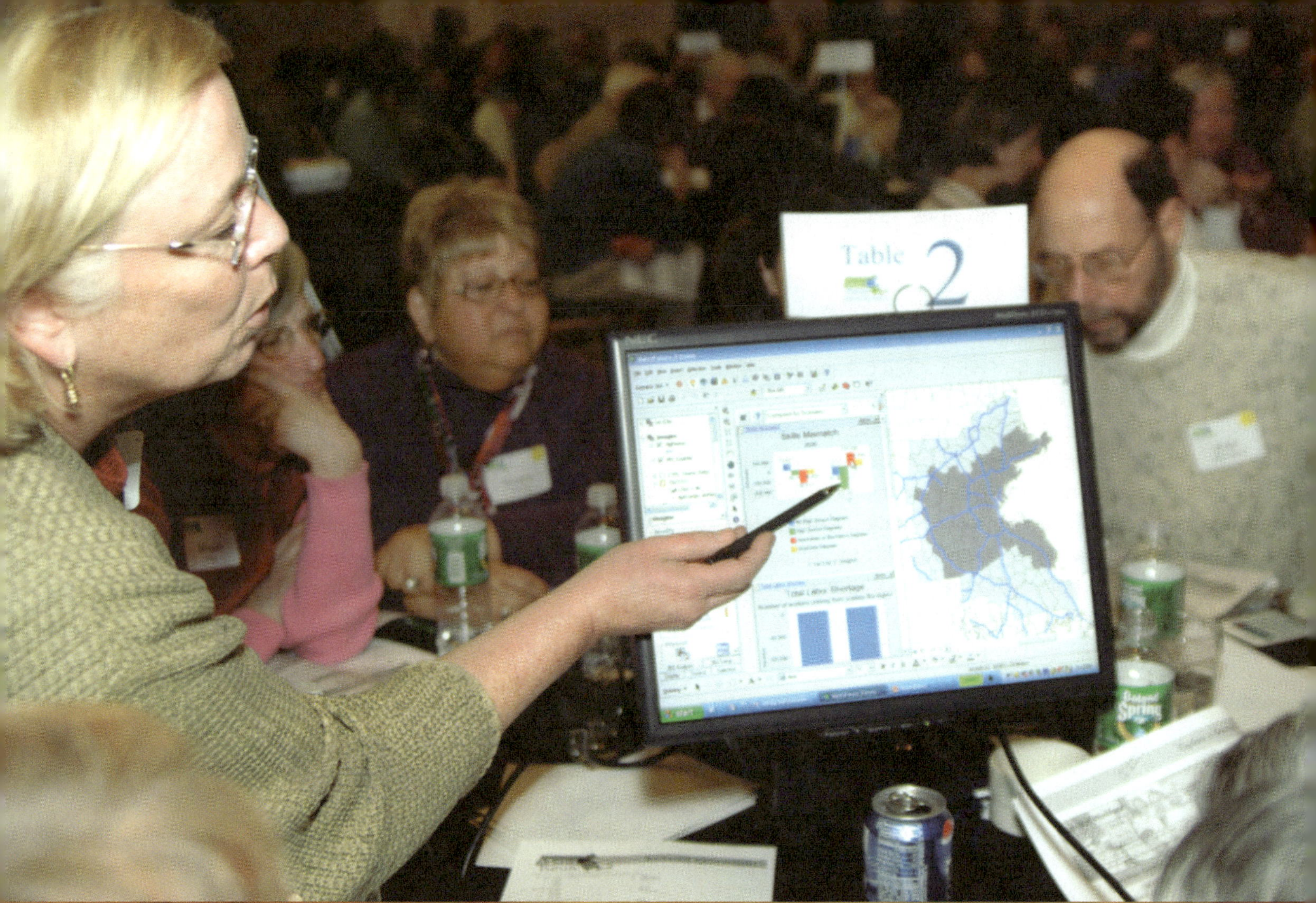
Table 2
Skills Mismatch
Total Labor Shortage

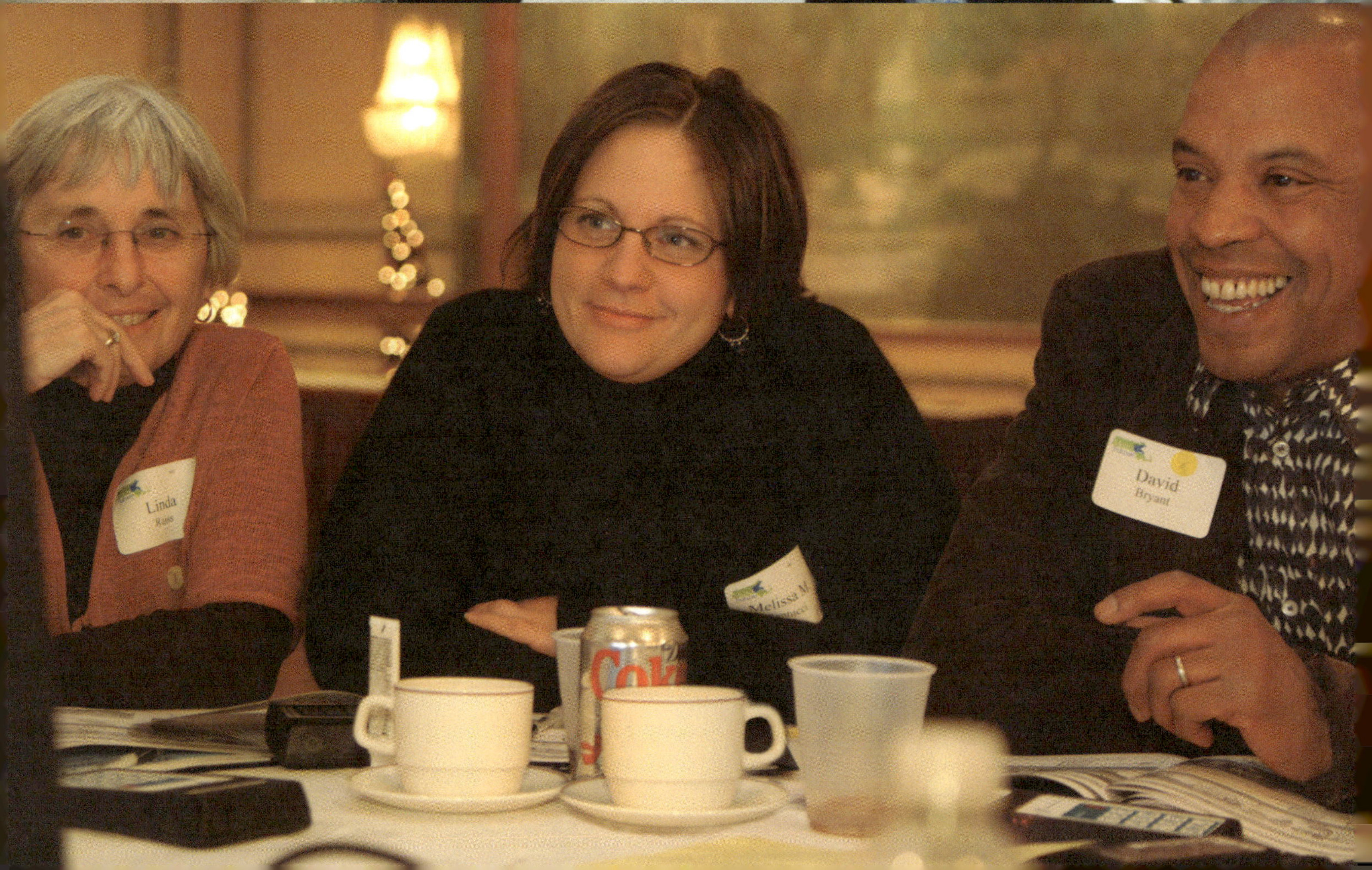
Linda
Ross
David
Bryant

SECTION II: COMMUNITY VISIONING, VALUES, AND GROWTH PROJECTIONS

NAVIGATING THIS SECTION

Section 2 describes how CommunityViz can help you start an effective comprehensive planning process with meaningful public participation. The initial steps include identifying what residents value and wish to see happen, what current trends suggest may happen, and how particular choices about growth and development might affect the future of the community.

Chapter 7, Visioning, presents techniques that planners often use in working with local residents to assess current conditions and to discuss potential future scenarios for their communities. Chapter 7 shows how CommunityViz can help support a variety of techniques ranging from low-tech methods such as paper map exercises to high-tech geodesign. This work often takes place in public meetings or charrettes. For more information about using CommunityViz in public settings, refer to Section 5.

Chapter 8, Growth Projections, begins with a survey of the primary CommunityViz tools for projecting the location and density of future development projects: Build-Out Wizard, Land Use Designer, TimeScope, and Allocator. The chapter then offers advice on why and when to use the tools alone or in combination. For more advanced build-out techniques, also refer to Chapter 14.

Chapter 9, Value Mapping and Special Places, explains how CommunityViz enables you to do value mapping as a way to identify those places that the residents value: their heart-and-soul resources. The chapter also discusses how you can make maps of heart-and-soul resources with CommunityViz.

BACKGROUND PLANNING CONCEPTS FOR THIS SECTION

In the Bible, Proverbs 29:18 says, "Where there is no vision, the people perish." While this statement may be extreme, it underscores the importance of having a sense of how you want your community to look, function, and change over the next several years. Often, a community will plan to create more jobs or more housing without considering the potential impacts on the community's appearance, finances, and public services. A community vision needs to be comprehensive. It sets a direction for the entire community, the residents, businesses, and elected officials. A community vision must also be realistic, not simply a list of wishes.

To develop a vision for the community, residents should first understand how the community has grown and changed in the past 20 years, and the trends, conditions, and challenges that are likely to continue into the future. Next, residents need to express how they want the community to change and which heart-and-soul features they want to retain. Finally, community members must figure out how to turn that vision into a reality. A key purpose of planning is to lay the groundwork for regulations, incentives, and public infrastructure that will influence trends so that the most desirable outcomes occur.

An effective way to begin the visioning process is to hold a public workshop or *charrette*.

At a charrette, which may take from several days to a week to complete, residents express what they like and don't like about the way their community looks and functions. They also discuss a variety of issues, such as downtown revitalization, historic preservation, roads, and housing design. CommunityViz can help you to engage participants in discussions about their values and the future of their community. CommunityViz enables you to educate participants by showing them data and illustrations of the community. The participants respond by expressing their preferences about their community. Then you can use CommunityViz to present a range of development options and elicit participants' responses for improving the appearance and operation of the community. Through this interactive process, a charrette often alerts residents and elected officials to the need for a new community plan, changes to land-use and design regulations, or new investments in public infrastructure.

Another visioning activity is to use CommunityViz presentations with a set of focus groups. Each focus group should have no more than a dozen people who represent a diverse cross-section of the community by age, gender, income, a particular interest, or prominence in the community. As with a charrette, the focus groups should discuss the physical aspects of the community as they affect current and future needs. You can use CommunityViz to show a focus group the community's current conditions and show sketches of several alternative futures in order to find out what participants like and don't like. The scenario-building capabilities of CommunityViz are especially helpful in illustrating options for alternative development projects and overall community development patterns. CommunityViz can enable an audience to "fly through" a neighborhood or throughout the community in different development scenarios.

The visioning process results in a vision statement, drafted by the local planning commission with public input, which expresses how the community should look and function over the next 10 to 20 years. The statement guides public investment and private development decisions, and it gives direction to the local comprehensive plan and land-use and design ordinances. The vision statement serves as an overall policy for the local government, and it sets the foundation for the general goals and specific objectives described in the comprehensive plan.

Many local comprehensive plans begin with a projection of population growth and the land-use needs of that growing population. Anticipated increases in population often drive local planning decisions for new retail space or office buildings, housing developments, and expanded public infrastructure, such as sewer and water facilities and schools. Also, many state and federal government grants are based on current and expected population levels.

One shortcoming of traditional comprehensive plans is that they are driven more by a sense of a need to accommodate future population growth than by a desire to maintain and retain those features of the community that make it a good place to live. That is, traditional comprehensive plans tend to overlook the community's heart-and-soul assets. At charrettes and focus groups, participants are asked to identify those elements of the community that they would not want to lose. These heart–and-soul assets can be placed on a community values map. The values map is helpful in determining where future development should take place, and the appropriate type and size of that development. Alternative scenarios created through CommunityViz can incorporate values maps to show the impacts to heart-and-soul resources under different development proposals. The goal is that new development or redevelopment not destroy or reduce the value of those resources. You can create values map as part of a community's comprehensive plan, neighborhood plan, or zoning ordinance update. In particular, you can include the values map data in drafting the future land-use map of the comprehensive plan, which then becomes the basis for the community's zoning ordinance.

7 VISIONING

KEY CONCEPTS AND TERMS IN THIS CHAPTER

- Charrettes
- Creating scenarios
- Geodesign and live sketching
- Map exercises
- Stages of visioning projects
- SWOT analysis (Strengths, Weaknesses, Opportunities, and Threats)

The process of creating a vision for the future of a community or region—known as *visioning*—lays the foundation for a public planning effort. Done well, visioning can bring people together, engender trust, generate optimism and excitement, build momentum for constructive planning actions, help define values, and focus priorities. But wishful thinking about the future must be tempered with data analysis and pragmatism. This chapter describes how CommunityViz can help make visioning a catalyst for effective community or regional plans, implementing ordinances, and infrastructure investment.

WHY AND WHEN

The saying "If you don't know where you are going, you might end up someplace else" is attributed to Yogi Berra. Our version is: "If you don't know where *you want to go*, you might end up someplace else." Leaders usually call for a vision when they sense that the community has lost its consensus on where it wants to go, or when new opportunities or threats arise that the existing zoning regulations or infrastructure budget cannot handle. Successful visioning establishes a clear long-term direction to guide subsequent comprehensive plans, day-to-day decisions about development proposals, zoning and subdivision regulations, and infrastructure investment.

Visioning often addresses land use and public education, economic development, and community identity. CommunityViz deals with physical and spatial planning and development design, so it cannot address the entire range of topics in a visioning process. But for issues involving public comprehensive plans, land-use regulations, and development design, CommunityViz can be a valuable tool. Figure 7.1 illustrates some typical steps in the visioning process and the role CommunityViz can play, particularly during scenario building and the process of selecting the desired future scenario.

Figure 7.1 CommunityViz support through stages of a visioning process

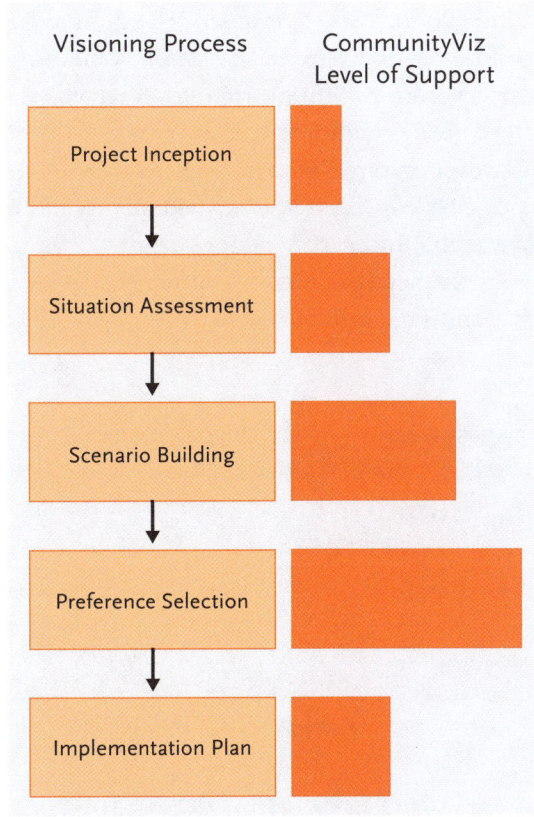

The primary contributions of CommunityViz are to: a) tell you the consequences of choices, b) illustrate not just the final plan but also choices along the way, and c) help you present and explain your work to diverse audiences.

Keep in mind that you do not need to use CommunityViz for every aspect of the visioning process. For sketching potential development projects, for example, sometimes using a marker with a flip chart is a simpler and more helpful way to communicate than geodesign with CommunityViz. CommunityViz works nicely with keypad polling, but sometimes the best way to collect public opinions is to have the audience put sticky dots on a map or on a list of development design and location alternatives. And, although an interactive CommunityViz 3-D scene can show how a future development might look, there may be times when a photo of an existing similar development will suffice.

BEGINNING THE VISIONING PROJECT

The early phase of the visioning process usually features organization and team building. At this stage, CommunityViz can help to articulate the call to action, a sense of urgency, and the need for a new vision. The call to action sometimes emerges from growth projections in which you might use CommunityViz to show a now-open landscape covered with houses or now-quiet roads clogged with traffic. A vivid picture of an undesirable future can compel people to think about the need for a new comprehensive plan and land-use ordinances. CommunityViz has strong growth projection capabilities, and Chapter 8 describes them in detail.

ASSESSING THE CURRENT SITUATION

Visioning should include an assessment of the existing conditions in the community, such as current land-use patterns, infrastructure problems, and the implications of recent growth trends. One popular exercise is a SWOT analysis, a report on the community's strengths, weaknesses, opportunities and threats (see Figure 7.2). Chapter 1 described ways to collect SWOT information.

Strengths and *weaknesses* describe current conditions, whereas *opportunities* and *threats* refer to the future. Therefore, when you represent SWOT information in CommunityViz, you need to show two scenarios, present and future. You can also use TimeScope to show a progression of changes from the present to the future (see Chapter 8).

If your community's strengths and weaknesses involve particular locations, map them. Create maps or map layers that show favorite places, natural assets, and economic assets, as well as least-favorite places, natural hazards, and blighted neighborhoods.

Residents often learn most effectively from regional comparisons that show how their community compares to others, so this is when creating maps that are larger than the study area makes sense. For example, a map that shows commuting times for places throughout the region may shed light on whether a community's commuting times are a strength or a weakness. If you need to do only simple mapping, you may

Figure 7.2 Sample SWOT analysis

STRENGTHS	WEAKNESSES	OPPORTUNITIES	THREATS
Community spirit	Poor relations with the county	New retail businesses	Population losses
Good educational system	Merchants not organized	Community block grants	Decrease of revenue from sales tax
Interstate highway location	Low incomes	Tourist accommodations	Lack of affordable housing
Preservation of downtown buildings	Unsightly entrances to the community	Regional craft fair held twice a year	Lack of sewer capacity

From Thomas L. Daniels et al., *The Small Town Planning Handbook*, 3rd ed. (Chicago: APA Planners Press, 2007), p. 38.

not need CommunityViz, but its Saved Views, Symbol Saver, and Scenario Comparison tools can make for smoother live presentations. You may also want to consider setting up alerts that highlight particular features on the map based on their attribute values—for instance, you could make an alert that identifies all counties in an agricultural region that contain at least 50 percent prime agricultural soils (see Figure 7.3). You can show strengths and weaknesses that are difficult to map on charts instead. For example, a balanced economy is a strength, and a pie chart illustrating the different economic sectors in the planning area will provide a visual representation of the size of each sector.

You can illustrate opportunities and threats in the same way you depict strengths and weaknesses—with feature maps, regional maps, alerts, and charts. In your presentation, be sure to distinguish the current conditions from any future scenarios. Audiences often assume that if information is being shown on a computer, it must be true or part of an already approved plan. Help them distinguish between the certainty of current conditions and the uncertainty of future projections.

SCENARIO BUILDING

There are no fixed rules about how to form a community vision; widely different strategies and practices have been used to elicit public input. Here, we will describe the three main methods. We do not promote any particular method; rather, we describe the ways you can use CommunityViz to support each one.

The most common visioning practices involve the drafting and evaluation of alternative scenarios. CommunityViz supports several ways to create: 1) scenarios to use in low-tech visioning; 2) scenarios which are generated by the public for higher-tech visioning; and, 3) scenarios for high-tech visioning, which are produced mainly by public planners or planning consultants.

LOW-TECH VISIONING

Some planners believe that you should be careful not to burden the visioning process with too much technology and predetermined structure.

Figure 7.3 Alerts being used to highlight geographic features of particular interest. Alerted features have a bright red outline.

Low-tech visioning often involves a facilitator who helps audience members reveal their desires for the future in response to a series of photos, graphics, and other visuals. The result is a series of sketches that relate to places on a map of the study area. Low-tech visioning makes little reference to current conditions, but rather focuses on arriving at an audience consensus of the desired future outcomes.

CommunityViz can support low-tech visioning only to a small degree. If the visioning process begins with maps and data about existing conditions, you can use population, economic, and land-use data compiled in CommunityViz for the study area profile (see chapters 1 and 2). Later, you can translate the series of sketches of the desired future into the CommunityViz framework in a few different ways:

- Scan or digitize any flat artwork, and then attach the files to points on a GIS map or in a 3-D scene using hyperlinks. People looking at the map or scene can click to see the artwork. You can also embed art in 3-D scenes in the form of images on the sides of buildings, or on signs or billboards (see chapters 5 and 6). For example, if the visioning process produced sketches of what children wished their school looked like, you could place those sketches on top of the existing school.

- Scan any maplike drawings and add them to your GIS map as image layers for ready reference and illustration. Note that the maplike drawings do not need to be geographically correct; you can simply include them as images at approximately the right place and scale. One particularly nice display technique is to start with the maplike drawing on top and then use the ArcMap Wipe or Transparency tools to gradually reveal a traditional map underneath.

- If the visioning process identified heart-and-soul resources, such as important and special places, map them as precisely as possible so you can use them in subsequent analyses.

- You can create CommunityViz indicators to capture important community values identified through the visioning process.

CommunityViz is clearly not a low-tech tool, so if you use it to support a low-tech visioning process, be sensitive to its methods and community attitudes toward computer technology. Here, the role of CommunityViz is to translate the artwork of desired designs into potential future results, not to replace the facilitator's task of arriving at a group consensus in the visioning process.

SCENARIOS CREATED BY THE PUBLIC

Planners agree that the public must be involved in any community visioning process. But there is debate about the specifics of the public's participation. The most open approach includes the public in all phases of the planning project, especially in creating scenarios.

One popular and effective method for creating scenarios is the map exercise, "growth challenge game," or chip game. During a public meeting, participants break into groups of between three and 10 members, and each group is given a large map of the planning area with grid squares overlaid on it. Each group suggests a plan by placing colored poker chips, board game pieces, or stickers representing types of development onto the grid squares. A simple scoring system linked to particular goals turns the map exercise into a game. For example, the object of the game may be for players to place on the map enough housing chips to accommodate projected population growth and enough commercial chips to maintain a good balance between jobs and housing. At the end of the exercise, all the participants reconvene to compare results and draw conclusions.

You can use CommunityViz to help you determine the chip game's parameters, such as how much growth players should aim for, or site suitability scores. Then at the end of the exercise, you can use CommunityViz to analyze the maps from each group so that participants can see the consequences of their proposals. A map exercise appears in the teaching example later in this chapter.

Live sketching is a high-tech method for the public to create scenarios employing live CommunityViz screens rather than paper maps. This method works well in a charrette when a computer is available to each small group, or where audiences have access to an electronic map table or portable display technology. Electronic map tables are kitchen-table-sized, horizontal displays with touch-screen technology that allows participants to gather around and interact with the map by touching and drawing on it. Portable displays range in size and design from tablet computers to chalkboard-sized devices that are usually vertical and also allow for audience interaction.

Taking advantage of the CommunityViz Land Use Designer or Scenario Sketch tools, or both, participants use the mouse to paint proposed land uses (using the Painter tool) or built features (using the Clone tool) directly onto a live map.

With live sketching, indicator results appear immediately on the CommunityViz displays. Also, participants can draw and redraw as much as they like, providing a more interactive experience. You can customize the painting palette—for example, a single brush stroke can apply not just residential and commercial units, but also associated government services, infrastructure, parks, and other details. This capability makes live sketching more flexible and sophisticated than the placing of chips on paper maps. Finally, you do not need to use grid squares with live sketching, so participants can work with oddly shaped features on the landscape, such as watershed boundaries or census blocks. The disadvantages of live sketching are that it requires more technical resources, and in some cases the additional detail and sophistication may be more than the participants want or need. To learn how to set up geodesign with live sketching, see the discussion in Chapter 8 of the Scenario 360 decision tool called Land Use Designer.

SCENARIOS CREATED INTERNALLY

You can form a team of about half a dozen people to draft a set of scenarios and then present the scenarios at a public meeting where you ask local residents for their reactions. This small team typically includes professional planners and CommunityViz analysts who can build models that are more complete, internally consistent, and perhaps more instructive than those created in large public settings. Including one or two citizen representatives on the core team may also enhance the scenarios.

In this case, you can use the guidelines for creating a preferred scenario described in Section 1. Keep the level of analysis broad at this visioning stage, and also consider the other best practices for creating scenarios, which are described next.

BEST PRACTICES FOR CREATING SCENARIOS

Here are several best practices for creating scenarios for visioning projects:

- Stay as high as you can for as long as you can. In other words, take the view from 1,000 feet; be general and avoid building an analysis that is too detailed. At the visioning stage, details are distracting, and setting them up adds unnecessary time and cost. You want to be able to make large changes quickly and easily, and you should not invest too much effort in any particular scenario. Consider using the thousand/thousand rule of thumb that: a) the number of features in the primary analysis layer should be less than 1,000, regardless of the size of the study area, and b) any 3-D models should be viewed from above 1,000 feet so that residents cannot make out their particular house, to avoid disputes about accuracy.

- Be bold. The vision stage is the best time to consider potentially dramatic changes and ambitious planning projects. Scenarios still need to be realistic, but they do not need to be cautiously incremental. Visioning is the art of imagining the possible over an extended period of time, and is not necessarily limited by current financial constraints or political gridlock.

- Pay close attention to presentation. Visions are for general audiences, so your analysis should be, too. Give scenarios evocative names, and design a small number of memorable, easily identifiable indicators that people will refer back to again and again.

- Do not let CommunityViz limit you. Be open to using other software tools, media, or techniques that can advance the visioning process.

SELECTING A PREFERRED SCENARIO

You will need to establish criteria by which to evaluate scenarios, compare scenarios, identify trade-offs, and set priorities, so that the community can select a preferred future scenario. Here are some ways to use CommunityViz to help the general public and decision makers compare scenarios and choose their preferred one:

- Create and display maps of each scenario using CommunityViz scenario tools, including the Scenario Comparison window. If you have created 3-D scenes, you can compare them as well.

- Measure and display important consequences and characteristics of each scenario using CommunityViz indicators. You can display the indicator values in charts, tables, and reports. If the process has suggested target values, you can show each scenario's performance compared to the targets.

- If your audience is a focus group of fewer than 25 people, you can allow participants to do geodesign by making small experimental changes to scenarios to learn their effects.

For example, a participant could use Sketch tools to change the land-use plan for several parcels of land or sketch in an alternative location for a transit stop.

- Invite discussion about important variables, assumptions, and subjective values that affect scenario indicator scores. Do so judiciously, remembering the "Stay as high as you can as long as you can" rule. Use assumption slider bars to demonstrate the sensitivity of the analysis to important but uncertain input values, such as future automobile fuel efficiency in miles per gallon; demonstrate the effects of changes to land-use regulations that are important enough to consider but not significant enough to justify their own scenario, such as height restrictions or steep slope ordinances; and capture and use subjective value judgments from the audience, such as quality-of-life priorities and heart-and-soul resources to protect (see Chapter 17 for more discussion).

IMPLEMENTATION PLAN

The final phase of a visioning process is to develop an implementation plan to make the preferred scenario happen. This phase has an unfortunate reputation for taking a long time and producing unimpressive results, but done well it can serve as a capstone for the vision and a bridge to the drafting of a new comprehensive plan and land-use ordinances, and the allocation of funds for new infrastructure investment.

The concept of designing for a living comprehensive plan is an important part of successful plan implementation (see Chapter 3). In addition, here are guidelines for using CommunityViz in the final stages of visioning:

- Move quickly. The energy and interest generated by a public visioning process will dissipate rapidly if visible results do not appear within a few weeks. CommunityViz allows you to perform final analyses of the preferred scenario and create final reports in a matter of days, and you should provide that information to the planning commission, visioning committee, or elected officials as soon as you can.

- Keep communicating. Take advantage of CommunityViz communication tools to publish the final preferred scenario and vision statement in many formats; these may include paper reports, web reports, maps, WebShots (see Chapter 18), and 3-D scenes. At the same time, remove from public display any working or in-progress versions to avoid confusion. A well-managed visioning project will keep the results in front of the public and decision makers, and build momentum for drafting and implementing a new comprehensive plan.

- Build on your earlier visioning analysis to create the comprehensive plan update. It is easiest to start the comprehensive plan analysis by creating a fresh new analysis file, but after the initial setup you can use CommunityViz templates to import parts or all of the analysis logic you used during visioning. A vision-oriented analysis is appropriately low on detail, but an implementation-oriented analysis in a comprehensive plan will need much more detail. You can use overlap functions to apply planned attributes of large areas on a future land-use map to smaller areas such as individual land parcels. Technical advice for changing resolutions appears in Chapter 11.

TEACHING EXAMPLE

This teaching example demonstrates the main steps we used to conduct a map exercise as part of a community visioning process. The exercise took the form of a game in which teams placed residential, commercial, and open-space chips on grid squares to show the location and amount of new development in a community. It identified some of the key planning issues of the study area.

STEP 1: CREATING THE MAP

The map began as a base map in CommunityViz with some standard layers—an aerial photo, roads, and waterways covering an area of 3 square miles (see Figure 7.4). For printing a paper map, we recommend you create a roughly square area.

Next, we used different levels of transparency to overlay color-coded layers representing fire hazards (tan), flood zones (purple), the water service area (lighter green), steep slopes

Figure 7.4   *Base map*

Figure 7.5   *Map with land-use overlays*

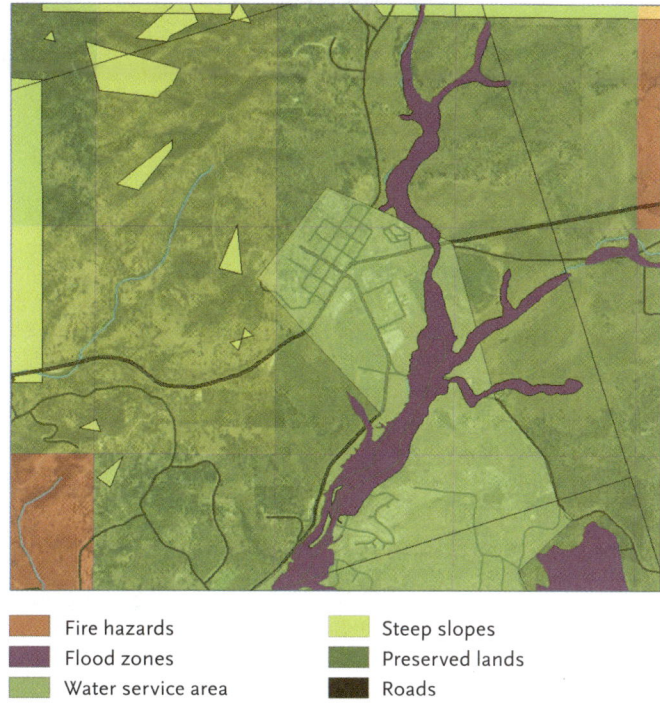

- Fire hazards
- Flood zones
- Water service area
- Steep slopes
- Preserved lands
- Roads

Figure 7.6   *Final map including grid squares*

(yellow), preserved lands (darker green), and roads (darkest green) (see Figure 7.5). In this case, the roads network and aerial photo gave participants enough information about existing buildings, but in a larger study area it is helpful to show existing buildings, or at least existing built areas, on the map as well.

Then, we created an analysis grid of squares, numbered 1 to 81, as shown in Figure 7.6. This pattern is sometimes called a fishnet. You can use any number of grid squares, but they need to be larger than the poker chips, board game pieces, or stickers the participants will place on the printed map during the exercise. Keeping the total number of grid squares under 100 made processing the results more manageable. In our example, each grid square represents an area of a little more than 70 acres in size.

STEP 2: SETTING UP THE ANALYSIS

Population estimates for this area suggested growth of about 1,000 people in the next 20 years, and using an estimate of 2.5 people per household, we projected a demand for 400 new dwelling units. We wanted each team to have about 60 residential chips to work with, so we initially decided each chip would represent seven dwellings. We made a variable assumption for "dwelling units per chip" for use in our analysis. That assumption would allow us to make changes later if desired.

We did not have a separate growth projection for commercial development. Our area profile had shown that most businesses in the area were retailers serving the local population, so we decided to use a coarse guideline that commercial space could reasonably grow as fast as the population but not much faster. That gave

Figure 7.7 Sample map exercise indicators

HOUSEHOLD TYPE
Average distance to main road
Average distance to town
Impervious surface remaining
New developed area
New dwelling units not on slopes
New dwelling units on infrastructure
New dwelling units on slopes
New dwelling units with high fire risk
New dwelling units with acceptable fire risk
New impervious surface
New jobs
Preserved acres
Study area acres
Sum of total vacant land
Total commercial space
Total dwelling units
Total jobs
Vacant land remaining

us an estimate of a maximum 180,000 square feet—about 4 acres—of viable new commercial space over the next 20 years. We decided to represent the new commercial space with 30 chips, each equal to 6,000 square feet, which we again set up as a variable assumption for our analysis. We purposely prevented commercial chips from representing very small spaces because commercial development is more successful in larger blocks than on scattered lots.

Because our grid squares were large, we also provided a way to site clusters of buildings amid open space. One open-space chip in the stack meant that one-quarter of the grid square was to be kept open.

STEP 3: PLAYING THE GAME

Several speakers introduced background-planning concepts to the group before teams at separate tables set to work. Stacking on a grid square was allowed: the higher the stack, the denser the development. We challenged the players to place all 60 of their residential chips somewhere on the map, and no more than 30 commercial chips. Players could include up to three open-space chips in any stack. We encouraged them to try to achieve optimal performance based on a number of indicators (see Figure 7.7). The idea was to place the chips to create more of the positive outcomes, such as new dwelling units not on slopes, and less of the negative results, such as new dwellings with high fire risk. In practice, most teams tried to maximize the number of new jobs and minimize the amount of new impervious surface. Each team had a score for each indicator in Figure 7.7. And each team had an overall score, which consisted of the sum of the scores for each individual indicator.

STEP 4: SCORING

After the teams had placed their chips, we gave each team a simple spreadsheet for entering the data for their proposed development pattern. In the left-hand column, we listed each grid square, from 1 to 81. We instructed each team to count the number of each type of chip in each grid square and enter it in the relevant right-hand columns, as shown in Figure 7.8.

Once the data were entered, we used the CommunityViz External Table Links capability to read the results and update the analysis. Each team had one scenario. One team was asked to create a business as usual scenario; the others

Figure 7.8 Map data entry table

GRID SQUARE	NUMBER OF RESIDENTIAL CHIPS	NUMBER OF COMMERCIAL CHIPS	NUMBER OF OPEN-SPACE CHIPS
1	10		1
2		2	
3	8	8	1
...	...	...	...
81	3	1	1

Figure 7.9 Chips placed by one team, shown as bar charts within each grid square

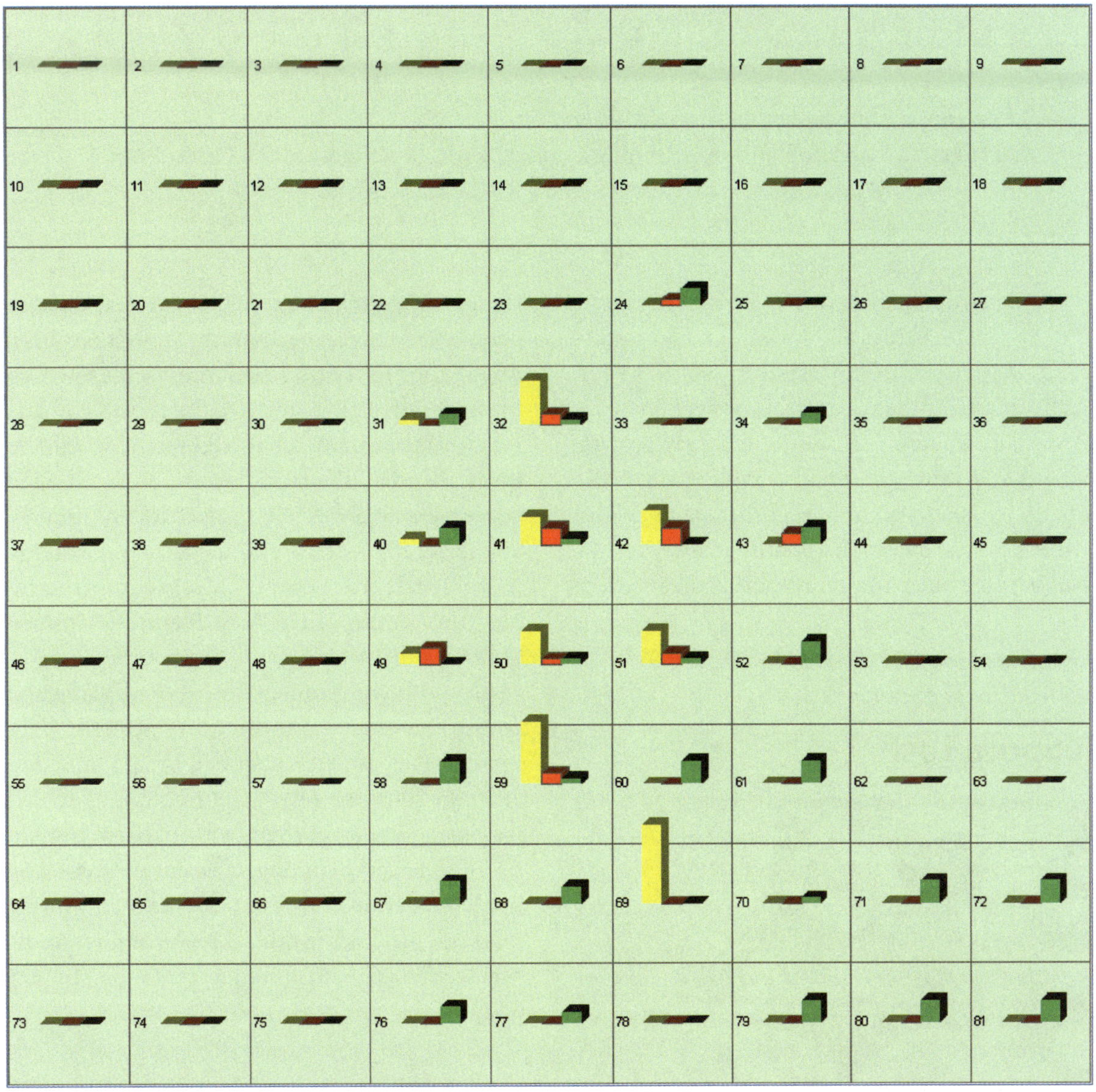

Note: Yellow chips are residential development, red chips are commercial development, and green chips are open space.

were free to place their chips wherever they wanted. Once we tabulated all of the results, we could easily generate charts and maps illustrating each proposal.

Figure 7.9 is a map showing where one team placed its chips. Figure 7.10 is an example of an indicator chart showing results from 12 teams that participated in the exercise. These graphics and indicators enabled us to engage the entire group in a conversation about planning choices and their implications.

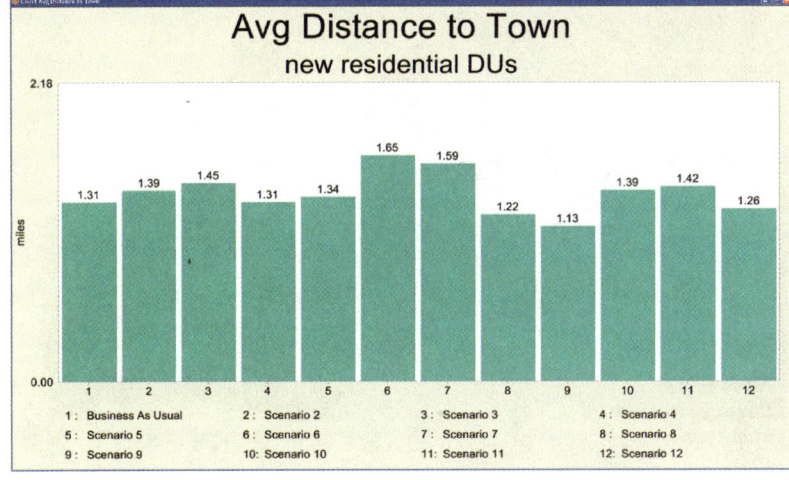

Figure 7.10 Sample indicator chart showing results from 12 teams

CASE STUDY
REGIONAL PLAN: METROFUTURE

Location: Metropolitan Boston, Massachusetts
Partners: Metropolitan Area Planning Council, with the support of the Orton Family Foundation and numerous other foundations and partners

Metropolitan Boston is a complex region of 164 cities and towns and had a population of 4.3 million people at the 2000 census. At the time of this project, in 2003, it was anticipated that slow and steady growth would add more than half a million new residents by 2030. As in many other parts of the United States, the population in greater Boston had become older and more racially diverse over the past 20 years. These trends were expected to continue. Moderate economic growth has been forecast for the region, with most job growth in business, education, and health services. Greater Boston faced many challenges as it sought to meet affordable housing needs, preserve open space (see Figure 7.11), protect water supplies, and make efficient use of transportation systems.

In 1963, the State of Massachusetts created the Metropolitan Area Planning Council (MAPC) to "prepare and, from time to time, revise both comprehensive regional plans and comprehensive economic development programs." The last such plan had been adopted in 1990. In 2003, the MAPC set out to update that plan using a new approach with an equal emphasis on technical planning, civic engagement, and implementation. The result was the MetroFuture plan, adopted as the official regional plan in the spring of 2008, with an implementation strategy adopted that fall.

Figure 7.11 Expected loss of open space in Greater Boston, 2000–2030, if current development trends continue

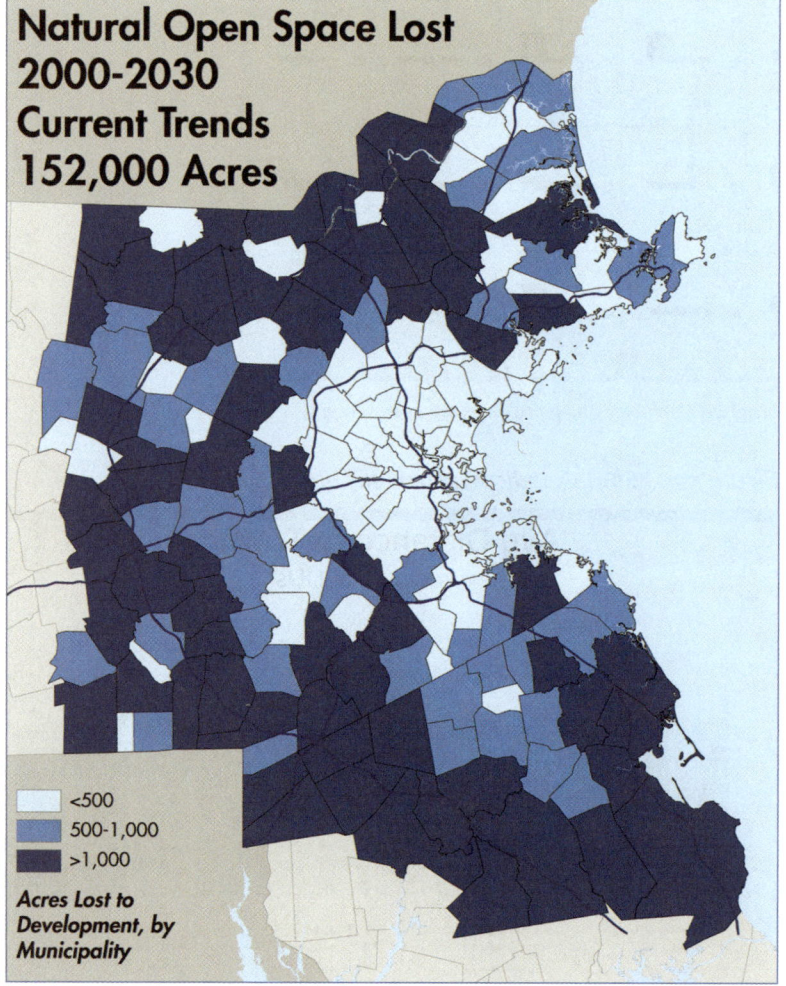

Project Description: The MetroFuture plan was developed in five phases: 1) initial visioning activities, 2) analysis of current trends, 3) development of alternative futures, 4) preference selection, and 5) development of implementation strategies. With a great deal of public input, MAPC produced four alternative growth scenarios—Current Trends, Little by Little, Winds of Change, and Imagine—and built them as models in CommunityViz. In the preference selection phase, two workshops were held in which 500 people had the opportunity to test the alternatives. Laptops on each workshop table allowed citizens to change assumptions in CommunityViz, discuss impacts among their fellow attendees, and vote on the alternatives using keypad-polling technology.

Figure 7.12 *Share of new residential growth by settlement if current development trends continue, versus MetroFuture plan*

	Existing Population	If Current Trends Continue	MetroFuture
Inner Core	31%	17%	35%
Regional Urban Centers	24%	21%	26%
Maturing Suburbs	23%	26%	24%
Developing Suburbs	21%	36%	16%

All images in this case study courtesy of MetroFuture

The "Scenario Exploration Guidebook" helped orient participants to each scenario and provided a framework for understanding the impacts of modified assumptions. Participants overwhelmingly rejected the Current Trends scenario; most preferred Winds of Change, which altered the distribution of growth in the region by focusing new development in designated smart-growth areas in urban and suburban communities. In addition to these workshops, smaller public meetings and surveys were conducted to vet and refine the alternatives. The preferred scenario, called MetroFuture, was ratified by 94 percent of the 400 people who attended a public seminar. The final phase of the project focused on drafting 13 implementation strategies on topics ranging from land use (see figures 7.12 and 7.13) to public safety and water policy.

The MetroFuture project involved collecting and analyzing large quantities of data, which became the foundation of the model built in CommunityViz. The model, which is intended as a living version of the plan, enables users to easily incorporate new data and update the plan.

Technology and Tools: CommunityViz served as the platform for creating and analyzing the alternative scenarios, and it enabled the public to experiment with assumptions and assess impacts (see Figure 7.14). In addition, the Boston Region

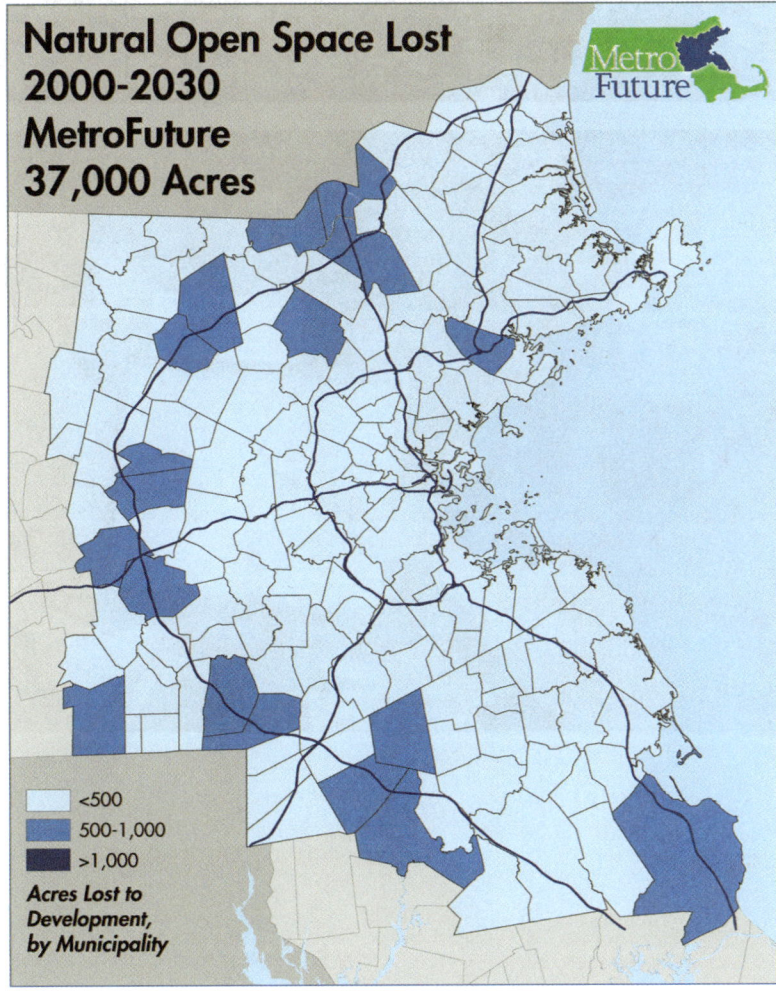

Figure 7.13 *Expected loss of 37,000 acres of open space in 2000–2030 under the MetroFuture plan. Current trends were projected to result in the loss of 152,000 acres of open space over the same period.*

Metropolitan Planning Organization (MPO), which is responsible for the region's transportation planning, was able to use the data generated from the CommunityViz model once it was modified into the Traffic Analysis Zones (TAZs).

Creating the MetroFuture plan captured the insights and opinions of more than 4,500 people and organizations through a variety of citizen engagement tools, including: visioning workshops; focus groups; a telephone poll; a survey administered through local papers, online, and in person; public briefings across the region; large workshops with workbooks, computers, and keypad polling; visualizations using Photoshop and aerial photos; a policy summit to address key policy areas prior to plan adoption; and a strategy summit to review draft recommendations prior to adoption of the implementation strategies.

Outcomes: Important implementation measures were introduced following the visioning effort. The Boston Region MPO adopted the MetroFuture plan as the basis for its 20-year regional transportation plan. The Massachusetts Department of Conservation and Recreation has used MetroFuture to forecast future water needs. Meanwhile, the MAPC began developing a program to help individual communities discover ways to implement MetroFuture, often using CommunityViz and the findings of MetroFuture.

Figure 7.14 MetroFuture workshop participants experimenting with CommunityViz

CommunityViz really helped our region's residents plan for their future.... CommunityViz's Scenario 360 had the geospatial components, equations, and functions that were flexible enough for our staff to model exactly what we wanted. The slider bars help our model be responsive to participants' concerns and incorporate their perspectives into the scenarios planning.

—Holly St. Clair
   Director of Data Services
   Greater Boston Metropolitan Area
      Planning Council

8 GROWTH PROJECTIONS

KEY CONCEPTS AND TERMS IN THIS CHAPTER

- Land Use Designer
- Build-Out Wizard
- TimeScope
- Allocator
- Desirability surface and pull factors

At the start of a planning effort, community members often ask themselves, "Where are we headed at the moment?" They want to know what their population growth rate is, what kind of developments their land-use regulations will allow, and where growth is likely to occur over the next few decades. In trying to answer these questions, they can derive other useful information, such as whether they will have sufficient infrastructure and services to support future growth, and what is to become of their quality of life and their community's heart-and-soul resources. It is valuable to estimate and understand growth trends, especially if the future is likely to pose major problems. In addition, expected growth trends serve as a baseline scenario for comparison with alternative growth scenarios that involve new plans, regulations, or infrastructure investments.

Once the current trends have been identified and understood, the next question is: "Where *could* we be headed if we took certain actions?" This is a fundamental planning question, because the answer can influence community decisions about land use regulations and infrastructure spending. Through planning, communities can influence the location, amount, and appearance of future development, rather than passively allowing expected growth trends to occur. In order to steer toward the outcomes it desires, a community needs to know the long-term consequences of alternative actions.

The answers to questions about where a community is headed are known as *growth projections*. The term *growth* is not perfect, because in some cases—such as shrinking cities or remote rural areas—there may not be any growth. While we use the term *growth projections* in this book, you may find it helpful to think of them as *change projections*. We are careful to use the word *projections* rather than *forecasts*, because projections imply less certainty than forecasts. For scenario planning and geodesign (see Chapter 3), projections must be accurate enough to provide a basis for making planning decisions and comparing different scenarios, but they do not need to be precise.

CommunityViz provides many tools for making growth projections including the Build-Out Wizard, Land Use Designer, TimeScope, and Allocator. This chapter describes these tools and discusses how to apply them, alone or in combination, to make growth projections and how to use them in the planning process. For details on the operation of each tool, please refer to the CommunityViz product documentation.

Figure 8.1 illustrates the trade-offs between the amount of time you invest and the sophistication of different growth projection tools.

LAND USE DESIGNER

Land Use Designer allows you to study the economic, environmental, and social impacts of alternative future land-use plans with just a few clicks of the mouse. Land Use Designer helps audiences get a feel for how land-use plans affect the future of a community. If your planning project is at an early visioning stage, Land Use Designer is often a good tool to introduce the community to planning software.

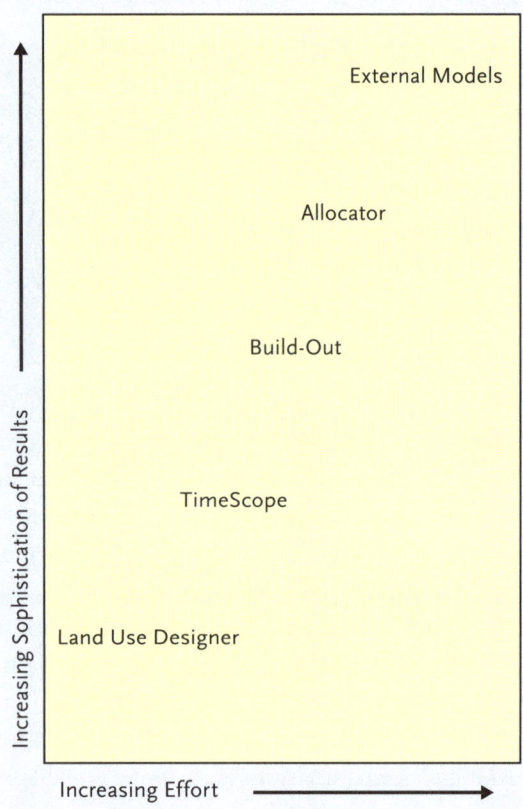

Figure 8.1 Conceptual comparison of several types of growth projections

A special dialog box lists predefined or custom land-use models (see Figure 8.2). Each model specifies the name and particular characteristics of a given land use, such as building density. When you "paint" a potential land use on a feature on the map (see Figure 8.3), the feature takes on all the specified characteristics, and CommunityViz automatically calculates the corresponding economic, environmental, and social impacts.

Land Use Designer provides a good alternative to a full build-out analysis when you are still at the community visioning stage. You need only one GIS layer of land-use polygons to get started, and Land Use Designer is fast, easy to use, and ideal for creating alternative land-use patterns. Almost anyone can use the Sketch tools to paint a proposed land-use pattern on the map. Land Use Designer is a good choice for charrettes, workshops, and visioning sessions. Later, when you are putting together the future land-use map in the comprehensive plan or revising the zoning ordinance, you will probably want to switch to the Build-Out Wizard for more-refined calculations of land capacity over time.

BUILD-OUT WIZARD

The Build-Out Wizard performs all the work necessary for a build-out analysis, the most common and basic type of growth projection. The wizard supports numeric, spatial, and even 3-D visual build-out analysis, and it can work a range of planning documents, from a simple land-use map to complex zoning codes.

Build-out analysis enables a community to look at the effects of its zoning regulations over time. The analysis shows you how many buildings and of what type could be built in any location, given a community's current zoning regulations on land uses, density, lot setbacks, height, and bulk coverage. The analysis seems hypothetical, because one rarely expects all the land to be fully developed to the zoning capacity. Yet a build-out analysis has many practical applications. For example:

- A build-out analysis provides an upper limit to any growth estimate and the resulting economic, environmental, and social impacts.

Figure 8.2 Land Use Designer dialog box with land-use models

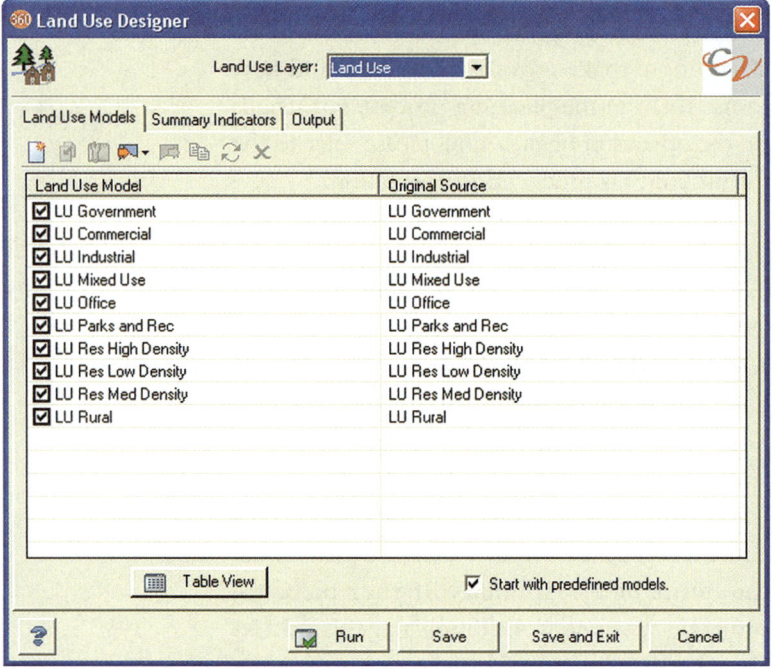

Figure 8.3 Map in Land Use Designer

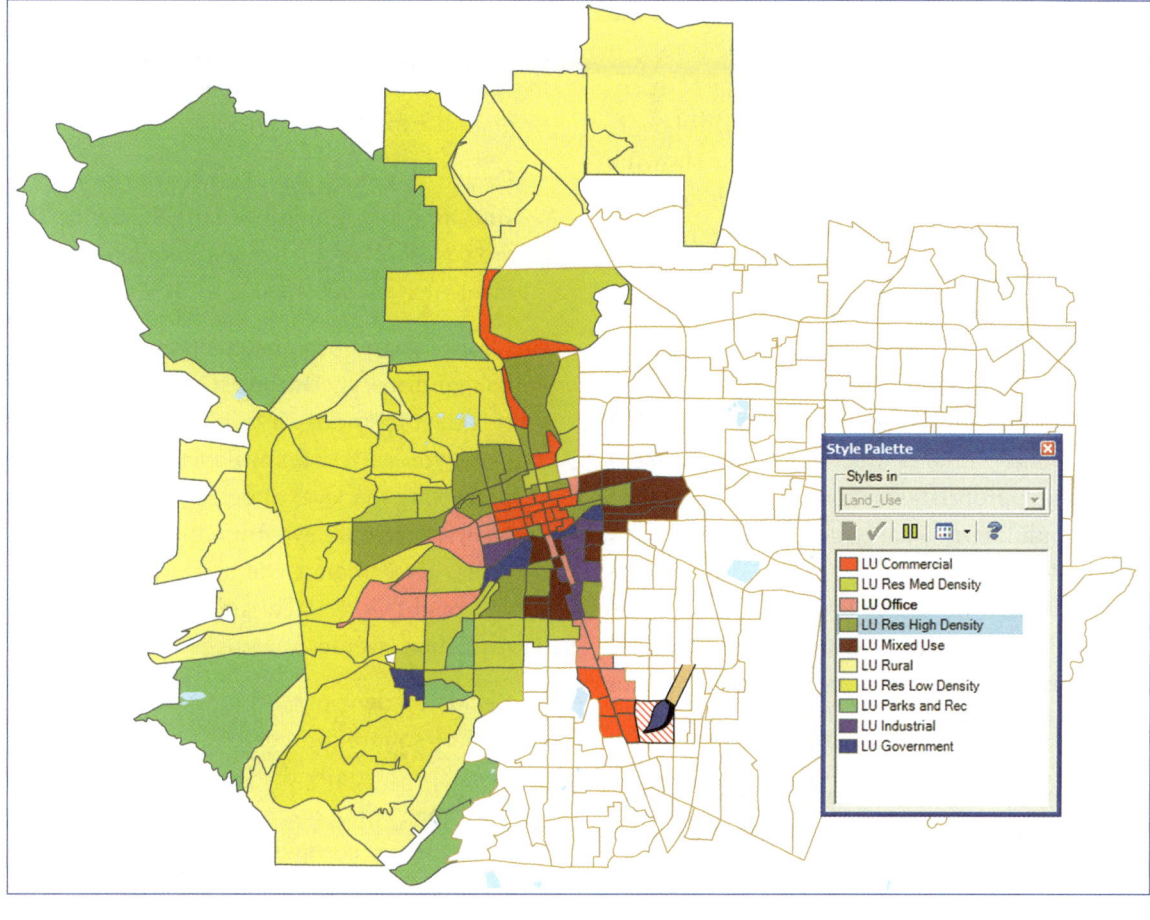

- It provides a basis for a subsequent analysis of growth *toward* build-out, using TimeScope or Allocator.

- It helps illustrate different densities and mixes of land uses.

- It shows realistic near-term results such as housing development in a specific part of the community.

Often, a build-out analysis presentation shocks audiences. By showing a map or 3-D model of what the community would look like if it were built out, you can draw the public's attention to the negative effects of poorly planned growth and weak zoning. Build-out analyses are now common, partly because of the Build-Out Wizard's array of functions. A build-out analysis was once a long and difficult manual process, but now you can perform the analysis much more easily and accurately.

You do not always need to do a build-out analysis, however, and here are a few cautions:

- Even with CommunityViz, a build-out analysis can be time-consuming and labor-intensive, particularly in the case of complex land-use regulations or large study areas.

- There may be easier ways to estimate building counts. For example, you can simply multiply the development density allowed in a zoning district by the area of the district.

- Build-out analysis focuses on new growth, when sometimes the focus of your study should be on existing development, such as in an area with failing septic systems.

If you decide to do a build-out analysis, create the base scenario near the beginning of your project from the existing land-use regulations. You are answering that first question—"Where are we headed at the moment?"—which will serve as the starting point for the rest of your planning study.

CommunityViz allows for three levels of build-out: 1) *Numeric* build-out produces mostly data on the number of buildings, 2) *spatial* build-out creates a point layer showing possible building locations, and 3) *visual* build-out sets up data that you can use to create a 3-D model (see Figure 8.4). Numeric build-out, the most basic type, is relatively quick to do and is the foundation for more detailed build-out analyses. Spatial build-out is useful to see on a map and provides a more refined building count. But spatial build-out takes much longer to run, so it may be inappropriate for studies with more than 30,000 buildings. Visual build-out offers an easy way to set up a 3-D model and allows viewers to see the new buildings by type and location. Three-dimensional models are very powerful for communicating results—see chapters 5 and 6 for more details.

Build-out analysis is such a rich topic that it has its own guide within the standard CommunityViz documentation. A general outline and some practical tips for doing a build-out analysis as part of a community-planning process follow. For more-advanced techniques, refer to Chapter 14.

BUILD-OUT STEPS

Think about how you, your client, or the general public will use the build-out analysis for revising plans or the zoning ordinance. Then, work through the following steps:

1. Decide on a study area. To make the best use of your time and to maximize the Build-Out Wizard's performance, choose the smallest convenient area you can, such as a city or county.

2. Choose a land-use analysis layer, such as the zoning districts. This must be a *polygon* layer. It is best to choose a level of resolution that gives you as few features as possible while preserving the level of detail you need for the analysis. If you have more than 100,000 features, performance will be slow enough that you might want to consider making a lower-resolution layer for analysis purposes.

3. Decide on density rules for dwelling units per acre or square footage of commercial space per acre. Usually these can come straight from the zoning ordinance, but if the density rules are too complicated or too coarse, you may need to tweak them (see Density Rules, below). Gather and prepare all the other build-out-related data you want or need to

Figure 8.4 Build-Out Wizard

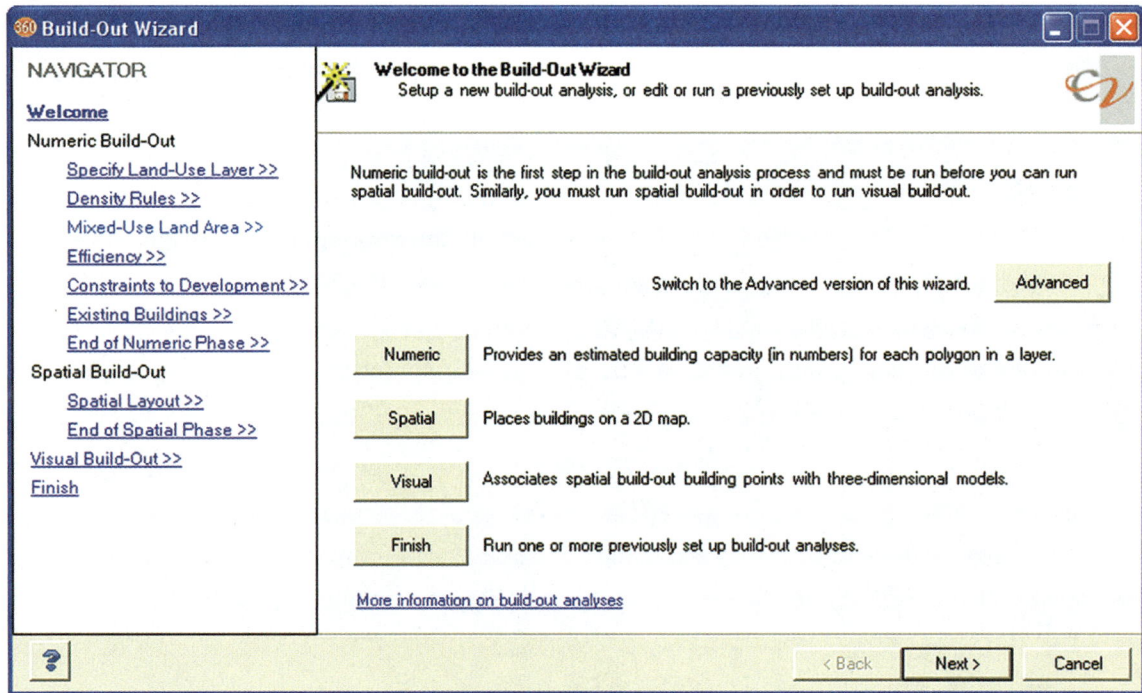

use (see Data Needs and Sources, below). You may need to:

a. Clip to the study area's extent, which means discarding features that lie outside the study area.

b. Re-project zoning data so that it uses the same GIS-projected coordinate system as all the other layers in your analysis.

c. Create polygon constraint layers from lines, points, or rasters. See the appendices, or ask your GIS professional for details. Recognize that these additional layers are optional.

4. Use the Build-Out Wizard to run a base scenario. Keep the scenario as simple as you can at first; you can always add details later. Run a numeric build-out first, and see if your numbers make sense. Once they do, move on to spatial and then to visual build-out if needed.

5. Look at the resulting map, charts, and reports. Do they make sense? You can go back and rerun the wizard as many times as you like, overwriting your old results. Try to get to a solid base scenario, which will serve as a benchmark for comparisons with other scenarios.

6. Design and create alternative scenarios by making small changes to the base—for example, adding or subtracting a constraint layer or slightly adjusting the density of a residential zoning district—or large differences, such as an entirely new zoning ordinance for the study area. Compare scenarios using reports and the many CommunityViz scenario-comparison tools. Figure on a maximum of five scenarios for a neighborhood study area or three for a citywide or regional study area. Carefully explore the consequences of possible zoning changes or different assumptions about pace of development.

DENSITY RULES

If you are doing a build-out analysis based on existing zoning regulations, you may need to simplify a complex zoning ordinance. For example, an ordinance containing dozens of zoning districts can and probably should be consolidated into a manageable number of density categories, perhaps no more than 20.

Another consideration for setting density rules in build-out is the "you've got to be kidding" test: Will reasonable observers, such as attendees at a public meeting, find the results credible and useful? For example, we know of a town that created an ordinance allowing garage apartments on *any* residential lot. The subsequent build-out analysis put a garage apartment on *every* lot and therefore showed a huge capacity for future growth. Although this analysis was technically correct and probably worth doing, we advised creating a second build-out scenario that put garage apartments on only a fraction of the lots and produced a more realistic and practical result.

COMMERCIAL BUILDINGS

In many cases, build-out analysis involves only residential development and excludes commercial development. This approach makes sense when:

- The study area is nearly all residential.

- Commercial considerations are not central to the possible changes in the zoning ordinance.

- Planners want to use different methods to calculate future jobs, commercial revenue, and other commercial-related economic data.

You will need to decide whether commercial build-out calculations are appropriate for your project. But keep in mind that on the one hand, they are not required by CommunityViz and on the other, they are not particularly difficult to do.

KEEPING PERSPECTIVE

The CommunityViz Build-Out Wizard provides tools for making many refinements to a build-out analysis. Yet, those refinements can sometimes make the process complex, time-consuming, and expensive. How much attention to detail and refinement are required depends on what the residents of the study area need to understand from the build-out analysis. A build-out analysis is simply a tool to aid planners, the public, and elected officials in decision making. If your resources are limited, it may be wiser for you to create five build-out scenarios in medium detail than one in high detail. Consider how the scenarios are going to be used and by whom, how much uncertainty exists in your initial assumptions about the pace and location of development and in your scenarios, and which is likely to be the preferred scenario that will be used to make planning decisions in the near future.

TIMESCOPE

TimeScope helps to answer the first question many audiences ask after seeing a build-out analysis: "Yeah, but what's *really* going to happen?" People are more interested in, and more likely to act upon, a realistic five- or 10-year growth projection than on a theoretical maximum of development for a zoning district or an entire community.

TimeScope lets you look at incremental changes year by year. Buildings and roads appear on the landscape; infrastructure capacity fills up; land uses change; and economic, environmental, and social impacts are updated. All of this takes place according to rules and assumptions you set. You can even use the results with Google Earth's "Timeline" control (a special slider bar that appears automatically when TimeScope data is included).

Unfortunately, projections of growth rates and locations almost never exactly predict future outcomes. Nevertheless, you will find TimeScope very useful for describing general development patterns and trends.

TimeScope depends entirely on your input; you provide the assumptions or growth models you want TimeScope to use. This means that you must understand the drivers of growth in your community or region before you can use TimeScope.

There are two ways to use TimeScope in making growth projections: 1) by itself, using premade or custom growth models, or 2) in conjunction with other tools such as the Suitability Wizard or Allocator.

Using TimeScope by itself is relatively straightforward. You provide assumptions about the rate of growth of development (for example, 3 percent per year) and the order of growth (for example, development of land closest to roads first), and TimeScope does the work from there, enabling you to set any year (for example, 10 years from now) on a slider bar and see the results (see Figure 8.5). This method is very effective for giving quick, conceptual illustrations of growth as the community approaches build-out over time. However, the models set up this way are not particularly sophisticated and produce only coarse estimates of when and where new growth will occur.

For a more refined model, use TimeScope together with other CommunityViz tools. The most common approach is to create a *desirability surface* with the Suitability Wizard (see Chapter 12). A desirability surface is a map showing the relative attractiveness of locations for development. It is called a surface because you can think of it as a terrain of mountains and valleys, with high points and low points corresponding to high and low desirability. The theory is that development generally occurs in the most desirable places first, with overflow to other locations as time goes by and more growth occurs. Desirability is calculated on the basis of any number of *pull factors*, or growth attractors, such as proximity to roads and sewer and water lines. It also includes *push factors*, or factors that discourage development, such as steep slopes. The Suitability Wizard provides a handy way to set up this calculation, and CommunityViz offers an easy way to link the Suitability Wizard with TimeScope to create a growth model based on a desirability surface.

One rule of thumb when creating a desirability model is that growth follows growth. Statistically, the best indicators of desirability are, in order: 1) proximity to existing buildings; 2) proximity to roads; and 3) proximity to centers, such as city centers or major intersections. Amenities also attract growth. Typical pull factors

Figure 8.5   TimeScope time assumption slider

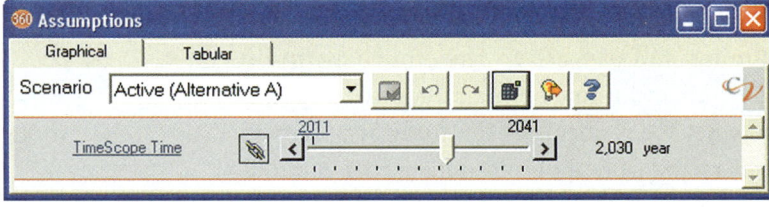

include airports, major transit stops, water and sewer infrastructure, water bodies, and natural areas or open space.

It is important to realize that growth patterns are influenced by a complex set of interactions within the local environment. For example, in an area where septic systems are common, sewers may be less important than in an area where septic systems are rare; and access to transit may be a more significant factor in congested areas. Furthermore, local governments can promote or discourage particular growth patterns through a variety of financial and regulatory incentives or disincentives.

If you use the Suitability Wizard to create a desirability surface, you can include the locations and amenities listed above as desirability factors, plus any others you see fit. The wizard will automatically create variable weightings for each desirability factor, so you can experiment with emphasizing or de-emphasizing each particular factor.

Planned unit developments (PUDs) are specially zoned areas that are developed as large, mixed use subdivisions. A PUD zone is a floating zone, meaning that it can be located anywhere in a jurisdiction, subject to the approval of the elected officials. As a result, a PUD may cause growth in places that would not have been predicted by TimeScope. If you know about existing or proposed PUDs ahead of time, you can usually separate them from the analysis. There is no consensus among planners on whether PUDs absorb growth from other parts of the community or create new growth of their own. Our feeling is that the larger the PUD, the more it tends to create new growth.

ALLOCATOR

Allocator helps determine where growth is most likely to occur over time. It uses the classic supply-and-demand approach and probability-based models to allocate new development to available building locations. A carefully designed analysis that combines Allocator with TimeScope (and perhaps also the Suitability Wizard) can provide a very credible model of future growth. You will need good data on current residential and commercial development and infrastructure, and access to a reliable model for pull factors in your study area.

To implement Allocator, you need an analysis layer that already contains the development desirability and development capacity of each feature. This information normally comes from the Suitability Wizard (for desirability) and Build-Out or Land Use Designer (for capacity). For guidelines on creating the desirability rating, refer to TimeScope, above.

To determine the amount of new growth to be allocated, you can work with a specific number or you can use an assumption tied to TimeScope. You set a year in the future, and TimeScope can calculate how many houses there will be in the study area.

Once you have the desirability, capacity, housing units, and time-frame inputs, running an allocation is straightforward.[1] This technique is an elegant way to model and view growth patterns over time. However, in large areas, such as multi-county regions, Allocator's performance may face challenges—refer to Chapter 11 and Appendix 3 for suggestions.

EXTERNAL MODELS

External models of growth can work very well with CommunityViz. At one end of the spectrum, you may find that U.S. Census Bureau population forecasts meet your needs. You can import these forecasts into CommunityViz quite easily, and then estimate people per household to project the number of new dwelling units there will be in the year of the Census Bureau's forecast. At the other end, there are very sophisticated modeling tools that may involve specialized expertise, computer simulations, or other methods that CommunityViz cannot provide. Examples include economic growth forecasting models such as those developed by Regional Economic Models, Inc. (REMI), multivariate allocators such as What If?, and Monte Carlo simulators. Because CommunityViz has many ways to exchange data with other programs, it can often use output from, or send input to, these external models. This connection allows you to employ the other models as specialized contributors to your overall CommunityViz analysis.

---

1. For details on options in the setup of an allocation, see the CommunityViz technical documentation.

Figure 8.6 Typical order of a growth analysis

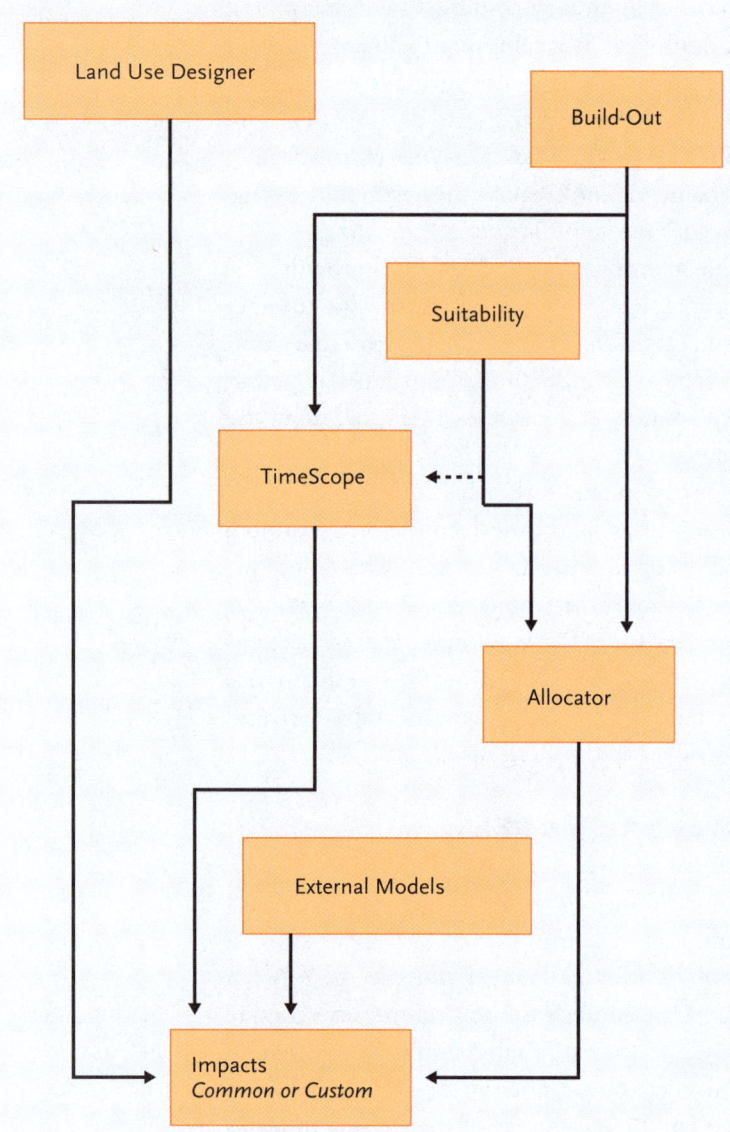

COMBINING GROWTH-PLANNING DECISION TOOLS

Combinations of the components described above are entirely possible, and they are often a good idea. Figure 8.6 shows a typical sequence. You start with some simple sketching and geodesign using Land Use Designer, which allows you to "paint" land uses on the map and see their impacts. When you are ready to do a more careful analysis, you run the Build-Out Wizard, which gives detailed calculations of future development capacity allowed by your future land-use map or zoning designations. Using the Build-Out Wizard results, you run TimeScope or Allocator to study likely development patterns over time. TimeScope is simpler, and Allocator is more sophisticated. Both TimeScope and Allocator can benefit from desirability maps that show where development is most likely to occur. One way to make desirability maps is using the Suitability Wizard. An alternative to TimeScope and Allocator is an external model, whose results you read into your CommunityViz analysis for further processing or display. Any impact models you make can include build year as a factor, so that you can look at how development impacts change over time based on the results of TimeScope or Allocator.

DATA NEEDS AND SOURCES

In general, when you make growth projections, the quality of the output depends on the quality of the input, so better data means better results. However, don't be discouraged by a shortage of data, and don't be overconfident that detailed data will automatically lead to more useful results.

Population growth projections make the most sense early in a decade, shortly after the latest national census of population. At that time, it is easy to identify population trends over the previous 20 years and to predict land-use needs if those trends continue over the next 20 years. However, it is difficult to predict the amount of people who will migrate into and out of an area, especially in suburban communities and rural boomtowns. For an American city or county, the U.S. Census Bureau[2] has a wealth of population data, including total numbers, population change over time, and in some cases, population projections. The Census Bureau also has data on gender, age, and ethnic background. For communities of fewer than 2,500 people, your state department of commerce or community affairs will have population data. Appendix 4 offers more suggestions about data sources.

Figure 8.7 gives some guidelines on where to find data, which data are most important, and alternative approaches ("work-arounds") to use if data are not readily available. For information on what to do if you have too much data or overly detailed data, refer to Chapter 11 and Appendix 2.

---

2. The U.S. Census Bureau's website address is www.census.gov.

Figure 8.7 Data sources for growth projections

	DATA	TYPICAL SOURCES	WORK-AROUNDS
Build-Out	Land-use polygons	Parcels, zones, master plan, comp plan	Sketched polygons; Land Use Designer
	Density rules for each land use	Land-use plan, zoning code	User judgment or variable
	Constraints (steep slopes, wetlands, habitat, etc.)	Local sources, USGS, conservation groups	Ignore
	Existing building points or footprints	Local sources, E911 (emergency 911 system administrator), extraction from aerial photo	Ignore
	Minimum separation distances/setbacks	Zoning code	User judgment or variable
	Roads	Local sources, developer's proposal, esri, USGS	Sketch or ignore
	3-D models of buildings	Model library, 3D Warehouse, self-made	Model library
	Mixed use building mix ratios	Zoning, developer's proposal	User judgment or variable
	Efficiency factors	Planner's judgment or variable	Default value
	Building information (DUs and Floor Area)	Developer's proposal	Default value
Land Use Designer	Land-use polygons	Parcels, zones, master plan, comp plan	Sketched vector grid
	Density rules for each land use	Land-use plan, zoning code	User judgment or variable
TimeScope	Development growth rate (e.g., 3% per year)	State demographer, US Census Bureau	User judgment or variable
	Future building locations	Build-out	Land Use Designer, custom calculation
	Layer(s) used to calculate growth order	Standard base layers like roads and cities	Ignore
	Other growth calculation	Suitability Wizard, Allocator, custom model	Ignore
Allocator	Analysis layer (usually land-use layer)	Parcels, zones, master plan, comp plan	Sketched polygons, vector grid
	Capacity of each feature in analysis layer	from Build-Out or Land Use Designer	Simple formula
	Desirability model such as weighted pull factors	Planner's/demographers expertise	User judgment or variable
	Layers representing pull factors	Local sources, USGS, esri	Manual desirability scoring method

Key: *White = must have   Light blue = nice to have   Dark blue = can use if available*

TEACHING EXAMPLE

The following fictional example walks you through a growth-projection analysis employing most of the CommunityViz tools described in this chapter. You do not need to do all of these steps, but you will want to choose the appropriate steps for your planning project. For examples of how growth projections have been applied in real-world planning situations, see the case studies at the end of this chapter.

STUDY AREA AND DATA

In this example project, we were interested in the future growth of a small town within commuting range of a rapidly growing metro area. Study areas do not necessarily need to correspond to any particular jurisdictional boundary such as a city or county, though they often do. In this case, we chose the 5,000-acre town boundary as our study area (see Figure 8.8).

Figure 8.8 Base layers in the study area

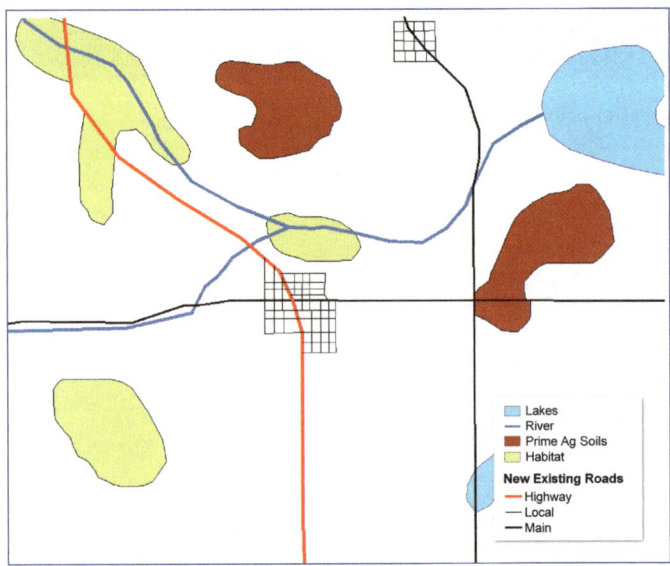

Figure 8.9 Painting land uses on a grid

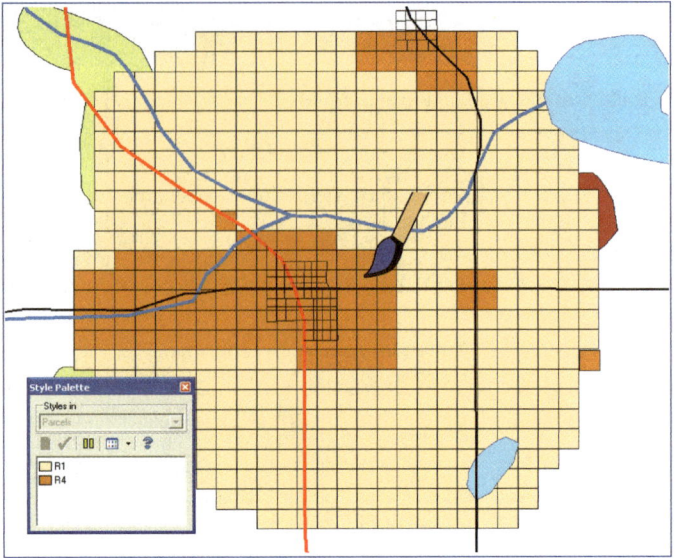

Figure 8.10 Land Use Designer indicator charts

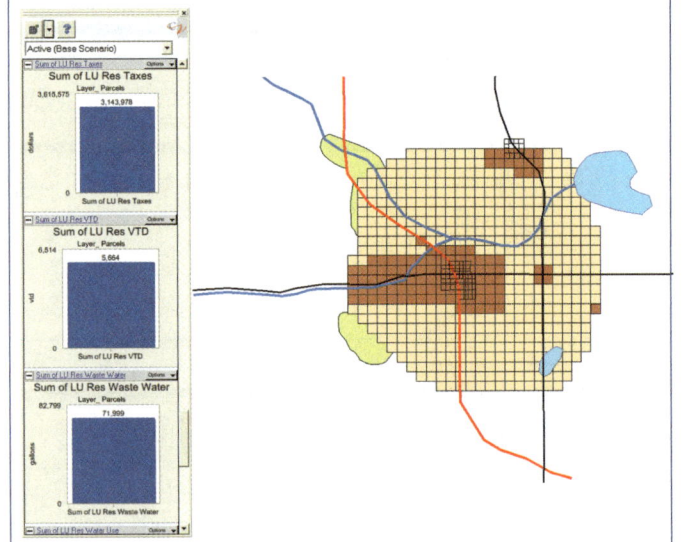

Figure 8.11 Build-out showing numeric and spatial results

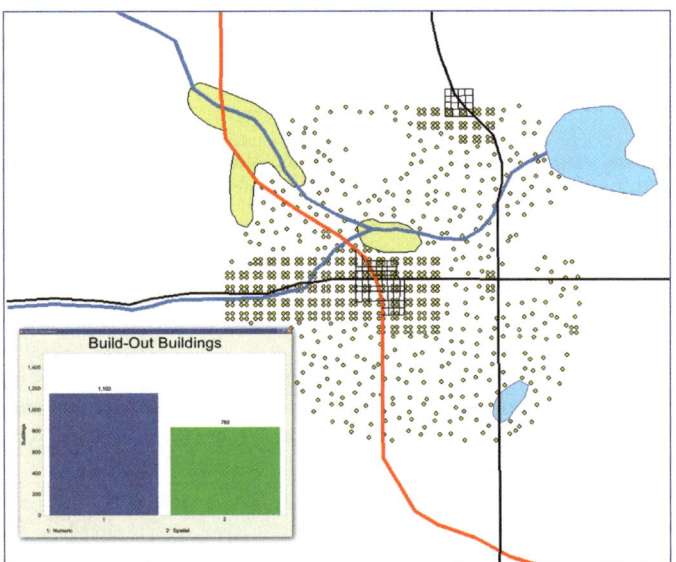

We decided to use a grid of 2-acre rectangles as an analysis layer, because the rectangles were readily available in digital form, unlike the town's land-use plan, which existed only on paper. We could have used census blocks or block groups, Traffic Analysis Zones (TAZs), parcels, or any other convenient polygon layer.

We were able to find free data online that provided the following layers: roads, lakes, rivers, critical wildlife habitats, and prime agricultural soils.

We sketched in points to represent the town centers and the school. We decided that the points representing town centers would be used as proxies for existing building points, which we did not know. We were careful to set up all the layers with a consistent, projected coordinate system.

LAND USE DESIGNER

Our land-use layer did not include existing local zoning designations. We could have entered this information in a number of ways, but we chose to use the Land Use Designer as a quick visual method. We set up land-use styles using the local density rules—R1 with one dwelling unit per acre, and R4 with four dwelling units per acre—and then painted them on the correct grid squares (see Figure 8.9).

Because we had land-use styles set up in Land Use Designer, we also made a test scenario and experimented with different land-use plans to see their effects on the indicators automatically generated by Land Use Designer (see Figure 8.10).

BUILD-OUT WIZARD

Returning to the base scenario, we ran an initial numeric build-out, first with all default settings and then again with the Prime Ag Soils layer as a constraint. Numeric build-out told us that 1,103 buildings were possible under the current town zoning ordinance. When we ran a spatial build-out, however, the number of buildings decreased to 780 because of minimum building setbacks from property lines (see Figure 8.11).

If we had had a layer of existing buildings, we could have included it in the build-out analysis so that our results would show only new growth. Instead, we approximated existing buildings by setting up a Sketch style that allowed us to paint the map by hand to show areas of existing development. We gave ourselves the option to specify "fully built," "50 percent built," and "empty." By visually cross-referencing to Google Earth, checking total building counts against property tax rolls, and applying our planner's local knowledge of the town, we developed a very good approximation of existing buildings within a few days. By combining the estimate of existing buildings with full build-out, we came up with a logical number for the remaining building capacity of each grid square in our study area.

Once we were satisfied with the build-out numbers, we were ready to create realistic alternative scenarios. One local topic of debate was whether landowners whose property contained prime agricultural soils should be allowed to sell to developers. Our Farm Development scenario kept the same zoning but allowed building on prime agricultural soils. Our Clustering scenario looked at a recommended planning practice of clustering development in small areas; it reduced density in most of the town to one dwelling unit per 10 acres, but increased allowable density in designated growth areas to 15 dwelling units per acre.

DESIRABILITY SURFACE

Our next task was to estimate where growth was most likely to occur. Using the Suitability Wizard, we scored each polygon in the Buildable Area layer (generated by the Build-Out Wizard) using the factors and weightings in Figure 8.12.

Figure 8.12 Desirability weighting factors

FACTOR	WEIGHT
Proximity to town centers (proxy for existing buildings)	8
Proximity to roads	5
Proximity to lakes	3
Proximity to rivers	1

After translating the desirability scores into colors ranging from yellow (least desirable) to blue (most desirable), we produced the map shown in Figure 8.13.

But after talking with local community members, we realized we were missing an important local factor: commuting time to the city. The shorter the commute, the more desirable a location would be. We could have addressed this by expanding the study area and using Network Analyst functions in CommunityViz to measure commuting times and distances. Instead, we decided to use the much simpler approach of creating a "city proxy" point. We placed this single point at the edge of our study area, along the main road to the city, in the south. Then we added "proximity to city proxy" as a highly weighted factor in our desirability analysis. Our new desirability map showed that the southern locations of the town were more desirable than was indicated in the first analysis (see Figure 8.14).

ALLOCATOR

Having created a capacity estimate and a desirability estimate for each feature in the analysis layer, we were almost ready to set up an allocation model. However, one task remained. We needed to know how many buildings to allocate—that is, the *demand*. The U.S. Census Bureau had listed population estimates for the town, as shown in Figure 8.15.

We used Excel to plot these data on a graph, which revealed a nearly linear growth rate of 23.5 people per year (1,225-755)/20. Assuming an average of 2.56 people per household, we estimated the construction of 9.2 new dwelling units per year. This number made it easy for us to create an "estimated dwelling units" indicator using the formula:

755 +([Assumption: TimeScope Time] – 2010) × 9.2

We used the result as the demand input to the Allocator. We could set the year of our study to any time in the future, let the Allocator run, and see the pattern of growth to that year—that is, how many buildings there would be on each grid square in the map (see Figure 8.16).

With this growth projection, we had a far clearer picture of future development trends and alternatives for the town.

Figure 8.13 *Desirability surface*

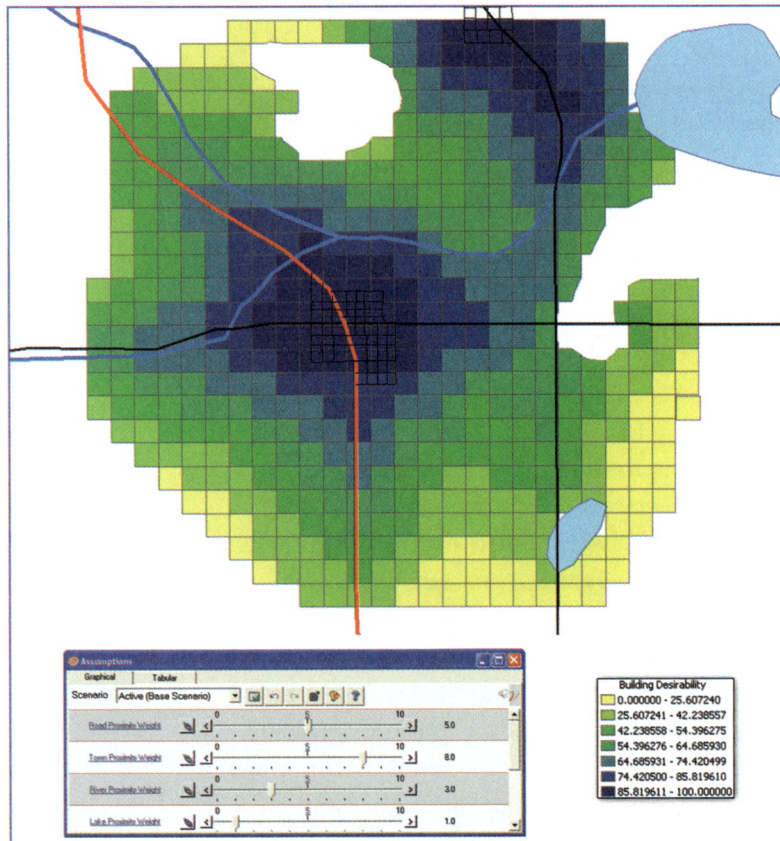

Figure 8.15 *Population estimates*

YEAR	POPULATION
2010	755
2020	982
2030	1,225

Figure 8.14 *Desirability surface after addition of city proxy point*

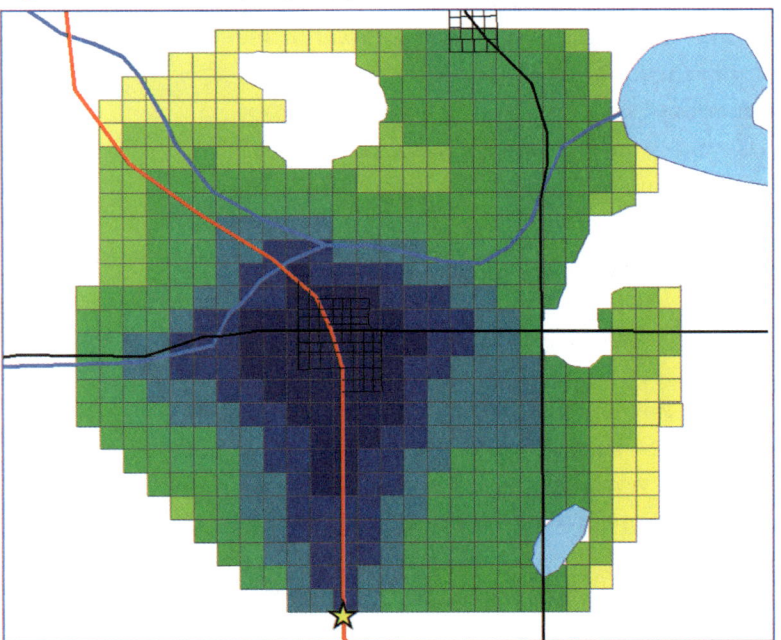

Figure 8.16 *Allocated growth over time.*

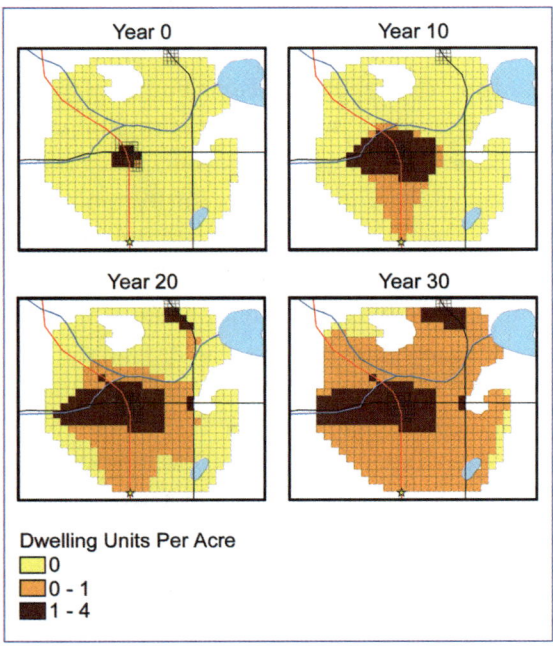

CASE STUDY
SMALL TOWN BUILD-OUT STUDY

Location: Middlebury, Vermont
Partners: Town of Middlebury; Community Oriented Geography

The Town of Middlebury lies in Vermont's wide Champlain Valley and covers 39 square miles. Best known for highly regarded Middlebury College and the historic village of Middlebury, the town is also defined by its working farms and agricultural services. In fact, more than one-third of the town is zoned for agriculture, which is considered vital to the town's present and future character and economy.

With a population of about 8,300, Middlebury had experienced steady population growth in the decades leading to this project, with increased suburban-style development at the edge of the village and in the rural areas. Population projections indicated continued growth and a need for 300 to 400 dwelling units per decade going forward. In 2006, the town began a review and update of its comprehensive plan. Planning commission members wanted a good understanding of the town's overall growth capacity. The town retained Community Oriented Geography to perform a build-out analysis to determine growth capacity associated with the existing zoning regulations. The town would use the results of the build-out analysis in updating the comprehensive plan and zoning ordinance.

Project Description: Community Oriented Geography conducted a detailed build-out analysis for the entire town, including residential and nonresidential buildings. Results of the analysis showed that build-out under the current zoning would allow for over 2,500 new dwelling units within the town, more than double the present number, and that there was plenty of land zoned for nonresidential uses. Figures 8.17 and 8.18 show examples of the analysis.

The real surprise was that more than 900 new low-density residences could be built in the agriculturally zoned areas, a finding of great concern given the town's goals of encouraging new development in growth areas and conserving agricultural lands (see Figure 8.19).

The town made a strong effort to engage citizens in the planning decisions. The planning commission and select board shared the build-out analysis at public meetings to discuss the comprehensive plan update and proposed zoning changes. Town planning staff made a special effort to reach out to owners of large parcels of land in the rural areas to ensure that the proposed zoning changes would still provide them with a reasonable economic use of their lands.

The build-out analysis was invaluable in helping to see the need for amending our zoning to a more appropriate density for our rural agricultural areas, and the visualization of the information proved highly valuable during the public review process.

—Fred Dunnington
Town Planner
Middlebury, Vermont

Figure 8.17 *CommunityViz screenshot showing spatial build-out points (red dots) and other build-out results for Middlebury.*

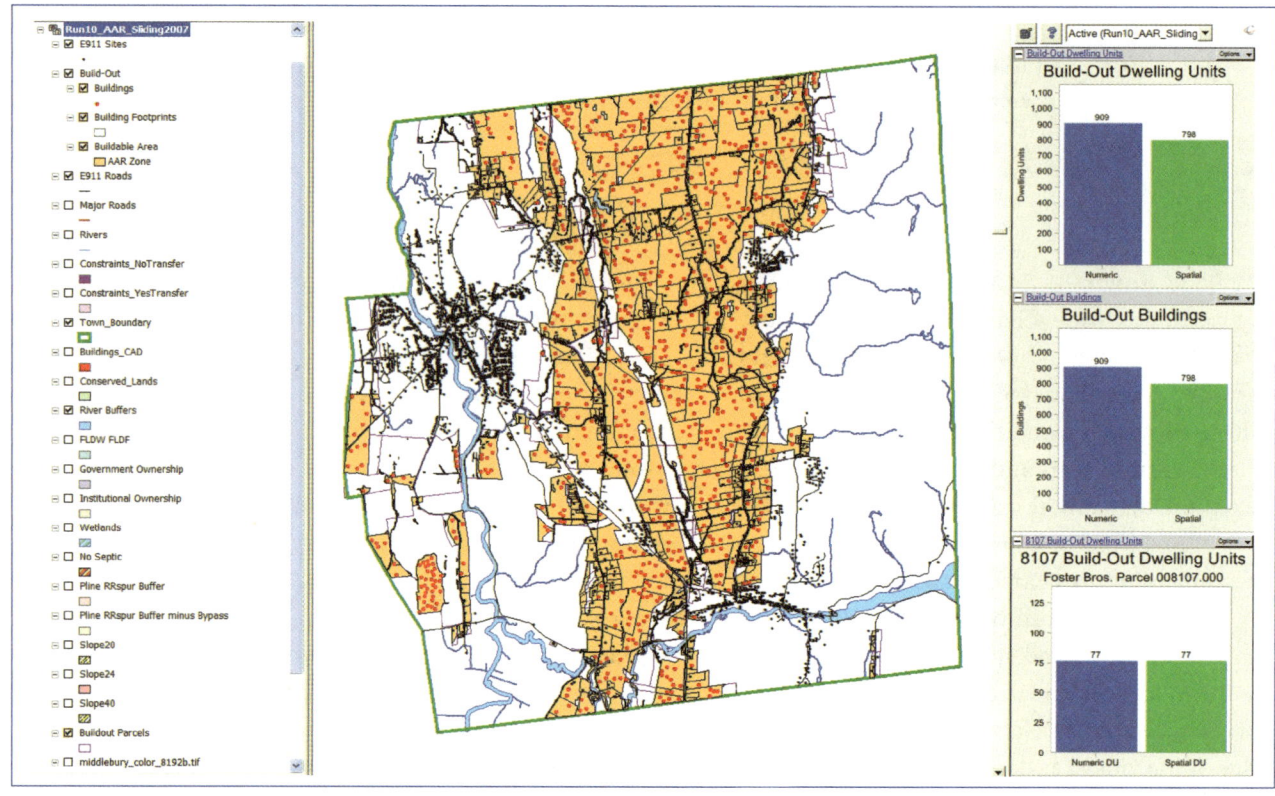

All images in this case study courtesy Community Oriented Geography

Figure 8.18 *Illustration of the Middlebury build-out analysis showing buildable areas color-coded by zoning district*

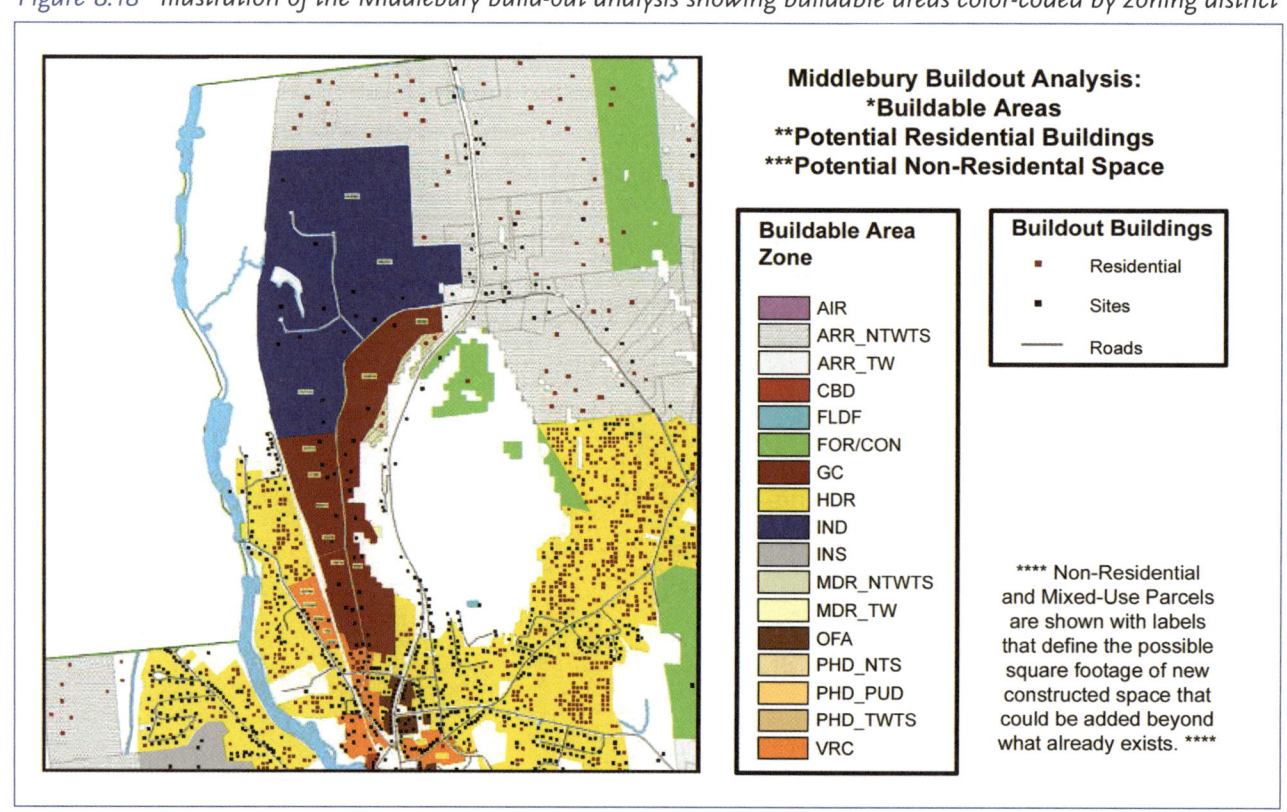

Technology and Tools: The project used CommunityViz, particularly the Build-Out Wizard. The town's planning commission and select board held public meetings.

Outcomes: The build-out study was completed during work on the new town comprehensive plan. In June 2007, the town adopted the updated comprehensive plan, with policies reflecting the results of the build-out. No new growth areas were added. Because the build-out had shown that an alarming number of new residences could be located in the town's agricultural district, the plan suggested further limitations on the amount of development in the agricultural district. This suggestion was implemented in 2008 when the town adopted an amendment to its zoning and subdivision regulations that substantially reduced the number of residential units permitted in the agricultural district, from approximately one per 10 acres to approximately one per 25 acres above a certain farm size.

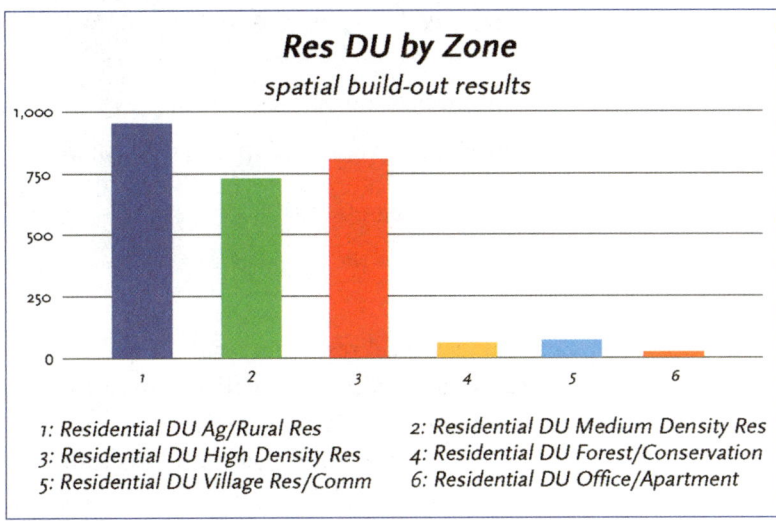

Figure 8.19 Residential dwelling units ("Res_DU") by zoning district. The blue bar on the far left shows the dwelling-unit capacity of agriculturally zoned lands. The green bar shows the dwelling unit capacity of lands zoned medium-density residential. The red bar shows the dwelling unit capacity of lands zoned high-density residential.

9 VALUE MAPPING AND SPECIAL PLACES

KEY CONCEPTS AND TERMS IN THIS CHAPTER

- Articulating values
- Connecting physical forms to values
- Heart and soul
- Mapping special places
- Value indexes
- Value trees, value elements, value drivers

If you ask local residents what they like about their community, they will rarely answer in planning terms—for instance, they're unlikely to say, "Love the floor area ratio." Instead, they talk about intangibles such as friendliness and small-town feel, or say things like "There's always something new going on." If you delve deeply into the responses residents give to community surveys, and what they say at storytelling workshops and neighborhood meetings, you will find that many people give the same answers. Part of the fabric of the community is a shared image about the unique characteristics and culture of the place where they live, which we call the community's heart and soul.

Many planners have an intuitive sense that the physical form of a city or town affects the quality of life of the residents. *Value mapping* is a way to make clear connections between the characteristics that residents hold dear about their town and its physical form. By including value mapping in your CommunityViz analyses, you give yourself a tool for planning that includes community sentiment and emotions. Alternatively, you can simply *map special places* that people value. This chapter describes both methods.

VALUE MAPPING
WHY AND WHEN

Value mapping is a useful exercise when a community is engaging in a visioning process at the start of updating a comprehensive plan. Value mapping adds a new dimension to the planning process by placing more emphasis on stewarding the unique physical character and social customs of the community. Moreover, local planning policies are derived from community values and culture as much as they are by planning law.

ARTICULATING CORE VALUES

The first phase of value mapping happens outside of CommunityViz. This is the value-gathering phase, when project organizers ask residents about their shared values about the community. Then the organizers summarize the shared values in a core value statement.[1] The statement usually consists of half a dozen carefully articulated core values that capture the essence of what residents treasure about their community. Each core value has a short title, such as Small-Town Feel, and a one- or two-sentence description. The planning project team must distill hundreds or thousands of individual opinions into specific values. Two tests for good value statements are: 1) most residents agree they describe something important, and 2) they are unique to that community and its heart-and-soul attributes.

VALUE MAPPING STEPS

After you have drafted a core value statement, CommunityViz can play a role in value mapping, which has the following steps:

---

1. Resources, tools, and examples relating to creating the core values statement are available online at the Orton Family Foundation website (www.orton.org).

Figure 9.1 Portion of a value tree (one branch fully expanded)

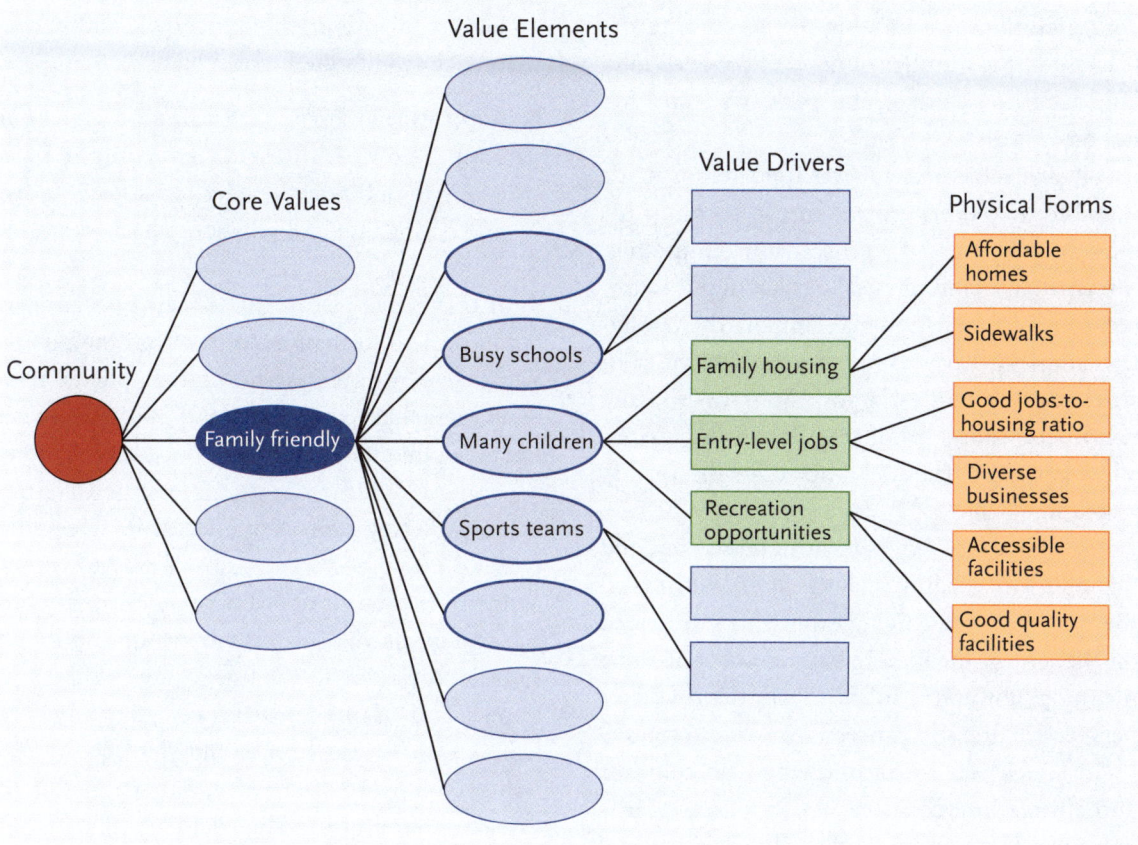

1. Validating core values
2. Identifying value elements
3. Identifying value drivers
4. Identifying physical forms that affect value drivers
5. Developing weighted value scores
6. Using value scores and interactive weighting to compare scenarios.

The discussions about values during the value mapping process are as important as the final results, because the purpose is to discover and describe the connection between planning and values in the community.

MAKING A VALUE TREE

A value tree resembles an organizational chart or a family genealogy. It organizes and illustrates the relationships between the community's core values, value elements, value drivers, and physical forms—all of which you are about to uncover as the value mapping process unfolds.

Figure 9.1 shows a portion of a value tree, with one of the branches fully expanded. (The complete tree is too big to reproduce here.)[2] The tree starts on the left, branching out to the community's *core values*, which make up the community's character. As an example, let's start with a core value of family friendliness.

The next level of the tree describes ways in which each core value is manifested in the community, which are called *value elements*. In the example in Figure 9.1, residents feel that family friendliness is evident in the large number of children in the community, its busy schools, and its abundance of youth sports teams.

Value elements arise from *value drivers*: factors that cause or contribute to the presence of value elements in the community. Regarding the value element of the large number of children

---

2. One convenient software tool for creating such large diagrams is FreeMind, available free of charge online.

in the community, perhaps it has arisen because young families are moving to the community because of the number of good entry-level jobs, affordable house prices, and attractive recreation opportunities.

Finally, value drivers are supported or made possible by *physical forms* in the community, including land-use patterns, historic buildings, infrastructure, and physical design. In our example, the physical forms that support the family-friendly value drivers are the high number of single-family homes, a good jobs-to-housing ratio, sidewalks, small neighborhood stores, adequate school facilities, and accessible, quality recreation facilities.

The value tree works in both directions, and planners will recognize that the physical forms on the right lead to the living experiences described on the left. In the step-by-step process of value mapping, however, you start from the residents' perspective first and proceed from left to right.

In Figure 9.1, we are showing neat columns and simple interconnections. In practice, it is common for a value tree to show additional complexity, with value elements, value drivers, and physical forms that overlap.

The following sections provide more details on value elements and their related value drivers and physical forms, and how you can combine all the parts of a value tree into a CommunityViz analysis of community values.

VALUE ELEMENTS

A value element commonly fits into one of four categories:

- **Tangible forms.** If a core value is "Western feel," some of the value elements might be the presence of cattle ranches, horses, historic buildings, and mountain views.

- **Behaviors.** If a core value is "friendliness," some value elements might include residents' welcoming attitude, openness to diversity, familiarity with one another, and habit of being helpful to neighbors.

- **System characteristics.** For a core value of "vibrant local economy," some of the value elements might be diversity of businesses, high median household incomes, and strong retail and entertainment activity.

- **Aspirations.** For a core value of "self-reliance," some value elements might be a desire for job growth, a desire for lower taxes, and opposition to regulation.

If this range of categories seems broad, it is because the information comes from the public. Value elements are descriptions of how the residents view their community and their lives there, not the opinions of planners or outside facilitators.

Value elements emerge from the original value-gathering process that identifies where the core values come from. A simple way to gather residents' opinions about a value element is to ask two questions: "If this core value continued to be a core value in the future, how would you know?" and "If this core value ceased to be a core value in the future, how would you know?" You will get a variety of answers, but the goal is to extract a handful of value elements that represent the bulk of the responses.

VALUE DRIVERS

As the value tree moves to the right from value elements to value drivers, the content changes from describing *what* people value about their community to *why* the community has those characteristics. Discovering important value drivers is a collaborative effort between professional planners and the public. To help residents identify value drivers, you can ask them these two questions: "Why is this value element part of your community today?" and "What supports or detracts from this value element?" These thought-provoking questions can sometimes elicit surprising and insightful answers from residents about how their community works. The local people can tell you: "We think it's friendly here because we all know one another, and we all know one another because we see one another as we go about our daily lives." In other words, they can tell you that a value driver for familiarity in their particular community is frequent daily encounters with other residents. In another community, the value driver might be something different, such as extended families or a strong church presence. In short, the residents of a particular community have specific local knowledge. On the other hand, planners tend to know more than most residents about how building patterns, long-term population growth, and regional economic change can affect the community. By working together, residents and planners can develop a better understanding of local value drivers and how they can influence plans, ordinances, infrastructure spending, and decisions about development proposals.

PHYSICAL FORM

Some, though not all, value drivers arise from the physical form of the community: its physical setting, land-use patterns, and particular buildings and structures. The best way to determine how physical form affects values is through collaborative analysis by planners and residents. The planner, for example, will connect the value driver "frequent daily encounters with other residents" to physical gathering places, but the local residents will know that in this town the post office and the gas station matter more than the library. Through CommunityViz, a planner may have insights into the effects of spatial relationships—for example, walking distances and regional trade areas—that may not come to mind for members of the public.

COMMUNITYVIZ VALUE INDEXES

You can make the process of building a value tree even more helpful by incorporating it into CommunityViz. Specifically, you can model the logic of the value tree in CommunityViz so you can evaluate geodesign sketches or compare future scenarios based on their likely effect on core values.

The CommunityViz analysis starts with the creation of indicators called *value indexes*. A value index represents how well a physical form in a scenario supports a particular core value. A lower score means poorer performance; a higher score means better performance. You derive value indexes by combining scores for each of the value elements that make up a particular core value. Those scores are derived from measurements of physical forms that affect the value elements. The steps for creating a value index are illustrated in Figure 9.2.

In practice, there are several points to consider. The most important point is that not all value elements are equally important. When setting up the CommunityViz analysis, include variable assumptions so you or your audience can set the relative importance—the weighting factor—of each index component. For example, if the core value is friendliness and two of the value elements are welcoming attitude and familiarity, your particular community may place much more importance on familiarity than on a welcoming attitude. In the combined friendliness index, the familiarity score might get a weight of 9 out of 10, while the welcoming attitude score might get a weight of 3 out of 10. Asking the public to help set these weightings is an excellent way to engage them in a deeper conversation about what really matters to them: their community's heart-and-soul attributes. CommunityViz slider bars are an effective way to control and display the weight given to each score. If you are working in a large group, you can use keypad polling to set the weight for each value.

You can also use weighting factors to balance the importance of different *physical* metrics. For example, if your analysis includes four similar measurements of distance to shopping but only one measurement of distance to restaurants, you would probably place higher weight on the restaurant metric to give it fair treatment compared to the shopping metrics. But weighting factors can

Figure 9.2 Value indexes

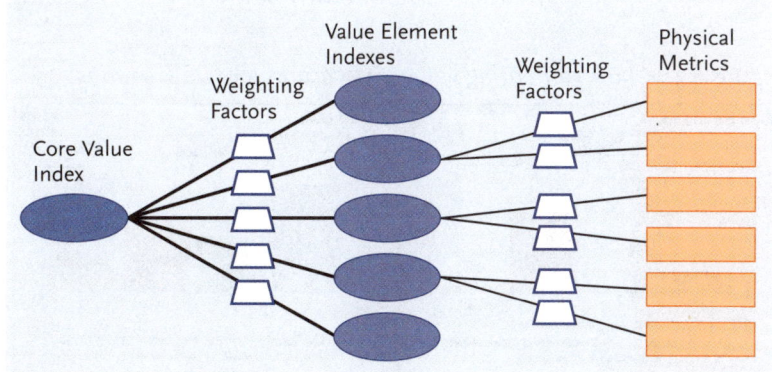

become confusing, so usually you do *not* expose weighting factors for physical metrics to an audience during a public presentation. In keeping with the CommunityViz philosophy of transparency, however, all weighting factors should be accessible to those who are interested.

Physical metrics include the distance between houses and shopping, ratios of public services to population, access to amenities, traffic counts, and so on. You can set up these metrics in CommunityViz using decision tools or custom indicators. You often find that a single physical metric applies to more than one value element. Before you use raw metrics in the index calculations, normalize them—that is, scale them so that all metrics have the same maximum and same minimum value (for more details, see Chapter 12).

Finally, consider how to present the value index scores. Because the entire value mapping process is subjective, we advise against presenting numbers that appear to be more precise or accurate than they really are. On the other hand, you need enough precision that you can compare scores between scenarios to see which scenario performs better on any particular value. We suggest that you present index values in charts with no numbers displayed, as illustrated in Figure 9.3.

You may also consider presenting value index scores on a very coarse scale, such as red, yellow, and green symbols indicating bad, okay, and good. Some practitioners advise not showing value *index* scores at all, but rather presenting a chart with the value *element* scores for each core value.

USING VALUE MAPPING

Value mapping provides a novel way to address the effects of planning on the character and values of a community and vice versa. By using CommunityViz to quantify values, you give a stronger emphasis to those values and offer a way for them to be considered alongside other planning issues, such as water supply and land for future housing developments. Our recommendation is to use value mapping to draw a wide audience into community planning efforts and as a way to discover the community's heart-and-soul assets. It serves as a supplement to, not a replacement for, the rest of the public planning process.

MAPPING SPECIAL PLACES

A more straightforward way to find out which aspects of a community are important to residents is to have them map the places they value. It can be fun and engaging for residents to create their own maps with features such as favorite fishing holes or hiking trails, best views, favorite restaurants, and so on. The mapping exercise can be done on paper at meetings, online, or using mobile GPS devices, including phones. You can also collect data on other matters of subjective opinion: least favorite places, areas of opportunity for redevelopment, neighborhood boundaries, and more.

Once you have maps of special places, you can use them in CommunityViz in many ways. The case studies at the end of this chapter give two examples, and here are some more ideas:

- Include "impact on favorite places" as an indicator when evaluating future growth scenarios.

- Count the number of people who will live within walking distance of favorite gathering places, or the number of parking spots or transit stops nearby.

- Count the number of people in the service area of favorite retail establishments to make sure vendors will have enough customers in the future.

- In 3-D scenes, check the future view from each favorite scenic place.

- Include proximity or overlap with favorite places when performing suitability analyses.

Figure 9.3 Chart comparing value index scores for two scenarios

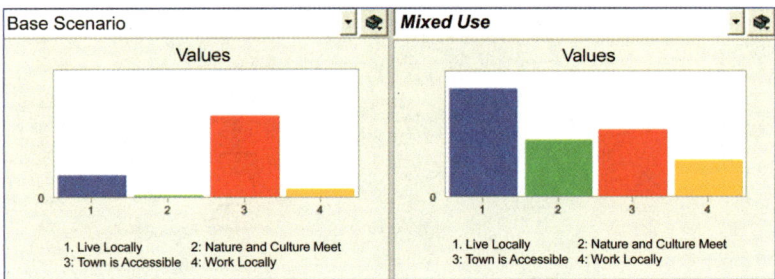

CASE STUDY
ALLEGHENY PLACES

Location: Allegheny County, Pennsylvania

Partners: Allegheny County; McCormick Taylor, Inc. as lead consultant; CommunityViz support provided by Donley & Associates, Inc.

Allegheny County, in southwestern Pennsylvania, is home to the City of Pittsburgh and 129 other municipalities. While Pittsburgh is the economic and cultural center of the county and region, the county's many municipalities contain great diversity. Old mill towns, new suburbs, river towns, and rural villages form a complex geographic, social, and economic landscape. Once reeling from the collapse of the steel industry, Allegheny County has been diversifying its economy and planning for its future.

Allegheny Places was Allegheny County's first comprehensive plan. The culmination of many years of hard work and an intensive public outreach effort, Allegheny Places established an overall vision for the future of the county and provided a road map to get there. Data collection and analysis was an important part of the planning process; however, attaining full participation from the county's many municipalities and diverse population was equally important. The What's Your Favorite Place? campaign was the key to attracting citizen interest, and it also inspired the name of the plan. Through the campaign, the county learned which places and qualities of life its residents valued most, and built on these values to create a vision for Allegheny County. In all, more than 3,000 people from around the county participated in shaping the plan.

Project Description: CommunityViz was used to merge public input and geographic information in order to measure how well different future land-use scenarios met the plan's goals and objectives. The public saw the results of the CommunityViz analysis through graphs, charts, and other illustrations.

The University of Pittsburgh Center for Social and Urban Research analyzed census data, local development data, population and employment trends, and recent development patterns and market trends. The amount and type of future new development and the expected losses of existing buildings were projected, mapped, and presented on a Trend Scenario map. There was a strong public reaction against the Trend Scenario. In response, four alternatives were developed: Good Old Places, Hot New Places, River Places, and Transit-Oriented Places.

Through CommunityViz, the performance of each alternative was evaluated according to factors such as congestion on county roadways, availability of water and sewer infrastructure, access to recreation and jobs, and acres of floodplains and greenfields developed. Equity and diversity were major focuses of the plan, so indicators such as "access to transit" and "amount of development in low-income communities" were also measured. The best

> *The use of the analytical and presentation tools in CommunityViz allowed us to combine the art of planning with the science of planning, resulting in a plan that has a good factual basis and the enthusiastic support of county residents.*
>
> —Leanne Doran
> Associate
> McCormick Taylor, Inc.

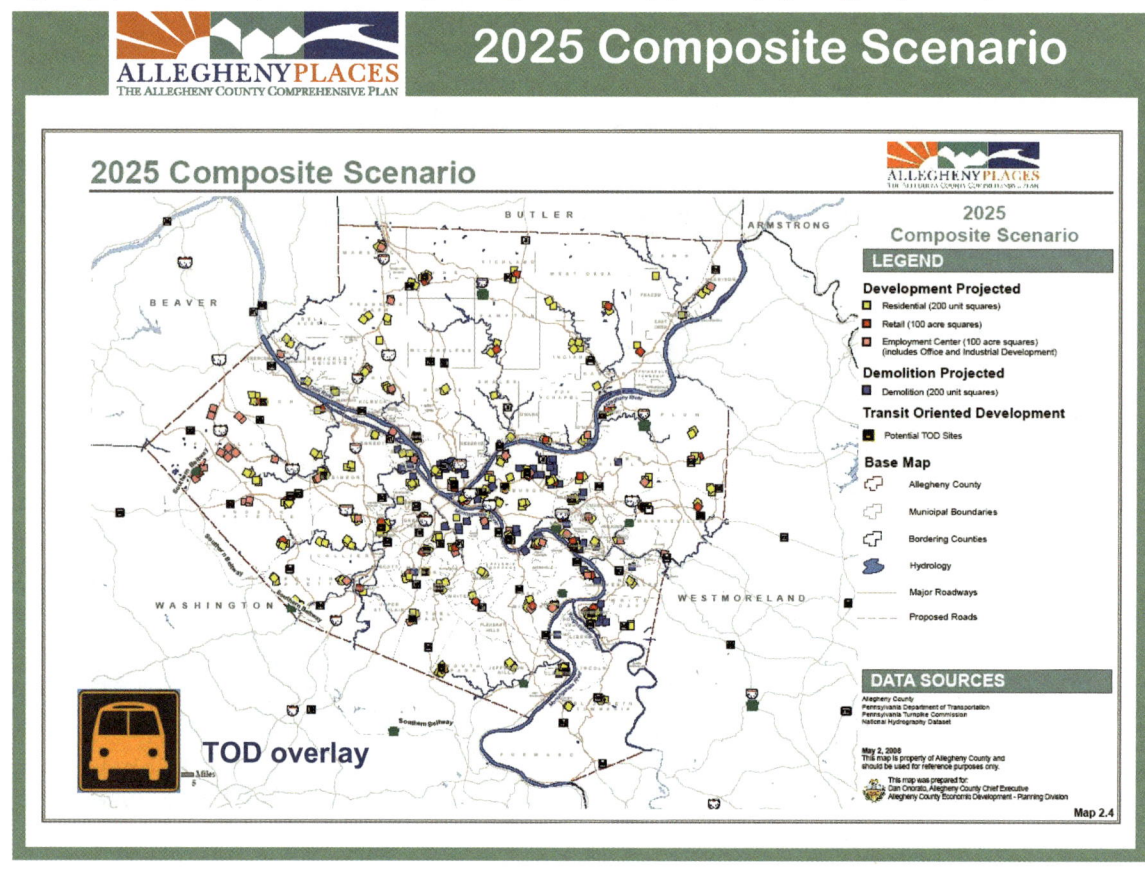

Figure 9.4 *2025 Composite Scenario for Allegheny County (courtesy of Allegheny Places)*

elements of each scenario were then combined into the 2025 Composite Scenario (see Figure 9.4) and tested again using CommunityViz. The resulting future land-use plan became the basis of the county's new comprehensive plan.

> *A major focus of Allegheny Places was creating a plan for the future in which all County residents would have equitable access to decent, affordable housing, safe neighborhoods, transit, good jobs, good schools, and recreation. CommunityViz gave us a way to actually test how well the future land-use plan met these important goals.*
>
> —Kay Pierce
> Manager, Planning Division
> Allegheny County, Pennsylvania

Technology and Tools: CommunityViz Scenario 360 tools—including the Common Impacts Wizard, the Suitability Wizard, and the Optimizer Wizard—were used to combine and analyze data, and to illustrate the analyses in several public venues. Other methods to engage the public included the What's Your Favorite Place? campaign (see Figure 9.5), outreach meetings, an interactive project website, youth outreach, and surveys. Public participation culminated in a series of public meetings held around the county, at which participants could place chips representing future development on maps to determine a preferred future land-use scenario. County executive Dan Onorato opened each public meeting with a 20-minute video presentation designed to educate citizens about planning and to encourage their participation.

Outcomes: Allegheny Places, the Allegheny County comprehensive plan, was adopted in

Figure 9.5 Public participation in the What's Your Favorite Place?

Courtesy of Allegheny Places

November 2008. It included a 170-page plan, a book of the plan maps, an executive summary, and a large-format poster plan—all of which were made available online.[3] An interactive online map viewer enabled the public to see the plan maps from both the county and the local scale. The extensive GIS database created for the plan was made available to the municipalities.

The plan has been used as a policy guide in the review of development proposals that would involve county resources and has provided support for two new initiatives: Allegheny Green, a countywide program to promote sustainability; and an effort to link Pittsburgh to Erie, Pennsylvania, via a trail along the Allegheny River. As Dan Onorato noted, "Allegheny County is home to the urban core of Southwestern Pennsylvania. How we plan for the future impacts all of our surrounding counties and our region."

---

3. Online resources for Allegheny Places can be found at http://alleghenyplaces.com.

CASE STUDY
VISIONS AND VALUES IN THE RURAL BORDERLANDS

Location: Exeter, Rhode Island

Partners: Town of Exeter; Dodson Associates; Foresee Consulting, Inc.; Consensus Building Institute; the Orton Family Foundation; The Nature Conservancy; and others

The Borderlands is a 20-town area of mostly undeveloped lands along the Connecticut–Rhode Island border. During the Borderlands Village Innovation Pilot, two communities sought to discover their heart-and-soul attributes and to build shared visions for the future. One of the pilot communities was the Town of Exeter, Rhode Island.

The initial visioning phase was called Developing a Game Plan for Our Future. During Phase 2, the town would research recommendations from the visioning, and in Phase 3 they would craft implementation strategies.

Exeter first appointed a local pilot team made up of town staff, residents, and business owners, and then hired a consulting team made up of Dodson Associates, the Consensus Building Institute, and Foresee Consulting to lead the project. A project coordinator staffed the project, and The Nature Conservancy and the Orton Family Foundation provided further assistance.

Project Description: A robust public engagement process included interviews with stakeholder groups and a citizen web survey to solicit input about Exeter's heart-and-soul characteristics and ideas for improving the town. In the first public visioning workshop, participants used keypads to prioritize local heart-and-soul resources and to respond to a visual preference survey. Small group discussions focused on local planning issues and opportunities.

In preparation for a second public workshop, Foresee Consulting used CommunityViz to create a build-out analysis for the town, which showed the likely amount and pattern of development under current zoning and development practices, and illustrated the likely impacts of the build-out on Exeter's rural landscape. In order to help people visualize the spatial extent and density of the build-out, Foresee used CommunityViz SiteBuilder 3D—an older component comparable to the newer Scenario 3D—to show a portion of Exeter with existing and potential new development overlaid on aerial photos.

At the second workshop, participants played the growth challenge game, or chip game: They placed chips representing new development on a map of Exeter showing a variety of features, including heart-and-soul resources. Working in five teams, participants wrestled with issues about where to place future development (see Figure 9.6).

The workshop produced five distinct alternatives for future growth, each of which improved upon the build-out scenario's potential impacts on important natural and cultural resources.

Workshop participants also completed a survey to gauge local attitudes toward two factors in land-use decision-making: landscape sensitivity and growth efficiency. Participants ranked protection of groundwater and environmentally sensitive lands as most important in analyzing landscape sensitivity, and they gave the highest efficiency rating to lands close to existing paved roads and public services.

Following the second workshop, Foresee Consulting used CommunityViz to analyze and compare the impacts of the five chip game alternatives against the impacts in the build-out scenario (see Figure 9.7). A final composite map showed areas most suitable for jobs and housing based on the results and values survey. Not content with the business-as-usual scenario, most participants showed support for clustering new growth into six or seven villages or mixed use centers, setting the stage for more-detailed Phase 2 discussions about the location and extent of targeted growth areas.

Technology and Tools: The Borderlands project was done with CommunityViz, including the Build-Out Wizard, Allocator, Impact Analysis tools, and SiteBuilder 3D. An ArcGIS tool called Model Builder was also used. Public engagement tools included focus-group interviews, resource allocation surveys, a project website, a web survey, workshops, heart-and-soul mapping, a visual preference survey, the growth challenge game (chip game), and keypad polling.

Outcomes: Phase 1 of Exeter's project resulted in the defining of shared values and concerns, and was the start of the process to develop a consensus about a shared vision for the future. The Exeter pilot team adopted a recommendation that the town council and the planning board integrate the findings of Phase 1 into the update of the town's comprehensive plan. Subsequently, the town council endorsed the vision and made it a part of the town's comprehensive plan, which was being updated. A work plan was created for Phase 2, during which the preferred vision identified in Phase 1 would be refined; and in Phase 3, when strategies for implementation would be developed.

Figure 9.6 Public meeting exercise in the Borderlands

Both images courtesy of Foresee Consulting

Figure 9.7 Portions of the Scenario 360 analysis

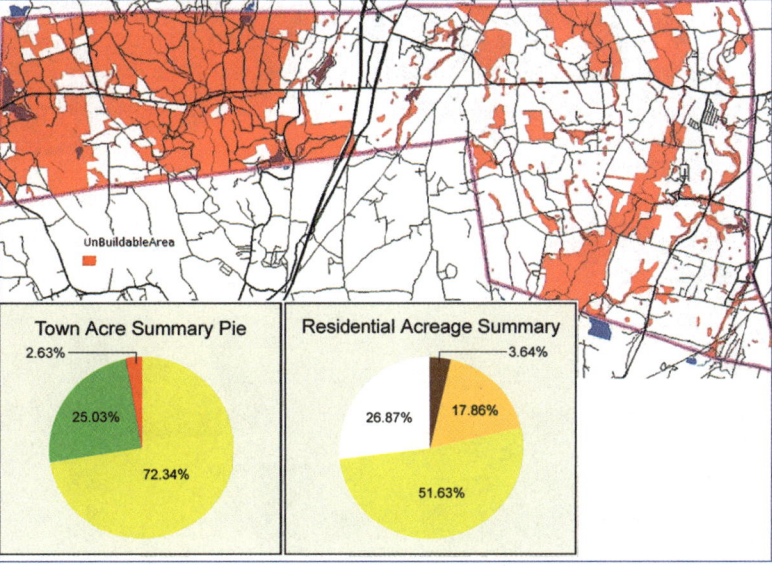

SECTION III
MAKING PLANS

NAVIGATING THIS SECTION

Section 3 shows you how to use CommunityViz to draft a variety of plans, including comprehensive plans, regional plans, transportation plans, and natural resource plans. Section 3 also contains a chapter on how CommunityViz can help with site selection and suitability analysis, which are helpful in creating development plans or conservation plans. The chapters in this section mostly stand on their own, so you can choose the particular chapter that addresses the work you are trying to do at a given time.

Chapter 10, Local Comprehensive Plans, explains how CommunityViz can help you analyze current land-use conditions and draft a future land-use map for a comprehensive plan. The chapter also describes how to use the Common Impacts Wizard to understand the economic, social, and environmental effects of a proposed future land-use map. The extensive teaching example focuses on transportation access and the mix of housing types. There is also a description of how to use a growth allocation spreadsheet as an alternative to sketching maps.

Chapter 11, Regional Land Use and Transportation Plans, looks at making plans at the scale of counties and regions, where land-use and transportation planning often go hand in hand. In addition to describing how CommunityViz can help draft these plans, the chapter also covers useful techniques for working at the regional scale. These techniques include analysis grids and scale-changing formulas that enable you to move GIS data between layers of different scales. Sketch tools for geodesign are also included.

Chapter 12, Site Selection and Assessment, details the wide variety of applications for the Suitability Wizard and related CommunityViz site assessment methods. These applications include the choosing of sites for particular purposes; the use of rating systems such as Land Evaluation and Site Assessment (LESA) and Leadership in Energy and Environmental Design (LEED); the estimating of patterns of future growth; and the evaluation of a community's vulnerability to natural hazards. We have included the chapter in this section because these analyses are often the building blocks of regional plans, resource plans, and local comprehensive plans.

Chapter 13, Resource Plans, discusses the creation of plans for natural areas and natural resources. Some of the topics include evaluating best management practices (BMPs), understanding conditions and targets, and working with raster data. The chapter also describes two CommunityViz tools, the LandFrag Wizard and the Optimizer. The chapter's teaching example is about forest management plans, but the example also illustrates some of the fundamental principles of multi-stakeholder collaboration supported by CommunityViz.

BACKGROUND PLANNING CONCEPTS FOR THIS SECTION

Planning can involve several different kinds of plans. The plans described in this section are the most common types: regional plans for two or more political jurisdictions, city or county comprehensive plans, land-use plans (which should be included in comprehensive plans), site plans, and natural resource plans.

A comprehensive plan incorporates the community's vision for the future with an inventory of population, economic base, housing, land uses, environmental features, transportation networks, and community facilities. A comprehensive plan contains goals for managing change over the next 10 to 30 years. It serves as a guide for residents, landowners, businesspeople, and public officials as they make both long-term and day-to-day decisions about development in the community. In addition, a comprehensive plan can be useful as an economic development tool, to attract businesses as well as to obtain state and federal grants for infrastructure projects.

It makes sense to do a new or updated comprehensive plan when the city or county is undergoing, or is expected to undergo, major changes in population or economic base, or when a new transportation project is about to increase accessibility. Also, it is a good practice to update a comprehensive plan every five to 10 years to reflect changes in community needs and desires. Because the comprehensive plan is the policy basis for the zoning ordinance, updating a comprehensive plan will compel a revision of the zoning ordinance to keep it current and consistent with the comprehensive plan.

The land-use section of the comprehensive plan consists of two parts: 1) the current pattern of the various land uses and densities in the city or county, and 2) the desired future pattern. The land-use section draws on the inventories in the other sections of the comprehensive plan and contains a current land-use map. The goals of the other plan sections are blended together to produce a future land-use map of the desired land-use patterns.

GIS and CommunityViz provide tools to help you organize, analyze, and present land-use data, and articulate community goals for a comprehensive plan. Geographic information systems offer a platform for combining and displaying land-use information—such as topography, soil types, and ownership patterns—that determine where development can go. CommunityViz enhances GIS by adding a rich set of capabilities, including geodesign, scenario planning, dynamic analysis, and public interaction. These capabilities help planners, the public, and elected officials understand complex land-use relationships and compare alternative land-use patterns for creating the future land-use map. The final future land use map should reflect the desires of the community. Later, this map will be used to update the zoning ordinance, which sets the rules for the location, mix, and density of different land uses.

Regional land-use and transportation plans have become increasingly popular over the past 20 years. A big boost for regional transportation plans in the United States occurred when Congress passed the 1990 Clean Air Act Amendments and the Intermodal Surface Transportation Efficiency Act (ISTEA) of 1991. ISTEA required each of the nation's more than 340 metropolitan areas to have a Metropolitan Planning Organization (MPO) in order to qualify for federal transportation funds. Each MPO is required to draft a 20-year regional transportation plan and a three- to five-year transportation improvement plan, with specific transportation projects that reflect air-quality concerns. The Safe, Accountable, Flexible, Efficient Transportation Equity Act: A Legacy for Users (SAFETEA-LU) of 2005 and its updates added provisions that encourage MPOs to use visualization in their proposed transportation projects and better integration of those projects with land-use plans.

Although regional land-use plans are usually not legally mandated, they offer many benefits. They have a close connection to regional transportation plans, and they can help guide the land use plans of their member jurisdictions. Creating a regional land-use plan is a good idea when the futures of two or more communities are closely linked. For instance, since 2000, to encourage more regional planning, the state of Pennsylvania has helped fund the drafting of multi-municipal plans. Drafting a regional plan also makes sense when you are planning for an environmental feature that crosses political boundaries, such as a watershed.

CommunityViz brings many of the same benefits to regional planning as it does to local planning. You can still apply techniques such as geodesign and dynamic analysis, though with some adjustments for scale. In addition, you can use CommunityViz to integrate and combine information across jurisdictions and technical disciplines.

Selecting a site and determining how and where to build on a parcel of land are key steps in real estate development and site planning. "Location, location, location" is the mantra of real estate developers, but the suitability of a site to support development in terms of slope, soils, water, and natural hazards is also important to consider. When planners choose a location for a new facility such as a library or a bus stop, they must often weigh a large number of factors. CommunityViz and GIS can help you combine all the relevant data and present clear information about preferences and trade-offs among alternative sites. At a broader scale, CommunityViz can help you create landscape-scale assessments that suggest desirable or likely areas for development, priority areas for particular land uses such as agriculture or conservation, and areas at risk for natural hazards. These assessments will help inform local and regional comprehensive plans.

CommunityViz is a popular tool for resource management and has an array of planning applications for water resources, environmentally sensitive areas, parks, agriculture, and forestry, among others. Resource planning is also a task for urban planners developing a comprehensive plan. A natural resource inventory is often recommended as a first step in the creation of a comprehensive plan. Even before making a population projection, you should understand the carrying capacity of the planning area—that is, the ability of the planning area to support population and development without causing undue environmental harm.

As part of the land-use section of the comprehensive plan, a planner can draft a resource plan to protect certain natural resources, such as farmlands, forests, wetlands, shorelines, water bodies, and wildlife habitats. Local residents will probably have identified some of these natural resources as important heart-and-soul assets.

A planner will need to inventory the location, amount, and quality of agricultural and forest lands, and waterways, wetlands, and wildlife habitats. Information on agricultural and timberlands may be found through searching property tax records, especially as active farms and forests qualify for use-value property assessments. Data on waterways, wetlands, and wildlife habitats should be available from your state department of the environment or natural resources. GIS technology is invaluable for collecting and managing data on natural resources, and CommunityViz lets you analyze that data and apply it to make better plans. Alternative development scenarios can show where and how natural resources may be impacted, and alternative management plans can help identify the best practices for managing particular natural resources, such as surface water.

10 LOCAL COMPREHENSIVE PLANS

KEY CONCEPTS AND TERMS IN THIS CHAPTER

- Common Impacts Wizard
- Growth allocation spreadsheet
- Transportation and access impacts

A city, town, or county drafts a comprehensive plan to determine long-term goals and policies. A comprehensive plan serves as the policy basis for zoning and subdivision regulations and public investment in capital improvements. Local officials use the comprehensive plan to guide day-to-day decisions on development proposals, land use patterns, infrastructure projects, and community design. The process of creating or updating a comprehensive plan closely parallels the process for creating a CommunityViz analysis, which is described in Section 1. This chapter focuses on how CommunityViz can help you analyze current conditions and draft a future land use map for a comprehensive plan.

WHY AND WHEN

A comprehensive plan usually needs to be updated every three to five years depending on state statutes and how fast the community is growing. The comprehensive plan's future land-use map must be updated to be consistent with changes in the zoning map. Ideally, you will create and maintain a living comprehensive plan that allows planners to monitor progress and make adjustments to the plan from year to year. Before beginning a comprehensive plan analysis, review Chapter 1 for more detailed information on the CommunityViz approach to scenario planning and Chapter 3 for suggestions on project design. Figure 10.1 illustrates the most important CommunityViz activities associated with a traditional comprehensive planning process.

You can use CommunityViz throughout the plan-making process, during specific phases of the process, or for specific comprehensive plan elements. For example, CommunityViz can help you, the public, and elected officials study future land-use alternatives to arrive at a preferred future land-use map; or study transportation and pedestrian networks to draft specific goals for the transportation element of a comprehensive plan.

DATA NEEDS

To analyze current conditions, you will need data about the existing population, land uses, transportation networks, utilities, natural environment, community services, economic base, housing, and the rest of the built environment. The more data the better, but the most common data needs can be ranked in general order of priority.

You *must have* the following data:

- **Land-use polygons.** Parcel data are preferable, but you can also use data covering larger areas, such as future land-use polygons. Ideally, the land-use polygon data will include attributes that show existing residential units and the floor area of nonresidential buildings. If these data are not available locally, you may be able to derive them from census data.

- **Current land use** or land cover by polygon.

The following data are *highly desirable:*

- **Road centerlines.** Roads and streets provide access and indicate an ability to support development based on location and traffic capacity. Road and street data include information on rights-of-way, level of service for roads and streets, and functional classification of roads and streets, such as arterials, collectors, or local streets.

- **Constraint areas.** Constraint areas are where building is restricted or prohibited. Typical constraints include floodplains, wetlands, water bodies, steep slopes, environmentally sensitive areas, historic buildings and landmarks, archaeological sites, prime agricultural areas, contaminated sites, and areas prone to natural hazards.

Figure 10.1 CommunityViz activities associated with the comprehensive planning process

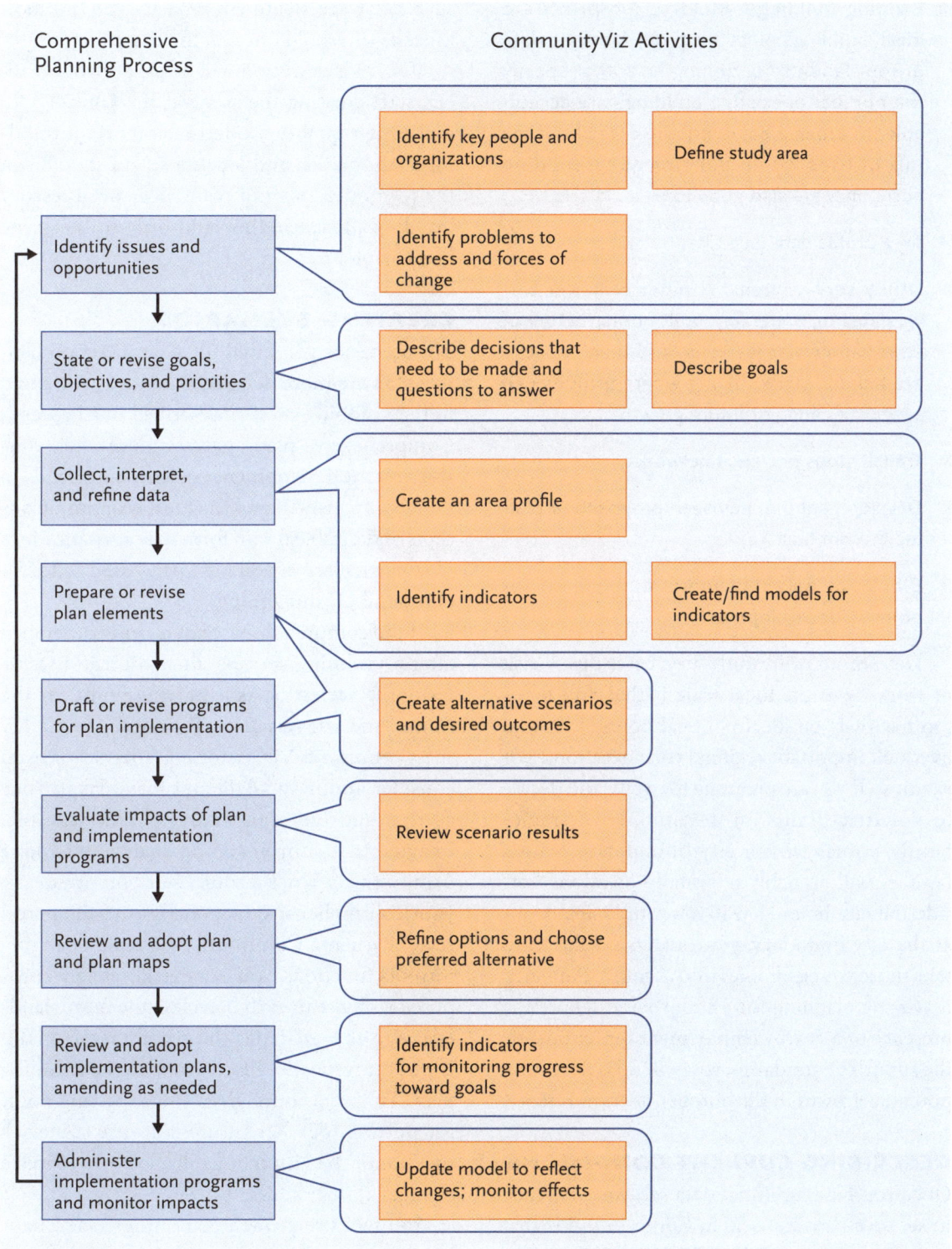

- **Land-use overlay districts.** A land use overlay district can provide an opportunity for additional development, such as a density bonus area, or impose additional constraints, such as steep slope overlay on top of a residential area.

It is *desirable* to have this data:

- **Existing buildings.** Building footprints are ideal; building points are good. Attribute data in your land-use or zoning layer that specify the number of existing buildings are acceptable. In urban areas, attribute data about the mix of uses within buildings and building occupancy are also good to have.
- **Area profile data** (see Chapter 1).
- **Utility service areas.** A water or sewer service area or, preferably, built infrastructure of sewer and water facilities, and their capacity are helpful in identifying where utilities can support existing or future growth.
- **Transit stops** or transit networks.
- **Development** that has been proposed or platted but not built.
- **Blocks or neighborhoods** designated for potential redevelopment.

Determine your study area carefully. A risk of working at the local scale is that you focus too narrowly on local political boundaries and overlook important regional considerations. For example, if you are planning for a city and decide to put strict limits on the number of single-family homes within city boundaries, young families will probably migrate to locations outside the city boundary. If your study area stops at the city boundary, your analysis will fail to take those young families into account. Similarly, if you are planning for a suburb and ignore the presence of a nearby employment center outside the suburb's boundaries, you will miss the future potential growth in the number of commuters.

DESCRIBING CURRENT CONDITIONS

Once you have an initial data set, you are ready to set up a base scenario in CommunityViz that shows current conditions in the planning area.

As you work, take time to check data quality, choose appropriate map symbols, and give layers meaningful names.

Set up indicators and charts to store and display important nonspatial information such as total population or public-service usage rates. If you know of important thresholds or limits, such as sewage-treatment capacity, you can show those as threshold lines on the charts.

If 3-D visualization will be part of your project, start creating the scene at this time. Try to make high-quality models of important buildings, landmarks, and locations. You should not try to model existing residences or accessory buildings, because they add little to the scene (see Chapter 6).

CREATING SCENARIOS

The scenarios you build for a local comprehensive plan are more detailed than those you build in the visioning process described in Chapter 7. Comprehensive plan analyses more often consider recent development patterns and trends in population growth and the local economy. Concepts of desirable urban form may also come into play, particularly if you use form-based codes for part or all of your zoning.

If the comprehensive plan is being developed after a visioning process, then you can use the visioning scenarios as a starting point for the future land-use scenarios. Do not try to modify the CommunityViz visioning analysis, but do consider adding its data and formulas to your comprehensive plan analysis. For example, imagine that your visioning analysis was done using census block groups but you are doing your comprehensive plan analysis at the parcel scale. By using CommunityViz scale-changing formula functions, you can quickly assign a proposed land use to each parcel on the future land-use map that matches the recommended land use of the respective block group in the visioning plan. This procedure gives you a starting point for putting together future land-use scenarios that honor the vision but still allow you to make changes at finer scales.

You will use growth projections (see Chapter 8) as part of your future land-use scenarios.

Figure 10.2   Potential sequence for using CommunityViz tools to sketch future land-use map scenarios

Land Use Designer → Build-Out Wizard → TimeScope and TimeScope Animator

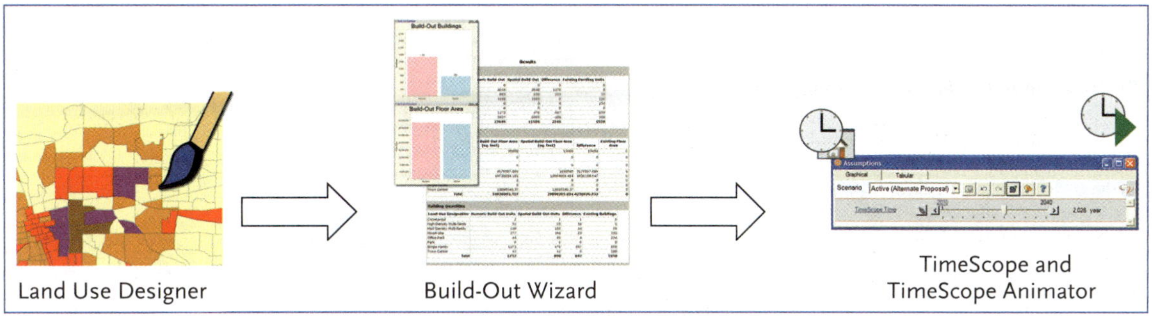

Figure 10.2 illustrates a potential sequence in which CommunityViz tools could be used to sketch future land-use map scenarios. For initial sketches of alternative scenarios, you can use the Land Use Designer. It enables you to "paint" land uses on the map and receive immediate feedback, in the form of charts and indicators, about the impacts of your future land-use scenarios. As you begin to narrow the scenarios down to a preferred scenario, you will probably want to use the more precise Build-Out Wizard. The wizard asks you for more-detailed information about development density, the mix of land uses and building uses, building constraints, and other factors. It then produces more-detailed estimates of the future capacity of each land-use polygon. It can provide numeric capacity estimates and, if desired, spatial estimates in the form of building points on the map. After the Build-Out Wizard gives you estimates of the ultimate development capacity for each scenario, use TimeScope to model growth during the planning horizon of the comprehensive plan, which is usually 20 or 30 years. TimeScope calculates where and when new development will occur based on assumptions that you provide about growth rates and growth patterns.

One effective method for visualizing development patterns over time is to use animations created with the TimeScope Animator. If you have access to property tax data for existing buildings or building permit data for lots, you can use the "year built" information to create an animation in TimeScope, in which buildings will appear on the map according to the year they were constructed. When viewed over a wide area, such as a county or region, the animation reveals patterns of growth, such as the tendency for new development to occur near roads. If you make another animation that shows future development projections, the patterns should flow logically forward from the present.

MODELING IMPACTS

The adjective *comprehensive* means "complete and broad," and one of the benefits of using CommunityViz in comprehensive planning is its ability to provide complete and broad impact analysis.

The *Common Impacts Wizard* is a good tool to start with, because it's very easy to use and provides credible rate-based impact models for a variety of economic, environmental, and social indicators (see Figure 10.3).

For a comprehensive plan impact analysis, however, the results from the Common Impacts Wizard may not provide enough precision. We strongly recommend that you inspect each indicator produced by the wizard and decide whether it meets the needs of your particular project. At a minimum, consider resetting the variable assumptions—the slider bars—to values that match your local conditions. For example, the Common Impacts Wizard uses a default value for household water use that is based on the U.S. national average. If water use is an important part of your comprehensive plan, obtain usage rates from the local water utility and plug in those rates in place of the default. One way to calibrate these settings is by using the Common Impacts Wizard to produce an analysis of existing buildings, and then comparing the results to your current conditions indicators. There should be a reasonably good match. If there is not a good match, you may need to fine-tune your analysis.

Figure 10.3 Screenshot of part of a Common Impacts Wizard Report

Indicator	Alternative A	Alternative B	Units
Common Impacts - Annual CO Auto Emissions	10,956,364	11,996,353	lbs
Common Impacts - Annual CO2 Auto Emissions	102,678	112,424	tons
Common Impacts - Annual Hydrocarbon Auto Emissions	1,383,909	1,515,271	lbs
Common Impacts - Annual NOx Auto Emissions	686,898	752,100	lbs
Common Impacts - Commercial Energy Use	2,733,774	1,965,786	million BTU / year
Common Impacts - Commercial Floor Area	30,041,469	21,602,046	sq feet
Common Impacts - Commercial Jobs	36,502	26,248	commercial jobs
Common Impacts - Commercial Jobs to Housing Ratio	3.24	2.13	commercial jobs / dwelling unit
Common Impacts - Labor Force	11,245	12,312	workers
Common Impacts - Population	28,605	31,321	persons
Common Impacts - Residential Dwelling Units	11,262	12,331	dwelling units
Common Impacts - Residential Energy Use	1,038,356	1,136,918	million BTU / year
Common Impacts - Residential Water Use	1,607,256,330	1,759,818,665	gallons / year
Common Impacts - School Children	5,406	5,920	school children
Common Impacts - Vehicle Trips per Day	67,009	73,369	vehicle trips / day

There will be impacts resulting from your comprehensive plan that need more-customized analysis than the Common Impacts Wizard can provide. An example is the fire response time analysis described in one of the case studies at the end of this chapter. For creating custom impacts, use the capabilities in CommunityViz for custom analysis, as described in Chapter 4.

ENGAGING THE PUBLIC

Here are some special considerations for engaging the public in updating or creating a comprehensive plan:

- In 2-D and 3-D displays, identify local landmarks and label them with their common local names.

- Use familiar local names to label neighborhoods.

- Even though a comprehensive plan is not legally binding in the way that zoning and building codes are, its land-use policies provide the legal foundation for zoning and subdivision regulations that affect private property. On the future land-use map of the comprehensive plan, Farmer Joe's favorite pasture may be designated for commercial use, or Landlady Laurie's apartment complex may be identified as a good site for a new parking garage. Try to work with landowners ahead of time to avoid surprises and anticipate major objections. Keep in mind that the zoning map is derived directly from the future land-use map of the comprehensive plan, and the two maps need to be consistent.

- You will be presenting information on a wide variety of impacts. Not everyone in the audience will immediately understand the implications of all the impacts, so plan to spend a little time educating the audience on each topic. At the same time, beware of overloading them with information. Use summaries to begin with and go into greater detail only if needed.

- Be conscious of the public's previous experience with local planning projects, and how CommunityViz can give the public better information and more detailed visual analysis than ever before.

- Be careful to identify the scale of impacts you model. While some of the impacts will be immediate and local, others will be regional or global; do not accidentally imply otherwise.

TEACHING EXAMPLE

This example describes highlights of an analysis undertaken to support an official community plan (OCP) for a growing Canadian city of a little more than 100,000 residents.[1] An OCP is essentially the Canadian counterpart to an American comprehensive plan, with elements that include goals, objectives, and policies for growth and development. As illustrated in the map in Figure 10.4, the city boundaries include both a city center (on the middle of the western shore) and sparsely settled outlying land. It lies on the eastern shore of a scenic lake.

The city expected to grow by more than 40,000 people over the next 20 years, and developers had already made several proposals for new projects. In addition to the new comprehensive planning study, the city wanted to pay particular attention to sustainability indicators. We have focused here on a few parts of the analysis that demonstrate some less common CommunityViz techniques.

PREPARING DATA

Our area profile included an overview of the city and its planning challenges. City staff provided good data for most baseline information. We used tax parcels as the primary land-use polygon layer, but for parts of the analysis, we worked with geographic sectors of the city and some smaller parcel collections called potential growth areas (PGAs) (see Figure 10.5).

Like many city GIS departments, this one stored current use information for multiuse parcels and some multifamily dwelling units as stacked polygons. Stacked polygons are multiple copies of a single polygon all placed at the same location on the map. Each copy stores information on a single use or owner, such as an individual story in a high-rise building. For our purposes,

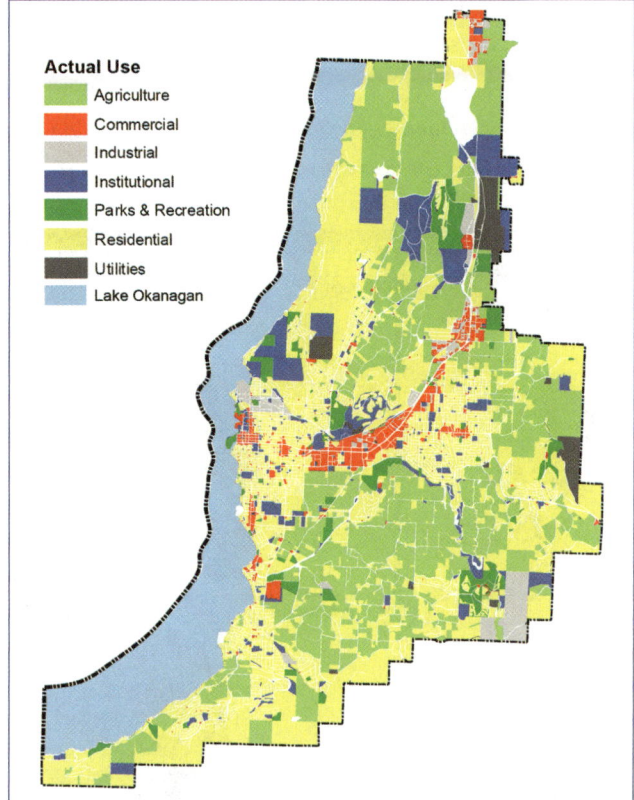

Figure 10.4 *Study area showing current land uses*

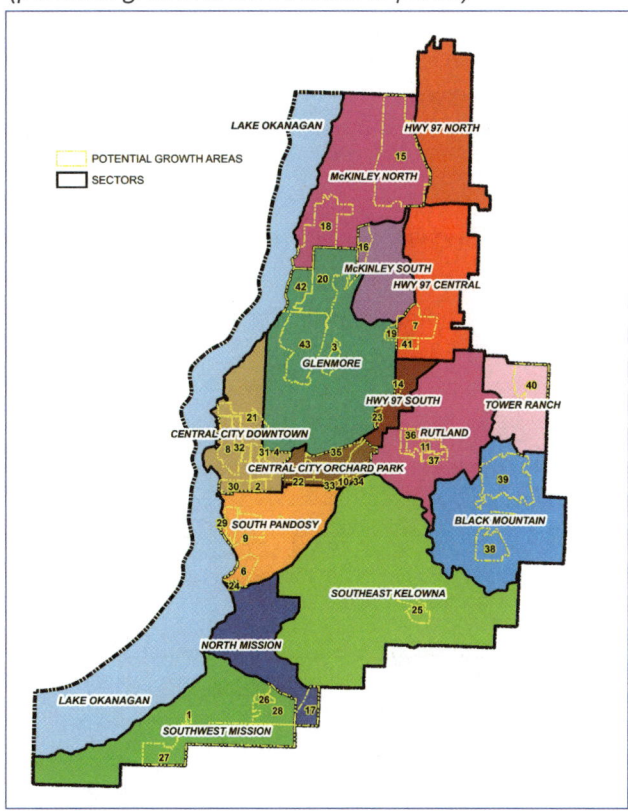

Figure 10.5 *Sectors (in solid colors) and PGAs (potential growth areas outlined in yellow)*

---

1. The example is drawn from work Placeways did with Urban Systems, Ltd. and others in support of an OCP process for Kelowna, British Columbia, Canada. Some details have been changed to make teaching points clearer.

we needed to flatten the stacks into a single polygon with multiple attribute fields for the various land uses and a count of dwelling units in a stack.

Figure 10.6 Four scenarios showing density of development (yellow to brown) and undeveloped areas (pale green). Lake Okanagan, to the left, is pale blue.

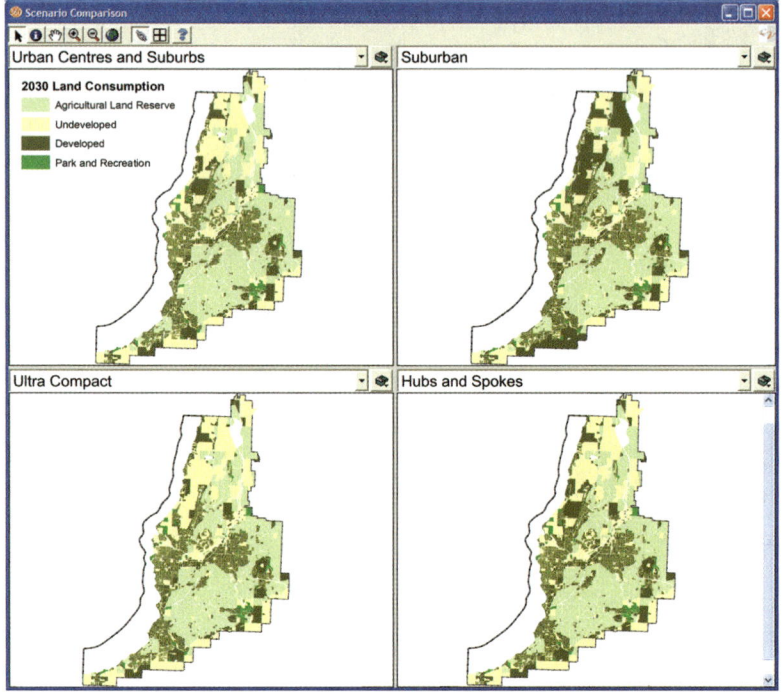

Figure 10.7 Growth allocation input spreadsheet (detail)

SECTOR/SUBSECTOR	REFERENCE: 2001–2008 TREND (UNITS)	% NEW GROWTH (PERSONS)
Black Mountain	4.5%	5.0%
Central City Downtown	11.6%	12.6%
Central City Orchard Park	11.6%	12.6%
Glenmore	18.9%	19.9%
Hwy 97 Central	2.0%	2.0%
Hwy 97 North	2.0%	0.3%
Hwy 97 South	.0%	2.0%
McKinley North	0.7%	0.7%
McKinley South	0.7%	0.0%
North Mission	5.6%	5.6%
Rutland	5.4%	5.4%
South Pandosy	13.4%	14.0%
Southeast Kelowna	3.3%	3.5%
Southwest Mission	12.9%	12.9%
Tower Ranch	5.4%	3.5%
	Must add to 100%	100.0%

CREATING SCENARIOS

After conferring with local planners, we developed four contrasting scenarios (see Figure 10.6):

1. **Urban Centres and Suburbs** was based on the future land-use plan from the 2020 OCP, which had already been adopted.

2. **Suburban** included all pending development requests. These had the overall effect of extending development outward from the city center and into undeveloped areas.

3. **Hubs and Spokes** channeled more growth into urban and village centers than was already called for in the OCP. It used growth boundaries and phasing plans to reduce growth in outlying areas.

4. **Ultra Compact** was designed to illustrate some new ideas. It prevented any growth from occurring in outlying areas.

We could have created these scenarios using Sketch tools in conjunction with growth projections. Instead, we chose an alternative method that gave planners more control over allocating specific amounts of growth to different geographic sectors. Our method was to create an input spreadsheet (see Figure 10.7). The total population growth forecast for the planning horizon was about 40,000. Using this spreadsheet, planners entered the amount of new growth they wanted to allocate to each sector of the city, and in some cases to potential growth areas (PGAs) within the sectors.

We fed the results into CommunityViz using External Table Links and performed further analysis and growth allocation (see Figure 10.8). We used the spreadsheet numbers as inputs to determine how much new residential growth would be placed in each sector and potential growth area. Next, we used the Scenario 360 Allocator to assign growth to particular parcels. In order to determine the required residential capacity of each parcel for each scenario, in Allocator we set up and employed scenario-specific assumptions about the mix of housing types, the rules for growth outside potential growth areas, and the possibility of mixed use residential redevelopment.

This project focused primarily on residential growth, but commercial development was also an important consideration. We mapped existing commercial uses and assumed that with a few specific exceptions, they would remain constant over time. Also, with the help of the local planners, we included new commercial and mixed uses in each scenario that were consistent with the residential plans.

ANALYZING IMPACTS

Once we built the scenarios, we could start analyzing impacts. One of the first questions was how much land would be consumed in each scenario. In urban and suburban areas, a parcel is usually considered consumed if it transitions from undeveloped to developed, regardless of how much building occurs on the parcel. In an area with large parcels, a single building does not necessarily consume all the land. In such a case, you may need to use an assumption that each building consumes, say, 1 acre of land. Figure 10.9 displays the results of the impact analysis, and it is a good example of the use of pie charts to show indicators that are expressed as percentages.

Another important set of indicators measured access to commercial services such as retail and offices. For this measurement, we used the ArcGIS Network Analyst extension to calculate five-, 10- and 15-minute walking times around the commercial parcels in each of the four scenarios (see Figure 10.10).

Once we had polygons for the walking times, a simple Scenario 360 formula let us count the number of dwelling units in each ring. As we expected, there were significant differences in results among the four scenarios (see Figure 10.11).

In theory, better access to services improves sustainability, because it reduces vehicle miles traveled and therefore reduces greenhouse gases from auto emissions. In practice, this effect cannot be measured directly; an estimation model is required. In this example, we assumed that the average household generated 5.95 vehicle trips per day. We reasoned that households with higher accessibility—that is, greater proximity to services—would make fewer vehicle trips per day because they could bike or walk instead of driving. We took into account their accessibility to: 1) commercial services, 2) institutional services such as schools and libraries, and 3) bus rapid transit hubs. The reduction in trips would be an estimate, so we set up two variable assumptions: one for the trip reduction in high-access areas (five minutes from services or frequent transit), and another for the trip reduction in medium-access areas (10 minutes to services or frequent transit) (see Figure 10.12).

Figure 10.8 Flow chart of growth allocation process

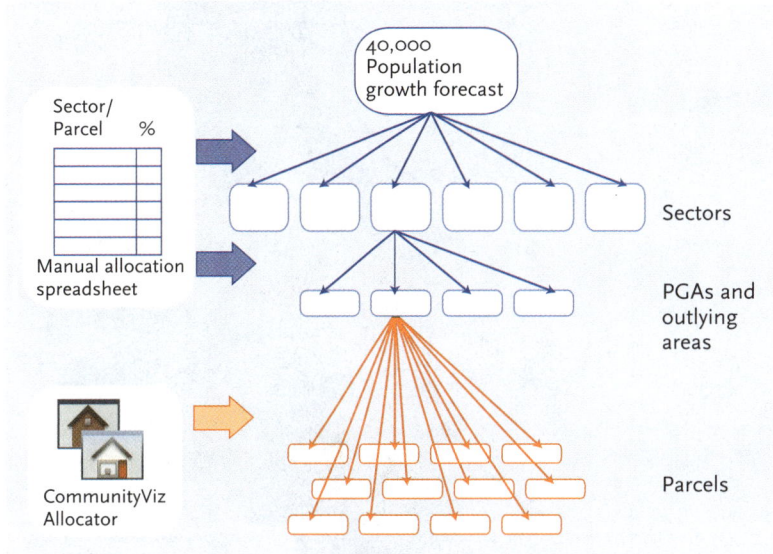

Figure 10.9 Land consumption scenarios in 2030. (ALR stands for agricultural land reserve.)

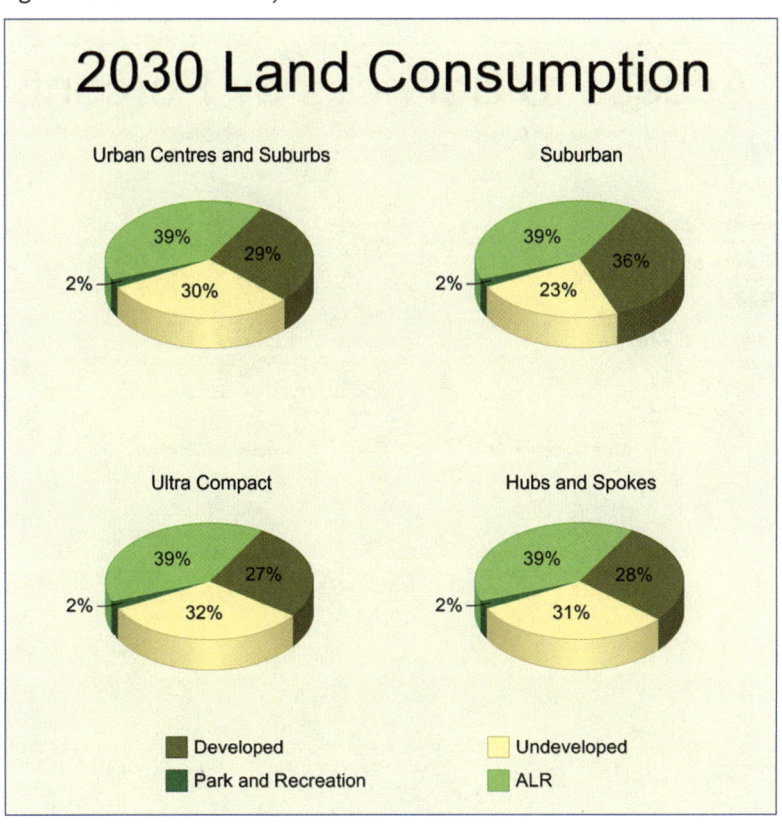

Figure 10.10 Access to services (red), showing walking times from five minutes (light yellow) to more than 15 minutes (dark blue) in one of the four scenarios

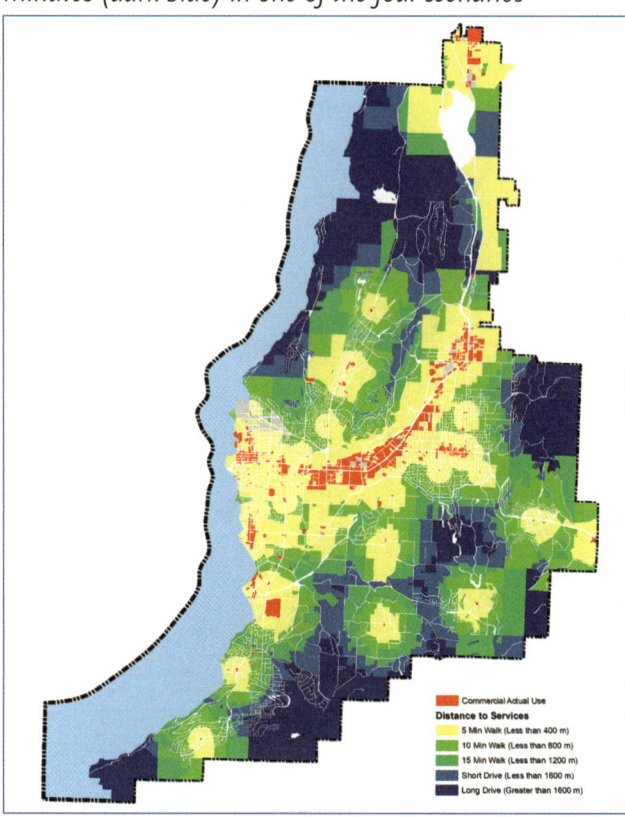

Figure 10.11 Access to services by scenario

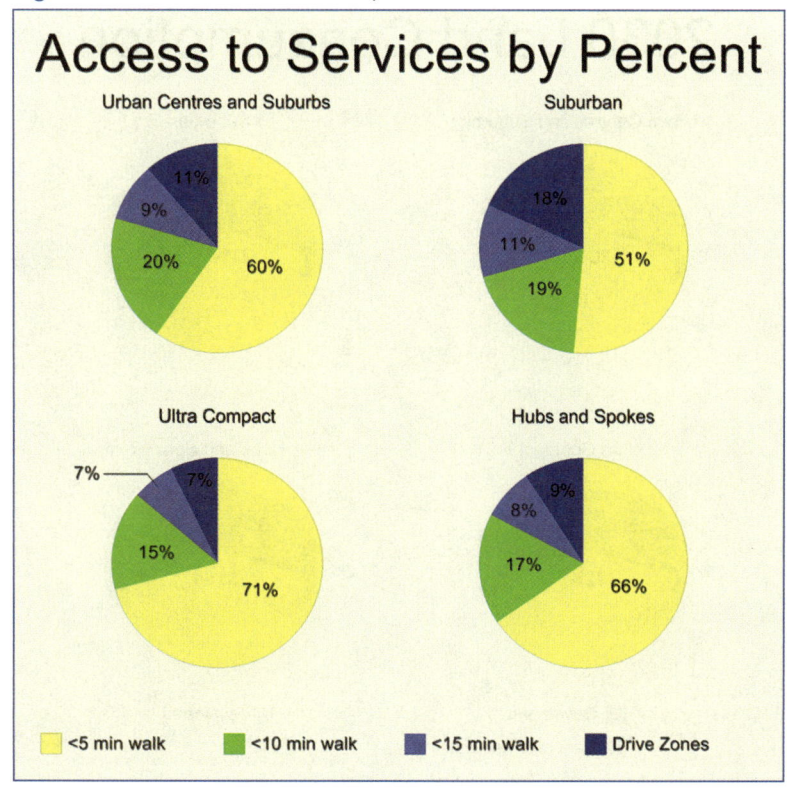

Figure 10.12 Variable assumptions for trip reduction depending on access to services

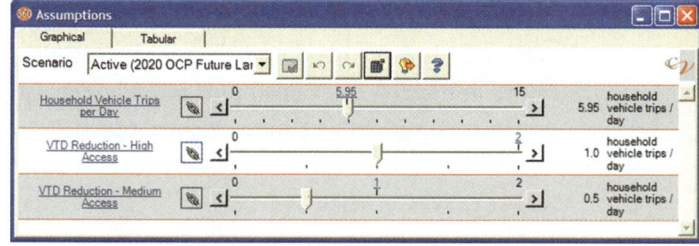

By applying those assumptions to our calculations of auto emissions, we were able to estimate the effect of trip reductions on auto emissions, as shown in Figure 10.13.

The city's population forecast included growth in the demand for various types of housing. Because of demographic and market shifts, a variety of housing types would be needed, from single-family homes to townhouses, from apartments to retirement complexes. Planners knew that it was important to match the details of the housing supply to the details of housing demand. They were concerned that an insufficient stock of single-family homes within the city limits would cause young families to locate outside the city boundaries and commute long distances to work in the city's employment centers. That pattern would exacerbate traffic and air-pollution problems as well as segregate the population.

To help the planners study the mix of housing types, we built additional indicators and assumptions into the analysis. Figure 10.14 shows one of the charts of future residential capacity, and Figure 10.15 shows how the four scenarios compared in the mix of single-family and multifamily dwellings. These analysis tools helped clarify the differences among the scenarios.

PRESENTING AND SHARING THE ANALYSIS

We developed this comprehensive plan analysis in cooperation with several organizations, including city staff and the consulting team. Thus we needed good ways to share work internally among team members. We also held review sessions with city staff and stakeholder groups, and at public meetings.

Within the team of CommunityViz users, we exchanged geodatabases and CommunityViz analysis folders. In a typical exchange, one analyst would build a model and make several Saved Views to illustrate its high points. She would then send the analysis to another team member, who would open it and review the work by stepping through the Saved Views.

To share information with team members who were not using CommunityViz, we frequently produced images of charts and maps showing work in progress. Images are easy to make, send, and view, and they do not have to show final results.

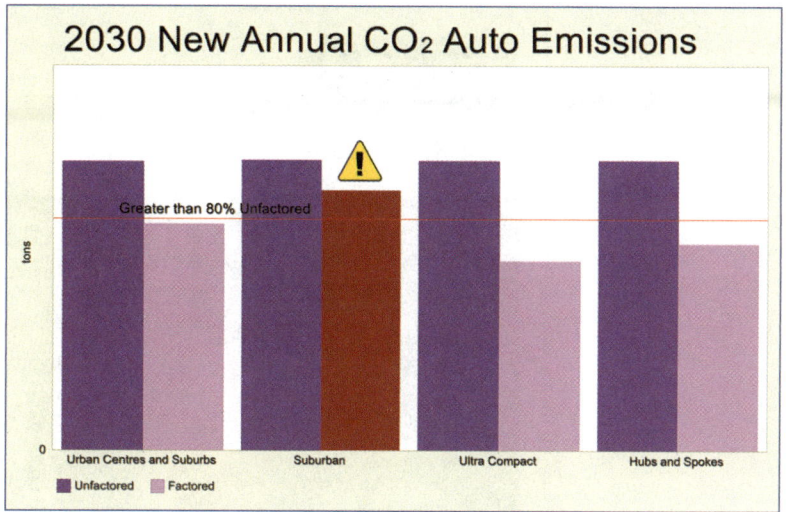

Figure 10.13 *Trip reduction impact on auto carbon dioxide emissions*

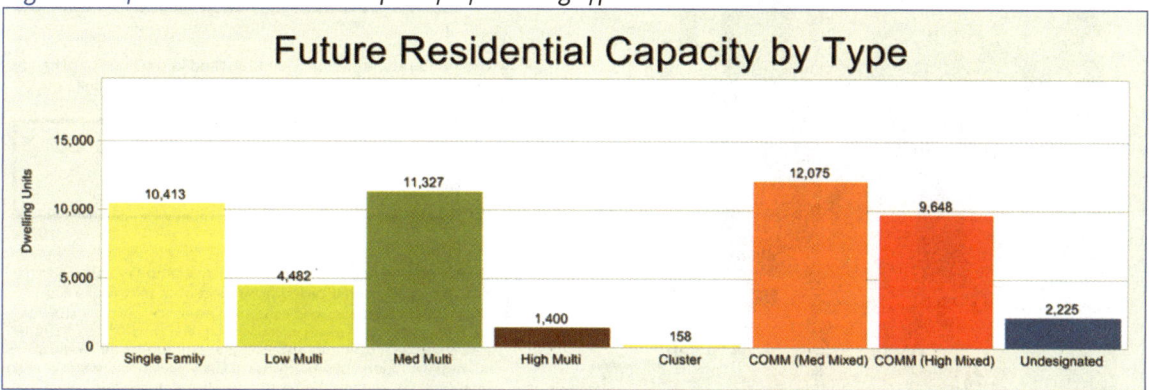

Figure 10.14 *Future residential capacity by housing type*

For public meetings and formal presentations, we supplemented CommunityViz display capabilities with additional media. For example, Figure 10.16 shows a sample poster used for gathering public reactions to aspects of the plan using red and green dot stickers. Later, we could add the public feedback collected on the posters to the electronic analysis. For formal presentations, we sometimes exported CommunityViz data to Excel to make more-specialized charts, and we created final maps using a combination of ArcMap, CommunityViz, and Photoshop image-editing technology.

This project demonstrated the successful use of CommunityViz to analyze, visualize, and communicate ideas. CommunityViz helped the public and elected officials make informed policy decisions during an effective comprehensive planning process.

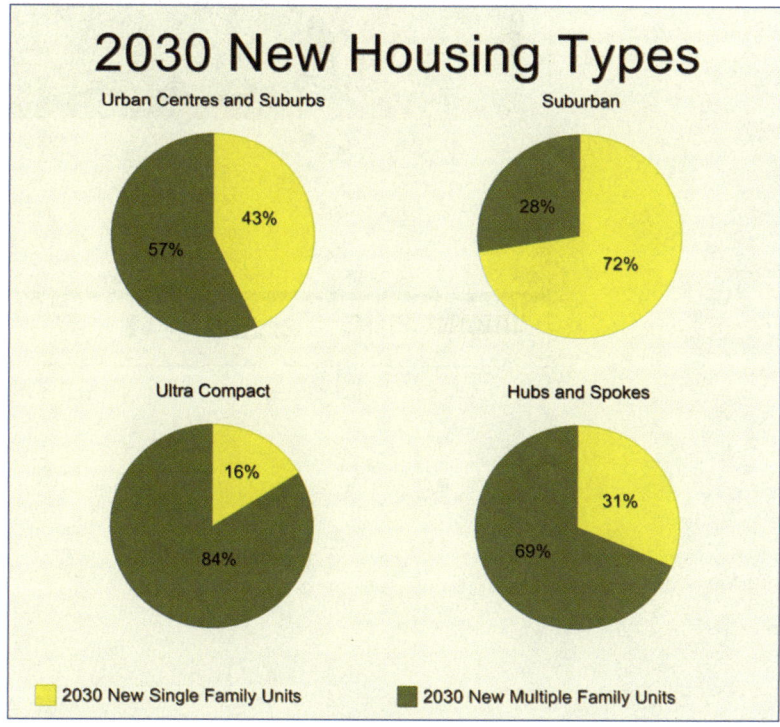

Figure 10.15 *Mix of single-family and multifamily units in 2030 by scenario*

Figure 10.16   Example of a public meeting poster

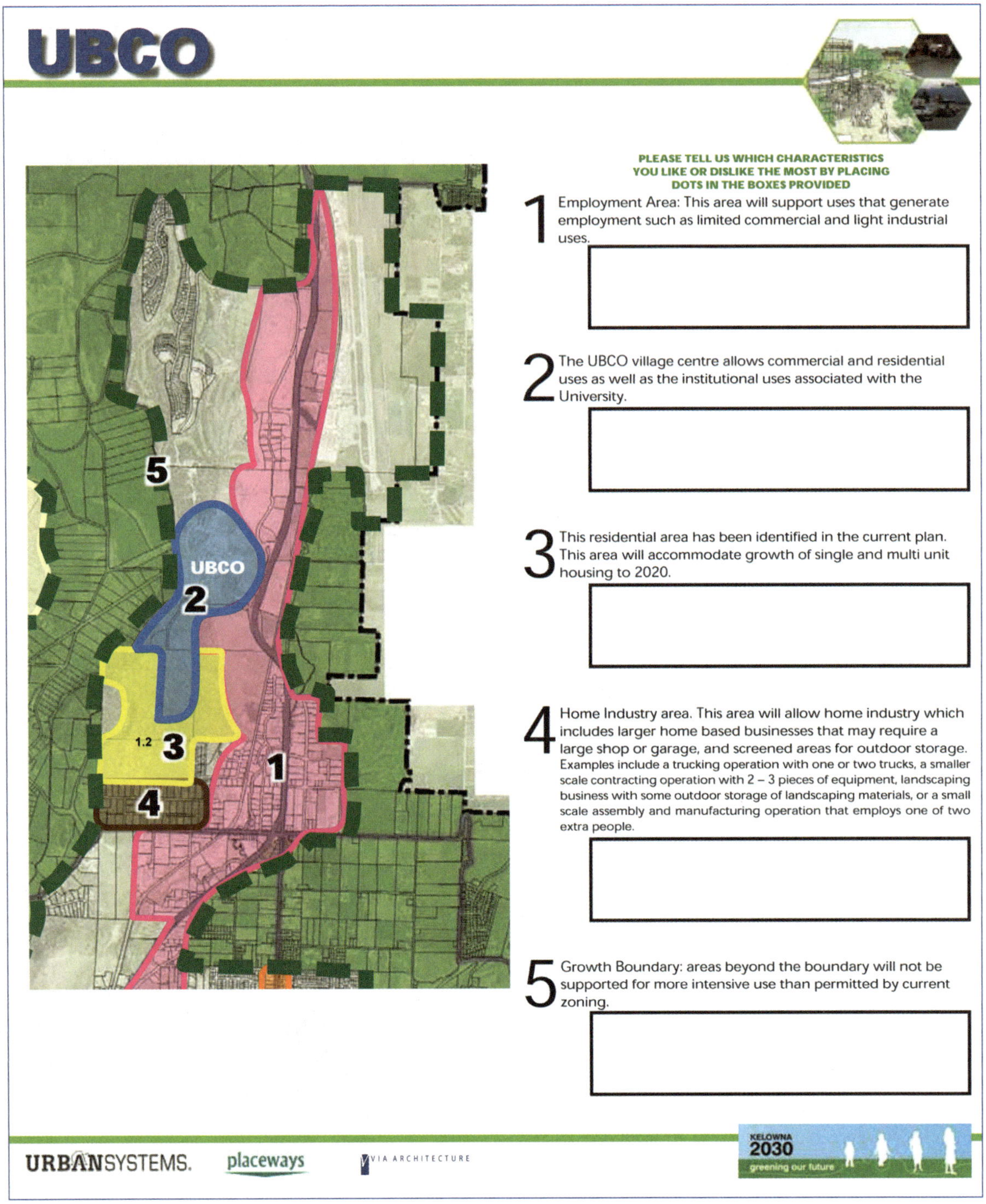

CASE STUDY
CITY COMPREHENSIVE PLAN

Location: Durango, Colorado
Partners: City of Durango; the Orton Family Foundation; Planning Works, as lead consultant; Donley & Associates, Inc. as CommunityViz consultant

The City of Durango, Colorado, lies in the Animas River valley, at an elevation of more than 6,000 feet and is surrounded by peaks of the San Juan Mountains (see Figure 10.17). With a population of about 16,000 people, and another 6,000 in the outlying areas, Durango had experienced rapid growth in the past decade. As described by the Orton Family Foundation, a partner in the project, "Durangoans were trying to preserve their city's heart and soul and avoid the 'anyplace syndrome' that they see creeping into neighboring communities and the region as a whole."[2] In 2005, city staff set out to create a new comprehensive plan guided by a broad-based citizens' review committee and input from a variety of residents.

Project Description: The project was notable for its intensity, inclusiveness, and innovation. The city hosted 20 workshops, which enabled the city, the consultants, and the public to work together to refine a preferred growth scenario. Early workshops focused on community values, and values such as authenticity and balanced growth came to the forefront. At later workshops, citizens played the chip game, placing chips on maps to allocate projected population and employment growth. Twenty maps were completed and later distilled into three distinct growth scenarios: 1) 1997 Plan and Subsequently Adopted Areas, 2) Growth Centers, and 3) Compact Growth. Subsequent workshops showed participants the economic, environmental, and social impacts of the alternative scenarios. Using keypad-polling technology and online surveys, participants rated the alternatives according to the values and vision developed early in the planning process. Ultimately, a preferred scenario emerged.

CommunityViz played an important role in the project by enabling many types of analysis and visualization. Near the beginning, a CommunityViz suitability analysis helped identify appropriate land uses through the evaluation of parcels and vacant undeveloped lands in terms of geologic hazards, wildlife habitats, airport noise, and more. A separate analysis was done for infill development. As alternative scenarios were created, CommunityViz helped the public meeting participants evaluate them in several ways. Build-out analysis and land-use allocation helped illustrate future development. Visualizations allowed people to "fly through" the landscape and see alternative future development patterns from several viewpoints. The fiscal and environmental impacts of each alternative were analyzed and re-analyzed dozens of times, thanks to the dynamic calculation capabilities of CommunityViz.

Figure 10.17 Greater Durango, Colorado

---
2. See http://www.orton.org/projects/durango.

Figure 10.18 Screenshot of Scenario 360 analysis showing estimated traffic according to traffic analysis zones for two scenarios

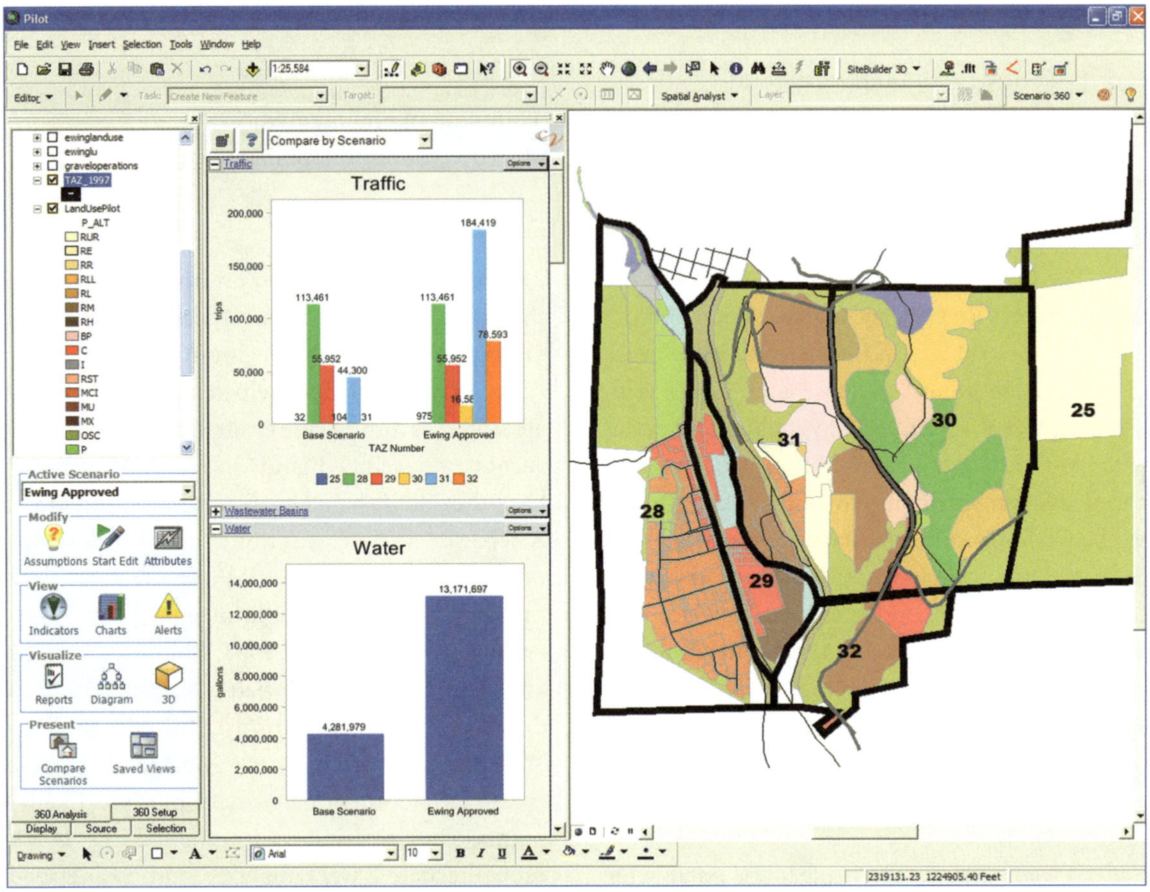

Courtesy of Donley & Associates

The model outputs included numbers of dwelling units and jobs by type, which were fed into a TransCAD model that estimated traffic impacts (see Figure 10.18). The traffic model results guided changes in land use patterns and transportation improvements.

CommunityViz was used to evaluate impacts on other infrastructure systems as well. For example, a wastewater analysis influenced densities in an outlying area. At the request of the fire authority, fire response times were analyzed (see Figure 10.19) to develop a phased plan for building new fire stations and upgrading existing ones. The revised fire station plan improved response times for new development under all three plan alternatives.

Technology and Tools: CommunityViz Scenario 360, including the Suitability, Build-Out, and Common Impacts wizards and Allocator tools, were used in the creation of the scenario framework and the undertaking of the impact analysis. Landscape visualizations were produced using CommunityViz SiteBuilder 3D, Google Earth, ArcGlobe, and ArcScene. TransCAD was used for traffic estimates based on CommunityViz calculations of jobs and housing. Network Analyst was used in the analysis of fire response times. The public was engaged extensively via a telephone survey, a project website with feedback capability, an interactive online mapping tool, a series of factsheets, and a series of workshops. At some of the workshops, keypad polling was integrated with real-time CommunityViz analysis; and at one workshop, attendees and television viewers at home could participate simultaneously in keypad polling.

Local Comprehensive Plans

> *The Durango Comp Plan project demonstrated CommunityViz's flexibility for responding to a wide range of community issues and community members' questions.*
>
> —Greg Hoch
> Director of Planning and Community Development
> Durango, Colorado

Outcomes: The comprehensive plan included some important new directions from the earlier 1997 plan, such as an increased focus on sustainability and the provision of adequate public facilities. Upon the recommendation of the planning commission, the Durango City Council adopted the plan in March 2007. The city then updated its land-use and development codes to implement the plan's growth management strategies. The city also increased its development impact fees as a result of the project's impact fee analyses. The project's fire response analysis led to a decision by the fire authority to eliminate one proposed station site and instead build stations in two other areas where greater need was projected.

Figure 10.19   *Map of estimated fire response times*

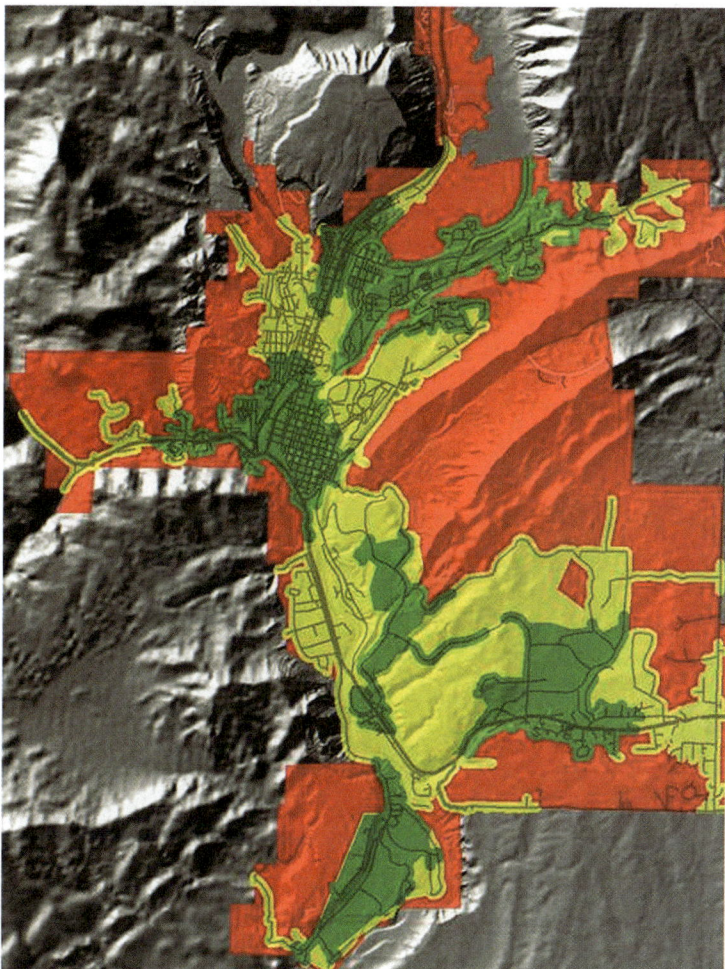

Screenshot from CommunityViz, courtesy of Donley & Associates

CASE STUDY
COMPREHENSIVE TRANSPORTATION PLAN

Location: Mooresville, North Carolina
Partners: Town of Mooresville; Kimley-Horn and Associates, Inc.; Mary Means and Associates, Inc.; North Carolina Department of Transportation

Mooresville grew from a tiny train stop in the mid-1800s, to a textile center in the early 1900s, to a fast-growing community of 27,000 people by 2007 (see Figure 10.20). By some estimates, the population was expected to double in the next 20 years. Within easy commuting distance to Charlotte, and offering amenities associated with Lake Norman, Mooresville has a mix of urban, suburban, and small-town living environments, as well as attractive locations for business and industry. Mooresville is the home of the Lowe's Corporate Campus and an expanding motor sports industry, earning it the nickname of Race City, USA.

Wisely recognizing the essential relationship between land use, urban form, and transportation decisions, the Town of Mooresville initiated three major planning projects in 2006: a comprehensive land-use plan (CLUP), a comprehensive transportation plan (CTP), and an update of its zoning ordinance. Following a suggestion by the Federal Highway Administration, the town decided to incorporate scenario planning to better link the three planning efforts.

Project Description: The town selected Kimley-Horn and Associates (KHA) to lead the development of the CTP; the study area of 130 square miles incorporated Mooresville and surrounding areas of influence. The CTP was drafted concurrently and in coordination with the CLUP project, led by Mary Means and Associates, and with the guidance of a citizens' transportation committee. The transportation and land-use project teams held two joint public workshops—the first to translate ideas and values into concrete goals, and the second to respond to plan recommendations as they were being formed (see Figure 10.21).

The transportation and land use plans emerged from a scenario planning exercise led by KHA. They first established urban form categories within a transect, which is the framework used by the Congress for the New Urbanism for organizing development patterns, intensities, and design elements in the built and natural environments. The urban form categories for Mooresville included: environmentally sensitive, rural, lakeside living, suburban, general urban, town center, and the Mount Mourne special district. Kimley-Horn and Associates used these categories to evaluate two extreme future development scenarios—a Sprawl Development scenario and a Compact Development scenario. Then KHA used CommunityViz to evaluate both alternatives and learn how the competing development alternatives would impact the efficiency of the proposed transportation system (see Figures 10.22 and 10.23).

Figure 10.20 Downtown Mooresville, North Carolina

Kimley-Horn and Associates transferred the CommunityViz outputs—dwelling units, population, and employment by type—into the 2030 Metrolina Regional Travel Demand Model to generate a comparison of daily travel characteristics across the two scenarios. The Compact Development scenario was shown to reduce congestion on major roads and increase the use of alternative modes of travel. The results served as the guiding framework for the CTP, which made detailed recommendations for investments in transportation programs, facilities, and services, and served as a key factor in the development of the future land use map included in the CLUP.

Matt Noonkester of KHA noted that by "using CommunityViz, we were able to communicate effectively with stakeholders, the advisory committee, and the general public on the inherent relationship between land use (demand), urban form (design), and transportation (supply) for improving the efficiency of the transportation system while promoting livability within the community. In addition, we were able to leverage the insights and measures of effectiveness generated through holistic analysis of competing

Figure 10.21 *A public meeting to discuss the transportation and land-use plans in Mooresville*

Courtesy of KHA

Figure 10.22 *Mooresville land-use profile being analyzed in CommunityViz*

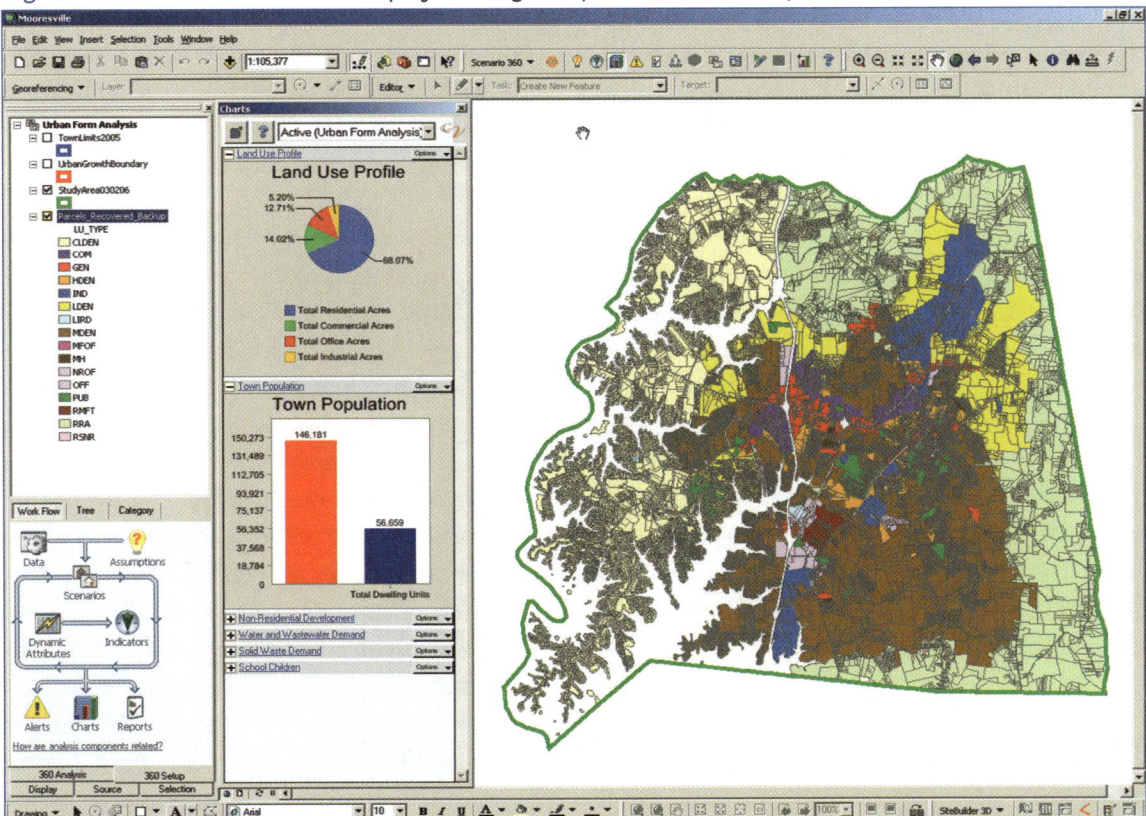

Courtesy of KHA

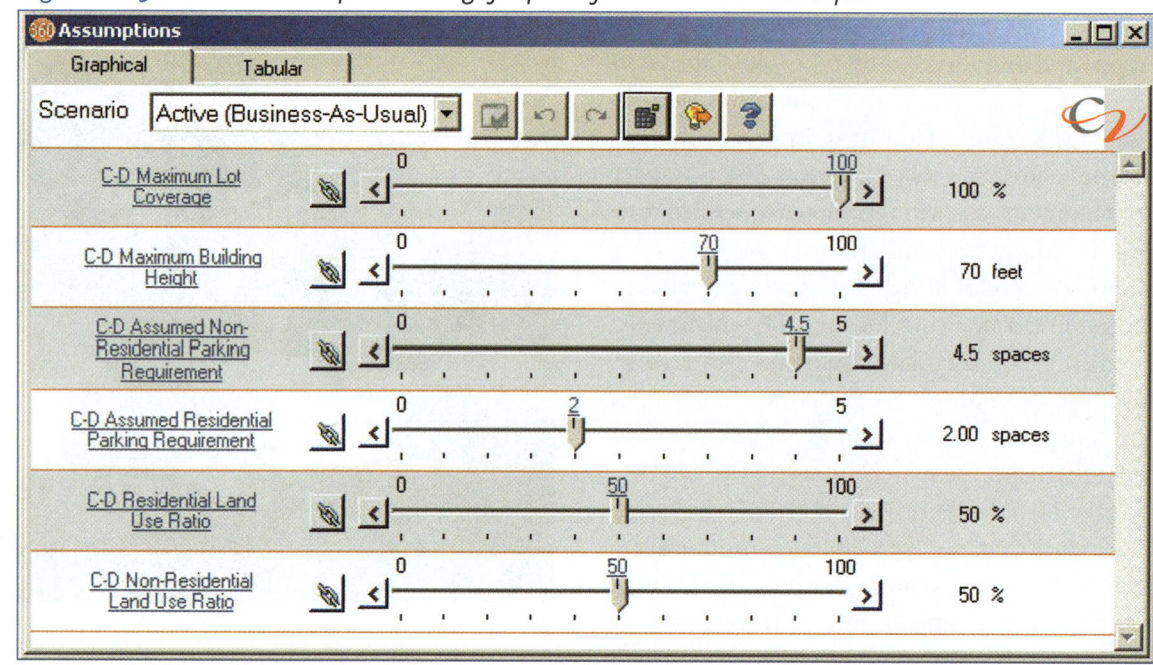

Figure 10.23 Variable assumption settings for part of the Mooresville analysis

Courtesy of KHA

development scenarios to provide mutually beneficial transportation and land use policy recommendations and implementing actions."

Technology and Tools: CommunityViz served as the platform for building and analyzing the alternative development scenarios. Tools used within CommunityViz Scenario 360 included the Suitability Wizard and Allocator. The categorizing of development patterns, intensities, and design elements observed in the built environment followed the transect advocated by the Congress for the New Urbanism. CommunityViz outputs were entered into the 2030 Metrolina Regional Travel Demand Model maintained by the Charlotte Department of Transportation. Methods to engage the public included: resource allocation surveys of members of the citizens' transportation committee and workshop participants, two project newsletters, two joint public workshops with the CLUP project, a dedicated project website, and publication of the plan on the town's website.

Outcomes: The Town of Mooresville adopted the CTP in 2007. The North Carolina Department of Transportation (NCDOT) adopted the plan maps in 2008. Mooresville adopted both the CLUP and the update of the zoning ordinance in 2008. The town started work on a series of alignment studies, as recommended in the CTP. The town is also implementing specific transportation recommendations, such as access management and development connectivity, in its review of development proposals. Kimley-Horn and Associates provided the CommunityViz model to Mooresville so that the town can maintain it and use it in future comprehensive transportation and land use planning efforts. The NCDOT is currently using the Mooresville CTP for in-house scenario planning training.

> *We were able to develop both a transportation plan and a land use plan in a way that truly made the relationships clear. CommunityViz provided the tool with which we were able to successfully bridge the two plans.*
>
> —Tim Brown
>   Director of Planning
>   Town of Mooresville, North Carolina

11 REGIONAL LAND-USE AND TRANSPORTATION PLANS

KEY CONCEPTS AND TERMS IN THIS CHAPTER

- Analysis grids
- Analysis templates
- Scale-changing formulas
- Sketch tools, including Palette, Painter, and Clone
- Traffic analysis zones (TAZs)

Transportation planning and land-use planning often go hand in hand at the regional or metropolitan scale. Each type of planning influences the other because growth tends to follow transportation networks, while transportation networks try to anticipate growth. Planning horizons are long, often 20 years or more, and the study areas are large. This chapter describes CommunityViz techniques and tools that are unique to regional land-use and transportation analyses. Figure 11.1 summarizes these and other regional plans and describes how CommunityViz supports them.

WHY AND WHEN

The drafting or updating of a regional transportation or land-use plan is the responsibility of a regional planning agency such as a council of governments, regional planning commission, or Metropolitan Planning Organization. Each plan update involves a major effort that may take years to complete. CommunityViz can play an important role in the drafting or updating of a regional land use plan or transportation plan. But for a detailed transportation study you will also need a travel-demand modeling tool and perhaps additional external models.

For transportation planning, CommunityViz is most helpful near the beginning of the process, when planners are considering general alternatives and sketching out possibilities. CommunityViz is a decision-support tool, not an engineering tool, so its strengths are in geodesign, visual communication, sketching, and rapid assessment of broad alternatives. After using CommunityViz to narrow your options, you can use more specialized transportation modeling tools for detailed assessment.

DATA NEEDS

In addition to current population and land-use data and a projection of future population, to draft a regional transportation plan you usually need data on:

- **Traffic analysis zones (TAZs),** or their equivalent. These are irregularly shaped areas whose sizes vary, but a typical TAZ has a population of up to about 3,000 and can range in size from a city block to a large area of rural land. A TAZ should share outer boundaries with specific land parcels, rather than cut through parcels. The TAZs' aggregate travel demand is used in transportation models.

- **Existing and proposed transportation networks** including roads, passenger rail, freight rail, bus, bike, and pedestrian routes, and any other important transportation modes.

- **Network access points** such as transit stops or highway interchanges.

In addition, it's often helpful to have the following, if readily available:

- **Data on pedestrian networks** and barriers near transit stops, as a measure of accessibility.

Figure 11.1 Regional plans supported by CommunityViz

TYPE OF REGIONAL PLAN	TYPICAL COMMUNITYVIZ SUPPORT APPLICATIONS
Long-Range Transportation Plan	■ Estimation of development growth patterns and future trip demand ■ Sketching and quick evaluation of transportation alternatives to narrow options for further study ■ Creation of sustainability and performance indicators including energy, environmental management, and community values ■ Accessibility analysis including walkability measures, populations served by proposed infrastructure, and 4D (density, diversity, design, and destinations) assessment *Comment: Often used in conjunction with a travel-demand model or transportation design and engineering tools.*
Regional Comprehensive Plan	■ Local plan consolidation and summarizing ■ Scenario analysis ■ Estimation of development growth patterns ■ Public engagement ■ The creation of indicators ■ Implementation of monitoring targets and indicators *Comment: Similar to local comprehensive plans (see Chapter 10).*
Regional Resource and Watershed Plan	■ Watershed planning, including estimation of impervious surfaces and water-quality impacts ■ Landscape fragmentation analysis ■ The setting of land conservation and preservation priorities ■ Strategic conservation planning ■ Resource utilization estimation *Comment: Can be used in conjunction with resource-modeling tools such as N-SPECT (for water quality) or NatureServe Vista (for biodiversity).*
Housing Plan	■ Spatial assessment of existing conditions and trends, such as cost distribution and job access ■ Planning for housing mix, inclusionary zoning, infill, specialized housing such as single-room occupancy and accessory apartments, etc. ■ Year-by-year growth and change analysis ■ Location desirability and suitability analysis *Comment: Strongest advantage is for spatial analysis; use in conjunction with conventional nonspatial tools.*
Regional Centers and Neighborhood Development Planning	■ Site suitability and location analysis for proposed centers ■ LEED certification checklist assessment ■ Studies of regional effects of urban growth boundaries, community area plans, and smart-growth concept plans
Regional Trails and Pathways	■ Assessment of route scenarios with scenario analysis and indicators *Comment: Well supported by regional 3-D visualization (see Chapter 6).*
Parks and Open Space Planning	■ Location suitability and value analysis ■ Site selection ■ Site planning *Comments: The Scenario 360 Optimizer can help you choose the best combination of candidate sites to fit a given budget. Suitability weighting factors provide a good mechanism for honoring the public's subjective preferences for park locations.*

- **Network type and routing data** for each transportation network. These are technical data that specify information such as how network routes connect to one another and how long it takes to travel a given segment. If you have this information, you can use it with the Network Analyst extension to do more accurate travel calculations.

- **Road lanes data**

- **Approximate cost information,** including construction and maintenance costs, for routes and nodes of all major transportation modes you are considering. This would include, for example, the cost per mile of light-rail tracks and the cost of a light-rail station.

- **Existing** comprehensive and strategic land-use or transportation plans for local jurisdictions, such as enterprise zones.

It is often difficult to obtain consistent data across the many jurisdictions within a region. Be prepared to spend time reclassifying land-use designations into a single common system, hand digitizing missing data such as existing land uses, or sifting through large libraries to find data for all parts of the region.

In some cases, the challenge is that you have *too much* data. At the early stages of the project, you want to work at a scale that allows fast analysis of many alternatives and you do not want to commit too many of your resources to data management or computer processing. Your goal is a regional umbrella plan, not a compendium of detailed local plans. Usually, instead of using small analysis polygons such as parcels or census blocks, you will want to use larger analysis polygons such as traffic analysis zones or an analysis grid.

COMMUNITYVIZ TOOLS

Regional plans are intended to guide plan implementation at both the local and regional levels. Therefore, regional plans need to reflect local conditions, needs, and intentions. CommunityViz provides several tools that are useful for working across and between jurisdictions.

ANALYSIS TEMPLATES

Creating a Scenario 360 analysis template enables you to reuse some or all of an analysis to analyze different data. If you are a regional planner, for example, and you create a custom analysis for urban shade trees in one of your member cities, you can reapply the same model to other cities in the region by using a template. The template stores all of the model's formulas, assumptions, charts, and other components in a special file format. To create a template, you create an analysis and then specify the components you want to include in the template. To use the template, you start a new analysis with fresh data and then apply the template.

Template files are completely portable, and you can share them with any other CommunityViz user. They are easy to share when the sender and receiver are using the same names for data layers and attributes, but there are options for translating between names. In regions where formats for some data types are consistent across jurisdictions, you can create a single model at the regional level and then provide the model to member jurisdictions.

SCALE-CHANGING FORMULA FUNCTIONS

Scenario 360 provides more than a dozen functions you can use to move data from a large scale to a small scale, or vice versa. In addition, you can write multifunction formulas that move data between layers in more complicated ways. Here is a list of commonly used scale-changing functions:

- CenterContains
- Contains
- Get . . . Where
- GetFromClosest
- GridOverlap
- Intersects
- IsCenterContainedIn
- IsContainedIn
- OverlapArea
- OverlapLength
- OverlapMost
- OverlapSum
- OverlapWeightedAverage.

Moving from a small scale (large polygons) to a large scale (small polygons) is usually straightforward except at the boundaries between large polygons: The smaller polygons simply take on the attributes of the larger polygons they lie within. Where one small polygon straddles two large polygons, you have to decide whether the small polygon will acquire the attributes of one large polygon, or the other, or some combined value of the two.

Moving in the other direction—from small polygons to large ones—often requires more judgment and analysis. For example, does a 100-acre analysis grid cell count as developed if it contains a single developed 1-acre parcel? What if it contains 50 developed parcels but they are small and clustered into one corner of the larger cell? To answer these questions, think carefully about the goals of the overall analysis and the decisions you are trying to support. Design an approach that gives you enough good information to make informed decisions, as described in Chapter 1. You can expect to lose some precision as you move from smaller polygons to larger ones.

You have five basic approaches to choose from:

- **Binary choice,** in which the larger polygon takes on the attributes of a single smaller polygon based on rules such as "largest" or "most." In the example above, you might decide to use a rule that the larger polygon counts as undeveloped unless it contains at least five developed parcels.

- **Blended choice,** in which the larger polygon takes on attribute values that are averages or other statistical combinations of all the smaller polygons. In the same example, you might calculate that the larger polygon is "5 percent developed."

- **Multiple-attribute tracking,** in which you use several different attributes in the larger polygon to keep track of different values of single attributes in the smaller polygons (see Figure 11.2). For example, you might give the larger polygon one attribute that specifies the number of developed parcels it contains, another attribute that specifies the number of undeveloped parcels it contains, and perhaps a third that specifies the number of parcels it contains that are designated as conservation lands.

- **Intermediate processing,** in which you perform a procedure or calculation on the smaller polygons to produce data that are easier to use for larger polygons. One example is when the attribute values of the small polygons are reclassified into a larger category—for example, several detailed residential land-use types could be reclassified into a single type called "low-density residential." This procedure sometimes makes it more attractive to run a subsequent binary-choice or blended-choice process. Another example of intermediate processing is the capturing of important spatial relationships within the large polygon. For instance, if it is important to know whether developed parcels are clustered together or spread apart, a simple way to measure this is to create a thin merged buffer around the small polygons. Within each large polygon, calculate the area of the buffer and divide it by the area of the small polygons. A higher ratio will mean less clustering of developed parcels.

- **Accessory analysis,** in which you analyze certain layers or attributes in their natural, high-resolution form without attempting to abstract their properties to the large-polygon level. There is nothing wrong with combining this approach with the others, and it's a sensible choice when your analysis requires precision that you would otherwise lose. Common examples of layers that need accessory analysis include transit networks and hubs, boundaries and coastlines, and important points such as hazardous waste sites or historic buildings.

Figure 11.2   Illustration of multiple-attribute tracking

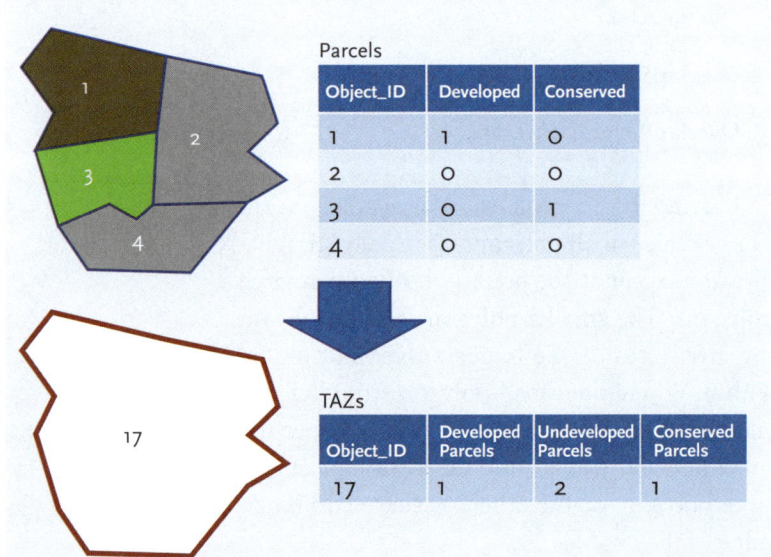

SKETCH TOOLS

Scenario 360's Sketch tools provide efficient ways to apply data to maps, create scenarios, and perform geodesign at the regional scale. With the Sketch tool Painter, you can apply any number of preset attribute values to existing features. You can use the Sketch tool Clone to apply copies of a particular shape, along with its specified attribute values. These tools complement the ArcMap Sketch tools and ArcSketch.

The Painter tool is commonly used to create and apply neighborhood types to existing analysis polygons. You start by setting up several styles, which are collections of attribute values that appear on the Sketch tools palette. A mixed use style, for example, might include attributes specifying commercial and residential densities, sidewalk ratios, parking ratios, energy use, traffic generation, and the number of civic buildings. If you are working with form-based codes, a style corresponds to transects or areas of the regulating plan, and the attributes specify building form standards. When you paint a polygon on the map with that style, its corresponding attributes are updated.

Painting can speed up data processing because you can precalculate many of the attribute values you will use. This advantage is particularly pronounced if you are working with an analysis grid that uses uniformly sized cells, which allows you to switch from area-dependent ratios to actual numbers and counts. For example, painting a medium-density residential style on 10-acre grid squares allows you to paint the number of dwelling units, population, water use, and many other attributes at the same time, with no further calculation. Keep in mind, however, that any good plan takes context into account, and therefore painting still requires at least some real-time spatial and numeric calculations.

The Clone tool enables you to create a palette of custom shapes that often have preset attribute values. At the regional scale, the most common application of cloning is sketching analysis shapes such as five-minute walk circles. For example, a clone shape called "transit hub" might come in the shape of a circle with a quarter-mile radius and might contain attributes such as construction cost, maintenance cost, and energy use. You could use it to sketch a series of proposed transit stations and then let the analysis calculate indicators of total costs, total energy use, and total population served.

LINKING TO EXTERNAL MODELS

With Scenario 360's External Table Links, you can connect your analysis to transportation modeling tools, travel demand models, and other regional planning tools. Chapters 4 and 15 provide details on these capabilities.

ANALYSIS GRIDS

Analysis grids are sometimes particularly useful at the regional scale. They are polygon layers that you construct as a framework for aggregating or disaggregating data and conducting an analysis. The simplest analysis grids consist of uniform squares, but you can also make more complex structures. One of the main advantages is that you can make the cells any size, so you can set the scale of analysis to the level of resolution you need. In urban areas, for example, you might use cells that are a few acres each, while in rural areas you might use cells of 100 acres or more. Once you have created the grid, you can use CommunityViz scale-changing functions such as OverlapWeightedAverage and GetFromClosest to populate each grid cell with attribute data from the underlying layers.

To make an analysis grid—also known as a fishnet—use ArcGIS geoprocessing tools or commonly available GIS utilities.

While many modeling tools use grids, CommunityViz is unusual in that it can easily work with mixed-sized grid cells (see Figure 11.3). A model whose calculations are based on quantities per grid cell, such as population or building count, needs to have uniformly sized grid cells. But in CommunityViz, you can do the same calculations based on quantities per unit area—for example, per acre. You calculate the quantity for each grid cell, and then you divide it by that grid cell's area using a simple dynamic attribute formula. This works with any size or shape of grid cell, but to maintain simplicity, experienced practitioners tend to prefer to use square cells and restrict themselves to only two or three sizes per analysis.

Figure 11.3 Analysis grid with mixed-sized grid cells. The dark area is more densely developed.

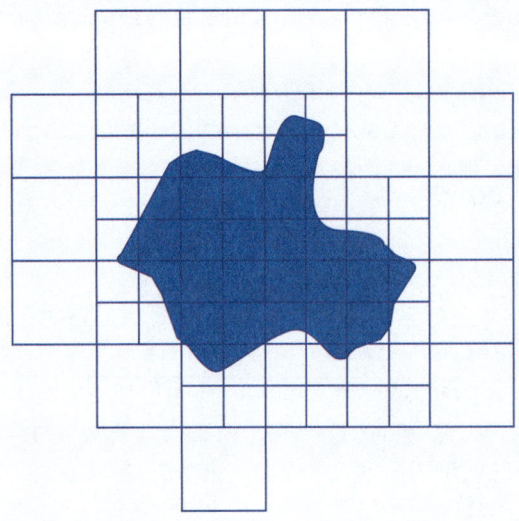

The primary reason you would create a mixed-sized grid is if your region has large variations in density or complexity. You want small cells in the dense areas, to provide sufficient resolution; and you want large cells in rural areas, to reduce the total cell count. Here is one method for creating an efficient mixed-sized grid in which each grid cell is a square in one of two sizes:

1. Create two uniform grid layers covering the entire study area: one with large square cells, and one with small square cells. Make sure the small square cells nest perfectly in the large square cells.

2. Sketch or otherwise develop a new polygon layer representing the areas that need small cells. This might be, for example, the city boundaries within a region.

3. Start editing the large-cell layer. Use ArcGIS selection tools to select the large cells that overlap the boundary polygon and delete them.

4. Start editing the small-cell layer. Select the small cells that overlap the remaining large cells and delete them. (Be sure to do steps 3 and 4 in this order. Starting with small cells can lead to gaps or overlaps.)

5. Merge the small-cell layer and the large-cell layer into a single analysis grid using the ArcMap Merge tool. Make sure the resulting layer has a projected coordinate system.

On some occasions, an analysis grid can increase, rather than decrease, the resolution of your study. Figure 11.4 demonstrates this point. It shows an analysis of walking distance to bus stops, which are designated by small purple dots. In the left-hand panel, the large parcel on the east is yellow, indicating excellent access to bus stops. The analysis yields this conclusion because it is measuring the shortest distance from any vertex on the parcel to any bus stop, and indeed the western boundary of the parcel is close to several bus stops. However, the parcel is well over one mile wide, so many parts of it are too far from a bus stop for residents to walk. The right-hand panel shows the same analysis using five-acre grid squares, which show a more accurate and useful result.

Figure 11.4 Side-by-side comparison of a distance-to-transit analysis, with and without grid cells

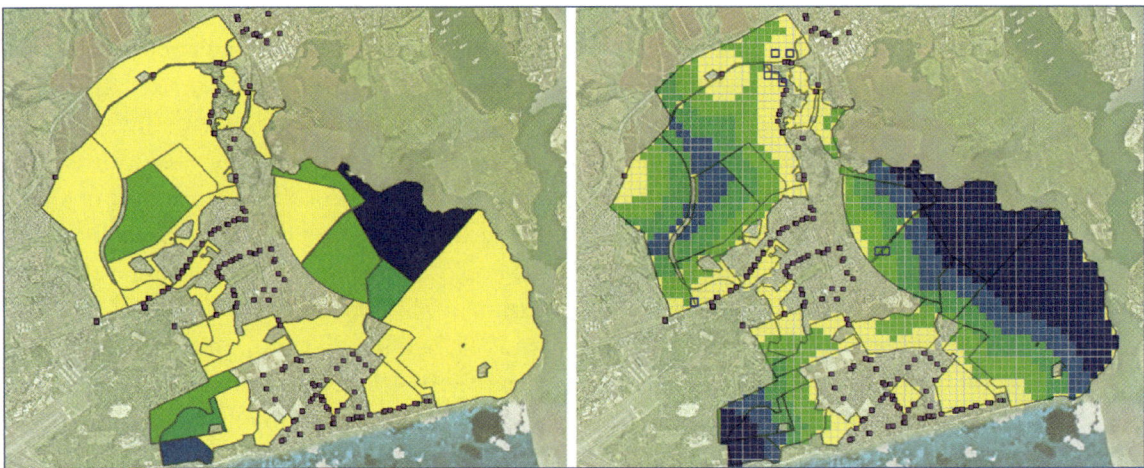

TEACHING EXAMPLE

This example is based on a regional transportation planning study of the interactions among transportation, land use, and environmental conservation in a study area covering two counties with a combined population of about 700,000 people. The population was expected to grow to more than 1 million during the 30-year planning period. We studied three scenarios: Business as Usual; an Enhanced Transit scenario, which tried to optimize regional transportation; and a Conservation scenario, which placed priority on protecting environmentally sensitive lands.

We used TAZ polygons as our primary analysis layer (see Figure 11.5), but we also did some work at the parcel level when required. As you can see, the area included both urban and rural areas, resulting in large variations in the size of the TAZs.

The existing urban zoning maps were too complex to use at a regional level. We reclassified about 25 urban zoning districts into five more general designations (see Figure 11.6).

We had a starting point for the Enhanced Transit scenario (see Figure 11.7) from a feasibility study that had already been done on potential light rail and bus rapid transit (BRT) in the two urban areas.

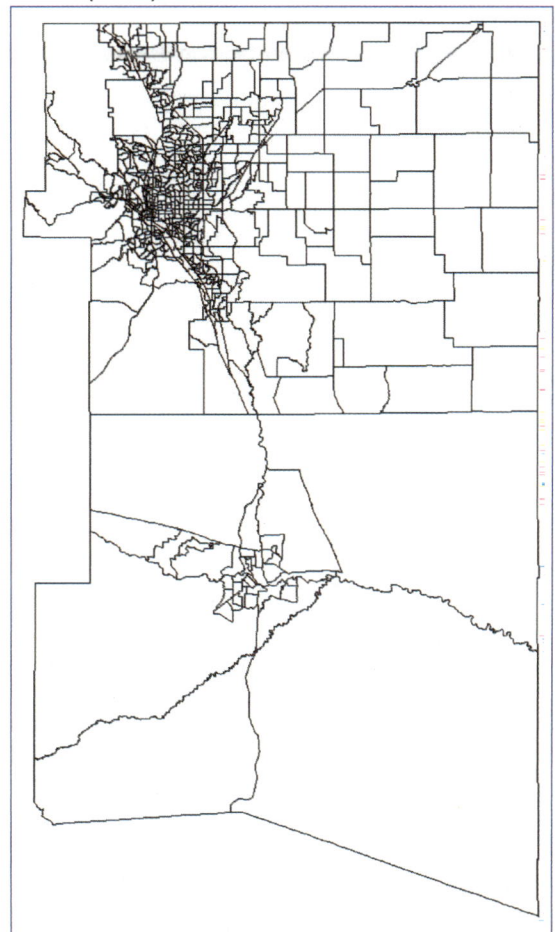

Figure 11.5 Study area showing Traffic Analysis Zones (TAZs)

Figure 11.6 Simplifying zoning classifications

Figure 11.7 Enhanced Transit feasibility study

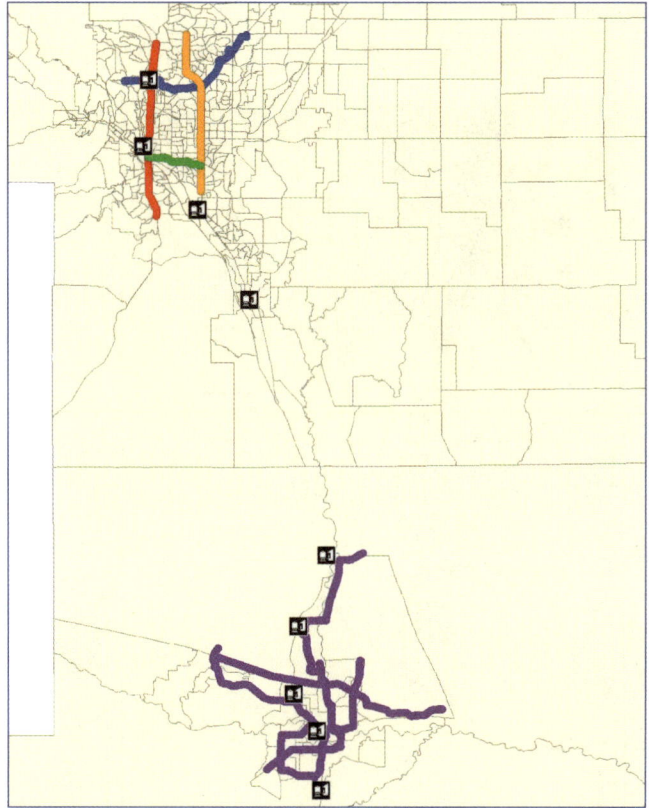

Figure 11.8 Zoning changes for Enhanced Transit

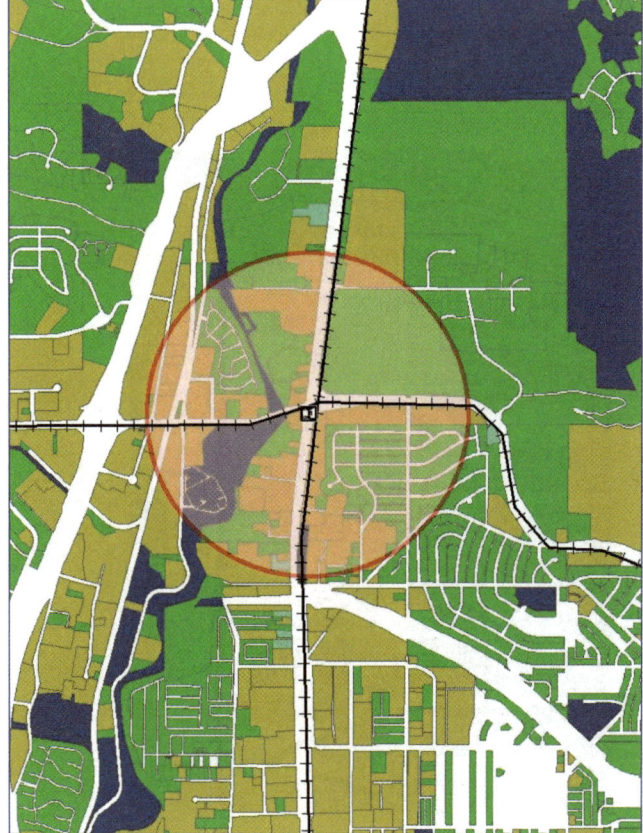

Our focus was on BRT, but we could have done a similar analysis for light rail as well. Using bus route maps and stations as starting points, we sketched density increases along the proposed routes (see Figure 11.8). Specifically, we increased density to an average of 15 dwelling units per acre within a half-mile circle of each bus station, and to 10 dwelling units per acre along the route corridors. We wanted people who were working with the analysis to be able to change designated stations and routes, so we used a combination of Sketch tools and analysis formulas. For stations, we made a new layer called Stations and a clone shape that was a simple circle of the correct size. We set the ArcMap Editor tools to place the centers of our circles onto existing roads (see Figure 11.8). For routes, we made a new attribute called "BRT" in the roads layer. Then we made a Sketch style called "BRT" that set the value to 1. We made another sketch style called "Not BRT" that set the value to 0 in case anyone wanted to erase BRT. Finally, we made a new dynamic attribute in the zones layer that we called "New Zoning." The formula for New Zoning set density to 15 dwelling units per acre if the zone was contained in a Stations feature; to 10 dwelling units per acre if the zone's distance to the nearest BRT route was less than 1,000 feet; and to the old density specification otherwise.

Creating the initial Conservation scenario was straightforward. We used data from an external assessment to select land areas that were particularly sensitive, and we simply redesignated the associated parcels as unbuildable.

Growth modeling came next. We took the region's 30-year population forecast as a given, and we focused our modeling efforts on the pattern of growth. To begin, we used the Suitability Wizard to create a desirability map that accounted for these factors:

- Downtown centers
- Planned unit developments (PUDs)
- Road density
- Conservation areas
- Employment centers

Figure 11.9 Desirability map (lighter colors show areas that are more desirable for development)

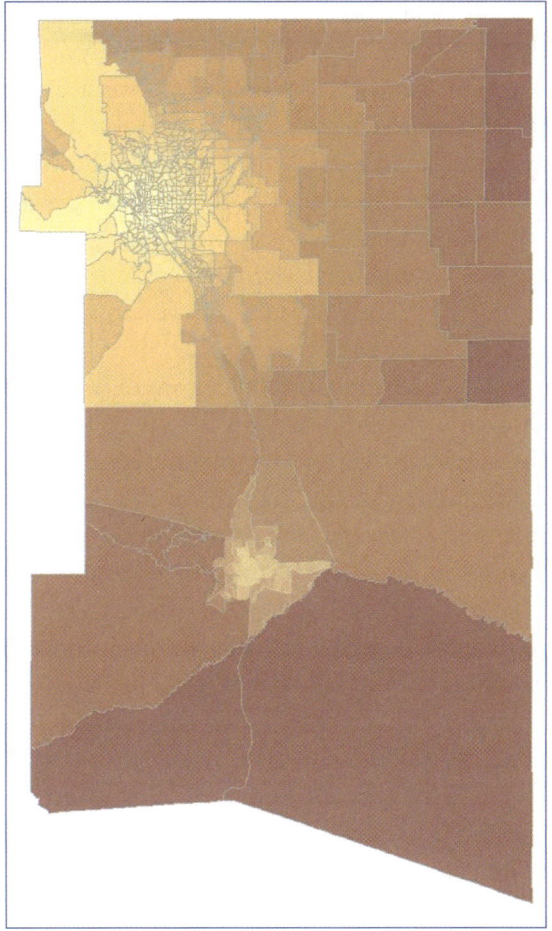

Figure 11.10 A development desirability map with areas unsuitable for development shown in black

- Open space
- Existing households
- Transportation stops and corridors

Usually, each of these factors would have the same weight across scenarios, but in this study we assumed that planners could use an array of policy incentives to encourage or discourage growth in different areas. Therefore, in the Enhanced Transit scenario, we placed extra weight on transportation stops and corridors to reflect the idea that incentives would make those areas more desirable for residential development. Figure 11.9 shows the resulting desirability map.

Next, we excluded areas that were unsuitable for development, including water bodies, road rights-of-way, conserved lands, and slopes of 10 degrees or more. This part of the work exposed a common challenge of regional planning: We had too much data. The terrain data we were using for slopes had half-meter resolution, which resulted in a very large data set for covering the entire region. Although it would have been possible to use the data in that form, we chose to use Spatial Analyst tools to create a lower-resolution terrain that was easier to work with. The resulting map appears in Figure 11.10.

We planned to use the Scenario 360 Allocator to distribute population growth across the map based on desirability scores we had just calculated and the capacity allowed by zoning. But we wanted to take into account two more considerations. One consideration was that the population forecast specified different growth rates for the two counties. The other was that a developer had announced plans to create a very large PUD with space for more than 180,000

Figure 11.11 Comparison of the growth patterns of two scenarios

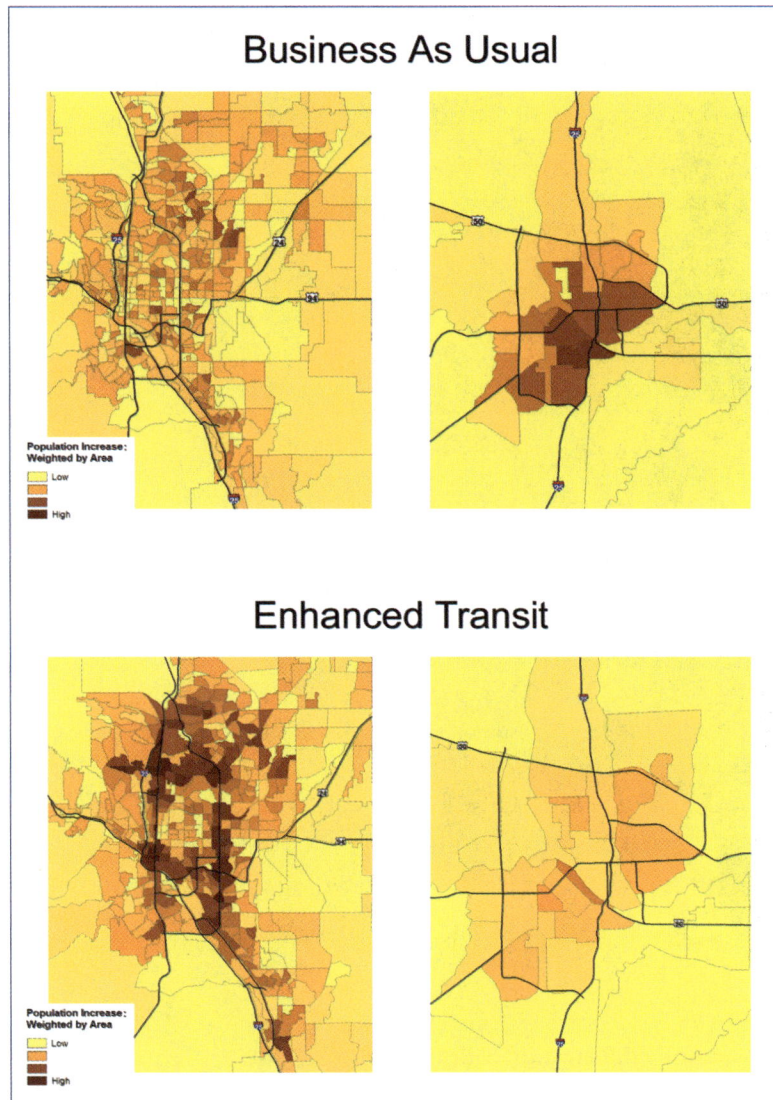

people. The proposed PUD had not been considered during the most recent population forecast work, and it did not lie within a highly desirable area according to our analysis. In consultation with local planners, we decided to assume that a) the PUD would not attract any additional growth to the region, but that b) it *would* capture part of the baseline growth and it would fill up by the end of the planning period. We removed 180,000 people from the population demand, and then we ran separate allocations for each county.

The resulting projected growth patterns showed differences among the scenarios, but the contrasts were not immediately obvious from looking at the maps. The problem was that the TAZs were very different sizes, so small changes in rural TAZs tended to look more significant than large changes in urban TAZs. We resolved this problem by zooming in on the urban areas and coloring the maps based on population increase weighted by area (see Figure 11.11).

Regional planning requires the ability to work across scales, jurisdictions, and disciplines to build an overarching plan. This project demonstrates how planners can use CommunityViz in a regional plan to span local and regional scales, work across jurisdictions, and integrate transportation and land-use planning.

CASE STUDY
LAND USE AND TRANSPORTATION INTEGRATION

Location: Greater Nashville, Tennessee
Partners: Nashville Area Metropolitan Planning Organization; Kimley-Horn and Associates, Inc.

The Nashville Area Metropolitan Planning Organization (MPO) is responsible for transportation planning in five counties plus parts of two other counties in central Tennessee. The MPO covers an area of approximately 2,900 square miles and is home to about 1.3 million people. The area is growing rapidly both in population and employment, with projected population growth in the seven-county area of approximately 17 percent between 2008 and 2015, and employment growth of about 11 percent during that same period.

In 2009, the MPO updated its long-range transportation plan. The MPO wanted to achieve a close linkage between transportation planning and land-use planning. Achieving this linkage required increasing the accuracy of the regional travel demand model for generating population and employment data, and allocating growth across the seven-county area. The MPO also wanted a robust database that would allow for convenient updates, support alternative land-use scenario planning and long-term visioning, and enable the MPO to work in partnership with the local member jurisdictions.

Project Description: The MPO retained Kimley-Horn and Associates (KHA) to develop a spatial data-planning framework to forecast development patterns together with socioeconomic data. Kimley-Horn and Associates used CommunityViz's mapping and data analysis component, Scenario 360, to evaluate competing build-out scenarios for the region, based on the carrying capacity of the land and policies that would guide future growth and development.

Data for the project included population and employment projections, census population estimates, available zoning maps and ordinances for each city and county in the planning area, available growth management plans, tax assessor data for the seven counties, and information from focus group meetings. The model used data for the region at the parcel level and allowed local governments to modify the model as needed. In order to process the large amount of data efficiently, seven micro models were created, one for each county.

Kimley-Horn and Associates used a three-step CommunityViz-based allocation model for growth. To estimate the amount of land available for development, they analyzed the carrying capacity of the land, taking into consideration constraints on development and areas of conflict for development. This resulted in an estimate of build-out potential for each micro model as measured by the number of dwelling units, retail gross square footage, office gross square footage, and industrial gross square footage supported by each of the parcels. Next, KHA analyzed the desirability of each parcel by assessing the physical features and proximity to roads, transit, and parks. They used supply, desirability, and demand (based on population and employment forecasts) to allocate projected population and employment by parcel, and created a development suitability map (see Figure 11.11).

Kimley-Horn and Associates selected the CommunityViz probability-based allocation method, which operates on the premise that the capacity of a parcel is used in proportion to its relative desirability. The information generated was aggregated up to the TAZ level for use in the macro area model for the planning horizon years of 2015, 2025, and 2035. The final step translated the results for input into the regional travel demand model.

Figure 11.11 *Development suitability map for Greater Nashville*

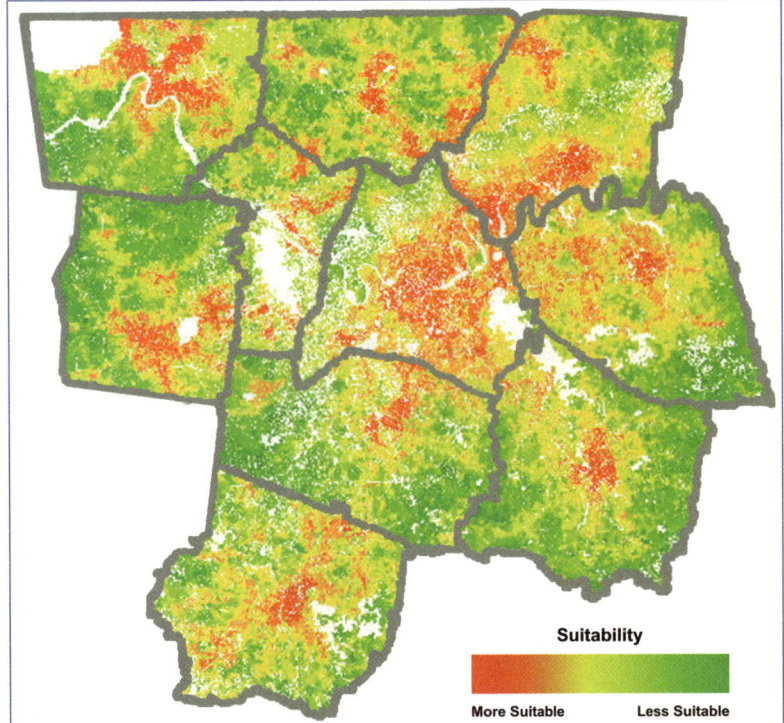

Technology and Tools: Kimley-Horn and Associates relied on CommunityViz to develop the spatial data planning framework and to forecast development patterns and intensities and socioeconomic data. The Allocator tool within CommunityViz helped KHA set up a supply-demand allocation based on a parcel's capacity and desirability features. The MPO will use TransCAD with the TAZ-level data to produce the regional travel demand model.

Outcomes: The MPO has become a data clearinghouse for GIS data, which has increased the interaction on land use planning issues between the MPO and its member communities. The growth model is now in the hands of the MPO, and it will be updated as new land use data become available. The MPO will loan out the growth model for use by county planners as they update their counties' growth management plans. The MPO is also expanding the growth model to include counties served by Cumberland Region Tomorrow, a nonprofit organization that encourages planning for growth management across a 10-county area of Tennessee.

Regional Land-Use and Transportation Plans

CASE STUDY: REGIONAL VISION

Location: Washington County, Utah
Partners: Washington County; Envision Utah; Winston Associates; Foresee Consulting, Inc.

Washington County, in Utah's southwest corner, is known as Utah's Dixie. This Sunbelt county nearly doubled in population in each of the three decades between 1970 and 2000, and according to some estimates, the population may triple in the next 30 years. Faced with growing concerns about the future, and spurred on by discussions about a proposed federal Washington County Growth and Conservation Act, Washington County decided to develop a regional vision that would maintain quality of life and ensure an affordable future.

Vision Dixie was about making choices, and the project used scenario planning at a big-picture scale to help people understand the consequences of present-day actions. Guided by a diverse steering committee and benefiting from the input of more than 3,000 residents, the project resulted in a set of Vision Dixie Principles and a Vision Scenario. The principles and vision scenario created a framework for voluntary implementation, which has been guiding elected local officials and residents as they make critical decisions about their local plans, development regulations, and development proposals.

Project Description: Vision Dixie engaged Envision Utah, which teamed with Winston Associates and others, to design and facilitate a series of public meetings and workshops. The project enjoyed extensive public input and media attention from its inception in October 2006. More than 1,200 residents attended 13 workshops to voice their ideas about how the county should grow. In addition to group discussions and keypad polling, participants engaged in a chip game by placing chips on large maps to represent development (see Figure 11.12).

The project team used an array of geographic, socioeconomic, and regulatory data to develop a baseline scenario founded on existing municipal plans, and three alternative scenarios reflecting the input of residents. They used CommunityViz throughout the process to evaluate desired development patterns (see Figure 11.13), allocate homes and employment,

Figure 11.12 A chip game in progress

Images courtesy of Winston Associates and Foresee Consultation

Figure 11.13 Map of development probability (in red) and public land conservation potential (in light blue)

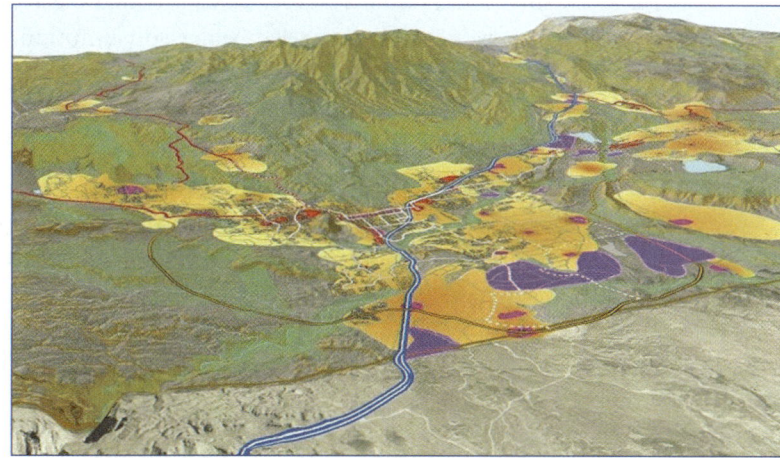

Figure 11.14 *Sample indicator charts showing land consumption and jobs within walking distance of transit for four scenarios*

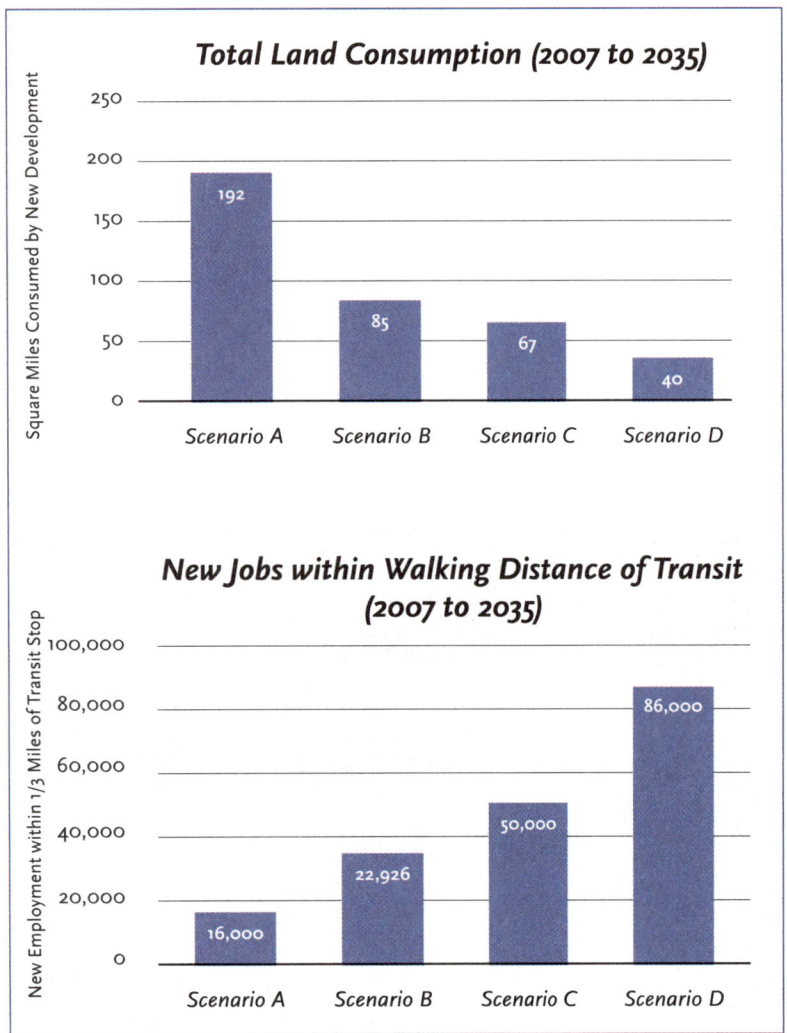

and conduct a variety of impact analyses for all four scenarios (see Figure 11.14). The impact analyses included measures of the compactness of development, land consumption, impact on sensitive land, amount of infill development, housing mix, vehicle miles traveled, water consumption, housing affordability, and impact on farmland.

In the spring of 2007, more than 500 residents attended one of nine Dixie Dialogue meetings, where they again used group discussion and keypad polling to respond to the scenarios and impact information. Another 800 residents evaluated the scenarios online. Hard copies of the scenarios were printed and widely distributed, and an independent polling firm conducted telephone interviews to gather additional opinions on growth issues and strategies. Based on all of these inputs, the steering committee developed 10 Vision Dixie Principles, as well as a Vision Scenario to illustrate one way the county might grow in line with these principles.

Technology and Tools: Winston Associates used CommunityViz Scenario 360 to evaluate development pressures, allocate development, and analyze impacts. They also used ArcGlobe, ArcScene, SketchUp, Google Earth and Winston's Vizhen for visualizations. At the same time, Envision Utah used its IMPACS (Integrated Model for Planning and Cost Scenarios) tool to identify water demands and localized infrastructure costs associated with growth. The public was engaged through a series of workshops and meetings, a chip game exercise, keypad polling, an interactive website with online scenario feedback, and an independent telephone survey.

Outcomes: While on-the-ground action will take a number of years to unfold, Vision Dixie is already influencing planning policy at several levels. The county commissioners formally adopted the final report, "2007 Vision Dixie, Making a Better Washington County," in 2008. The Vision Dixie Implementation Committee—composed of a county commissioner, two mayors, the executive director of the Five County Association of Governments, and a citizen representative—was formed and has met with each of the 15 municipalities in the county to present the Vision Dixie project and principles. By mid-2009, about one-third of the municipalities had adopted the principles. A participant in the Vision Dixie project raised funds to form a new nonprofit organization, FormTomorrow, to provide nuts-and-bolts planning support to local communities in concert with the Vision Dixie principles. At the federal level, the Washington County Growth and Conservation Act was passed by Congress in early 2009 and was signed into law by President Obama. The act designated hundreds of thousands of acres of land around Zion National Park as wilderness area, created two new national conservation areas, and requires consultation between the federal government and the county on any proposed land development.

12 SITE SELECTION AND ASSESSMENT

KEY CONCEPTS AND TERMS IN THIS CHAPTER

- Categories
- Land Evaluation and Site Assessment (LESA)
- Leadership in Energy and Environmental Design (LEED) and Smart Locations
- Suitability Wizard
- Weighting factors and location factors

CommunityViz provides a rich set of tools to answer questions such as: Where is the best site for a particular project? Where are people or resources most vulnerable to hazards? Where will growth occur over time? This chapter describes how to use the CommunityViz Suitability Wizard and other tools to help decision makers plan where to locate development and choose which lands to protect from development.

Suitability analysis is the determination of which sites meet certain criteria for development or have physical constraints that restrict development. Suitability usually refers to the assessment and selection of particular sites in a study area. But suitability analysis can also be used for hazard assessment, vulnerability assessment, desirability assessment, or identifying lands for conservation.

In suitability analysis, a *suitability score* is assigned to each location under consideration for development. First, scores are assigned for a number of factors at each location, such as its cost, size, physical limitations such as steep slopes, and proximity to other sites. The scoring system allows you to emphasize some factors over others by assigning them a higher weighting. For example, the location of a site may be twice as important and have twice the weighting than the size of a site. The score for a factor is the factor's assigned score times its weighting. By combining the score for each factor, you arrive at the location's suitability score.

Suitability analysis has its roots in overlay analysis, a technique pioneered in the 1960s by University of Pennsylvania professor Ian McHarg, who drew individual map layers of environmental features on transparent Mylar sheets and then placed the maps on top of one another. Modern GIS systems are descended from McHarg's layers approach. Students of GIS often learn a form of suitability analysis in which a number of raster layers—soils, topography, water, wildlife habitats, and vegetation—are overlaid on one another to produce a new composite suitability layer. The CommunityViz approach is similar in concept, but it uses attribute values in a single layer rather than multiple raster layers. As a result, in CommunityViz it is easier to make changes and to give different weightings for factors in a suitability analysis. In addition, CommunityViz allows for a much broader range of suitability considerations besides simple overlays, such as cost and proximity.

WHY AND WHEN

You can use suitability analysis on its own and as part of other analyses. Here are some of its most common applications:

- Selection of sites for development projects
- Ranking of parcels for development suitability, conservation value, or hazard risk
- Ranking of the development desirability of parcels as part of an analysis to project future growth patterns.

You can do a suitability analysis at any time. All you need to begin is a layer containing features representing sites whose suitability you want to study.

SUITABILITY CONCEPTS

CommunityViz suitability analysis assigns a suitability score to each site you are considering. The suitability score is a dynamic attribute based on Scenario 360 formulas: changing the formula, weighting of a factor, or the assigned factor scores, can instantly change the score. Often the score is a number between 0 (not at all suitable) and 100 (most suitable), though you can use other scales.

A site's suitability score comes from how a Scenario 360 formula combines the site's assigned scores and weightings for several factors. As an analogy, think of how a student's grade point average is calculated: The factor scores are like the student's grades in each subject, the weighting for each factor score is like the number of credits the course is worth, and the suitability score is like the student's GPA.

In the example in Figures 12.1 and 12.2, the site received a score of 25 on the cost factor, a score of 75 on the accessibility factor, and a score of 50 on the hazard factor. The overall score, however, is usually not just a simple average of the factor scores. Some factors can be weighted more heavily than others. Weightings are usually changeable assumptions, and changing the weighting changes the overall suitability scores. Figure 12.1 shows that the overall score is 50 if cost, accessibility, and hazard are all weighted equally.

But if accessibility has a weight of 8 out of 10, and cost and hazard each have a weight of only 2 out of 10, the overall suitability score is 62.5 (see Figure 12.2). The formula for the overall score is the average weighted score divided by the average factor weight.

Factor weights are important because they affect the final score. In many cases, however, there are no clear rules for determining the factor weights. Depending on your project, you may set them based on scientific models, standard scoring systems, or subjective opinions. In a CommunityViz analysis, factor weights are often set up as changeable assumptions that you can easily change using slider bars during the analysis process if appropriate.

A factor score measures how well a possible site performs relative to that factor. A factor score usually comes in the form of a number, a ratio, or a Boolean (yes or no) answer. This allows for a wide range of calculations. When measuring distances, for example, you can use both Boolean overlap calculations, such as "within the right-of-way buffer of a road," and non-Boolean proximity calculations, such as "x feet from the road."

Figure 12.1 **An example of a suitability score with equal weighting**

FACTOR	FACTOR SCORE (OUT OF 100)	FACTOR WEIGHT (OUT OF 10)	WEIGHTED SCORE
Cost	25	5	125
Accessibility	75	5	375
Hazard	50	5	250
(Averages)		5	250
Overall Score	50		

Figure 12.2 **An example of a suitability score with unequal weighting**

FACTOR	FACTOR SCORE (OUT OF 100)	FACTOR WEIGHT (OUT OF 10)	WEIGHTED SCORE
Cost	25	2	50
Accessibility	75	8	600
Hazard	50	2	100
(Averages)		4	250
Overall Score	62.5		

Figure 12.3 Sample factor measurements

FACTOR	MEASUREMENT
Cost	Number of dollars
Transit access	Distance (in miles) to nearest stop
Transit stop efficiency	Number of dwelling units within ¼ mile
Senior population density	Number of residents over age 65 divided by area
On steep slope	If more than half of parcel has slope >30%, then yes; otherwise, no (vector-based calculation) *or* If average slope of parcel is >30%, then yes; otherwise, no (raster-based calculation)

Figure 12.3 illustrates some sample factors and ways they might be measured.

There are two kinds of factor scores. The first is the *raw score*, and the second is the *normalized score*. A raw score is a direct measurement of a factor, such as a cost in dollars or a distance in miles, as shown in Figure 12.3. Raw scores are easy to understand, but you cannot combine raw scores from different factors, because they use different scales. Maybe one million dollars is a relatively low cost, but one million miles is a very long distance! You need to normalize the raw scores by translating them to a comparable scale, such as the 0–100 range in Figures 12.1 and 12.2.

One easy way to normalize a range of scores is to express them all as a percentage of the maximum possible score. For example, if you were studying land prices, you could find the price of the most expensive parcel and express all other prices as a percentage of that value. One flaw in that approach is that the scores will not necessarily be spread evenly between 0 percent and 100 percent. The least expensive parcel may get a score of, say, 79. When the cost scores are combined with scores from other factors, the cost scores will all be relatively high compared with the other factors. The effect will be the same as if cost had been given a very high weight. To overcome this problem, you can express each score as a percentage of the range between maximum and minimum. In this method, the score for a particular feature is calculated using the following formula:

$$\frac{(Feature's\ score) - (Minimum\ score)}{(Maximum\ score) - (Minimum\ score)} \times 100$$

Even this method may not perfectly reflect all the subtlety in your factor scores, but it works well enough for most kinds of analyses and it is the method used in the Suitability Wizard. If you are curious about the distribution of factor scores or overall suitability scores in your analysis, you can view a graph of attribute values by using the ArcMap Statistics tool available in the attribute table.

Normalizing Boolean factor scores is easy: "Yes" gets 100, and "no" gets 0. However, you need to be clear about whether your Boolean factors are *considerations* or *requirements*. If a factor is a consideration, it can be weighed along with all the other factors and a "no" will simply reduce the overall suitability score. If a factor is a requirement, it is overriding and a "no" will make the site completely unsuitable regardless of any other factors. If you are working with suitability factors that are requirements, process them separately. Calculate scores based on other considerations first, and then override them with requirements if needed. The easiest way to do the override is to make the requirement factor scores 1s and 0s. Multiply the combined consideration suitability score by all of the requirement scores to get a final result. If a site fails a particular requirement and there are no analysis changes that would enable it to pass, you may be wise to remove the site from your analysis. This method is shown later in this chapter in the teaching example.

COMMUNITYVIZ TOOLS FOR SUITABILITY ANALYSIS
SUITABILITY WIZARD

Scenario 360 includes a decision tool called the Suitability Wizard that provides an easy way to set up a standard suitability analysis. You tell the Suitability Wizard the name of the layer containing the features that represent the sites you want to evaluate, and then you specify any number of factors you want to include in the analysis. The features can be points, lines, or polygons. If your factors are based on standard calculations such as proximity and overlap, the wizard will automatically set up formulas for them. Otherwise, you can write your own formulas and then point the wizard to your results. One of the main advantages of the wizard is that it automatically sets up a normalized, weighted factor analysis. You are free to inspect the components and formulas the wizard creates, and you can change and improve them later if desired. The Suitability Wizard also sets up changeable assumptions for factor weights, making it easy for you to set specific values or experiment with different factor weights.

An alternative to using the Suitability Wizard is to set up your own analysis structure using standard Scenario 360 custom analysis, as described in Chapter 4.

You can use the Suitability Wizard more than once. For example, you might want to do one suitability analysis that rates parcels on their wildlife habitat value and another that rates parcels on their desirability for development. The wizard allows you to set these up as two separate analyses on the same layer. This method is also useful for nested suitability analysis, described next.

NESTED SUITABILITY

Suitability factors can be complex. A single factor called "agricultural value" might depend on soil types, drainage, slope, aspect, and other factors. Even the soil-type factor might be broken down into more-detailed categories of soil composition, depth, and so on. When doing an analysis at this level of detail, you have two choices. One is to develop static factor formulas that take into account all the contributing factors you need to consider. The other is to create what might be called a sub-suitability analysis that allows you to place variable weights on the contributing factors. You can do several sub-suitability analyses and then roll their results into the overall suitability analysis. This is known as *nested suitability*. The hazard assessment and planning case study at the end of the chapter provides an example of this approach.

CATEGORIES

Scenario 360 categories are like folders in a filing cabinet or tags on a blog. You can assign every component in your analysis—indicators, assumptions, dynamic attributes, and so on—to a particular category, and then you can sort and find components by their category designations. Organizing components by categories is particularly handy for suitability analysis, which tends to create a large number of related components that often have similar-sounding names. Categories help you sort out the components. In the nested suitability example above, for instance, you could make one category called "Agricultural Value" and another called "Soil Types." All the assumptions, indicators, dynamic attributes, and charts associated with the Soil Types sub-suitability analysis would be tagged with the Soil Types category, so they would be easy to find.

The Suitability Wizard automatically creates categories using the names you give it. If you are doing a nested suitability analysis, be especially careful to give each sub-suitability analysis a distinct name.

ALERTS

If you are using suitability analysis to select or identify a small number of sites from a large number of candidates, Scenario 360 alerts are often useful. You can easily set up an alert that is activated whenever a site's suitability score falls above or below a certain threshold. The features corresponding to the alerted sites are automatically highlighted on the map. For instance, you could set up one alert that highlighted the most suitable sites in green and another alert that highlighted the least suitable sites in red.

ASSUMPTIONS AND CHARTS

Assumption slider bars are the standard tools for setting weights in a suitability analysis. They are easy to use and visually informative. One caution is that factor weights are proportional: Setting all weights to 2 is the same as setting all weights to 8. For this reason, we recommend displaying a pie chart at the same time that shows each factor's weighting percentage.

SYMBOLOGY TOOLS

Part of the art of suitability analysis is your visual presentation of the results. Fortunately, 2-D and 3-D maps are ideal for presentations if you use them well.

The most straightforward way to display suitability results on maps is to assign symbols to sites based on their suitability scores, usually with a color range going from one shade (lighter) for low scores to another shade (darker) for high scores, as in Figure 12.5. You will also want to pay attention to the number of *classes* used for symbols. Classes are the ranges of values used for each symbol, such as 0–10 for lightest green, or 90–100 for darkest green. It's usually helpful to use at least five classes—that is, five separate divisions—for a score range of 0 to 100. You may need to look at the default divisions to make sure they make sense for your data. For example, if all your suitability scores are bunched between 90 and 100, it may be best to have a single class for all scores below 90, then five or six classes for values over 90. Keep in mind that suitability scores change as you work with the analysis, so you need to design symbols that will work across a range of values.

During a presentation, you will often need to change symbols to make another point. For example, if you have done two suitability analyses on the same layer, you will want to show both results. Scenario 360 provides two methods for making the transition quickly: the Symbol Saver and Saved Views. The Symbol Saver is a simple utility that memorizes the symbols you have set up for one or more layers, gives those symbols names, and enables you to quickly reapply them at a later time. Saved Views is broader; it also memorizes most other aspects of the display, including the charts and assumptions you are showing, the map's extent, the scenario, and so on. Scenario 360 automatically creates Saved Views for each category in your analysis, but you may also want to set up your own views to illustrate particular points.

SCORING SYSTEMS FOR CENTERS AND NEIGHBORHOODS

Planners can use a number of objective points-based systems to rate neighborhood plans or development proposals. These rating or scoring systems include: ICLEI's Star Community Index; the Leadership in Energy and Environmental Design (LEED) system of the U.S. Green Building Council; more recently the LEED—Neighborhood Development, and LEED—Sustainable Sites; and the Land Evaluation and Site Assessment (LESA) system from the U.S. Department of Agriculture's Natural Resources Conservation Service (see Figure 12.4).

CommunityViz is a good tool for estimating how well a neighborhood plan or development proposal scores on these rating systems,

Figure 12.4 Part of a sample LESA system site assessment for a 150-acre farm

SITE ASSESSMENT FACTORS	WEIGHT ASSIGNED	SAMPLE FARM POINTS	TOTAL POINTS TIMES WEIGHT ASSIGNED	MAXIMUM POSSIBLE POINTS
Percentage of land in agriculture within 1.5-mile radius	2.0	9	18.0	20
Percentage of land in agriculture adjacent to the farm site	1.5	8	12.0	15
Percentage of farm site in agriculture	1.5	9	13.5	15
Percentage of farm site zoned for agriculture	2.0	10	20.0	20
Distance from a city or village	1.5	8	12.0	15
Distance to public sewer or water	1.5	5	7.5	15
Size of farm vs. average farm size in county	2.5	8	20.0	25
Road frontage	1.5	8	12.0	15

From Daniels and Bowers, Holding Our Ground: Protecting America's Farms and Farmland *(Washington, D.C.: Island Press, 1997), 79.*

Figure 12.5 *Smart location map. The pie chart shows the scoring system.*

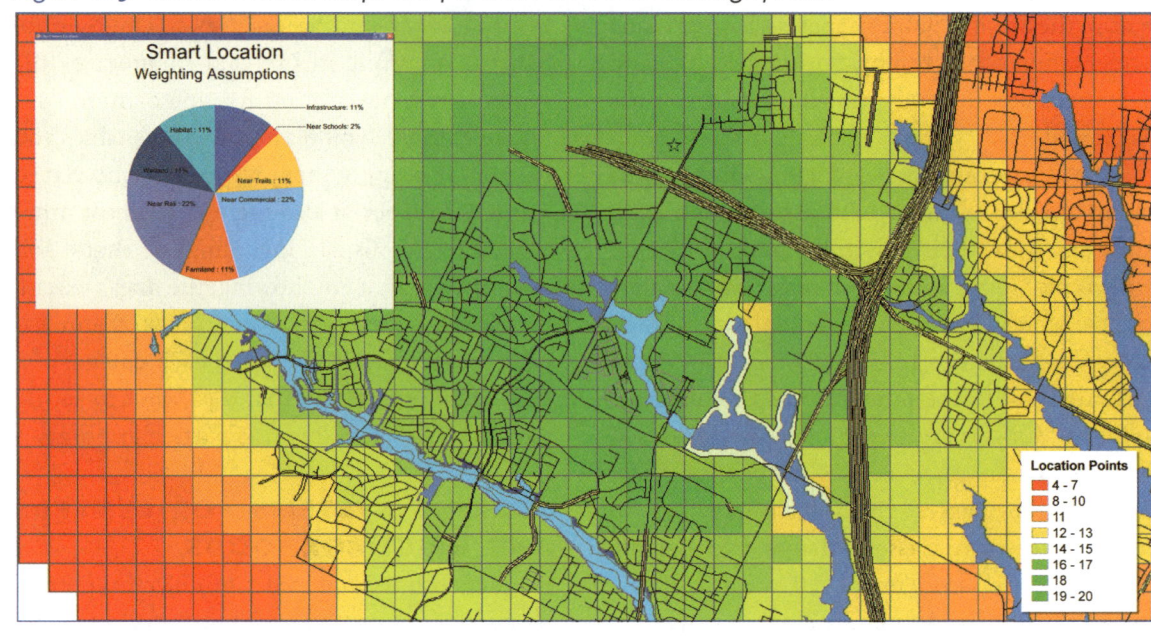

Figure 12.6 *Potential neighborhood (bounded in dark purple line) receives location scores*

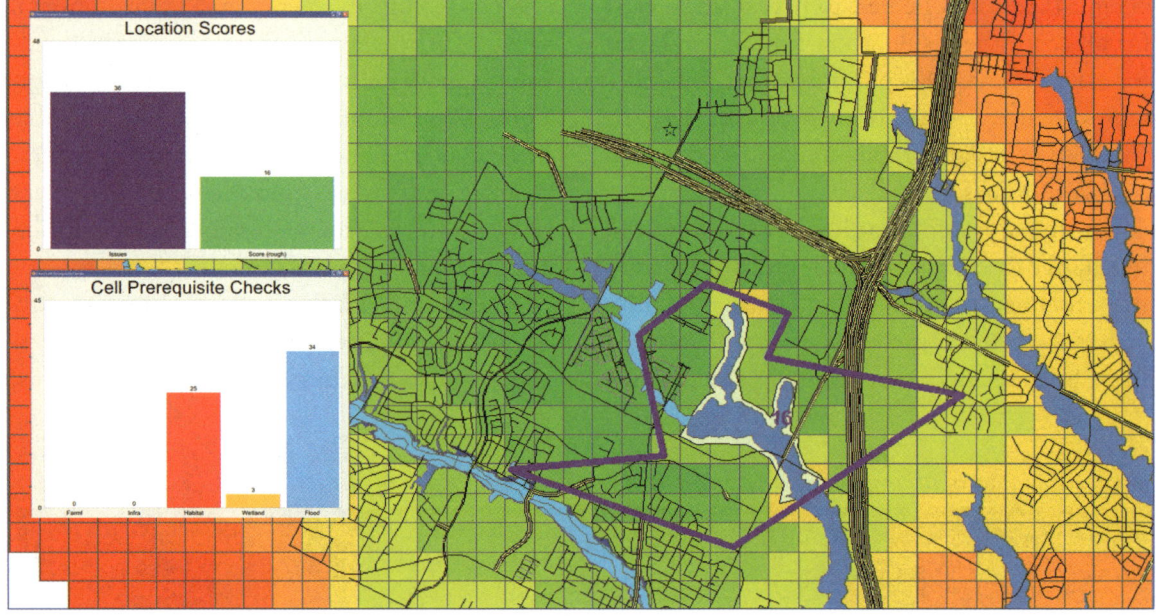

particularly for spatial factors. To create a rating analysis, first choose an analysis layer. The analysis layer may be made up of parcels or blocks, or you can use an analysis grid that covers the study area (for more about analysis grids, see Chapter 11). If you are using an analysis grid, create dynamic attributes that give points to the grid cells on each factor in the rating system. Typical factors to take into account include proximity to infrastructure and services, location in or near hazard areas, and agricultural soil productivity. Most rating systems provide simple rules for calculating the points score on each factor. Then use a lookup table or other method to multiply each point score by the weighting in your rating system. Add up the results to arrive at a total score for each grid cell. In some cases, the scores will be considerations, and in others they will be requirements. If a grid cell fails a requirement, you may need to give it a score of 0. Based on the scores, you can color the map in order to create a *smart location map* (see Figure 12.5). The map in Figure 12.5 indicates the most suitable general locations for the proposed neighborhood development.

Next, create a new layer if required and sketch potential boundaries of the neighborhood. Using overlap formulas, you can calculate the number of requirement violations, or issues, in the neighborhood and the average location score of grid cells in the neighborhood (see Figure 12.6). As you experiment with edits and changes to the neighborhood, you will see new location scores appear. This process is a good example of geodesign.

Finally, create scenarios for the neighborhood using Scenario Sketch tools, the Build-Out Wizard, or other methods. Once you have the neighborhood designs to work with, you can make indicators that provide information on many other scoring criteria, such as land use mix and distances from house points to services (see Figure 12.7).

TEACHING EXAMPLE

This fictional example involves finding appropriate sites for commercial redevelopment in a distressed urban neighborhood. It highlights some of the most common methods for site selection and assessment in CommunityViz using geodesign and the Suitability Wizard. As you can see from the parcel map (Figure 12.8), the area has a large number of vacant and abandoned lots intermixed with commercial, office, civic, and residential uses. The city was consider-

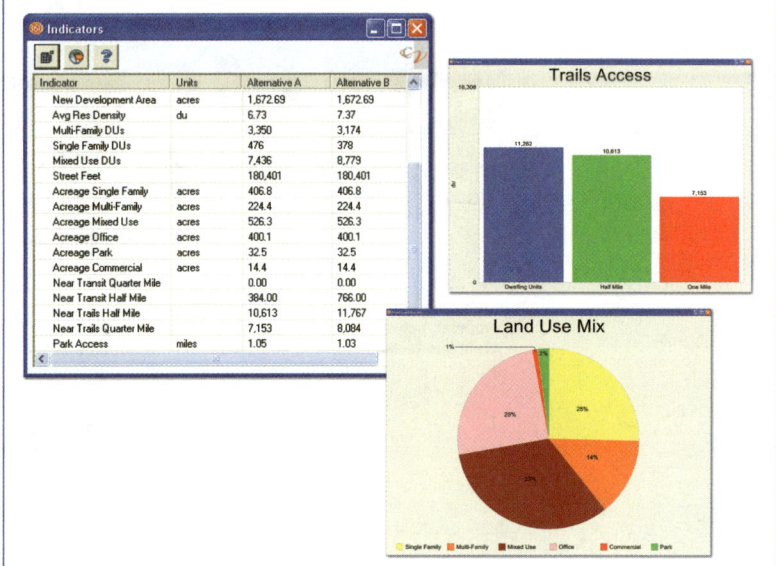

Figure 12.7 *Sample neighborhood scoring indicators*

ing an expansion of its light-rail system into the neighborhood, together with other initiatives that the city hoped would revitalize the area. The proposed light-rail stops are shown on the map, along with major intersections, which are marked with crosses. As usual, we made certain that all layers in our map were using the same projected coordinate system.

To rate the suitability of each lot for commercial development, we decided to use three factors: proximity to proposed light-rail stops, proximity to major intersections, and proximity to existing commercial properties. We felt that the closer a property was to these assets, the greater its chances for success.

We considered only vacant properties. In CommunityViz terms, vacancy was a *requirement*.

Figure 12.8 *Site map showing existing uses, major intersections, and proposed transit stops*

Figure 12.9 Map showing vacant parcels rated for redevelopment suitability

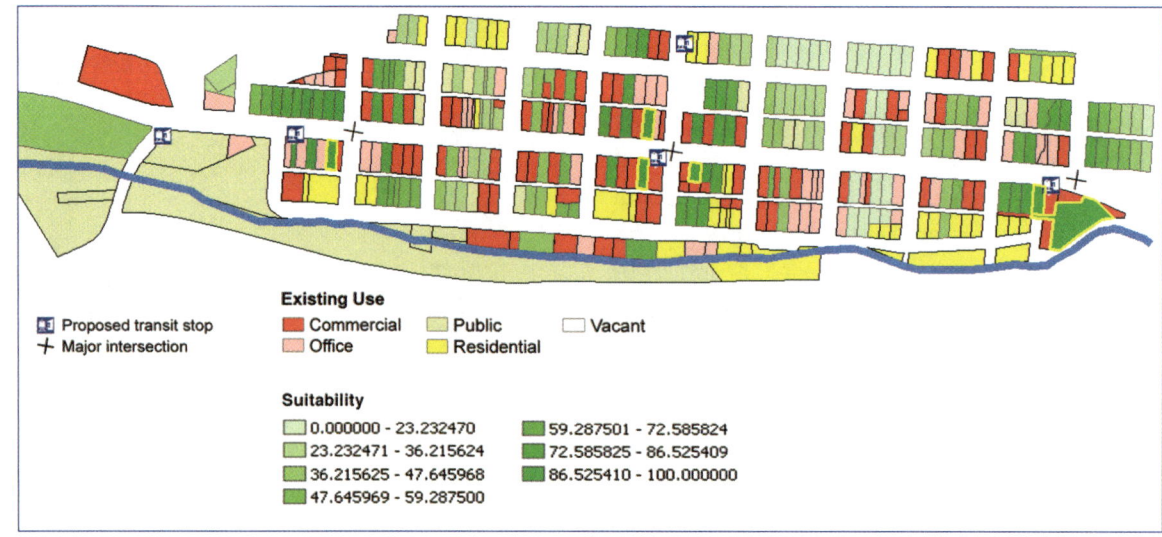

And because there were so many vacant properties to work with, we decided to make a new layer consisting of only vacant properties and do our analysis on that. To make the new layer, we used ArcMap to select the vacant properties, and then we exported the selected features.

We used the Suitability Wizard to create the analysis in our new Vacant Properties layer. Setting up factors for proximity to light-rail stops and major intersections was easy; we specified that higher suitability scores would result from closer proximity. The Suitability Wizard automatically set up formulas that measured the distances between each vacant parcel and its closest rail stop and intersection. Next, the Suitability Wizard created normalized factor scores, weight assumptions, and other components we needed for the analysis.

Setting up a factor for proximity to existing commercial properties was slightly more complex because we did not have a separate layer containing only commercial properties. The layer we were using was the original parcels layer, which contained residential, civic, office, and vacant parcels as well. Therefore, we used the Suitability Wizard feature, which allowed us to add a *Where condition* to the formula. A Where condition is part of a formula that specifies a subset of features in a layer. In our case, we specified that we wanted to use only those parcels where the existing use was commercial.

After setting up the final factor, we ran the Suitability Wizard and then resymbolized the vacant properties on the basis of their suitability score. The resulting map appears in Figure 12.9. The most suitable parcels (darkest green) were, as expected, close to intersections, transit stops, and existing commercial buildings.

As an added refinement, we created an alert that highlighted the parcels with a suitability score of higher than 95. In Figure 12.9, those parcels are outlined in bright yellow.

When we reviewed our preliminary results with the city planner, we could use the geodesign capabilities of our analysis. The planner asked three questions, two of which we were ready for and one for which we had to do a little more work. The first question was, "If the light rail project doesn't happen, then which sites would be best?" To answer that question, we simply changed the weight on the "light-rail proximity" slider to 0 and updated the analysis.

The second question was, "What if a particular rail stop doesn't go in, and another one is moved two blocks west?" In response, we simply edited the map to delete one rail stop and move another. When we saved the edits, Scenario 360 updated the results and showed a new set of best choices.

The third question was, "Can we take two parcels out of consideration? Those locations will probably be redeveloped into new city parks." We could have responded to this question by deleting those parcels from the Vacant Properties layer, but to make it easier to answer similar questions in the future, we decided to add another feature to our analysis. We created a new non-dynamic attribute in the Vacant Properties layer that we called Excluded. Then, we created two Sketch styles: one called Exclude, which set the value of Excluded to 0; and one called Include, which set the value of Excluded to 1. We modified the Suitability Wizard's formula for suitability slightly to multiply the old answer by the value of Excluded. As a result, we could easily paint on the map to exclude certain parcels temporarily from the suitability analysis. Those parcels would not disappear, but their suitability rating would go to 0. When we were finished asking "What if?" questions about what would happen if those parcels were excluded from consideration, we could return them to their original status by painting over them with Include (see Figure 12.10).

Our suitability analysis and geodesign tools were now working well from the planner's perspective. But when we entered into conversations with prospective developers, we found that another factor was important to them: site mitigation costs. The vacant sites had a variety of potentially costly problems, including old structures that would need to be demolished, damaged infrastructure, and hazardous materials. These would require detailed engineering studies later in the process, but for now we wanted a way to estimate the magnitude of the costs at each candidate site. We had two options: 1) create a sub-suitability analysis that treated each problem as a contributing factor, or 2) create a static set of formulas—also called a model—that estimated the cleanup cost for each site based on those factors. We chose the latter, a static model, because neither planners nor the public would know much about the cleanup costs. In consultation with an engineer, we wrote several formulas that eventually created a single dynamic attribute for each site that we called Site Mitigation Costs. Armed with this new information, we modified the existing suitability analysis in the Suitability Wizard to add a fourth factor that was based directly on the value of the attribute Site Mitigation Costs.

Figure 12.10 *Painting on the map to temporarily exclude parcels from consideration*

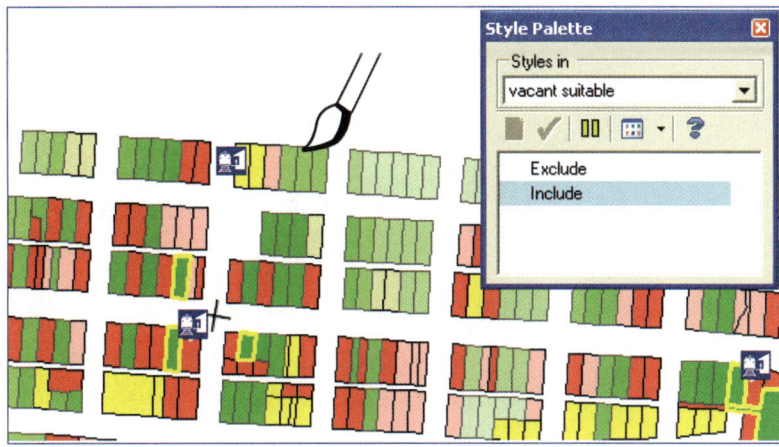

Finally, we had a suitability analysis that helped identify best sites for commercial redevelopment. It took into account several considerations in several different ways:

- **Simple location factors,** in our case proximity to major intersections and transit stops. To measure these, we used standard Suitability Wizard functions. We did not happen to use overlap functions or raster functions in this example, but we could have done so.

- **Conditional location factors,** in our case proximity to parcels where the existing use was commercial. For these we also used the Suitability Wizard.

- **Requirements,** in our case vacancy. For these we used the technique of eliminating site candidates from the analysis layer.

- **Conditional requirements,** in our case the possibility that some parcels would be designated as parkland. For these we used Sketch tools and modified the Suitability Wizard's formulas.

- **Complex factors,** in our case site mitigation costs. For these we employed a separate model whose results became a simple numeric input to the Suitability Wizard.

CASE STUDY
HAZARD ASSESSMENT AND PLANNING

Location: Squamish, British Columbia, Canada
Partners: Natural Resources Canada; District of Squamish; Smart Growth On the Ground; TerraCognito GIS; University of British Columbia Design Centre for Sustainability

The District of Squamish is located where the ocean meets the mountains in the Sea-to-Sky Corridor, midway between Vancouver and Whistler, in the Canadian province of British Columbia. Within commuting distance of greater Vancouver, Squamish has shifted from a reliance on traditional natural-resource-based industries to become a fast-growing exurban center, known as the Outdoor Recreation Capital of Canada.

Located at the confluence of five major river systems at the head of Howe Sound and flanked by a dramatic mountain landscape, Squamish was faced with the challenge of managing new development in a setting exposed to several natural hazards. These hazards include low-probability but high-consequence earthquakes and volcanic eruptions; slope stability hazards such as a large-debris-flow landslide hazard; periodic flooding; storm surge threats in the downtown waterfront area; and wildfire threats along the interface between the built and natural environments.

Project Description: Natural Resources Canada (NRCan) has a longstanding research program aimed at reducing risks from natural hazards. One of the program's objectives is to make vulnerability and risk assessment methods more widely available for decision making by agencies responsible for hazard mitigation and planning. In 2007, NRCan agreed with the District of Squamish to examine the conditions of natural hazard vulnerability and risk of floods, earthquakes, and landslides. Specifically, NRCan would study how these conditions could change over time with ongoing growth and development. Partnering with the district gave the research team a deeper understanding of the realities that community planners faced. The process built on previous information gathering, comprehensive plans, and long-term visioning work undertaken by the district.

The project partners established a working group of district staff, social agencies, educational agencies, emergency response groups, realtors, and community members to identify and prioritize community assets at risk, identify assets that might contribute to resilience, and discuss risk reduction strategies. These conversations took place during face-to-face workshops where participants had access to objective hazard information and also brought their own local knowledge and experience to bear on devising a risk management strategy for Squamish.

Natural Resources Canada developed an assessment framework now known as Pathways-DM (Decision Making). It includes methods for problem framing, priority setting, visualization, and exploration of viable policy alternatives through a process of participatory planning, integrated assessment modeling, and formal decision analysis. The project incorporated a wide variety of data, including geotechnical reports on flooding and landslide potential, as well as government data on earthquakes. Natural Resources Canada also used HAZUS-MH, a hazard assessment model developed by the U.S. government's Federal Emergency Management Agency (FEMA).

The Pathways-DM framework used a series of nested indicators that were all integrated within CommunityViz. There were four high-level decision criteria that aligned with the National Disaster Mitigation Strategy for Canada: socioeconomic security, public safety, resource efficiency, and equity. Within each of these four criteria, there were eight high-level management objectives measured by indicators and 27 related model parameters for measuring progress toward policy goals. All of these were modeled in scenarios that illustrated growth management choices and the vulnerability associated with population increases in certain areas (see Figure 12.11).

Technology and Tools: The project team used CommunityViz Scenario 360 for hazard potential analysis, growth analysis, suitability analysis, TimeScope analysis, social vulnerability analysis, and overall integration of the results from other modeling tools. CommunityViz SiteBuilder 3D and Google Earth were used for landscape visualization and interactive exploration of model results (see Figure 12.12). To analyze physical

Figure 12.11 CommunityViz screenshot showing risk profile analysis in progress

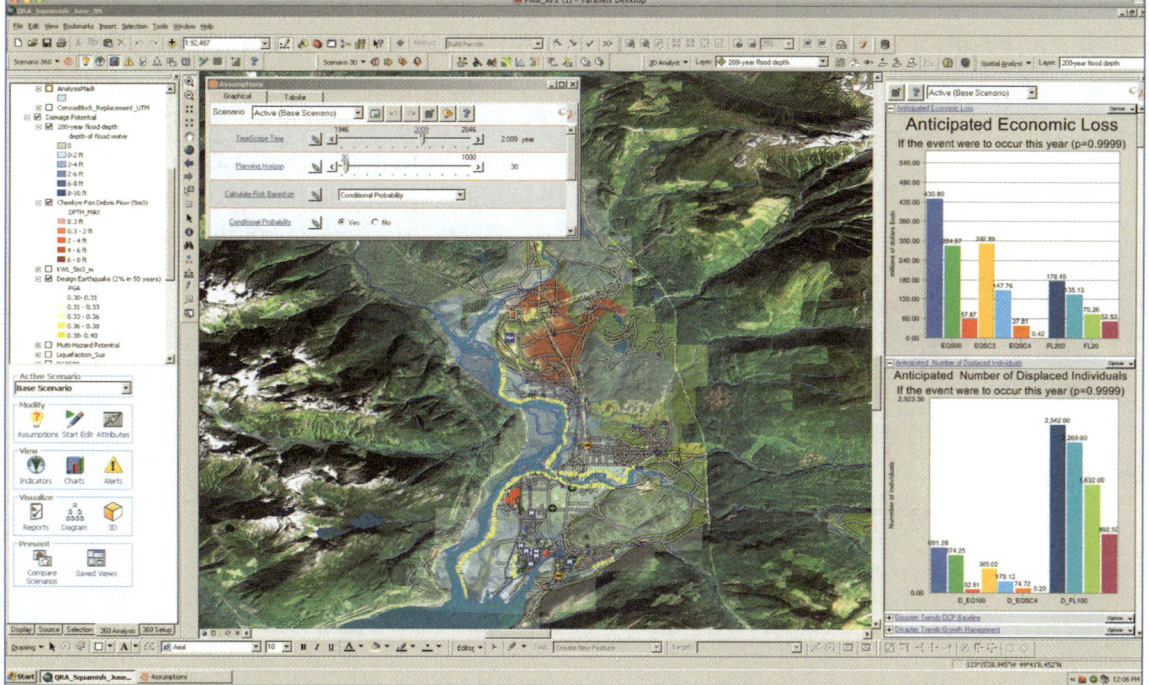

Images courtesy of Natural Resources Canada

Figure 12.12 Two screenshots showing development patterns and risk profiles exported to Google Earth. The inset web diagrams show risks on several dimensions.

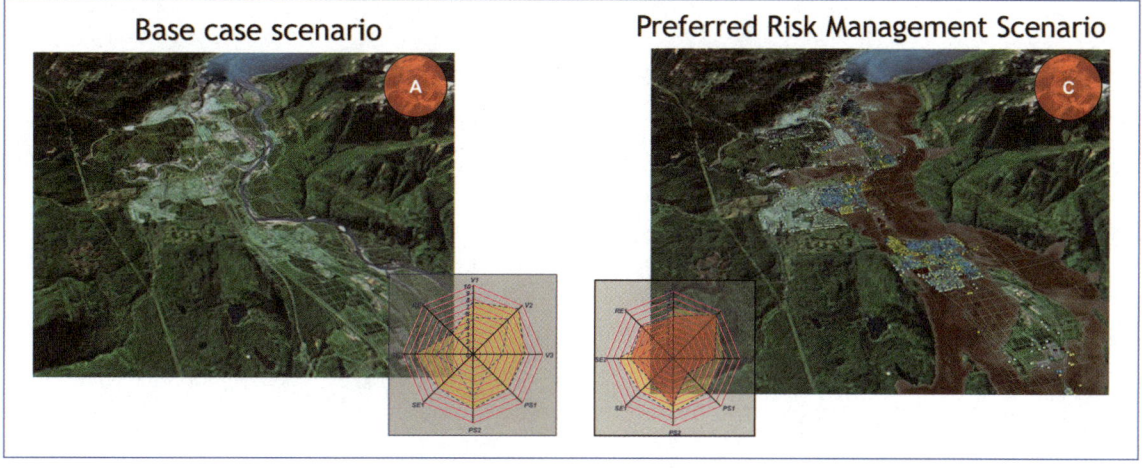

Figure 12.13 Map of the calculated risk profile for Squamish

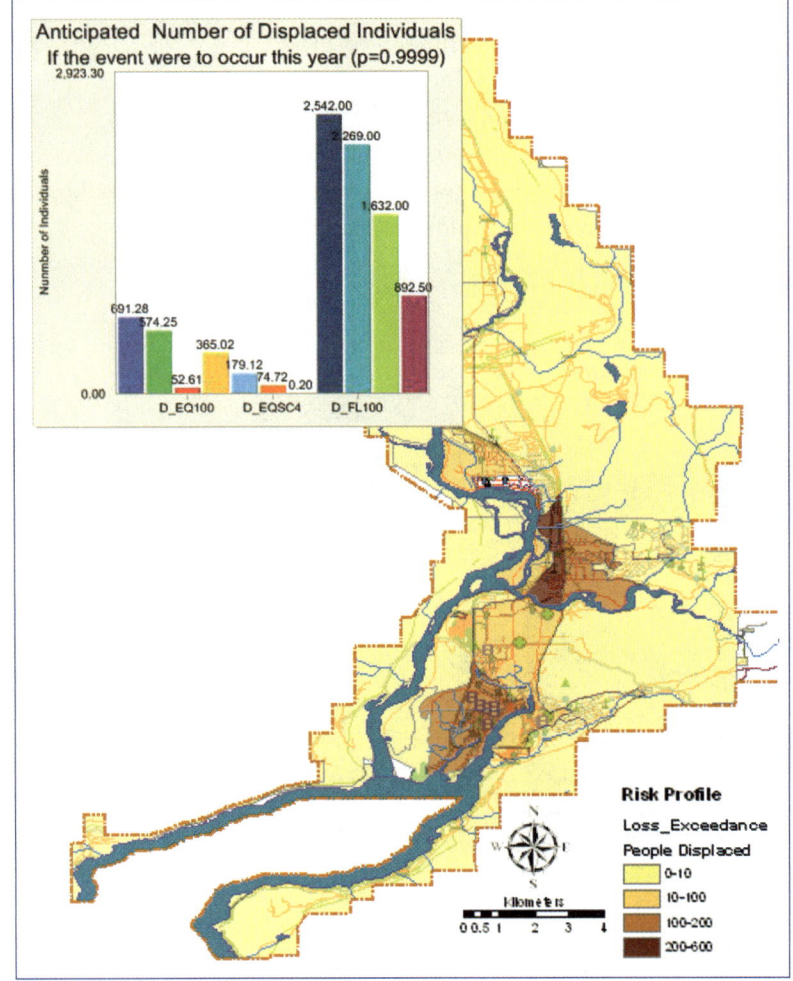

vulnerability analysis—that is, damage potential—and estimate losses, HAZUS-MH was used. Outputs of HAZUS-MH were entered into CommunityViz to illustrate risks associated with the future scenarios, and into the USGS Land Use Portfolio Model for a cost-benefit analysis.

Outcomes: Natural Resources Canada completed its analysis and planned to work with the District of Squamish to explore policy responses to the identified risks the community might face as it grew over the next 30 years (see Figure 12.13). The project helped to inform the district's drafting of a new official community plan with an expanded discussion of anticipated hazards. To reach a broader audience, NRCan planned to publish the framework and case study results for Squamish, which may inform ongoing strategies for regional risk assessment throughout Canada.

Site Selection and Assessment

CASE STUDY
PLANNING FOR AGRICULTURE

Location: Calumet County, Wisconsin
Partners: Calumet County; University of Wisconsin; U.S. Department of Agriculture; Wisconsin Department of Agriculture

Wisconsin, known as America's Dairyland, takes great pride in its agricultural landscape. In addition to providing valuable food and forestry products, agricultural lands also attract tourism and help maintain the state's environment and quality of life. But Wisconsin is losing farmland at an alarming rate. According to the U.S. Department of Agriculture, more than 2 million acres of Wisconsin farmland were converted to other uses between 1982 and 2007. The state has proposed a number of strategies to protect its working lands, and a consortium at the University of Wisconsin is addressing agricultural land issues through research, training, and outreach. The consortium undertook the Targeting Working Lands and Operations pilot project to provide local decision makers with the tools and training they needed to identify "important farms and farmlands where protection efforts are desirable and help attain community goals and objectives." Calumet County and La Crosse County served as the two pilot regions.

Project Description: The pilot project was intended to provide local decision makers with research, tools, and educational materials to help them prioritize agricultural lands worthy of protection, and to communicate the results to elected officials and the general public. In addition, the University of Wisconsin wanted to test the capabilities of CommunityViz to weigh local priorities and values in assessing agricultural lands.

Recognizing that local people know their counties the best, the project team engaged a committee of local volunteers to inform a LESA system. A LESA system consists of two parts: *land evaluation* factors, such as soils and slope, which relate to the physical productivity of the land for farming (see Figure 12.14); and *site assessment* factors, which describe farm support infrastructure and non-farm development pressures.

Ratings for the two sets of factors are added together to produce an overall rating of the desirability of maintaining the farmland for farming (see Figure 12.15). The LESA rating system has a

Figure 12.14 Sample map from the LESA analysis showing soil quality scores by parcel

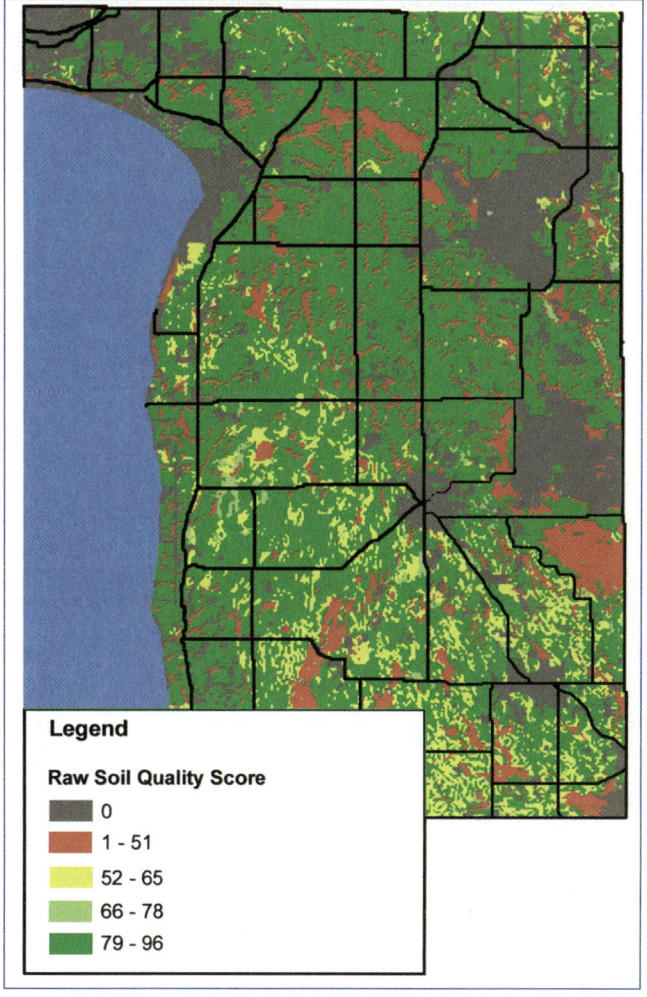

Images courtesy of University of Wisconsin/Tom McClintock

cut-off level below which a farm is deemed to be of relatively low value for farming over the long run. Farms that score above the cut-off level are considered to have long-term potential for farming and thus should be protected by zoning or preserved through the purchase of development rights.

In Calumet County, the LESA system comprised seven suitability layers of factors such as quality of soil, compatibility with surrounding land uses, distance from urban features, and proximity to protected working lands. The analysis included some 50 assumptions and 55 dynamic attributes, which were used to calculate suitability scores for each undeveloped parcel in the county (see Figure 12.16). The LESA committee assigned weights, or values, to the factors so that important factors had more influence over the final result than less important ones. The analysis results were reviewed and tested in comparison to committee member field observations and personal knowledge. Then, the LESA committee formally recommended the Calumet County LESA system for use by the county.[1]

Technology and Tools: The project team used CommunityViz and ArcGIS to perform the LESA analyses. Within CommunityViz, the suitability calculations were done using a combination of the Suitability Wizard and standard Scenario 360 dynamic analysis functions. The LESA system developed by the U.S. Department of Agriculture in 1983 was used as the framework for the CommunityViz analysis. A LESA committee was formed to guide the project and to design and recommend a LESA system appropriate for Calumet County.

Outcomes: In the pilot project, local professionals made effective use of GIS and CommunityViz to build LESA models that can be understood by citizens and policy makers alike. In Calumet County, the project team built a coalition of local citizen advocates that encouraged the county and state to use the technology to help identify farmlands worthy of protection. In the long term, project partners anticipate that the technology, coupled with public participation, will help increase public support for farmland protection policies. Project leaders also anticipate that more communities will invest in the technology to build their own LESA systems, and that land trusts will become active partners with local counties in using the technology to achieve common objectives. To that end, the University of Wisconsin is developing a workshop to teach other communities and organizations to use CommunityViz in creating and applying LESA systems.

Calumet County published a draft 2009–2019 Calumet County Farmland Preservation Plan to guide agricultural zoning and farmland preservation efforts and to heighten public awareness about agricultural issues. The plan notes the value of the CommunityViz LESA model and encourages its further development and use.

Figure 12.15 A Scenario 360 chart showing the distribution of LESA scores

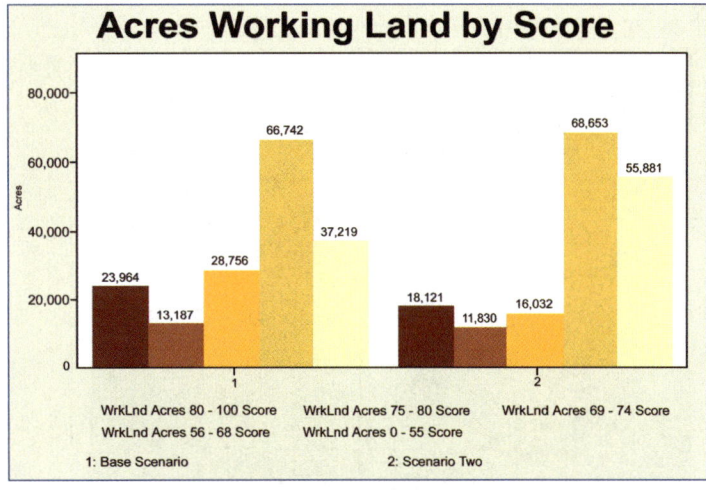

Figure 12.16 Sample weighting factors used in LESA analysis, displayed as CommunityViz variable assumptions

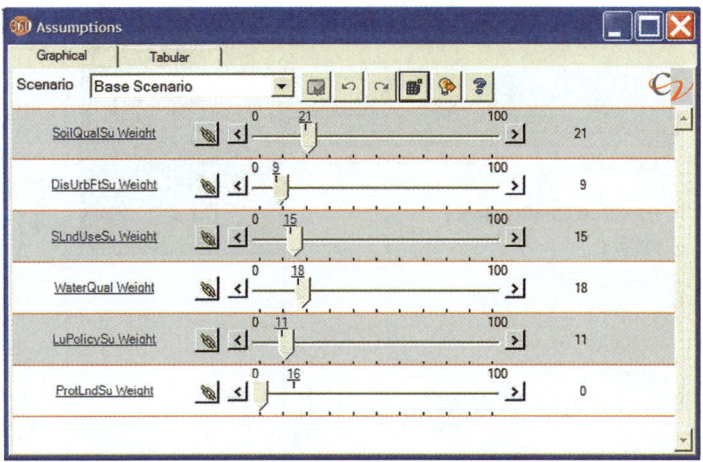

---

1. Details of its work are available online at: www.co.calumet.wi.us/uploads/document/_OFFICIAL_FP_CB_changes_1009.pdf.

13 RESOURCE PLANS

KEY CONCEPTS AND TERMS IN THIS CHAPTER

- Best management practices (BMPs)
- LandFrag Wizard
- Conditions and targets
- Optimizer
- Raster data
- Using special places maps

Resource planning involves the use of plans and analyses to manage and protect natural resources and natural areas. Some resource plans identify and create strategies for protecting environmentally sensitive areas such as floodplains, wildlife habitats, and steep slopes. Other resource plans focus on protecting and managing working landscapes of farmland, ranchland, or forest.

CommunityViz supports resource planning at several levels. For scientific modeling, it provides an analytical framework. For placing values on natural areas and understanding their functions, CommunityViz offers scenario planning and indicators. And for promoting collaborative decision making among diverse stakeholders, CommunityViz has interactive tools that help everyone understand the decisions that need to be made. This chapter covers all of these applications of CommunityViz for resource planning.

DATA NEEDS AND SOURCES

Resource planning begins with the collection of data about existing natural resources. Developing objective, scientific resource maps and inventories is usually not the role of CommunityViz. But once you have the data about a particular natural resource, CommunityViz can use the data in a planning analysis. Also, CommunityViz can help you develop data about natural resources whose values are more subjective, such as favorite places or scenic areas.

The information you need about a natural resource typically includes:

- Description
- Location
- Value, such as economic, environmental, social, and subjective
- Condition, such as size, capacity, quality and so on
- Condition targets
- Role in the systems you are modeling, including how the natural resource affects and is affected by use or depletion
- How the natural resource is impacted in alternative scenarios.

Some of this information will be available at the start of your project, and some you will develop over the course of your analysis.

Here are some examples of natural resources for which you can usually find objective data:

- Forests
- Agricultural lands and soils
- Public parks and open spaces
- Watersheds, aquifers, inland and coastal wetlands, and wellhead protection areas
- Wildlife corridors and habitats for wildlife (both animals and plants), especially those designated as threatened, rare, or endangered

- Ecosystem services areas, such as tidal wetlands that protect against coastal erosion

- Natural hazard areas, such as steep slopes, earthquake fault zones, avalanche areas, and floodplains.

Common sources of objective natural resource data include federal and state government agencies, local resource managers, state universities, and local scientists and experts. Make sure you understand the sources, limitations, and uncertainty of any data you use.

Gathering and analyzing subjective resource data requires more judgment about the value of the resource. Here are a few examples:

- Valuable historic or archaeological sites and structures

- Scenic areas

- Gathering places

- Heart-and-soul places that have value to local residents, such as favorite fishing holes, scenic vistas, or holy sites (see Figure 13.1).

Analyzing and gathering data about subjective resources requires more human interaction than collecting objective data does, but the goals are the same: to arrive at descriptions, locations, values, and indicators of status. The best way to get this information is to ask the public, through public meetings or through online surveys, kiosks, and booths at public events. To the extent you can, ask for all the information in the list above, not just the description or location. Local residents can often tell you a great deal about how a special resource functions in the community.

WORKING WITH RASTER DATA

Compared to data about the built environment, GIS data about natural resources and landscapes more often exist in raster and image formats. If your data include many raster layers that you want to use for any purpose besides display, you will need the Spatial Analyst extension to ArcGIS. You will also find that ArcGIS Model Builder is a good way to do preliminary data processing and consolidation of raster layers.

Figure 13.1 Places of the Heart map of Exeter, Rhode Island. Such information can be captured in CommunityViz and used for analysis.

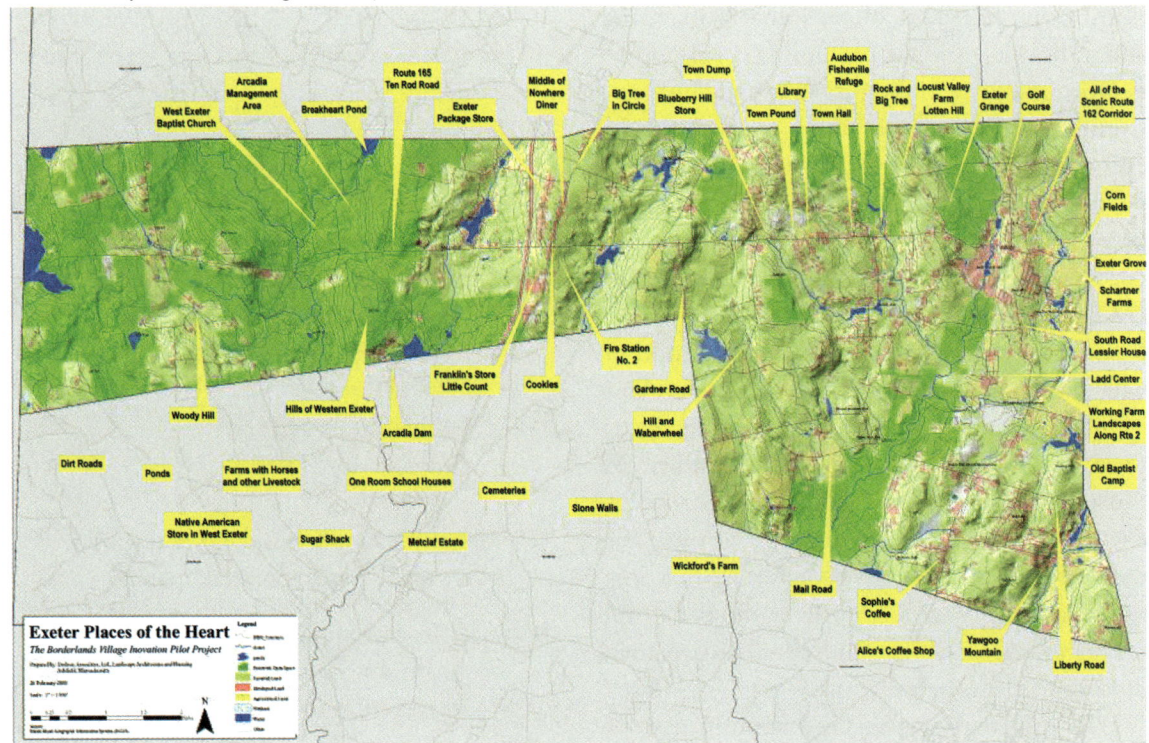

Courtesy Foresee Consulting

The Scenario 360 analysis engine only works on vector data: points, lines, and polygons. However, you can use raster data for reference and even include them in formulas and models. Another name for raster is *grid*. Scenario 360 Grid functions let you transfer raster data into vector layers based on overlap calculations. These functions include GridMax, GridMean, GridMin, GridMost, and GridOverlap. For example, the GridMean function finds the average value of the raster in the area underlying a vector feature such as a polygon. You could use GridMean to populate an Average Slope attribute in a parcel layer when you have raster data that gives slope. In other cases, you may need to convert raster layers to vector layers using Spatial Analyst's raster-to-features conversion utilities.

When you design your analysis, consider whether you can increase efficiency by pre-processing raster data to reduce the size and complexity. Common techniques include rearranging data into fewer classes, increasing raster cell sizes, reducing the extent of the study area, and merging multiple layers.

VALUING RESOURCES

To create a resource plan, you need to put values on the resources. Do this carefully, because a simple model does not always capture all the relevant values. Consider analyzing:

- Direct tangible values, such as revenue from sales of the resource

- Indirect tangible values, such as value of crops irrigated by a water resource

- Direct and indirect intangible values, such as scenic beauty.

For example, consider a publicly owned hay field at the edge of a growing town. It has direct value as part of at least two systems. As an economic resource, it generates a small profit from the sale of hay. As an environmental resource, it provides food and habitat for birds and insects, and it enables groundwater recharge. You can measure these amounts and show them as indicators in your analysis.

The hay field also has indirect value. For example, the field provides income to the farmer who is hired to work it. Perhaps it also contains an informal path that serves as a shortcut for people walking to the post office. These are indirect benefits that do not need their own indicators, but they may contribute to other indicators in your analysis. Here, for example, your analysis would show slightly higher farm pay and slightly better walkability scores when the hay field is present.

Finally, the hay field reinforces the town's self-image as a place with a strong agricultural heritage. This value is intangible, but it may still be important. Try to capture it, either directly—with a variable assumption slider bar called something like "value of hay field for self-image"—or as part of a value map, as described in Chapter 9.

One of the best ways to quantify the value of a resource that has a variety of benefits is to do a suitability analysis. You can use the Suitability Wizard or other tools to give a location a composite value score that takes into account a number of disparate factors (see Chapter 12).

CONDITIONS AND TARGETS

Natural resources are not static. A nonrenewable resource, such as a limestone quarry, can be partially or completely depleted. A renewable resource, such as a wetland, can be degraded, destroyed, or restored. Consequently, a resource plan typically pays extra attention to methods for monitoring and managing the *condition* of the resource, not just its preservation or destruction. The plan often sets specific, quantifiable targets for the condition.

An aquifer is a common example. People who depend on groundwater sources need to have a good understanding of how much water their aquifer can safely supply. As they make plans for water consumption based on population growth and economic activity, regional planners need to ensure that water supplies are sustainable. With CommunityViz, you can easily build a model that compares future water demand to existing water supply. To calculate demand, combine your growth projections with assumptions about the water consumption rates of various agricultural, residential, and commercial uses. To quantify the water supply available from the aquifer, use estimates provided by local water providers or water utilities. If demand exceeds supply in any given scenario, you can trigger an alert on the condition of the resource because the target has been exceeded. The alert will cause decision makers to reject the scenario or look for other implementation options, such as water use restrictions or additional water sources (see Figure 13.2).

Not all resource systems are that easy to quantify. If the resource issue is water quality, for example, supply and demand do not apply. Instead, you might think in terms of vitality and affronts to the water's condition. The vitality in this case is water quality as measured by the absence of pollutants. The affronts are pollutant loads that arise from urban runoff, soil erosion, fertilizers, and discharges from sewage treatment plants and factories.

Class A waters are considered drinkable. Class B waters are safe to swim in but not to drink. Class C, D, and E waters are impaired and are not safe for drinking or swimming. If the surface waters are rated Class C, for example, planners and the community must agree on whether to set Class B or Class A water quality as a reasonable target. At the same time, there is no simple formula that ties population growth rates and land-use patterns to water quality. You will need to use indirect models and perhaps specialized external modeling tools to obtain sufficient information to guide actions to improve water quality.

CommunityViz scenarios and dynamic analysis tools can be especially helpful when you are faced with complicated natural resource planning challenges. One of the strengths of scenario planning is that it gives you a way to capture the interrelations among economic, environmental, and social systems at the same time in a single location. Your analysis will automatically reveal connections between water quality, building patterns, and agriculture, because indicator values are updated automatically when anything that affects them changes. Displaying the indicators simultaneously is also a good way to support a community conversation about natural resource targets. Stakeholders who may start with strong preferences for one indicator tend to be more willing to compromise after they come to understand the bigger picture. The teaching example at the end of this chapter illustrates the use of indicators for natural resource targets.

ASSESSING IMPLEMENTATION STRATEGIES

Implementation strategies for natural resource plans can include guidance from visioning exercises, comprehensive plans, land-use regulations, financial incentives for land preservation or conservation, and resource-specific best management practices (BMPs).

COMMUNITYVIZ TOOLS

Resource planning draws on most of the capabilities of CommunityViz. This section describes CommunityViz tools and techniques commonly used in making natural resource plans as well as to assess the effectiveness of any or all of these implementation strategies.

SCIENTIFIC MODELING

Sophisticated scientific models exist for understanding and analyzing natural resource systems. The models can come in the form of software

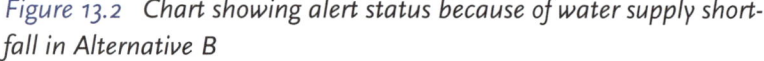

Figure 13.2 Chart showing alert status because of water supply shortfall in Alternative B

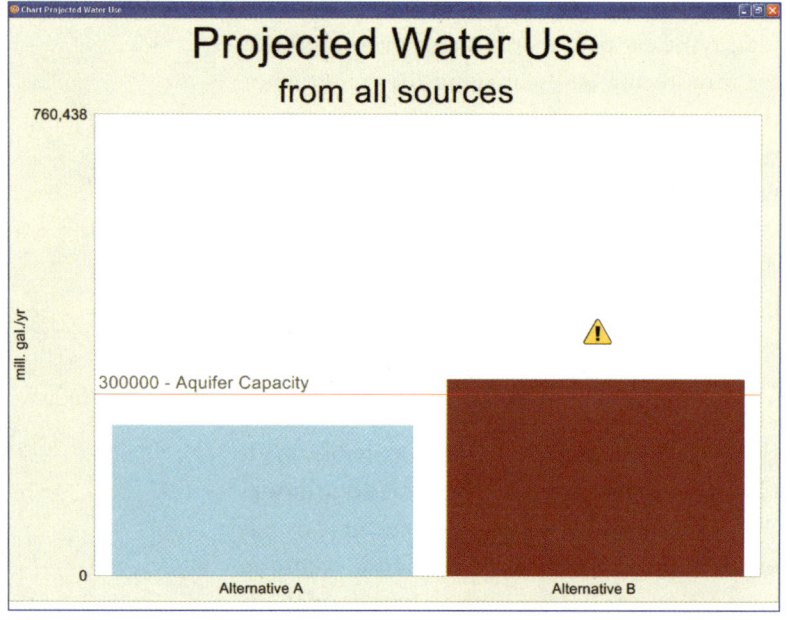

applications, algorithms, interactive databases, and more. There are models for surface water runoff, soil erosion, biodiversity impacts, forest health, fire risk, and many others. If you have access to these models and you need the level of accuracy and sophistication they provide to give you enough good information to make a decision, we encourage you to use them. There are several ways you can employ scientific models within a CommunityViz analysis, ranging from exchanging data with a separate stand-alone tool, to building an algorithm with internal CommunityViz formulas. For details, refer to Chapters 4 and 15.

In creating natural resource plans, first make sure you understand the limitations and uncertainties associated with the scientific models you are using. If you are using the model's results, its uncertainties become your uncertainties, so you need to know what they are. Second, remember the "enough good information" rule from Chapter 1. If the model causes your project to become bogged down with details, consider finding ways to simplify or generalize its results.

EVALUATION OF BMPS

The evaluation of BMPs is a way to estimate the effects of resource management methods such as the use of controlled burns to manage forests, roadside swales to reduce storm water runoff, and cattle fences to protect riparian buffers. With CommunityViz, you can use geodesign to experiment with potential BMP implementation strategies to estimate their cost and effectiveness before you decide on particular practices and an overall resource management plan.

To evaluate a BMP, start by learning its direct costs and benefits. Costs may include materials, labor, time, expertise, and other factors. You should be able to quantify benefits in terms of improvements from the baseline condition of the resource. Where possible, express costs and benefits in terms of rates, such as cost per mile or benefit per acre.

Next, create a way to sketch BMPs onto your map. In some cases, the most efficient approach is to make a new layer for each BMP. To apply the BMP, you sketch new features in that layer. In other cases, it may make more sense to create a Sketch style that you can apply with the Painter or Clone tool. Once you have a layer or attribute to work with, you can create an analysis and indicator formulas that reflect the direct costs and benefits of the BMPs you sketch.

Include any important indirect costs or benefits in your analysis. Will the BMP affect some other natural resource or environmental system in your study area? If so, how? These indirect impacts may appear automatically in your analysis if the BMP happens to affect a feature or condition you are already analyzing. But if these impacts do not appear automatically and they seem important, adapt your analysis to account for them.

Once you are sure your model is complete, experiment. Sketch a variety of BMPs, and study their outcomes. If you are able to set cost and benefit targets, do so.

Finally, use the CommunityViz analysis you have just created to design, assess, and finalize your BMP plans.

OPTIMIZER

Optimizer is a Scenario 360 decision tool that helps you choose the best combination of sites to satisfy certain goals, such as which parcels to conserve by purchasing conservation easements given a finite budget. Optimizer's Modified Simplex Method algorithm allows you to work with a large number of features in a short time, even on an ordinary desktop computer. In addition to choosing resource sites, Optimizer works well for choosing combinations of BMPs.

To use the Optimizer, you need a feature layer containing resource sites such as parcels, or BMPs such as settling ponds. The Optimizer works on only a single layer at a time, but a single layer can contain several different BMPs—for example, settling ponds and swales. Each feature needs a numeric attribute of its value or benefit. Each feature also needs numeric attributes of its cost, size, or any other factor for which you have projectwide limits. For example, if you are buying parklands and you have a fixed budget, you will need to know the cost of each parcel. If you also have a minimum acreage goal, you will need to know the area of each parcel.

Optimizer can use these inputs to calculate the combination of resource sites or BMPs that will achieve maximum benefit within the budget or other constraints you set. It may recommend, for example, that instead of purchasing the highest-scoring parcel, you would derive better results by purchasing three second-place parcels.

The Optimizer is very useful for quick initial assessments of resource planning priorities. It frequently finds answers that are not immediately obvious, and it runs fast enough that you can consider many alternatives. Be aware of the limits of Optimizer, though. First, its answers are not always mathematically optimal: It is possible that a bigger computer running for a longer period of time could find a better answer. This situation is most pronounced when you are working with a small number of features. The second limit is that processing time goes up quickly as you increase the number of features, so that an optimization on more than 500 features may take over an hour. The Optimizer's sweet spot is between 10 and 500 features or sites.

LANDFRAG WIZARD

The LandFrag Wizard helps you calculate and classify the fragmentation of an existing land-cover raster based on the pattern of land cover in surrounding cells. Fragmentation is a way to measure whether land cover is arranged in large contiguous blocks or broken up into small discrete pieces. A common application is the measuring of forest fragmentation, which is a threat to plant and animal habitats. But the LandFrag Wizard works on any land cover, and it can be used to study land-use fragmentation in the built environment. You can use the LandFrag Wizard in an analysis to measure existing fragmentation and to measure the potential fragmentation effects of alternative land-use scenarios or growth rates over time.

Landsat satellite imagery is the most common source for LandFrag analysis, though you can use other sources. LandFrag includes an easy method for reclassifying land-cover designations into the three simplified classes, such as forest, nonforest, and water. When LandFrag runs, it generates a new raster that specifies each pixel's position relative to the rest of the forest: in the core, on an edge, in a perforated area, and so on. With this new data, you can create maps, indicators, and charts that quantify the level of landscape fragmentation in an area.

TEACHING EXAMPLE

The mission of CommunityViz is to promote informed, collaborative decision making, and this is illustrated in the following resource planning example. Called "Vegetation Treatment," it is drawn from an elegant demonstration developed by Brenda Faber in the early days of CommunityViz. Over the years, we have used it in various forms for training, demonstrations, and documentation, and it remains a favorite of our staff. Vegetation Treatment tells the fictional story of a resource management challenge and how CommunityViz helped address the technical and human dimensions of the problem.

The context was a national forest in the West. The forest manager was responsible for making decisions in the best interests of the forest, and in particular for designing a program of silvicultural management, or vegetation treatments, that could include clear-cutting, thinning, and controlled burns. Unfortunately, she was confronted with a number of seemingly conflicting priorities. A stakeholder represented each priority, and you might imagine four angry people sitting around the conference table, arguing with the manager about what to do:

- The financial manager saw the forest as a financial resource. Its value came from the sale of timber; its costs came from timber harvesting. The financial manager's goal was to generate as much revenue with as little expense as possible. The best option to achieve that result was the clear-cutting of trees, and the second best was the selective thinning of trees. Controlled burns would not be useful in the near term.

- The fire manager saw the forest as a hazard area. This forest was particularly susceptible to dangerous crown fires, which can spread rapidly through the treetops—the crowns—when trees grow in a dense pattern. The fire manager's goal was to decrease the areas of dense crown. The best options were clear-cutting and controlled burns. Thinning would provide a partial benefit.

- The forester saw the forest as a long-term resource and wanted to maintain its health. He was particularly worried about dwarf mistletoe, an invasive species that was infecting the trees. The forester's goal was to improve forest health by reducing or eliminating the mistletoe. The preferred treatments varied among the forest stands, but in general, controlled burns and clear-cutting of the infected areas would be most effective.

- The recreation manager looked at the forest as a place for people to hike, camp, and fish. She objected to burning and clear-cutting because of their impacts on the appearance of the forest and the quality of water in rivers and streams. Her preference was for selective thinning or no cutting of trees at all.

The forest manager built a CommunityViz geodesign analysis to help her decide what to do. For data, she had detailed maps that had been gathered in the field, using mobile GIS, of areas of dense crown and mistletoe. She also had a coarse terrain raster that she decided to include for reference and in case she needed slope information later in the analysis. Combining those layers gave her the map shown in Figure 13.3.

As an experienced CommunityViz practitioner, the forest manager wisely asked herself what decisions needed to be made and what questions needed to be answered. She realized that the decision would come down to a treatment plan that showed where to burn, clear-cut, and thin. The forest manager did not yet know where the treatment polygons would actually be placed and which of the three treatments they would specify. Figure 13.4 is an example of a treatment plan map.

The questions to answer would come from her stakeholders: The financial manager would want to see indicators of revenues and expenses; the fire manager would want to see indicators of effects on dense crown; the forester would want to see indicators on the health of the forest

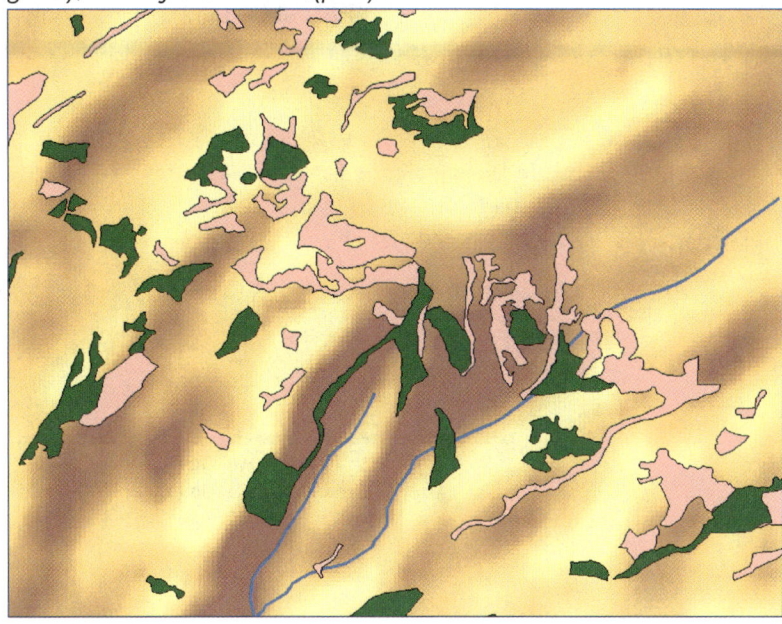

Figure 13.3 Base layers showing terrain (golden), dense crown (dark green), and infected stands (pink)

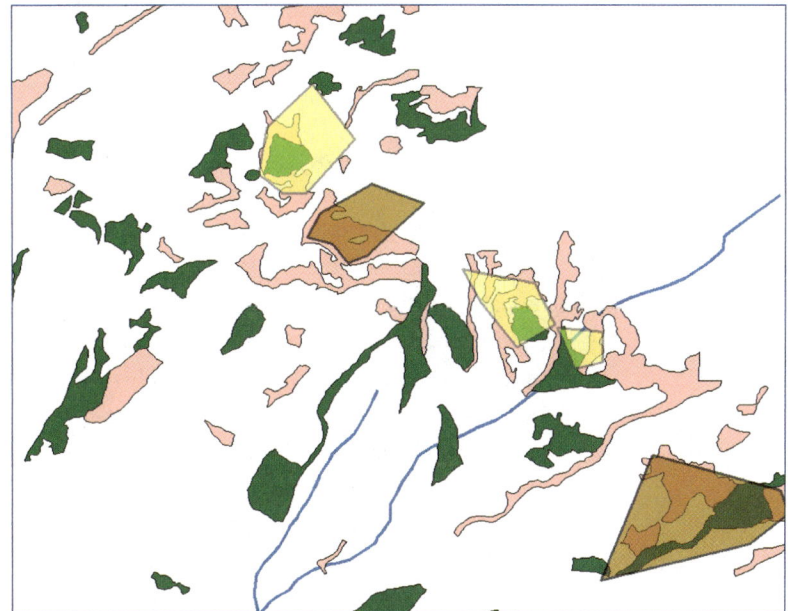

Figure 13.4 Sample of a treatment plan map, showing areas of clear-cutting (brown) and thinning (yellow). No burning is included in this treatment plan.

and the amount of mistletoe; and the recreation manager would want to see indicators on recreation opportunities. The forest manager showed those results in the charts in Figure 13.5 so that she could provide the group with immediate visual feedback about the effects of proposed treatment scenarios. She was careful to have at least one indicator for each stakeholder.

Figure 13.5 Impact indicator charts

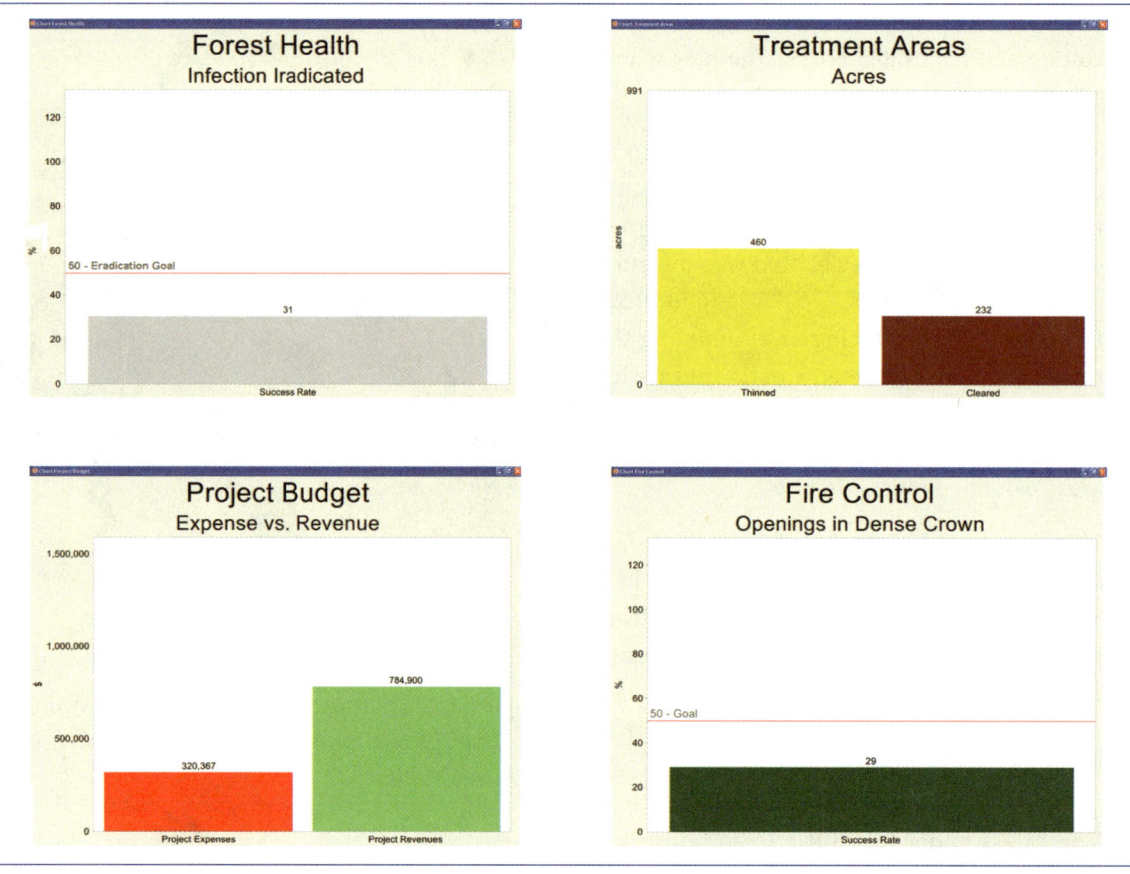

The forest manager set up her analysis and added a new, dynamic layer that she would use for sketching possible treatment areas. Then she created formulas to calculate the attribute values and indicators she required. Many of the results she needed came from multipliers based on the area and type of treatment. Thinning, for example, generated a certain amount of revenue per acre and had a certain cost per acre. However, the value of the multipliers could change because of several factors. Timber revenue, for example, varied by season and by market conditions. Therefore, she set up all the key multipliers as changeable assumptions (see Figure 13.6).

When the manager first showed her analysis to the team, everyone was very interested because she had quantified each stakeholder's concerns. Their first reaction was to focus on their own indicators and check whether the results made sense. The forest manager recognized that her calculations were reasonable but not completely accurate. She was using averages, and she knew that in some cases her model would under- or overestimate actual costs and results. The forester, for example, was uncomfortable with using a single number (45 percent) when estimating the effectiveness of thinning on reducing mistletoe infection, because he knew that the exact results of any treatment would vary. In response, the manager demonstrated that she could easily change the assumptions. Small changes, it turned out, made little difference in the results. The one exception was timber revenue per acre, where small changes could sometimes tip the balance between profitable and unprofitable operations.

The forest manager let each stakeholder spend some time with the model and invited each to sketch scenarios representing their own proposals for treatment plans. As each person worked with the model, they convinced themselves that it produced reasonable results for their particular area of concern. After that, they grew more interested in considering additional points of view. It became clear to the recreation manager, for example, that a small amount of thinning would have little benefit for any of the other stakeholders. More detailed treatment would be needed; the question began to transition from "whether" to "how much and where."

That kind of deeper thinking led most of the stakeholders to bring up suggestions for more detailed data to include in the model. The recreation manager, for example, suggested they add maps of the local hiking trails and try to find treatment areas that were not visible from the trails. Almost everyone agreed that they should avoid steep slopes and river crossings because of a combination of increased costs and environmental impacts. The forest manager, who was glad to see the conversation becoming more collaborative, added Scenario 360 alerts to the analysis to flag proposed treatment areas that were in poor locations.

Finally, it was time to start using the model as a base from which to create alternative scenarios and make choices. After discussion, the manager set a target for each indicator. The levels she set represented some compromise from what each stakeholder might have considered ideal, but this far into the discussion they all understood

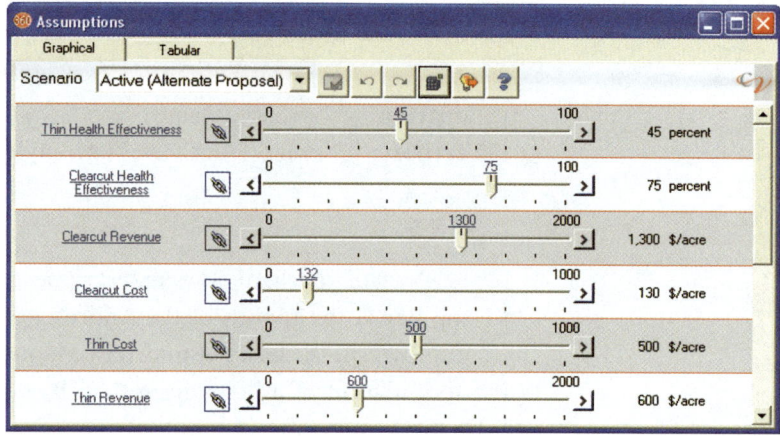

Figure 13.6 *Sample assumptions for the Vegetation Treatment exercise*

the need to make trade-offs. The team worked together to sketch several alternative scenarios and see how they performed compared to the targets. In each case, they were careful to test the implications of small changes in timber prices, because they now knew that these changes could be important.

In the end, they agreed on a vegetation treatment plan that met or came close to their targets. They had succeeded in making an informed, collaborative decision about a complex resource management challenge.

CASE STUDY
TOPSHAM NATURAL AREAS PLAN

Location: Topsham, Maine
Partners: Town of Topsham; New England Planning Concepts; Spatial Alternatives

The Town of Topsham borders Merrymeeting Bay at the mouth of the Androscoggin River, in the heart of midcoast Maine. With a population of a little more than 9,000 people, the community is a mix of historical neighborhoods, suburban residential development, and rural fields and forests (see Figure 13.7). Early development focused on the village of Topsham, while more recent development has occurred on large lots in the town's rural areas.

Topsham's 2005 comprehensive plan noted that while the town was rich in important natural resources, an inventory of those resources had never been completed. The plan recommended that the town "plan for the protection of important natural and scenic resources" and create "a more formal and comprehensive approach" to protection efforts. In 2006, the town formed the Natural Areas Planning Committee (NAPC).

Project Description: As a result of early public input, the NAPC decided to include a focus on community values pertaining to natural areas, in addition to a more traditional focus on the physical attributes of the land. The NAPC retained New England Planning Concepts and Spatial Alternatives to assist with the project. The consultants started by undertaking an inventory and detailed GIS mapping of the town's natural resources, analyzing each resource in relation to its functions: Environmental/Health and Safety, Habitat, Land Productivity, Recreational, Water Quality, and Wetlands (see Figures 13.8 and 13.9).

Following the inventory work, the NAPC held three public workshops to discern community values about natural areas. *Value voting,* a type of value mapping, was used, in which each participant figuratively spent $100, allocating it across values such as environmental health and safety,

Figure 13.7 A natural area in Topsham, Maine

Figure 13.8 Part of Topsham's water system

and habitat protection. This process yielded a weighting of the participants' values. In a CommunityViz analysis, the consultants mapped the town's resources based on the objective inventory data and the expressed community values. The resulting Matrix Analysis with All Values showed the combined approaches and also made clear the distinct resource focus areas within the town (see Figure 13.10).

The final part of the project was to use the results of the inventory, analysis, and public input to develop a set of recommendations. Recommendation number one was that "the Town directs the majority of its conservation resources, in whatever form (money, staff time, citizen effort, political capital, etc.), toward the focus areas and that the Town continues to use the methodology for identifying priority areas."

Technology and Tools: CommunityViz was used to analyze citizens' values about the town's natural resources. In addition, the consultants and NAPC held public workshops featuring small group discussions and value voting using keypads.

Outcomes: With the assistance of the consultants, town staff, and a multitude of community members, the NAPC prepared the Topsham Natural Areas Plan and presented it at a public meeting. After minor revisions were made to the plan, it was ready to become part of the town's comprehensive plan upon approval at the annual town meeting. In the meantime, the priorities expressed in the plan have already begun to inform discussions and priorities of the Topsham Conservation Commission and the Brunswick-Topsham Land Trust.

Figure 13.9 Agriculture in Topsham

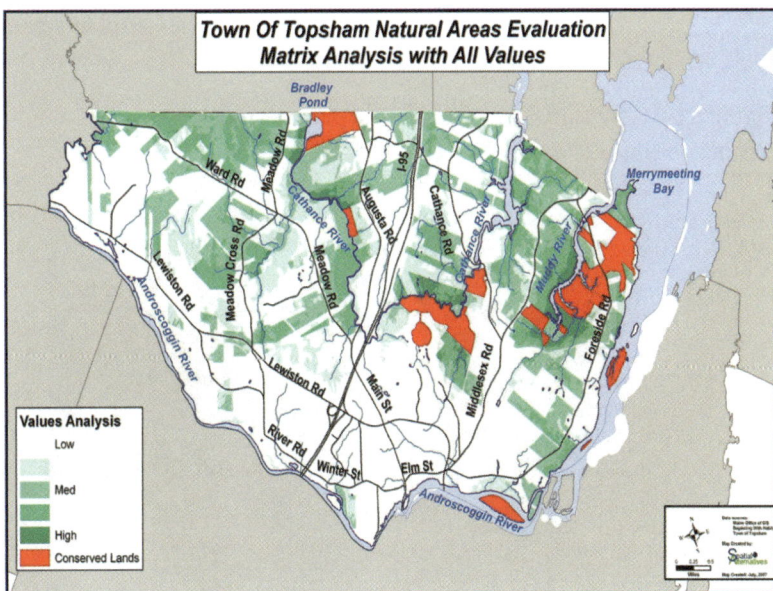

Figure 13.10 Map of Topsham showing areas of community-generated conservation value

CASE STUDY
DELMARVA ATLANTIC WATERSHED NETWORK

Location: Sussex County, Delaware; Worcester County, Maryland; Accomack and Northampton counties, Virginia

Partners: Delaware Coastal Management Program; Maryland Coastal Program; Virginia Coastal Zone Management Program; Maryland Coastal Bays Program; Center for the Inland Bays; Sussex, Worcester, Accomack, and Northampton counties; CommunityViz support by Donley & Associates, Inc.

The Delmarva Peninsula includes parts of Delaware, Maryland, and Virginia and lies between the Chesapeake Bay and the Atlantic Ocean. The peninsula boasts a strong agricultural economy based on corn, soybeans, and poultry production. The eastern shoreline offers historic communities, environmentally sensitive bays and estuaries, and rare species of plants and animals. The peninsula is increasingly being developed for new homes and tourism. In 2005, concerns about coastal development, tourism, water quality, public education, agriculture, and wildlife habitat led area leaders to form the Delmarva Atlantic Watershed Network (DAWN) to tackle issues of mutual concern. The network's mission was to look at the four-county area from a regional perspective and to identify cooperative efforts that could help protect the peninsula's natural resources in the midst of a growing population.

Figure 13.11 Density (in dwelling units per acre) for existing conditions and build out

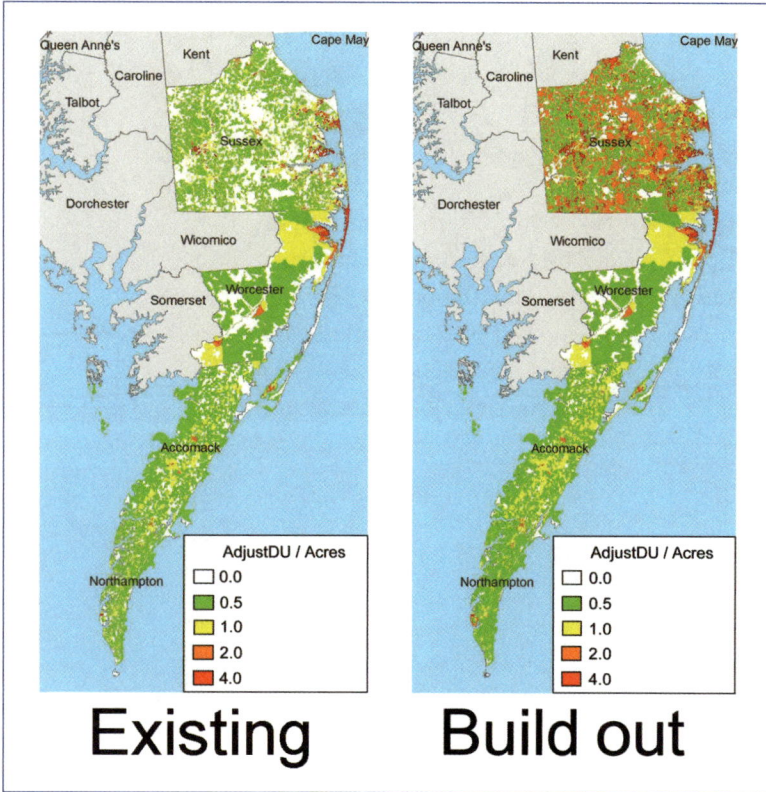

Project Description: In 2007, DAWN retained Donley & Associates, Inc. to undertake several resource-related analyses using CommunityViz, and to train people in the four counties to use the software. For the project, a series of build-out scenarios was developed for each county (see Figure 13.11) based on: zoning regulations; prime agricultural soils; green infrastructure; rare, threatened, and endangered species areas; floodplains; sewer service areas; groundwater recharge areas; and nutrient load by sub-watershed.

The analyses allowed people to see the amount of land in agriculture or forestry, as well as the development permitted under current zoning in each county and the anticipated impacts of that development on nutrient loads (see Figure 13.12). The results varied widely among the counties. In Worcester County, Maryland, a build-out population of 80,000 was projected, roughly double the 2007 population; the projection for Accomack and Northampton counties in Virginia was a combined build-out population of about 100,000, up from 44,000; and Sussex County, Delaware, faced a build-out of about 2 million residents, more than 10 times the 2007 population of 184,000. Impacts on agricultural lands and other indicators were significant—for example, Sussex County would lose more than 80 percent of its agricultural lands and 80 percent of its forestlands if current land-use trends and zoning regulations continued.

Public education was an important part of the project. Information about the project was disseminated through regional newspapers, mailings, and presentations to leadership groups, local civic organizations, state and federal political representatives, and on radio and television. Informational workshops were held for the public, planning staffs, and county commissioners in all four counties. Online CommunityViz training workshops were held for county planners.

Technology and Tools: A key tool was CommunityViz, including its Build-Out Wizard. A variety of outreach and educational tools and processes were also used, including written information delivered through news media, drop boxes, and mailings; PowerPoint presentations; radio and television presentations; public workshops; a project website; and an interactive heart-and-soul website for Sussex County.

Outcomes: The project gave rise to a number of other projects. In Sussex County, the county government and the University of Delaware collaborated on more-detailed county-level and sub-area planning, using CommunityViz to "paint" alternative land-use scenarios and analyze the results. In addition, the Sussex County Heart and

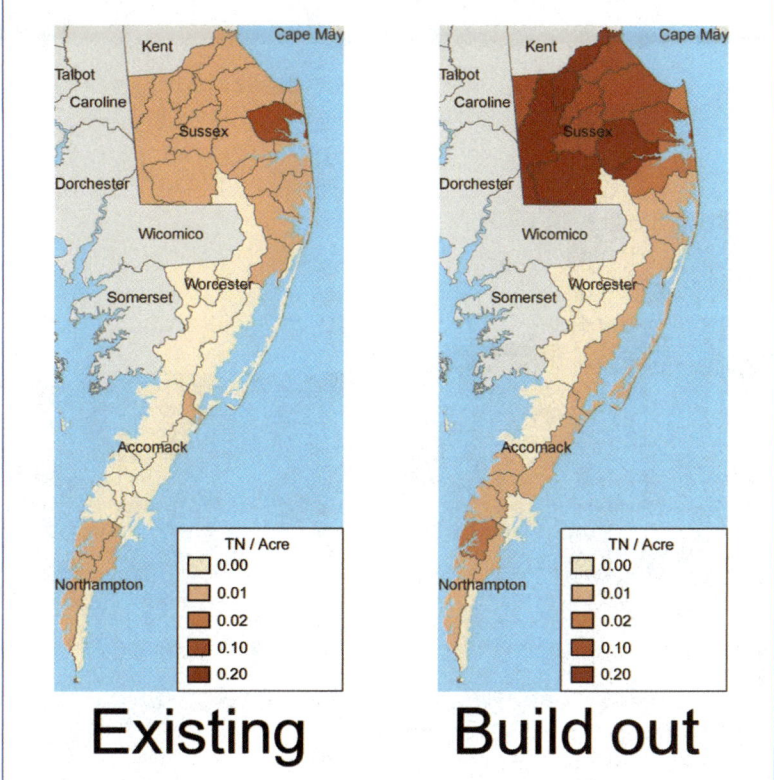

Figure 13.12 Nitrogen per acre (also known as nutrient load) estimated for existing conditions and build out

Soul project engaged citizens in public discussions about their desires, enabling future land-use decisions to be informed by citizen-defined heart-and-soul values.

Accomack and Northampton counties in Virginia also engaged in more-detailed analyses of future planning scenarios, and county staffs developed a road show to demonstrate how their counties might change for the better. The Delmarva Atlantic Watershed Network's build-out scenarios helped in the creation of a new comprehensive plan in Accomack County, and zoning amendments in Northampton County.

SECTION IV: REVIEWING REGULATIONS AND DEVELOPMENT PROPOSALS

NAVIGATING THIS SECTION

Section 4 explains how CommunityViz can help you gauge development potential and evaluate development proposals through the analysis of zoning regulations, estimation of public service costs, pro forma analyses, and design reviews.

Chapter 14, Analyzing Zoning Regulations, describes advanced uses of the Build-Out Wizard and other techniques that enable you to conduct detailed assessments of development capacity.

Chapter 15, Cost-of-Services Analyses, Capital Improvements, and Pro Formas, demonstrates ways to estimate the financial impacts of development and infrastructure from both the public and private perspectives. The chapter includes a description of the Custom Impacts Wizard and details on how to use External Table Links to connect to spreadsheet-based financial models.

Chapter 16, Design Reviews and Form-Based Codes, shows how you can use both 3-D modeling and numerical analysis when reviewing development proposals. The chapter describes design measurements or indicators, how to make 3-D models of proposed developments, and how to use these models to apply form-based codes or to enhance design reviews.

BACKGROUND PLANNING CONCEPTS FOR THIS SECTION

Zoning is the most common land-use control in the United States. A zoning ordinance consists of two parts: a text and a zoning map, which is based on the future land-use map of the comprehensive plan. The zoning ordinance usually divides the planning area into zoning districts, such as R-1 Single Family, C-1 Downtown Commercial, and MU-Mixed Use (commercial and residential), although other innovative types of regulation are also used.

Each zoning district has regulations governing permitted land uses, the density of those uses, the height of buildings, the setbacks of buildings from property lines, and how much of a site can be covered by buildings. In form-based codes, less emphasis is placed on land uses but more specifications are given for building design.

There should be a tight connection between the zoning ordinance and the comprehensive plan, because one of the main purposes of the zoning ordinance is to put the goals and objectives of the comprehensive plan into action as a way to promote orderly growth and change. Whenever the comprehensive plan is updated or entirely rewritten, it is important to update or revise the zoning ordinance to keep the two documents consistent with each other. Thus, the zoning ordinance, like the comprehensive plan, should be updated or revised at least every five to 10 years to reflect changes in community needs and desires.

Another purpose of zoning is to avoid or minimize conflicts between properties that have different uses. These conflicts can affect not just property values but the health and safety of residents. In particular, conflicting land uses may impact one or more of the community's heart-and-soul resources. CommunityViz and GIS can indicate places where conflicting uses are likely to exist. Identifying such conflicts can alert the public and elected officials of the need to change the zoning ordinance.

A valuable exercise to evaluate a zoning ordinance is a build-out analysis, which estimates how much new residential development can be accommodated in a residential zoning district. The question behind a build-out analysis is: "Does the community have enough residentially zoned land to accommodate future growth over the next 20 years, or is there too much residentially zoned land?" Typically, many cities and inner suburbs have little vacant residential land. Rural areas often have enough residentially zoned land to accommodate growth for several decades and add many more people than the community really wants.

Traditional build-out analysis was tedious and time-consuming because it involved many manual calculations and estimates of future growth. CommunityViz has transformed build-out analysis by automating most of the calculations and enabling detailed estimates of future development. Planners can now run build-out calculations that assess current zoning capacity and predict what would happen under a variety of possible changes to the zoning regulations.

Subdivision and land-development regulations are designed to ensure that land can safely support development. Subdivision is the legal process of dividing land into lots for future sale and development. Land-development regulations refer to standards for providing infrastructure such as roads, sewer and water facilities, and utilities to one or more parcels of land, and how buildings are placed on that land.

By using CommunityViz with up-to-date data on subdivision activity and building permits, you can monitor the rate of land development over time. In addition, as new development occurs, you can estimate the impacts on roads, water and sewer, utilities, and the environment. You can also anticipate needs for new infrastructure or for adjustments to land development regulations.

Capital improvements are the public investments in infrastructure that support current and future development. A Capital Improvements Program is a three- to five-year schedule of which infrastructure will be built or repaired and when, where the infrastructure will be located, and how it will be paid for. A Capital Improvements Program (CIP), like the zoning ordinance and subdivision regulations, serves to put the comprehensive plan into action. All four of these documents should be up to date and consistent with one another.

A CIP enables a community to set priorities for public infrastructure investments, budget for them, and build or maintain them in an orderly fashion. A well-crafted CIP will greatly assist in formulating the community's revenue needs, tax rates, and annual budget.

CommunityViz can show the location of infrastructure in relation to existing development and areas planned and zoned for future growth. How those future growth areas are developed will affect the amount, type, and cost of infrastructure. CommunityViz can calculate and illustrate the costs and revenues of different development patterns.

Infrastructure and government services such as schools, police, and fire protection required by new development cost money, and a study of those costs is known as a *cost-of-services analysis* (or a fiscal impact analysis). A formal cost-of-community-services study shows how much each land use contributes to the community's property taxes and how much it demands in public services. More than 80 cost-of-community-services studies have been conducted across the United States. They have all found that agricultural, commercial, and industrial land produce much more in property taxes than they demand in services, whereas residential land demands more in services than it generates in property taxes, mainly because of the need to educate the children of homeowners and renters.

Local cost-of-services analyses are used for many purposes, including comparisons of public service costs for different types of development, negotiations between a community and developers, and budget planning. CommunityViz provides a good platform for cost-of-services analysis because it can incorporate cost models as well as spatial information, such as road lengths. For example, when local officials are contemplating a ballot measure to raise public funds to preserve farmland, CommunityViz can illustrate where the farmland is and show how the community's revenues would change if some or all of the farmland was converted to residential development.

The design of the built environment and public spaces affects the community's appearance, historic character, tourism, pedestrian access and safety, and heart-and-soul resources. Communities can regulate many aspects of building design through design review guidelines, standards, or form-based codes.

Design review guidelines and standards usually apply to specific zoning districts, such as commercial districts and historic districts. A form-based code typically is applied to an area poised for redevelopment or a new development altogether. Design review ordinances and form-based codes both specify how new buildings or major alterations to existing buildings must relate to the neighboring buildings and public spaces in terms of height, setbacks, materials, color, orientation, roof type, and even architectural style.

The local government appoints a design review board of three to five members. Good candidates for a design review board are an architect, landscape architect, and local historian. The design review board inspects all architectural drawings and any CommunityViz presentations submitted by the developer, and it makes a recommendation to the elected governing body.

If form-based codes are being used, the planning commission has review authority, though it may work in tandem with the design review board. The planning commission can carefully compare the proposed development to the building form standards specified in the code. A review based on a design review ordinance should use objective data such as a historic buildings survey and the community values map discussed in Section 2. CommunityViz Scenario 3D is an excellent tool for illustrating a proposed building or new public space in the context of the rest of the neighborhood. Scenario 360 can also help provide information about typical existing development in the community. The design review board can then make recommendations about changes to the proposal to improve its conformance with design standards and its fit with nearby structures.

14 ANALYZING ZONING REGULATIONS

KEY CONCEPTS AND TERMS IN THIS CHAPTER

- Advanced Build-Out Wizard techniques
- Capacity calculations
- Zoning development capacity analysis

From time to time, planners need to evaluate how well zoning regulations are implementing the goals and objectives of a comprehensive plan. Their analysis can include a review of the zoning districts that seem mismatched with the future land use map of the comprehensive plan; a detailed assessment of future development capacity in one or more zoning districts, such as R-3 Multifamily, for example; and projections about the future mix of land uses in particular zoning districts. An analysis of zoning regulations is more detailed and precise than a visioning exercise or the future land-use element of the comprehensive plan, in part because a zoning ordinance is a local law.

CommunityViz provides helpful tools for analyzing a zoning map and the written zoning district regulations. The CommunityViz Build-Out Wizard provides an array of capabilities for evaluating the performance of zoning districts over time. In addition, you can use CommunityViz custom analysis to address special needs and unique situations.

WHY AND WHEN

A zoning development capacity analysis is a little like spring cleaning: something to do on a regular basis but also a bit of a chore. Not only can CommunityViz make the task easier, it can help you arrive at new insights. We recommend you undertake a zoning development capacity analysis: a) if your community is experiencing rapid growth; b) as part of a general revision of the zoning ordinance; or c) if an update to the comprehensive plan and the future land-use map will result in changes to the zoning map and text.

A zoning development capacity analysis gives you a clear picture of what kinds, amount, and location of development your zoning regulations allow. It looks in detail at your current zoning regulations, existing development, and recent development trends to assess your capacity to absorb new development and redevelopment. An up-to-date zoning development capacity analysis lets you identify gaps between the supply of and demand for commercial- and residential-zoned land for development. You can also anticipate future needs and locations for public services.

DATA NEEDS

To begin a zoning development capacity analysis you need the current zoning map and the text of the zoning regulations. If you have parcel data in digital form, use them; if not, use the individual zoning districts. You will also need GIS data representing any features mentioned in the zoning regulations, such as roads, rivers, floodplains, and steep slopes. Most of this data should be readily available, but if not, you will need to find good sources. Unlike broad-brush planning exercises, zoning capacity analysis does not work well with work-around data or hand sketches.

ZONING DEVELOPMENT CAPACITY ANALYSIS USING THE BUILD-OUT WIZARD

Chapter 8 explained how to use the Build-Out Wizard as part of a community planning process. Here we describe how to use the wizard to calculate the capacity you will need for analyzing the zoning regulations. For details on how to operate the Build-Out Wizard, consult the guide in the standard CommunityViz documentation.[1]

To calculate development capacity based on current zoning regulations:

1. Decide on a study area. To maximize the Build-Out Wizard's performance, choose the smallest convenient area you can, such as a city's boundaries or the boundaries of a particular residential subdivision. For a larger area such as a county, consider performing separate analyses on geographic subsections.

2. Choose a land-use analysis layer. For a zoning development capacity analysis, you normally use zoning districts or parcels. In this description, we will use the term *parcels*. For this layer, be sure to use the same GIS-projected coordinate system as you have for all the other layers in your analysis, and discard any parcels that are not part of your study. Check the data for quality, paying particular attention to the following items that you will need to fix before proceeding:

   a. Empty (null value) fields
   b. Slivers or overlaps where parcel boundaries do not align perfectly
   c. Duplicate or stacked parcels
   d. Parcels that straddle zoning districts and need to be split into two
   e. Unique zoning districts that break up parcels into smaller zones, as often occur in planned unit developments (PUDs).

3. Define zoning designations. You will need a single attribute in each parcel giving its designation, which is usually the same as its zoning district. However, if the number of zoning districts is more than about 40, consolidate them into a smaller number of generalized zoning designations. Later, you may add some artificial designations to help you address situations such as partial density constraints or overlay districts. If your parcels do not already contain attributes giving their zoning designations, use CommunityViz scale-changing functions such as GetFromClosest to pull in the designation from the underlying zoning map (refer to Chapter 11 for details on scale-changing functions).

4. Decide on density rules (see Figure 14.1). Ideally you will be able to enter these directly from the zoning ordinance, either manually or from an input table or attribute in the parcels layer. The most common formats for density designations are simple rules such as dwelling units per acre and floor area ratio, but the Build-Out Wizard can also use lot sizes, specific numbers of units per feature, and specific amounts of commercial space per feature. If zoning regulations are not straightforward, you will need to do additional analysis:

   a. Reduce density ranges to a single number. For instance, regulations may call for low-density residential development of between one and four dwelling units per acre. For analysis purposes, this needs to be set at one specific number. Use the highest allowable density for a conservative (that is, high) build-out estimate, or

Figure 14.1 Density rules screenshot from the Build-Out Wizard

Designation	Dwelling Units		Floor Area	
	Quantity	Measurement	Quantity	Measurement
Commercial	0	None	30000	Floor Area (sq feet)
High Density Multi-family	30	DU per acre	0	None
Med Density Multi-family	10	DU per acre	0	None
Mixed Use	10	DU per acre	0.5	FAR
Office Park	0	None	1.5	FAR

---

[1] This is available online at http://placeways.com/communityviz.

an intermediate density (2.5 dwelling units per acre in this example) for a likely estimate. There is no easy way to vary the density during analysis, because any change in density requires a completely new run of the Build-Out Wizard.

b. Precalculate condition-dependent density values. If allowable uses depend on previous or current uses, the presence of an overlay district, historic designations, utility service areas, or similar conditions, calculate these effects ahead of time so that you can enter a single value for the parcel.

5. Consider mixed uses. If zoning regulations call for a simple mix of residential and commercial densities, no special processing is required. However, you will need to provide the Build-Out Wizard with additional information if:

   a. Regulations specify a particular mix of uses within buildings; or

   b. Regulations set aside a certain percentage of area within a parcel for a particular use, such as open space.

6. Document multifamily designations. If regulations specify two or more dwelling units per building, you will need to enter that information into the Build-Out Wizard.

7. Document building constraints and gather relevant data about constraint areas (see Figure 14.2). Take into consideration that:

   a. The Build-Out Wizard will automatically exclude unbuildable areas such as water bodies, floodplains, or right-of-way easements from the analysis, but you must provide polygon layers representing those areas. If your data contain only constraint points or lines, such as centerlines for roads or rivers, you will need to make a new polygon layer by buffering the points or lines.

   b. The Build-Out Wizard will need to know whether density transfer is allowed—that is, whether a parcel that includes unbuildable areas is allowed to have the same number of buildings as it would without that constraint, or the unbuildable area is netted out so that only the density in the remaining buildable area applies. Note that we are referring here only to density transfer within a given parcel. If you need to analyze transfers of development rights between parcels, set up a custom analysis outside the Build-Out Wizard.

   c. If the constraints are partial—for example, building is allowed but at a reduced density—you will need to create separate pseudo-parcels ahead of time and assign them a land-use designation with a reduced density, or else do a custom analysis as described later in this chapter.

   d. If regulations specify a minimum buildable lot size, such as 1 acre, you will need to specify that size in the Build-Out Wizard. This feature can be useful for excluding the development of small slivers of land left over from clipping out constraints.

   e. If regulations specify lot-line setbacks, you have several choices: You can use the Build-Out Wizard's spatial component to

Figure 14.2 *The Build-Out Wizard's constraints to development*

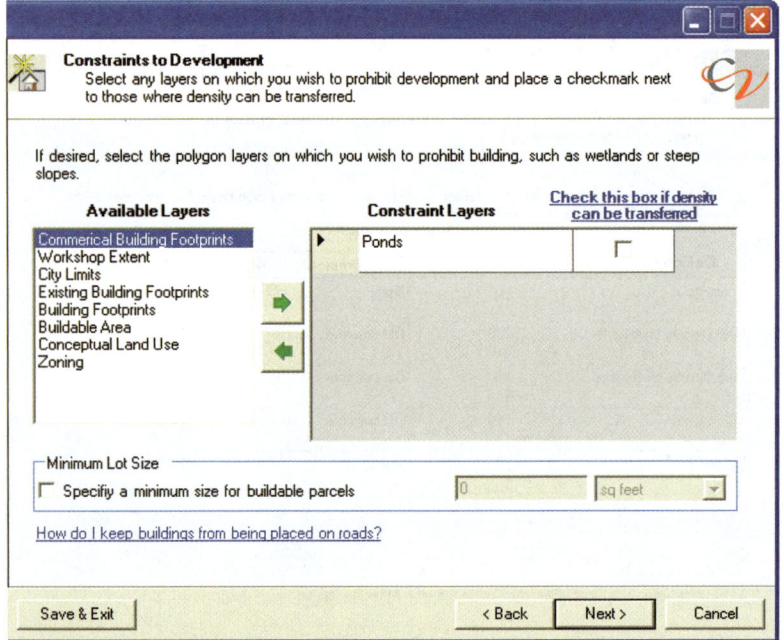

estimate effects. Spatial build out takes into account road setbacks, building separation distances, and lot-line setback distances to determine how many buildings can fit onto a lot. However, its results are only estimates. Other alternatives are to create constraint layers that represent setback areas by buffering roads and lot lines, and using custom analysis.

f. If regulations specify height restrictions or building envelopes that you cannot translate into a floor area ratio, you will need to use custom analysis.

8. Decide on efficiency factors, which enable you to take into account additional building restrictions that you have not explicitly included in the analysis. There are three main types, but we recommend that you use only the first two in the Build-Out Wizard:

   a. **Statutory factors,** such as a 20 percent open space requirement for new residential subdivisions

   b. **Accessory land uses,** such as access roads, parking, and utilities rights-of-way

   c. **Planner's judgments** about a development's likelihood, timing, or form. Because these judgments tend to be subjective, we recommend that you apply them *after* completing the more objective parts of the analysis so that your assumptions are more transparent and easier to change.

9. Assemble data about existing development. Here are some guidelines:

   a. If your parcel layer already contains attribute information about existing development, you do not need to use the Build-Out Wizard to recalculate it. To calculate remaining development capacity, simply subtract the existing development from the Build-Out Wizard's total capacity calculations.

   b. If your parcel layer does not contain information about existing development, you can tell the Build-Out Wizard to use information from a separate point layer such as an emergency services address map. Each point should be attributed with the number of dwelling units or amount of commercial space it represents.

   c. If you know footprints of existing buildings, you have several choices. You can run an overlap calculation that populates the parcels layer with information from the footprints it contains. Alternatively, you can convert the footprint polygons to *centroid* points using an ArcMap feature-to-point edit, and then provide the point layer to the Build-Out Wizard. You can also do custom analysis as described later in this chapter.

   d. If you anticipate redevelopment of existing structures or areas, consider omitting them from your existing buildings data, or else treat them as partial constraints.

Once you have developed and compiled this information, you can use it to run an analysis in the Build-Out Wizard. Look carefully at the results for each zoning district. It is normal to uncover mistakes or problems in the first few iterations; do not be concerned if it takes several cycles of refinement to achieve credible results. Two of the many benefits of the wizard are that you can run it as many times as you like and you can quickly and easily modify your analysis. For example, if you decide to eliminate one or more of your constraints from consideration, you can do so with a single click in the wizard.

Just as you may have done preprocessing before running the Build-Out Wizard, you may also want to do post-processing. If you did not use an Existing Buildings layer, for instance, you may need to create some formulas to calculate remaining capacity. Similarly, you will probably want to create a number of summary indicators that provide an overview of zoning capacities and current uses. Start with the default indicators that the Build-Out Wizard provides, and then add indicators as needed.

ZONING DEVELOPMENT CAPACITY CALCULATIONS OUTSIDE THE BUILD-OUT WIZARD

You may also do some or all of your development capacity calculations using custom Scenario 360 analysis tools. Reasons to use custom analysis for capacity calculations include:

- There is little uniformity in zoning in your study area, so that the number of distinct land-use designations is very high (100 or more).

- Significant parts of your study area are developed, and most of the analysis has to do with redevelopment or infill potential.

- Density rules within a zoning district vary based on the characteristics of each parcel.

- You need a detailed lot-by-lot analysis of building envelopes or buildable footprints.

Custom analysis is very flexible and enables you to design an analysis to meet your needs. Your goal is to create attributes in the parcels layer that provide the allowable development capacity for each type of use the zoning allows.

For area calculations, calculate factors that reduce the gross area of a parcel to its net buildable area. Here are some typical limiting factors and suggestions for analyzing them:

- **Constraint layers** such as steep slopes, floodplains, water bodies, wetlands, riparian buffers, environmentally protected areas, hazardous areas, and rights-of-way. If these are no-build constraints, it's helpful to merge the layers into one layer before doing further analysis. Consider creating a New Parcels layer that is like the original Parcels layer except that constrained areas are clipped out. (This is the method the Build-Out Wizard uses.) If you choose not to use clipping, be careful to account for overlapping constraint layers. You may mistakenly double-count constrained areas if you are simply summing overlaps from individual constraint layers.

- **Setbacks,** including road setbacks and lot-line setbacks. Often, lot-line setbacks are uniform on three sides and larger on the side facing the road. If so, you can buffer the side and rear lot lines to make one constraint layer, buffer the road to make another constraint layer, and then merge the two. If lot-line setbacks vary between side and rear, you may need to construct a new line feature that traces all the rear lot lines, and then buffer that line to create the back-of-lot setback.

- **Building footprint coverage limitations.** If there is a straightforward requirement such as no more than 15 percent lot coverage or at least 90 percent lot coverage, you can multiply that ratio by the area of the parcel to find the size of the footprint. Pay attention to minimum sizes; if the buildable footprint is too small, it may not be feasible to construct a building. To find the buildable capacity, multiply the footprint by the number of floors allowed.

- **Set-asides for open space or agriculture.** Set-asides are usually easy to calculate because they are specified as percentages of the parcel area. However, they typically apply to commercial developments and residential subdivisions, where many other factors influence the built capacity. For large PUDs, it's best to estimate residential and commercial development capacity in conjunction with a design review (see Chapter 16).

Methods for specifying density vary widely. If ordinances are written in common formats such as dwelling units per acre, minimum lot size, and floor area ratio, the calculations are straightforward. However, those formats are not always used. In urban areas, for example, the primary restriction on capacity is usually building height. In suburban areas, regulations may specify minimum building separation distances. In addition, ordinances may impose complicated conditions on density that you will need to account for using a series of calculations. (See the teaching example at the end of this chapter.)

One advantage of custom analysis is that it allows you to design fine analysis controls related to density, such as zoning overlay districts. If you are including overlay districts in your analysis, be certain to include indicators and other reporting data that allow you to keep track of the source of your ultimate development capacity for a zoning district.

A possible result of a careful zoning development capacity analysis is the discovery of zoning nonconformities or inconsistencies, such as areas where development is clearly intended but is not possible because of zoning restrictions. This information is important. Highlight it in your analysis by using alerts and reports. You can also employ the analysis capabilities of CommunityViz to suggest and design remedial measures.

ESTIMATING CAPACITY UTILIZATION

Once you have used the Build-Out Wizard or custom analysis to calculate the remaining development capacity in your study area, you can begin estimating how that development capacity will be taken up over time. Such a development-timing estimate involves considerably more guesswork than a development capacity analysis for a zoning district. You must clearly distinguish between the relative accuracy of the two analyses whenever you present your results.

Chapter 8 covered methods for projecting the timing and location of development. If you have done a thorough zoning development capacity analysis, you can refine those development projections with the additional information you now have. In particular, look for:

- Underdeveloped parcels—that is, parcels zoned for much more capacity than they currently use
- Parcels whose capacity has recently changed because of the addition of an overlay district
- Parcels where public policies encourage or discourage new development or redevelopment, such as in a tax increment financing district or a historic preservation district
- Areas with abundant remaining development capacity in highly desirable areas, which you can identify by doing a desirability assessment, described in Chapter 8
- Parcels that appear to be unbuildable because of zoning constraints.

TEACHING EXAMPLE

This example is of a residential land inventory and capacity analysis for a midsized city in Canada.[2] The example includes basic principles for a zoning development capacity analysis. Moreover, it highlights techniques for studying redevelopment potential and complex zoning regulations. It's a good example of an advanced analysis performed outside the Build-Out Wizard.

The city provided us with a Parcels layer and a property database. The Parcels layer included an identifier attribute that allowed us to join it to the property database, providing us with reliable data about existing development conditions and zoning designations. Prior to the zoning development capacity analysis, a future development projection had been conducted for the city. The development estimates from this forecast, and the city's current population, gave us a good baseline for comparison with the existing development numbers from the property tax assessor. Building constraints were also straightforward: This was a well-established urban area where the only unbuildable areas were clearly designated parks or public facilities.

There were hundreds of distinct zoning designations, so one of our first steps was to compress them into a smaller number of classifications. This was laborious, but since many of the unique characteristics of the districts involved accessory uses or minor differences in setbacks, we found that combining uses by density and floor area ratio was effective in reducing the number of zoning designations without reducing accuracy. We decided on approximately 18 residential classes, and because nonresidential development was not our focus, we decided that single classes for commercial, civic-recreation, and industrial were acceptable. The resulting map appears in Figure 14.3.

Calculating the potential residential development capacity of each parcel was complicated. In principle, a parcel's capacity is its area times its allowed density. If you subtract the existing dwelling units from the total capacity, you get the remaining development capacity. Here, however, there were complications to that simple formula.

---

2. The example is drawn from work Placeways performed with Urban Systems, Ltd. for Victoria, British Columbia, Canada. Some details have been changed to make teaching points clearer.

Figure 14.3 *Generalized zoning map*

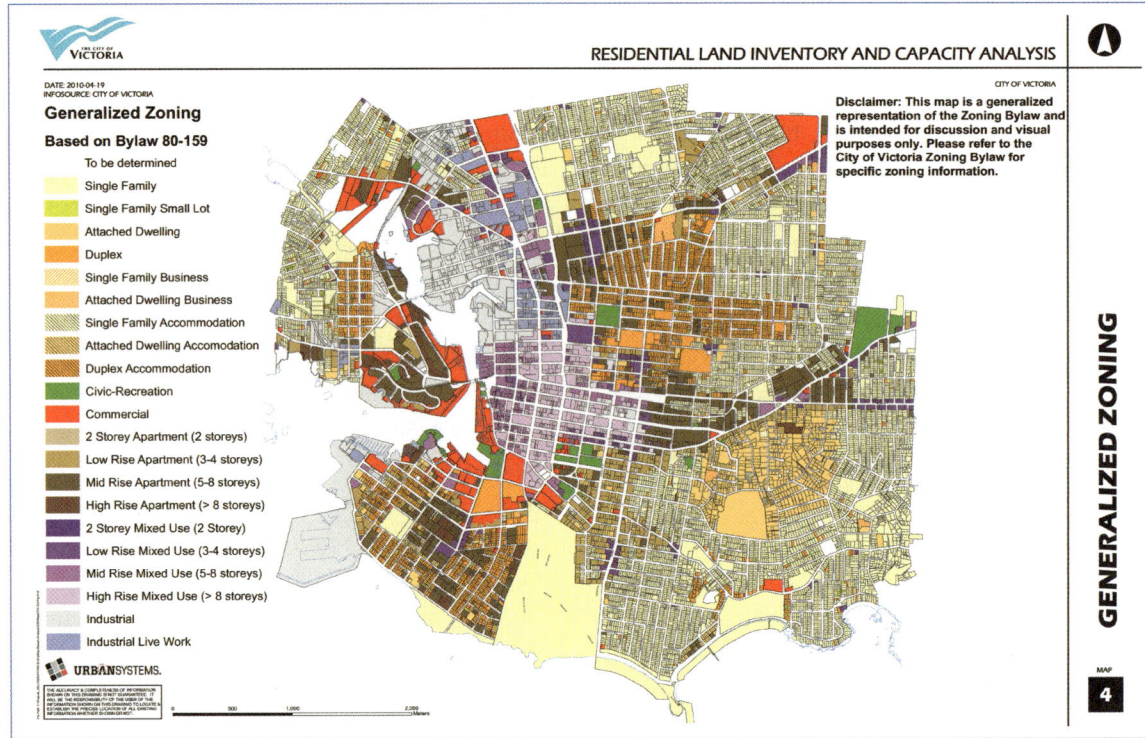

Images from this example courtesy of City of Victoria

The primary consideration was the prevalence of redevelopment. In this mature city, most of the residential development activity involved redeveloping existing structures into denser housing. Examples included converting single-family units to multifamily units, converting older multifamily units into new larger multifamily units, or converting older commercial buildings into mixed use developments. But we could not do our analysis on the broad assumption that every parcel would be redeveloped to its maximum potential, because a variety of constraints might apply. These included the following:

- Historic designations

- Actual use that was perpetually nonresidential—such as parks and government buildings—despite residential zoning

- Site-specific zoning that reflected current actual use

- Multifamily zoning on parcels that were too small to support multifamily construction

- Actual use that was a recent single-family-to-multifamily conversion but still below capacity.

An example of the last item was a new three-unit apartment on a parcel that allowed four units. The zoning code specified almost uniformly across all single-family zoning districts that if a single-family home was built prior to 1931 it was eligible for a conversion to a multifamily building. However, if it had been converted to multifamily after 1984, the owner could not conduct another conversion that would increase the number of units.

To manage these considerations, we developed a CommunityViz analysis based on a flowchart, shown in Figure 14.4. You do not need to study the chart in detail; it illustrates that we evaluated each parcel by checking for various restrictions that allowed us to calculate its development capacity.

When the analysis was complete, we had a map of the city's remaining residential development capacity, shown in Figure 14.5.

We could also map and analyze the remaining capacity in terms of types of units (see Figure 14.6), lot coverage, building age, and other factors. This gave the city an excellent view of its inventory.

Figure 14.4 Capacity calculation flowchart

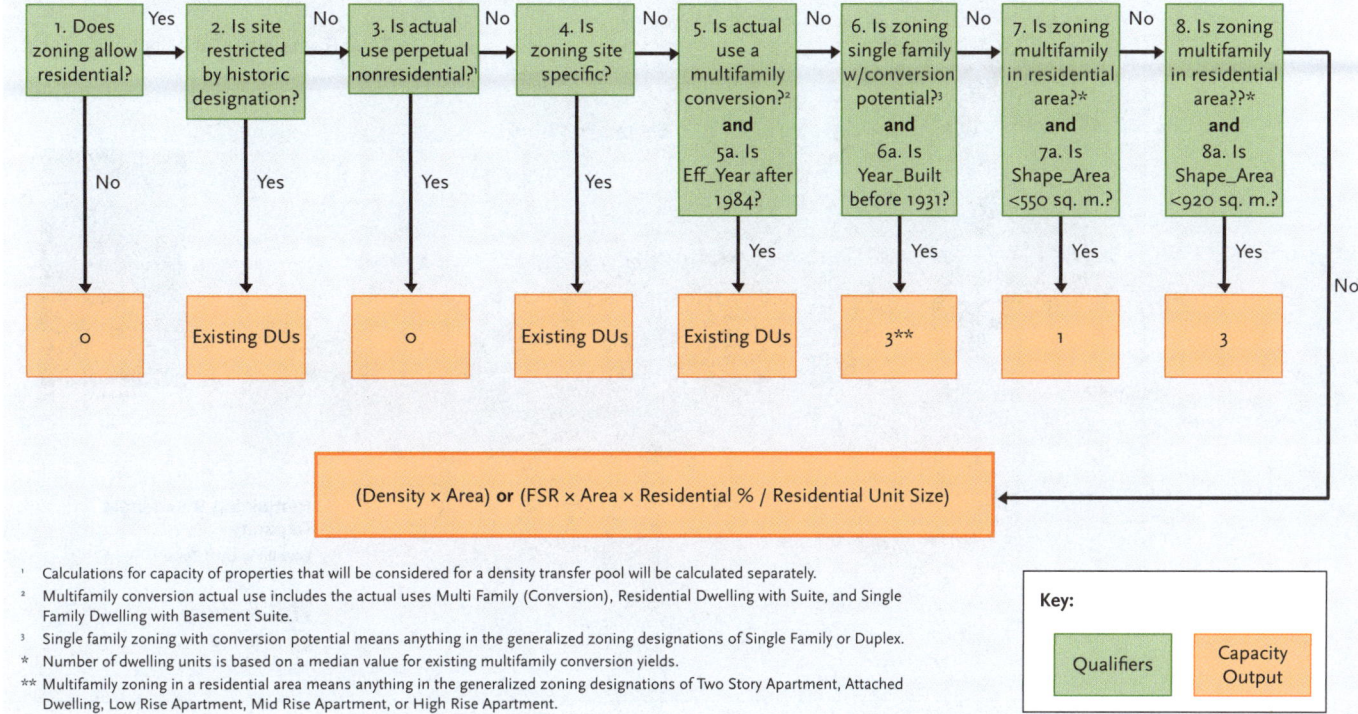

[1] Calculations for capacity of properties that will be considered for a density transfer pool will be calculated separately.
[2] Multifamily conversion actual use includes the actual uses Multi Family (Conversion), Residential Dwelling with Suite, and Single Family Dwelling with Basement Suite.
[3] Single family zoning with conversion potential means anything in the generalized zoning designations of Single Family or Duplex.
[*] Number of dwelling units is based on a median value for existing multifamily conversion yields.
[**] Multifamily zoning in a residential area means anything in the generalized zoning designations of Two Story Apartment, Attached Dwelling, Low Rise Apartment, Mid Rise Apartment, or High Rise Apartment.

The city was also interested in estimating future development patterns to understand how the remaining development capacity might be used over the following 30 years and how well the available supply of buildings and land would be able to meet the forecast needs.

For that purpose, we created a CommunityViz Suitability Wizard analysis that allowed the city to consider a number of factors that could affect the likelihood of development:

- **Remaining residential development capacity.** The more capacity, the higher the likelihood of development.

- **Building age.** We assumed that older buildings were more likely to be redeveloped.

- **Lot coverage.** Parcels with more available land were more likely to be developed.

- **Heritage restrictions**. Many parcels were limited by historic register designations and other historic considerations. The city found that these restrictions dissuaded development but did not entirely prevent it.

Figure 14.5 Map of remaining residential capacity by units

Our suitability analysis automatically set up changeable weighting assumptions so that the city planners could see the relative effects of these and other factors on the patterns of likely development (see Figure 14.7).

Figure 14.6 Map of remaining residential development capacity by dwelling unit types

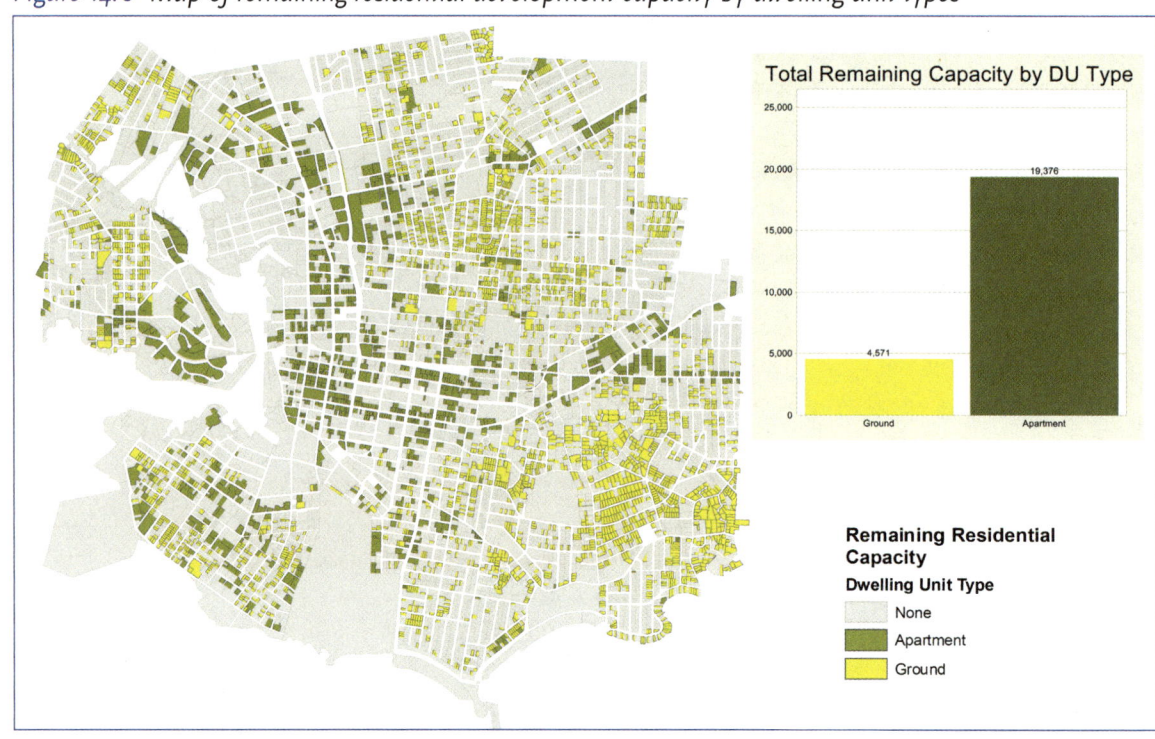

Figure 14.7 Analysis of development likelihood

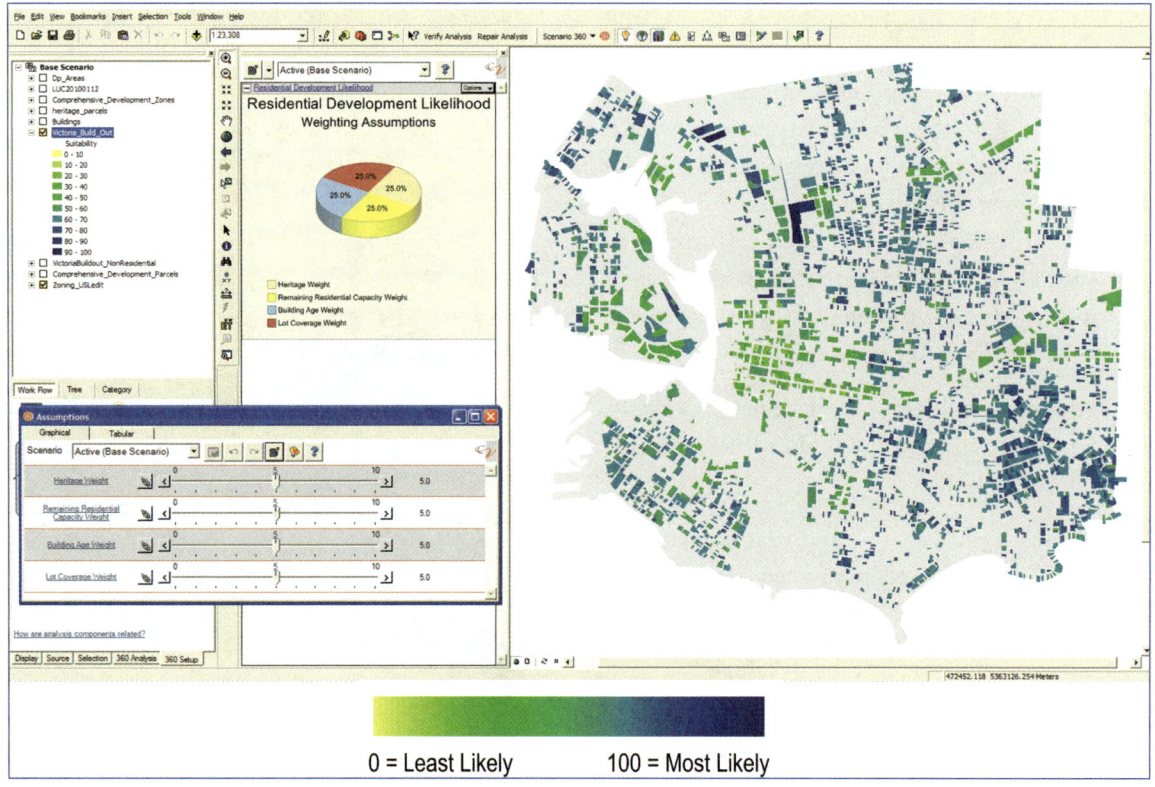

We also ran a Scenario 360 Allocator analysis that combined the likelihood of development with our capacity calculations and the previously forecasted demand to produce a map of future development and density. Using a timeline slider incorporating allocations at 10-year increments, we created an interactive map that allowed planners to change the year and see the changing density of their city. An example of a density map for 30 years in the future appears in Figure 14.8.

This example of zoning development capacity analysis demonstrates how useful CommunityViz can be for interpreting complex zoning codes and for understanding redevelopment potential in an urban area. CommunityViz is also excellent for evaluating zoning development capacity in areas where zoning is simpler and redevelopment is less common. In those cases, the Build-Out Wizard does most of the work. Whether your needs are simple or complex, CommunityViz makes zoning development capacity analysis easier and faster to do and more interactive, and it provides richer, more useful results.

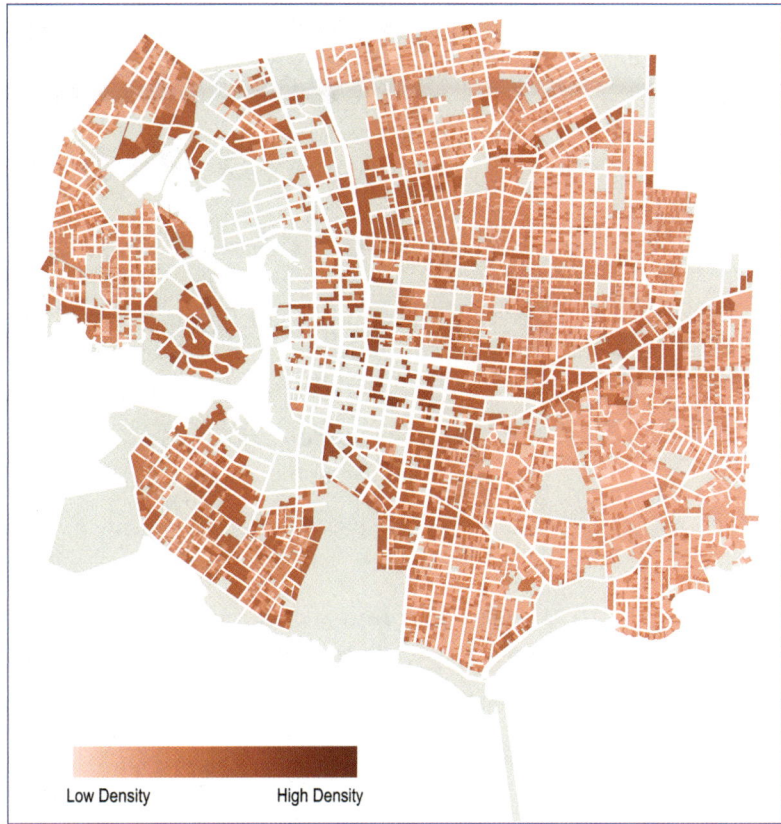

Figure 14.8 *Projected residential density in 30 years*

 COST-OF-SERVICES ANALYSES, CAPITAL IMPROVEMENTS, AND PRO FORMAS

KEY CONCEPTS AND TERMS IN THIS CHAPTER

- Custom Impacts Wizard
- External Table Links
- Impact models: rate-based, spatially dependent, and external
- Spreadsheet models
- Subdivision and land development regulations

Population growth and land development result in significant infrastructure costs for local governments. Local governments typically provide roads and transportation networks, municipal water and sewer, police and fire protection, libraries and schools, and land for parks. Infrastructure costs come in the form of initial capital outlays, debt service, and ongoing operating costs. A capital improvements program is a schedule of which infrastructure the local government will build, replace, or repair, when and where, and how the infrastructure will be paid for. Local governments plan to recover their costs through taxes, user fees, and possibly grants from the state or federal government. Developers of large-scale private projects typically pay for at least some, and often most, of the initial infrastructure costs associated with their projects. But even in those cases, local governments need to understand the financial implications to the public purse of the construction, maintenance, and operating costs of the necessary infrastructure. Studies of this kind are often referred to as cost-of-services analyses (or fiscal impact analyses).

Developers have similar needs in estimating the cost of building and selling a development project. They, too, commit to significant costs, with uncertain returns over the long term. In addition to the cost of building, developers need to invest in land, obtain development approvals, improve the site and install infrastructure, and market what they build. Returns come from sales revenues, but again there are complex financial considerations. Developers generally use a real estate *pro forma analysis* to present an overview of the financial costs and returns for a development project.

The financial analysis and CommunityViz tools used to understand development and infrastructure costs and revenues are similar. This chapter focuses on cost-of-service analysis, and also describes pro forma analysis.

When you use CommunityViz for financial analysis, you gain two major advantages. First, you can tie sophisticated spatial analysis together with complex financial analysis. CommunityViz provides the spatial analysis tools, and its ability to link to external spreadsheets gives you simultaneous access to advanced financial tools. With CommunityViz, a cost-of-services analysis does not need to be based solely on *how much* development there is; it can also take into account *where* that development occurs.

Second, you can use geodesign. You can sketch a project and design necessary infrastructure. Once you have set up an analysis, you can edit the map to move projects to new locations, expand infrastructure, compare scenarios, change your time horizon, and much more. You get immediate feedback each time you edit the sketch.

DATA NEEDS AND SOURCES

There are three main kinds of information you need for a cost-of-services analysis:

1. **Level of service required.** For example, how much park space per person does the city require? If local regulations do not specify levels of service, you can use multipliers based on current rates or you can use standard planners' guidelines.

2. **Operating costs and capacities for government services.** For example, you need to find or estimate the average cost of educating an elementary school student, and you need to know the maximum capacity of your schools to estimate when one or more new schools will be needed. Available capacity of the sewage treatment plant and the drinking water source are important for determining the ability of the local government to accommodate new development. This data usually comes from local government staff.

3. **Capital costs for new facilities.** These are the initial costs of constructing new buildings, treatment plants, and so on. Cost-of-services analysis often uses annual amortization costs that include debt service rather than lump sum up-front costs. Estimating initial capital costs for major projects usually requires close cooperation with the local government's engineer or the developer, so consult the government's financial planner for amortization rules and borrowing costs.

SETTING UP A COST-OF-SERVICES ANALYSIS

Like other impact models (see Chapter 4), cost-of-services models come in a variety of forms:

- *Rate-based impact models* are the simplest and most common. They are used to estimate costs of a unit of infrastructure, such as school cost per household or road maintenance cost per mile.

- *Coefficient-based impact models* use a number of different numerical factors in a single calculation. Examples include net present value analysis of purchasing new equipment, sewage treatment plant capacity, and police and fire department staffing requirements.

- *Spatially dependent impact models* require spatial calculations of things such as distances, areas, and overlaps. For example, the cost of providing sewer and water to a new development in town is less than the cost of providing it to a new development far outside of town, where infrastructure is not yet in place.

- *External impact models and simulations* include transportation network analyses, local retail trade simulations, and other complex calculations that exceed the capability of either CommunityViz or a spreadsheet.

Most cost-of-services analyses use a combination of rate-based, coefficient-based, and spatially dependent models. If your analysis is simple enough, you can implement it easily with the Custom Impacts Wizard or as a custom analysis within CommunityViz. If your analysis requires external impact models or simulations, follow the directions for external models here and in Chapter 4 and add the results to the rest of the analysis. Figure 15.1 provides an overview of the information flow between CommunityViz and the external model. We will focus on spreadsheet models here, although you can also use other database tools as well.[1]

To set up a cost-of-services analysis:

1. Start with a spreadsheet and set up operating cost models. For now, we will focus on a single scenario. Organize all the cost factors you want to consider, decide on the modeling method you want to use for each one, and collect operating data such as cost rates and capacity limits. When you come across data inputs you need for each model, such as total population or road miles, put in placeholder values and highlight those cells in a

---

1. A particularly good technique for advanced users is to use Scenario 360 CustomScript functions that allow you to "call" external VBA scripts. ("Calling" a script means sending it data, causing it to run, and receiving results in return.) External scripts allow you to manage and use much more complex external models, databases, and database collections than the simple spreadsheets described here.

Figure 15.1 Flow diagram for external spreadsheet cost models

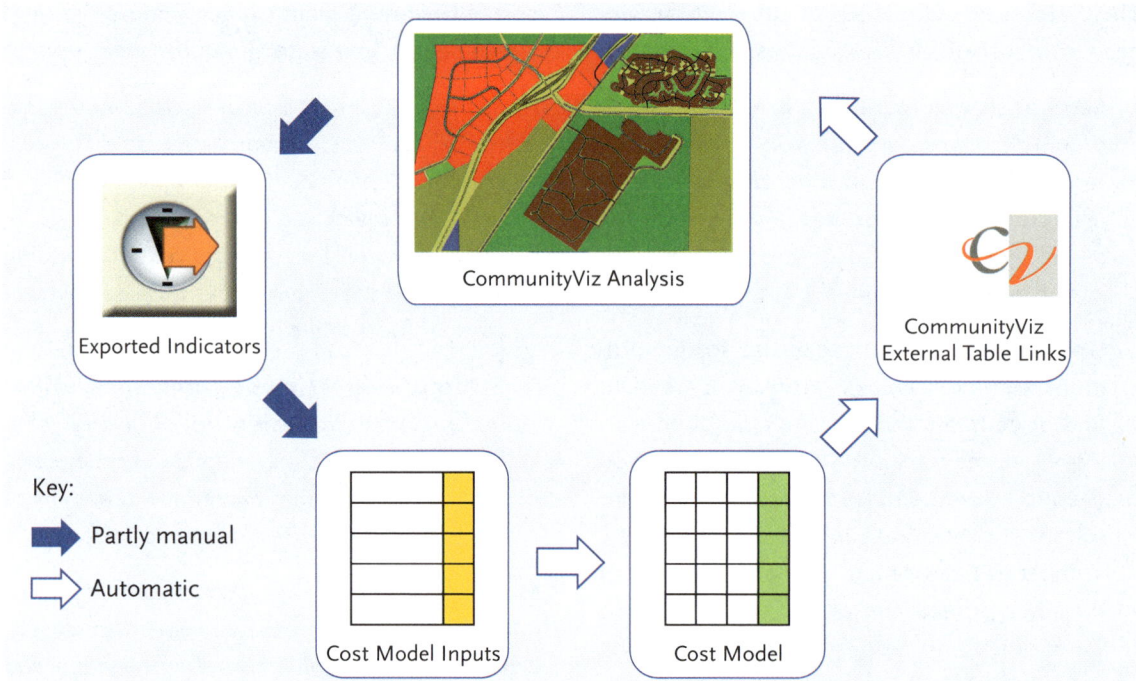

prominent way (we used yellow highlighting in our examples). Build the spreadsheet so that it produces cost estimates for your entire study area, not just one person or one road at a time. Figure 15.2 gives a simple example.

2. Once you have constructed all the cost model spreadsheets, review the inputs you require. Some models will require only a single number, such as population, while others may require more details, such as miles of roads broken down by road class. Make a new spreadsheet in table form that captures all the inputs you need (see Figure 15.3). Connect the inputs in your Scenario 360 cost models to the values in the spreadsheet input table using External Table Links as described in Chapter 4.

3. Turn your attention back to CommunityViz. The input table you created in the spreadsheet tells you the indicators you need to create in the CommunityViz analysis. Create all the indicators you need, and then organize them into a single indicator list that you can export as a table in comma separated values (CSV) format. Connect your spreadsheet input table to the CSV table. From now on, every time you export a new set of indicators, your cost model spreadsheet will calculate new values.

4. The final step is to read the spreadsheet results—or outputs—back into your CommunityViz analysis for display, reporting, and further calculations. Use External Table Links and it will happen automatically.

Figure 15.2 Example of a simple cost-of-services spreadsheet table for schools (using fictional data)

TOTAL POPULATION	AGE GROUP	PERCENT OF POPULATION	STUDENTS	OPERATING COST PER STUDENT	TOTAL COST
1,000	Grades K–5	6.2	62	$8,500	$527,000
	Grades 6–8	6	60	$9,200	$552,000
	Grades 9–12	6.7	67	$9,500	$636,000
	Totals		189		**$1,715,000**

Figure 15.3 Example of a spreadsheet input table

INPUT PARAMETER	VALUE
Dwelling Units - High Density	63
Dwelling Units - Low Density	410
Dwelling Units - Medium Density	129
Population	1,000
Road Miles - Arterial	27
Road Miles - Collector	15
Road Miles - Local	72
Road Miles - Rural Res	63
Water Main Feet - 12 inch	42
Water Main Feet - 8 inch	135

The description above was for a single scenario. For multiple scenarios, the easiest approach is to create copies of the modeling spreadsheets so that each spreadsheet handles a single scenario. The only difference between spreadsheets is that each one uses a different column from the indicator list: The first spreadsheet uses the column containing values from the first scenario, the second spreadsheet uses the column containing values from the second scenario, and so on.

USING A COST-OF-SERVICES ANALYSIS

You can use a cost-of-services analysis just as you would any other CommunityViz analysis or geodesign tool. It's an excellent tool for sketching subsequent development proposals and analyzing their costs. Here are a few points to keep in mind:

- Try hard to maintain transparency. Show your audience the spreadsheets you are using, and feel free to use Excel charts to complement CommunityViz charts.

- Pay special attention to maintenance. Your analysis probably calls on cost models that are used by many different government departments, all of which update their methods from time to time. Check to make sure that your models stay up to date.

- Remember that you are using a planning tool. The number-intensive character of cost-of-services models tends to make people think they must have engineering-level accuracy. But even the most detailed cost models still rely on averages and assumptions, and there is still uncertainty in the results. Make sure your audience understands those limitations.

ANALYZING SUBDIVISION AND LAND-DEVELOPMENT REGULATIONS

In the land-development process, subdivision and land-development regulations spell out the standards and requirements for infrastructure. These regulations are designed to ensure that land can safely support development. Subdivision is the legal process of dividing land into lots for future sale and development. Land-development regulations refer to standards for providing infrastructure such as roads, sewer and water facilities, and utilities, and how buildings are placed on the land. Subdivision and land development regulations require that a site plan review be conducted for a proposed development. The review is carried out by planning staff and the planning commission, who determine if lots have been properly sized and surveyed; how sewer and water will be provided; whether roads or streets will be built, and if so, whether they meet the standards; the siting of buildings in relation to setback requirements; and stormwater drainage patterns.

A community of more than 1,000 people, especially if it's experiencing a population growth rate of more than 2 percent a year, should have a subdivision and land-development ordinance. The ordinance may need to be updated every few years if the growth rate exceeds 3 percent a year.

For an analysis of subdivision and land-development regulations, you need property tax maps, building permits, infrastructure capacity, and environmental data. The tax maps, assuming they are kept up to date, indicate where subdivision activity is occurring in the community. Building permits linked to a GIS database can show where development is happening. The community, planning staff, and elected officials need to determine whether development is happening in places where development is desired and where adequate infrastructure exists to support it.

For example, in a rural area, an increasing number of houses using on-site septic systems and wells may alert planners and elected officials that future extensions of central sewer and water lines may be needed to avoid groundwater pollution or overdraft of the aquifer. Similarly, in a suburban area, if the local sewage treatment plant is close to maximum capacity, new development may have to wait until the plant can be expanded. Storm-water runoff is a major source of water pollution. If local lakes are experiencing declining water quality, storm-water runoff from new development may be a cause. In turn, this may signal a need to revise the subdivision regulations to require better storm-water management through the use of detention ponds, grass swales, vegetation, or pervious pavement, or limits on impervious surfaces.

CommunityViz can help you analyze the performance of subdivision regulations by keeping track of new development through tax maps and building permits. It also enables you to create custom impact models that measure the effects of new development on roads, water and sewer, utilities, and environmental quality. The custom impact models will have the same structure as cost-of-service models but may not always measure effects in financial terms. As development occurs over time, the impact indicators you have created will allow you to keep track of performance and stay alert to any needs for additional capacity or revisions to your subdivision and land-development regulations. You can use the same models to forecast impacts into the future, according either to current trends or to alternative scenarios. These forecasts will not be highly precise, but they may help you to better anticipate infrastructure needs.

PRO FORMA ANALYSES

Setting up and using a real estate pro forma analysis is similar to doing so for a cost-of-services analysis. The techniques for estimating costs are the same: You use CommunityViz scenario sketching linked to external cost models when needed.

In estimating revenue, pro forma analyses often work on the basis of the retail sales potential of a given dwelling unit. House model A might have a sales potential of $200,000, model B a potential of $250,000, and so on. A development's overall sales potential depends on the number of each type of model in the project. The sales potential is uncertain, so it's important to consider a range of possible selling prices. To set this analysis up in CommunityViz, make variable revenue assumptions for the value of each building model. Also set up a cost calculation for each model using standard cost modeling techniques such as construction cost per square foot; these two will combine to give you gross profitability figures on the models. To make the analysis more interactive, create Sketch styles to use with the Painter tool or Clone tool (see Chapter 11) so that you can easily do geodesign by experimenting with changing the models on the map. As you change the model designation for each site, you will see new cost and revenue results.

The timing of costs and revenues is an important part of a pro forma analysis. Large developments are often built in phases to reduce risk and improve cash flow, and smaller developments often take time to build out as well. Scenario 360 TimeScope is ideal for managing the time-dependent parts of your analysis. For example, if your project phases are based on particular geographic areas, you simply specify the construction dates for each phase area, and TimeScope will automatically apply those dates to any buildings you plan in that area. You can also use finer-grained controls to specify construction dates for individual buildings or other parts of the project. Once those construction dates have been set, you can use them in CommunityViz formulas or external models. You can also use the TimeScope time assumption slider to set the virtual month or year in your analysis. As you change the date, you will see on the map which parts of the development have been built, and you will see in charts and indicators the status of your finances and other impacts.

TEACHING EXAMPLE

This fictional example looks at two alternatives for development next to a new highway interchange being built to serve a growing town in Wyoming.[2] The two alternatives appear in Figure 15.4.

---

2. We are grateful to Scott Lieske of the University of Wyoming for contributions to this example. Data and cost rates in this example are fictional; you should not use them for a real analysis.

Figure 15.4 Two scenarios for new development around a highway interchange

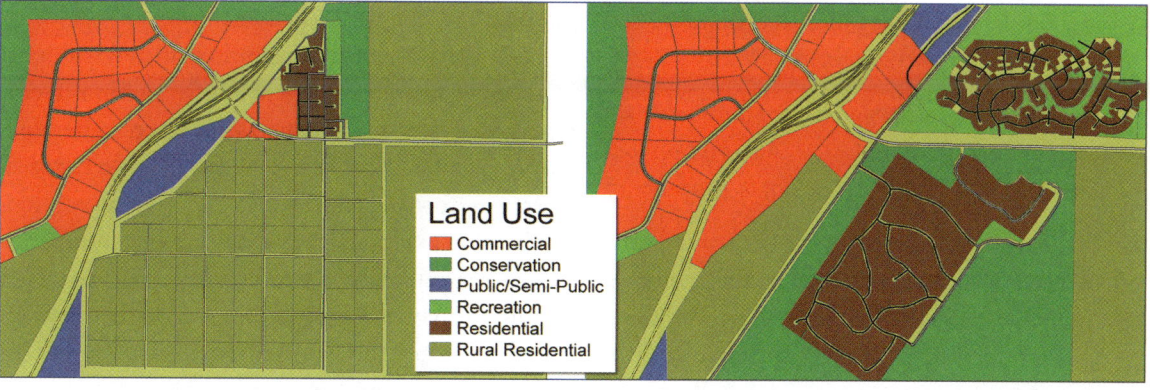

Most of the commercial district to the west of the highway was already developed, so our focus was to the east. As you can see, the Business as Usual scenario (above left) anticipated a small, dense residential subdivision in the northeast corner of the interchange, and large-lot rural residential development to the southeast. This pattern was consistent with other development in the region over the previous 20 years. The Alternative scenario (above right) featured two larger, curvilinear residential subdivisions with additional land designated for conservation and recreation. Both scenarios included some additional commercial development to take advantage of the interchange.

The scenarios posed a number of interesting planning questions, but here we will focus on the comparative cost of services. We modeled costs for roads, schools, sewer, and water.

We modeled road costs using road type and road length, as shown in Figure 15.5. Notice that our model incorporated construction costs using an annual amortization expense and that it distinguished between summer and winter maintenance costs. As you can see from the table, the model used the total length, in feet, of each type of road as an input. This told us that we would need to create indicators in CommunityViz that gave road lengths for each scenario.

We sketched the scenarios in enough detail so we could measure road lengths directly from the map.

If our design had not included that much detail on roads, we could have used the rule of thumb that road length per parcel in a subdivision is given by:

0.42 × (parcel area)

Our model for school costs incorporated operating costs and capital costs. For operating costs, the model was similar to that shown in Figure 15.2. To calculate the number of students in each scenario, we had two choices. One was to use estimates based on ratios of the overall population, as shown in Figure 15.2. The other, which we preferred for this case, was to use estimates based on households and density. In most areas, there is an inverse correlation between children per household and density: The higher the density, the fewer school children per household. Ratios vary, so we decided to use variable assumptions set to 0.7 children per household for the rural residential areas and 0.6 children per household for the higher-density residential areas. Later, we

Figure 15.5 Example of a road cost spreadsheet table

TYPE	FEET	AMORTIZATION	SUMMER COST	WINTER COST	COMBINED	ROAD COST
Collector	10,672	$16	$140	$160	$316	$3,372,266
Local	6,507	$12	$100	$120	$232	$1,509,567
Rural Res	33,386	$40	$80	$100	$220	$7,344,823
Minor Arterial	20,943	$24	$200	$240	$464	$9,717,445
Principal Arterial	10,845	$26	$220	$260	$506	$5,487,523

would vary those assumptions to see how sensitive our results were. Using these ratios, we created an output indicator whose formula was:

(Assumption for rural children per household) × (number of rural households) + (Assumption for subdivision children per household) × (number of subdivision households)

We used that value as in input to the operating cost model, which now looked like Figure 15.6.

This model made sense, but it had one flaw: Every time we changed assumptions about student-per-household ratios, we had to re-export the number of students to the spreadsheet model to get a new result. This illustrated a point that sometimes arises with external models: They are not always as flexible as internal CommunityViz analysis. However, you can often tune the design so that the changes you are most likely to make during interactive analysis are handled internally. In our case, we noticed that the spreadsheet model always gave the same average cost per student, regardless of the number of students. We took advantage of that fact by importing that single number using an External Table Link (see Figure 15.7) and then multiplying it by our internally calculated number of students. Our analysis would still be updated if the cost spreadsheet changed, but it would not need to cycle through the cost spreadsheet each time someone changed an assumption.

It was clear that the influx of new students would so overwhelm the existing school facilities that new classrooms would need to be built. We calculated construction costs using ratios of square feet per student at different grade levels—for example, 100 square feet per elementary school student—and construction costs per square foot. We ignored land costs because we assumed that the required expansion would take place on existing school grounds.

For water and wastewater, we wanted to account for the following costs:

- Water treatment
- Wastewater treatment
- Water mains
- Sewers.

The models we had available for water and wastewater treatment worked on the basis of the number of dwelling units at given densities (see Figure 15.8).

The density ranges did not happen to coincide with our land-use classifications, so we created new indicators in Scenario 360 that counted the number of dwelling units in each of the model's

Figure 15.6 Example of a school cost spreadsheet table starting from number of students

TOTAL STUDENTS	AGE GROUP	PERCENT OF STUDENTS	STUDENTS	OPERATING COST PER STUDENT	TOTAL COST
423	Grades K–5	35	148	$8,500	$1,258,425
	Grades 6–8	30	127	$9,200	$1,167,480
	Grades 9–12	35	148	$9,500	$1,406,475
	Totals		423		$3,832,380

Figure 15.7 Example of a student cost spreadsheet table modified to calculate an average cost per student

TOTAL STUDENTS	AGE GROUP	PERCENT OF STUDENTS	STUDENTS	OPERATING COST PER STUDENT	TOTAL COST	AVG COST
100	Grades K–5	35	35	$8,500	$297,000	
	Grades 6–8	30	30	$9,200	$276,000	
	Grades 9–12	35	35	$9,500	$332,000	
	Totals		100		$906,000	$9,060

Figure 15.8 Example of a water treatment spreadsheet model

DENSITY	DWELLING UNITS	DEMAND PER UNIT	TOTAL DEMAND	COST PER GALLON	WTR COST
< 1 DU per acre	148	450	66,586		
1 to 2 DU per acre	5	420	2,100		
3 to 5 DU per acre	11	400	4,400		
6 to 8 DU per acre	10	250	2,500		
9 to 14 DU per acre	275	250	68,750		
> 14 DU per acre	88	250	2,000		
Totals	457		146,336	$10	$1,463,361

Figure 15.9 Example of a spreadsheet cost model for water mains and sewers

ROAD TYPE	FEET	WATER MAIN TYPE	WATER UNIT COST	WATER MAIN COST	SEWER TYPE	SEWER UNIT COST	SEWER COST
Collector	10,672	8	8	$85,374	8	60	$640,304
Local	6,507	8	8	$52,054	8	60	$390,405
Rural Res	33,386	8	8	$267,084	8	60	$2,003,134
Minor Arterial	20,943	12	16	$335,084	12	100	$2,094,277
Principal Arterial	10,845	12	16	$173,519	12	100	$1,084,491
Totals				$913,115			$6,212,610

categories. We used the same method to estimate sewage treatment costs. We assumed that the treatment plants had sufficient capacity to handle the new demand. If either of the new scenarios had created new demand that exceeded available capacity, we would have added an additional capital analysis to cover the construction of additional plants.

For water mains and sewers, we used a common method for estimating the length and size of the infrastructure: We assumed that the water network would follow roads, and that smaller roads would be associated with 8-inch mains while larger roads would correspond to 12-inch mains. Therefore, we could use the same road-length data we had used earlier. The spreadsheet cost model appears in Figure 15.9.

Once we had set up these cost models and linked them to indicators and charts in our analysis, we had an excellent framework for presenting results and doing geodesign and scenario analysis. See, for example, the Scenario Comparison window in Figure 15.10.

These examples illustrate three of the major costs we considered. In another part of the work, we also addressed the costs of commercial development, and we set up simple per-resident multipliers to capture a variety of other costs such as public safety and library services. Later, we set up an analysis that estimated revenues from permitting and sewer tap-in fees, property taxes, commercial sales and use taxes, and other sources. When these were all combined, local planners had an excellent tool for analyzing the financial implications of the scenarios, suggesting adjustments to the proposals, and negotiating with developers.

What we set up was a "living" analysis: Local planners continued to use the same framework for the next several years to evaluate new development proposals as they arose.

This example demonstrates how to set up a powerful cost-of-services analysis framework using CommunityViz together with spreadsheet cost models. It demonstrates several different techniques for modeling costs, and it also illustrates that you have a great deal of flexibility in designing approaches that meet your particular needs for level of detail, processing speed, and types of models.

Figure 15.10 Scenario comparison including cost of services

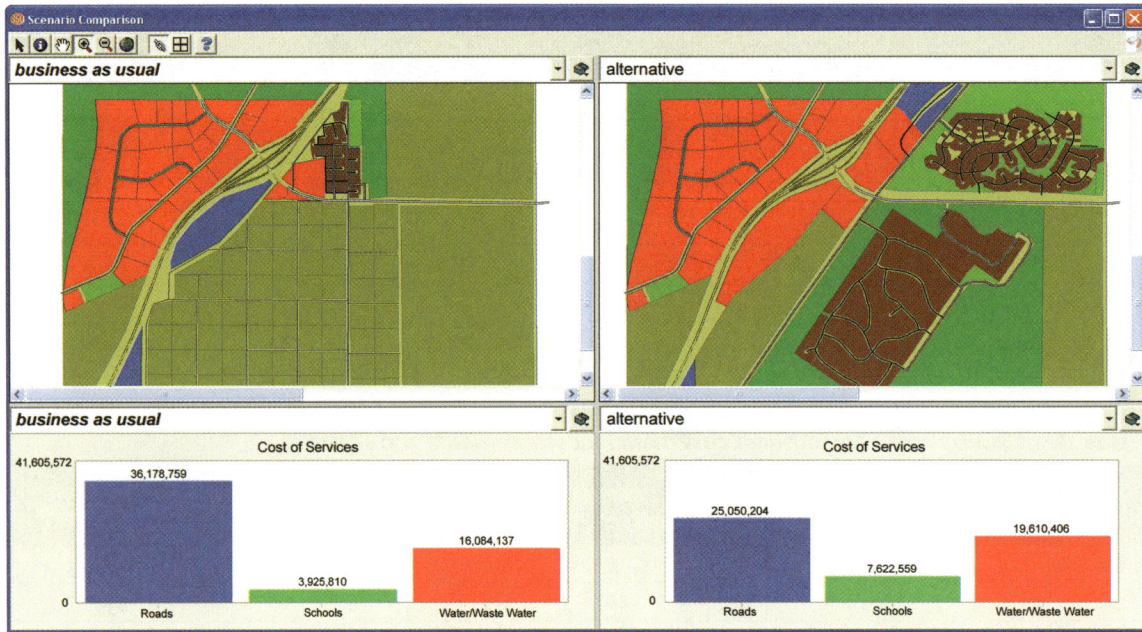

16 DESIGN REVIEW AND FORM-BASED CODES

KEY CONCEPTS AND TERMS IN THIS CHAPTER

- Three-dimensional modeling for design reviews
- Comparative community indicators
- Design guidelines
- Displaying 3-D scenes
- Form-based codes
- Indicators for design reviews
- SmartCode

A design review enables a community to examine the appearance of a proposed project before it is built. It gives planners, design professionals, and design review board members the opportunity to study a development proposal and determine how well it will fit into its surroundings. The focus of the review is usually on aesthetics, architectural design, and compatibility with neighboring buildings. But community heart-and-soul and site-planning criteria—from the zoning, subdivision, and land-development regulations—can also come into play. Even though design reviews often consider matters of opinion, the process must not be arbitrary. Planners should try to give landowners and developers clear guidance by establishing design standards in a design review ordinance, or a set of guidelines adopted by reference in the zoning and subdivision ordinances.

A *form-based code* is a set of regulations accompanied by illustrations that planners can use to guide developers to build well-designed buildings that fit in with the surroundings. Form-based codes are an alternative to traditional land-use regulations and zoning. Used primarily in urban settings, they emphasize physical forms such as building heights, facades, street cross sections, and landscape design rather than specific land uses, floor area ratios, or residential density. The principles of form-based codes are incorporated into the SmartCode system and the concept of the *transect*, which is a diagram that shows appropriate development types and densities ranging from the urban core to the countryside. Form-based codes have been adopted in more than 300 communities in the United States, but they may not be appropriate for all communities. We leave it up to you to decide whether a form-based code is appropriate for a particular project.

CommunityViz has both visual and analytical tools to support design reviews and the drafting of form-based codes. Scenario 3D can produce realistic 3-D models of the community setting and the proposed project or urban form. Scenario 360 can assist you with setting up community indicators and conducting an analysis of site plans or proposed form-based codes. CommunityViz is especially efficient for conducting successive design reviews so that each new development proposal requires only a small amount of additional work.

ABOUT 3-D MODELING FOR DESIGN REVIEWS AND FORM-BASED CODES

If a 2-D drawing of a design is a window onto the development project and a CAD rendering is a statue of the project, then a Scenario 3D scene is an in-person visit to the site. Done well, a 3-D scene *feels* like the place where the project is being proposed. You, as the visitor, can go anywhere, look anywhere, see new things, and learn new information. It's an excellent environment for conducting design reviews and drafting form-based codes.

Figure 16.1 Scenario 3D screenshot of a street with small setbacks

Figure 16.2 The same street as in Figure 16.1, with wider setbacks

Other CommunityViz 3-D tools, such as Google Earth Exporter and the ArcScene extension, can be helpful for conducting design review and drafting form-based codes, but they are not quite as well suited as Scenario 3D. Scenario 3D produces a more realistic-looking scene and gives you finer control over the appearance of the objects in the scene.

But even Scenario 3D has limitations. It cannot provide as much fine detail or as realistic a rendering of the site as a carefully created CAD model or a photo simulation. For studying details smaller than about six inches, Scenario 3D is not suitable as a primary tool. Also, Scenario 3D does not allow the artistic interpretation and subtle suggestion of a hand drawing, and we do not recommend trying to replace hand drawings and other well-established design tools. But Scenario 3D does present a useful combination of high realism, spatial accuracy, interactivity, and low cost.

Here are some aspects of design review and form-based codes that Scenario 3D helps you address:

- Alternative scenarios
- Alternative building forms, such as stepped-back upper stories (examples of "wedding cake" design)
- Lines of sight from various positions
- Placement alternatives, such as small setback and large setback (see figures 16.1 and 16.2)
- Screening, such as fences and hedges
- Parking, loading, sidewalk, and other access options
- Special structures, such as micro wind towers and water tanks

You may find that a Scenario 3D scene is a useful visual aid as you review other design guidelines or form-based code elements such as:

- Signage
- Neighborhood conditions
- Transportation network access, including pedestrian, bicycle, vehicular, and transit networks
- Public spaces
- Public art
- Energy-efficient site design

However, you may want to consider using tools other than CommunityViz for evaluations of:

- Architectural details such as cornices, railings, and insets
- Historical authenticity
- Landscaping materials
- Lighting design
- Entryway design
- Accessibility standards
- Fire safety standards

We encourage you to use Scenario 3D as a complement to other tools, applying each tool for its best purpose.

USING 3-D FOR DESIGN REVIEW

This section describes best practices for using a 3-D scene in a design review. For details on how to create the Scenario 3D scenes described here, refer to Chapter 5.

MODELING PROPOSALS FOR DESIGN REVIEWS

Start with a Scenario 3D scene of existing neighborhood conditions around the proposed development project. The neighborhood must be easy for local residents to recognize, and they should be able to quickly find the project site. It's helpful to have models of both the existing project site and the proposed new development so that you can illustrate before and after conditions. However, your priority is how the site will appear after renovation or new construction.

If the developer has a 3-D model of the project in electronic format, try to incorporate it into your model. Most 3-D modeling tools can export files in a format compatible with Scenario 3D, though in some cases large file size may be a problem. If the developer cannot provide a 3-D model, you will need to create one in SketchUp using the developer's drawings. For Scenario 3D applications, tolerances of about six inches are usually acceptable, so you do not need to make a perfect model. Be sure to consult closely with the developer before displaying your version of the model in public. If you know of any variations of the design, model those as well so that you can show them during the design review.

There are three main parts of a development model, each of which has special considerations:

1. **Built structures and hardscaping** such as buildings, outbuildings, bridges, roads, parking lots, sidewalks, and retaining walls. These are the easiest parts to handle in 3-D modeling software, and they usually receive the most attention. It is important to verify that all structures and hardscaping have accurate dimensions and placement. Architectural details, colors, textures, and other visual criteria should also be fairly represented, though it is not practical to render them in great detail.

2. **Landscaping and water features that are included in the proposal,** such as specific vegetation, plantings, grading, streams, rivers, and lakes. Because of their organic shapes, these elements are more difficult to model with 3-D software than built structures and hardscaping. However, landscaping and water features should not be ignored, and Scenario 3D provides some tools that will help you (see chapters 5 and 6). Trees are particularly controversial, because they are visually important but they take time to grow to their ideal height. A design review board may feel slightly betrayed by the visual model when the project is first built, because the trees will be so much smaller than imagined. For this reason, many 3-D modelers include trees at two or three different levels of maturity to show the transformation over time. Vegetation of any kind can significantly affect the appearance of a computer-generated scene, so take care that the base model includes precisely what is specified in the proposal. You can add accessory elements later.

3. **Accessory elements.** These are not part of the proposal but are included in the scene to create a realistic view. They include people, vehicles, additional vegetation and signs, street furniture, and other elements that contribute to the sense of scale and activity. Accessory elements add visual appeal to a scene, but use them with great caution. There is a saying that "kids and balloons" can make any project look attractive. The goal of your 3-D scene is to provide an objective picture of the project, not one that makes it look better or worse than it would in reality. Be sure that you can turn accessory elements on and off when displaying the scene.

DISPLAYING THE SCENE

When you first show a 3-D scene during a design review, it will naturally become the center of attention at the meeting. That attention is to be expected, but it's not your long-term goal. After 10 to 15 minutes, you want the audience's fascination with the scene to give way to a discussion about the development proposal under review. The scene can serve as a useful reference for answering questions as they arise. Remember that the design review is about the development proposal, not about the 3-D scene.

For suggestions on how to present the scene initially, refer to Chapter 17. You should describe the scene's sources and limitations. In a design review, place extra emphasis on explaining how you can change the scene to illustrate specific points. For example, explain that you can:

- Turn certain features such as awnings and planters on and off
- Change the field of view, lighting, and other environmental effects
- Change the maturity of trees
- Show the project with and without landscaping or accessory elements
- Make foreground objects partially transparent.

Be prepared for questions about the technical accuracy of the scene. Audiences that are not familiar with GIS will need some education on how it works and how much trust can be placed in the distances and positions shown in the scene. It is often helpful to add visual aids to the scene to verify scale and measurements. Examples include a person who is exactly 6 feet tall, a semitransparent plane suspended in the air that demonstrates the horizontal alignment of rooftops, or a 15-foot arc on the sidewalk outside a door.

Review the development proposal ahead of time to check for any exceptions to your design guidelines or form-based code. If you find any, make sure they are clearly illustrated in the 3-D scene. For example, if the width of an opening is too small, make sure the 3-D scene shows the width correctly and does not obscure it with trees or cars. Then, during the presentation, visit that particular location and discuss the possible exception.

USING 3-D FOR DRAFTING AND APPLYING FORM-BASED CODES

Scenario 3D can help you and others visualize the implications of a proposed form-based code for the built environment. You can make 3-D scenes that show not just a single street or cross section, but entire neighborhoods as they might appear under the new code. You can illustrate alternatives for variables such as setback distances, sidewalk widths, building heights, and landscaping. And you can overlay possible future buildings on top of illustrations of existing conditions. Scenario 3D's ability to simulate walking down the street and being immersed in the virtual setting often helps people understand the proposed regulations.

If your community is considering the adoption of a form-based code, start with conventional code-drafting techniques such as following the SmartCode and generating hand drawings. Then you are ready to create 3-D scenes that illustrate the proposals more dynamically. In general, the process of creating a scene for a form-based code proposal is the same as for a design review, described above. Here are a few additional guidelines:

- For building models, use SketchUp or other tools to create building forms that incorporate the specifications of the form-based code. Form-based codes often specify heights, window sizes, doorway frequencies, and other details that allow you to sketch basic shapes. However, fine architectural details are not specified, and there are two schools of thought on what to do with them. One point of view is that you should show the simplest possible model of any detail that is not specified; for example, walls should be flat and gray if no building materials are specified. Another point of view is that you should choose realistic details—for example, red brick walls similar to an existing building in that area—so that the 3-D scene feels more realistic. If time and resources allow, you can do both, and simply turn on one version or the other as you view the scene.

- For streets and sidewalks, consider modeling one block at a time in SketchUp and then importing the model into the Scenario 3D scene. Using SketchUp makes it easier to exert fine-grained control over lane widths, curb heights, and road striping.

- If you are modeling a large area, ensure you have the ability to show three or four stages of gradual growth. A fully built-out city neighborhood that uses all the height and lot coverage allowed by a form-based code can be visually overwhelming when first viewed. Showing stages of growth is both more realistic and easier for general audiences to absorb.

INDICATORS FOR DESIGN REVIEW AND FORM-BASED CODES

You can use Scenario 360 to rate a development proposal or a proposed form-based code on a range of indicator targets, including numeric values, site-specific features, and neighborhood impacts. Although many development impacts in a design review do not require the analytical strength of the indicators available in Scenario 360, others do. Here we will describe two primary categories of indicators. These categories are not mutually exclusive, but we have divided them up as a convenient way to organize the many available indicators.

SITE-SPECIFIC INDICATORS

Most design indicators in design guidelines or form-based codes relate to the project, its site, and the surrounding neighborhood. Here are some common examples of indicators and targets that Scenario 360 can help you calculate:

- Traffic generation (trips per day)
- Open space percentage
- Required parking area based on dwelling units or square footage of commercial space
- Requirements based on dimensions, such as the requirement for a sidewalk when the lot line exceeds a certain length
- Lot coverage
- Fire service access rules for the site, such as maximum distance between buildings and curbs, turning radii for vehicles, maximum length of dead-end roads, minimum width of access roads, and maximum height of buildings
- Site engineering requirements based on factors such as slope, drainage, and utilities
- Tree counts and street lamp counts based on spacing requirements

COMPARATIVE COMMUNITY INDICATORS

A common theme of design guidelines and form-based codes is their emphasis on the project's "fit" within the neighborhood. People generally want a project to be consistent with the surrounding development patterns and character of buildings, and some design guidelines include measurable indicators of how the design of the proposed development compares to its surroundings. Scenario 360 can help you to set *comparative community indicator* targets that measure the fit of existing buildings within a neighborhood, and use the targets to assess the proposal's fit. Here are some examples:

- Massing guidelines recommend that new houses be about the same size as existing houses in the neighborhood. Similar rules can apply to height, street frontage, lot coverage, and so on for both residential and commercial structures. To set targets for these guidelines, map the neighborhood and create Scenario 360 indicators that calculate local averages and ranges for any particular characteristic. For example, you might calculate the average building footprint for all existing houses within a one-mile radius of the project site. Then compare the average building footprint to the building footprint of the proposed development.

- Proximity guidelines involve distances such as setbacks and driveway lengths, and distances to historic districts and special places.

Often these distances are set as targets for certain zones or land uses, but sometimes they are described in terms of comparisons to nearby land uses. Treat proximity guidelines as you would massing guidelines.

- Community character or heart-and-soul guidelines can range from a sophisticated value index (see Chapter 9) to simple rules regarding the preservation of special places. You usually set targets ahead of time based on a communitywide analysis, which you can perform in CommunityViz. You can measure the fit of a proposed development both at the site level and in terms of its cumulative impact on the communitywide indicators.

TEACHING EXAMPLE

This example involves a proposed hotel and commercial development near a highway interchange in a New England town.[1] The site appears in Figure 16.3. As you can see, an interstate highway runs roughly north–south along the western side of the image, and the interchange makes the location a good fit for hotels and related businesses. The existing conditions included a gas station and a few small restaurants at the junction, as well as a large retail store (the green rectangle) that had recently closed. The hotel was proposed for vacant land on a small rise east of the store.

A general site plan of the proposal (see Figure 16.4) called for a new access road running northeast from the local highway and passing first the hotel and then a restaurant. Farther back and up a hill, a self-storage complex was suggested, and other building pads were sketched in for possible future development.

An administrative review had already confirmed that the proposal met the zoning requirements. For the design review, the town wanted to understand how the development would look, how it would relate to the nearby busy intersection, and what impacts it would have on quantitative community indicators. The project budget was limited, and not much local data were available, so we needed to use a number of cost-saving techniques.

To create a 3-D model, we started by choosing the smallest study area we could without losing context. We obtained a good-quality aerial image of the study area, and the town provided building footprint data. If footprint data had not been available, we would have had to hand sketch footprints from the aerial image. The town gave us their TIGER streets data, but when we added them to our analysis we found that the resolution was too coarse for our purposes: In some places,

Figure 16.3 Aerial view of the project site overlayed with rectangle showing size of Figure 16.4

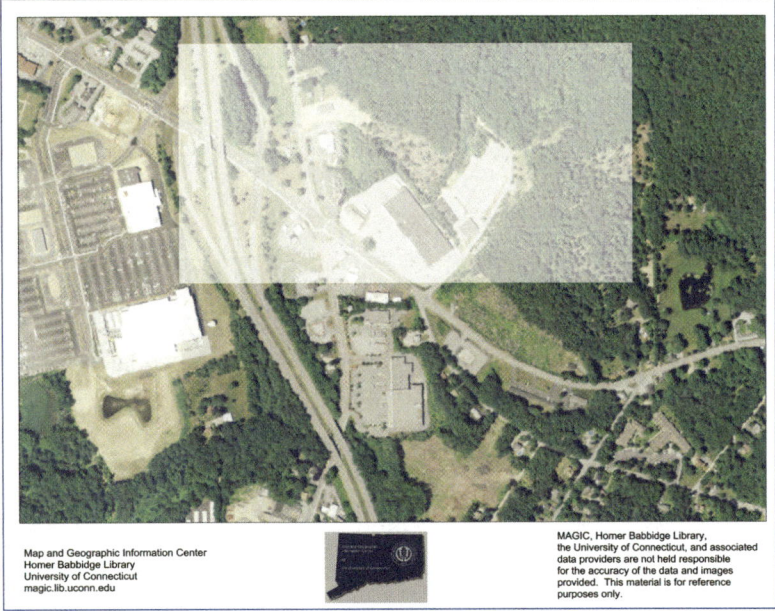

Figure 16.4 General site plan of the proposal, showing hotel, restaurant, and storage complex

---

1. This is a fictionalized version of a real project in Killingly, Connecticut. We are grateful to the Northeast Connecticut Council of Governments for its assistance.

the TIGER lines were more than 20 feet away from the roads in the aerial image. In response, we hand digitized our own Local Streets layer. This task was not particularly difficult, because we had chosen a compact study area. For terrain, we started with 20-meter contours that were freely available from the U.S. Geological Survey, but later we were able to switch to a one-meter digital elevation model (DEM) that improved the visual quality of the scene.

We knew we would not be able to model the entire area in detail, so we talked to local residents, who helped us identify high-priority features, especially around the busy intersection closest to the proposed hotel and self-storage units. We learned that a large old oak tree had been the subject of a recent preservation campaign, and many people mentioned the famous Zip's Diner, housed in a 1950s railroad car. We also noted that when people told us how to find the intersection they often added, "You can't miss it. It's the one with the big Dunkin' Donuts sign." From comments such as these, we knew which features we would need to make custom models of using SketchUp. We obtained local photographs, and made models accordingly.

The local photographs gave us information about the appearance of the area from ground level. In particular:

- There was a gas station at the corner that would not look right as a simple block model, but because none of the local residents had mentioned it by name or otherwise remarked on its unique appearance, we decided that we could use a generic gas station model.

- We noted that the traffic signals at the intersection were important visual elements, especially as you looked toward the proposed hotel site, and overhead utility poles also occupied some of the visual space. It was easy to place these vertical elements in the scene by sketching points on the map corresponding to the base of their shadows in the aerial image.

- Trees were abundant. We carefully placed tree points that were close to the road, try-

Figure 16.5 *Screenshot of the interactive 3-D scene showing existing conditions near the proposed development. The project site is behind the big oak tree.*

ing to match the aerial image as accurately as possible. For trees that were farther away, we used a thinner, more random distribution that would still look realistic, and for trees on the distant hillside we created tree fences (see Chapter 6), which reduced the complexity of the scene while still suggesting the presence of thousands of trees.

Finally, we were ready to create the 3-D scene in Scenario 3D. We used our terrain data, aerial image, extruded building footprints, and custom models for a few key objects. We decided not to model roads explicitly, because our aerial image was reasonably clear and we needed to save time. However, we did add some generic cars—placed by hand on top of their corresponding images in the aerial image—and we also added curbs to help define the edges of the roads. A snapshot of the result appears in Figure 16.5.

When we showed this scene to local residents, they immediately confirmed that they recognized the location, which had been our primary goal.

Next, it was time to model the site of the proposed development. We made a new scenario, working off the current conditions analysis. The

Figure 16.6 Model of the hotel proposal (screenshot of an interactive 3-D scene)

Figure 16.7 Hotel site showing existing conditions (screenshot of an interactive 3-D scene)

Figure 16.8 Hotel site showing proposal (screenshot of an interactive 3-D scene)

existing area was wooded, so we deleted the old tree points in the area and made new ones that would match the design of the proposed development. Using the developer's rough site plan, we sketched in the proposed roads and parking lots by hand. If the developer had had a geographically correct rendering, we would have brought that into our analysis as an image and used georeferencing (longitude and latitude coordinates) to position it properly in the scene. For the hotel, we used a SketchUp model. We put cars in the parking lot and, after checking with the developer, placed trees in the parking lot where they were specified. We also added simple models of the restaurant and storage complex to the scene (see Figure 16.6).

With this model in place, we had everything we needed for the visual aspects of the design review. When it was time to present our results, we started by introducing the audience to Scenario 3D and talking about our data sources and limitations. We gave a brief tour of our model of existing conditions (see Figure 16.7) to get everyone oriented with the area and comfortable with the technology. Then we panned up and back to show the project site in context (see Figure 16.8). Finally, we turned on the proposed new development and zoomed back in to look at details, sight lines, and so on.

The town was interested in a number of indicators associated with this proposal. Our response called on a variety of techniques:

- Jobs were illustrated in a simple data display. Jobs were very important to the community, and the town maintained an annual jobs target based on population. The town wanted to know how many jobs the proposed hotel and commercial development would produce, and how much closer those jobs would get them to their target. We could have estimated jobs using a variety of techniques, but in this case we simply asked the developer. With that data, we made a chart (see Figure 16.9) in Scenario 360 that showed the job impacts. While the design review board could have found the jobs data in other places, it was helpful to display it alongside the other information we were presenting.

- Stormwater runoff from impervious surfaces was a concern for the town, and the proposed parking lots and access road would increase the impervious area. We used Scenario 360 to calculate the required parking area, which matched the design we had modeled. Then we derived an impervious surface ratio for the project by finding the area of all the impervious surfaces in the proposal and dividing that by the area of the overall parcel. We also set an alert at the town's impervious surface ratio target of 14 percent. In this case, the alert was triggered, which led to a discussion about the need to limit stormwater runoff (see Figure 16.10).

- Lot coverage was an example of a comparative community indicator. The town had no set target for a given site, but there was a guideline that lot coverage be proportional to the surrounding area. To get baseline data for this indicator, we used a separate map of a larger area and drew a circle with a one-mile radius around the site. Then we used Scenario 360 analysis, together with the Building Footprints layer and a Parcels layer, to produce statistics about lot coverage in the area.

- Calculating traffic and access indicators involved employing a mix of techniques. Using a simple multiplier for hotels, we estimated the vehicle trips per day the hotel would generate. One way to reduce trips was to encourage walking, and we hand sketched likely pedestrian routes to nearby points of interest and measured the walking distances. This exercise pointed out that pedestrians walking to Zip's Diner from the hotel would be strongly tempted to jaywalk!

After we had shown the 3-D scene, we introduced several indicators about the impacts of the proposed development. The design review board found they had much more information and a far better understanding of the proposal and its impacts than they would have had without CommunityViz.

Figure 16.9 Job indicators

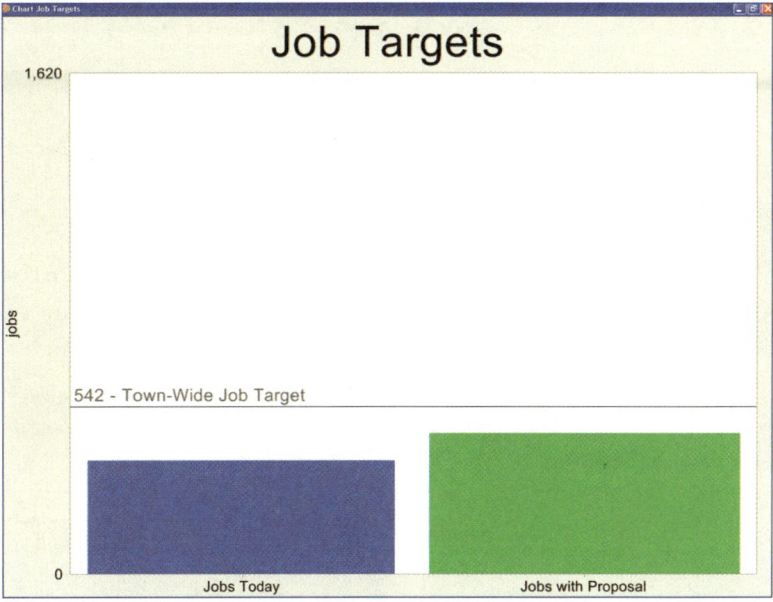

Figure 16.10 Impervious surface indicator and alert

CASE STUDY
TRANSIT-ORIENTED DEVELOPMENT

Location: Westminster, Colorado
Partners: City of Westminster; Van Meter Williams Pollack, LLP; Donley & Associates, Inc.

Context: The City of Westminster is a northwestern suburb of Denver with a population of just over 105,000 people. Westminster is a highly desirable place to live and work, but it does not attract the same level of attention as Denver. Changes are coming down the track, as FasTracks, a new commuter rail service, is planned to connect Denver with Boulder to the north, passing through Westminster. A FasTracks station is planned for South Westminster, in what is now an underutilized industrial-commercial area ideally located and targeted for redevelopment. The Denver Regional Transportation District (RTD) anticipates opening the line in 2015.

To be proactive in the revitalization of South Westminster, the city's community development department drafted a mixed use transit-oriented plan for the 100-acre site around the proposed station. The plan was intended to help people visualize what was possible on this site within the city's designated urban renewal area, and to attract investment to the area.

Figure 16.11 Overview of the transit-oriented development (screenshot from an interactive 3-D scene)

Images courtesy of Donley & Associates

Figure 16.12 Detail of the 3-D scene showing a potential rail station (screenshot from an interactive 3-D scene)

Project Description: The city retained Van Meter Williams Pollack, LLP, to develop a 2-D transit-oriented redevelopment plan for the area, and Donley & Associates, Inc., to translate the plan into a detailed 3-D model. Donley & Associates used CommunityViz to develop the 3-D model, available both as static images and interactive scenes that people could "fly through" in order to see the site from different vantage points (see figures 16.11 and 16.12).

Donley & Associates also used CommunityViz to develop an impact analysis model to evaluate the proposal in terms of land use, tax revenues, and parking requirements (see Figure 16.13). Based on assumptions regarding the initial mix of uses, the development was expected to generate $2.3 million annually in tax revenues to the city.

The city incorporated the plan and the visualizations into presentations given at public

Figure 16.13 Plan view and impact analysis of the development in a screenshot from Scenario 360

workshops in the neighborhoods surrounding the transit-oriented development (TOD) area, giving residents the chance to see and comment on what a mixed use redevelopment proposal would look like. Similar presentations to the city council and to a variety of other groups were made, with the intent of attracting mixed use TOD worthy of this prime redevelopment site. Both the visualizations and the impact analyses can be updated, so the city has a flexible tool for evaluating more-detailed development plans as they emerge.

Technology and Tools: Donley & Associates used a digital version of the site development plan to digitize the building footprints using ModelBuilder 3D; then they extruded footprints and applied textures. They used SiteBuilder 3D to develop the 3-D visualization, and CommunityViz Scenario 360 for the impact analyses.

Outcomes: The city incorporated the visualizations into informational presentations to the public and city leaders, and into presentations targeted at prospective developers. The city will use the visualizations on its forthcoming website devoted explicitly to this transit-oriented redevelopment opportunity. In the meantime, the Regional Transportation District has been refining the design of the FasTracks station. The city planned to use CommunityViz to evaluate any needed adjustments to the redevelopment plan because of the visual and economic impacts of the station. According to the Westminster revitalization projects coordinator, "The impact assessment model built in CommunityViz gave us an essential tool with which to estimate costs and benefits of the current plan, while giving the city the capability to analyze development options relative to increasing or reducing density. Through this analytical capability the city will be able to establish optimal development and zoning allowances within the TOD area."

SECTION V: COMMUNICATING AND INTERACTING

NAVIGATING THIS SECTION

Communicating with audiences is an important part of most CommunityViz projects. Section 5 shows you how to employ CommunityViz in public meetings, workgroups, and online. We also provide some examples of how to use CommunityViz for planning across government departments.

Chapter 17, Public Meetings, Presentations, and Charrettes, presents best practices for making large and small group presentations with CommunityViz. It includes sample agendas for several kinds of public meetings and tips on working more interactively with small groups. The chapter also covers a variety of display and interaction tools, including analysis diagrams, keypads, and Saved Views.

Chapter 18, Reports, Displays, and Websites, reviews the many CommunityViz features for creating printed and visual materials you can share with other people, including online content and 3-D scenes.

Chapter 19, Beyond Planning Projects, emphasizes that CommunityViz does not have to apply only to individual projects. You can use CommunityViz to assist with many day-to-day planning activities. The chapter also provides short descriptions of many applications of CommunityViz that extend across local government departments.

BACKGROUND PLANNING CONCEPTS FOR THIS SECTION

Getting more than a few local residents involved in the planning process is a common challenge. It is not that people do not care about their community but that they tend to care only when changes are proposed in their neighborhood, on an adjacent property, or to the zoning of their land. And a planning commission meeting is not known as an entertaining way to spend an evening. Yet if the quality of planning decisions is to improve and if those decisions are to reflect the desires of a broad cross section of the community, then more residents need to be brought into the planning process and the process needs to be transformed to reach more people.

First, residents must feel that their opinions and desires are heard and taken seriously by planners and elected officials. Public meetings are a traditional way to start an update to a comprehensive plan or zoning ordinance. A shortcoming of typical public meetings is that only a vocal few participate in a meaningful way. Planners have worked to create more interactive forums by using small groups and table exercises. With the advent of interactive technology such as CommunityViz, keypad polling, and online forums, it is finally possible to have widespread, meaningful involvement in the process so that everyone is heard and can feel that their participation makes a difference.

Planners and elected officials are naturally cautious of public participation, because it exposes the planning process to scrutiny and uncertainty. In America, there is also lingering confusion about the difference between participating in a planning workshop, which is advisory, and voting on a ballot measure, which is legally binding. These considerations mean that the purposes of public meetings and workshops need to be carefully explained, so that the participants know where their role stops and the planner's responsibilities begin. The best planning outcomes occur not when planning is thrown completely into the hands of the public but when there is meaningful dialogue and a mutually respectful conversation among planners, experts, elected officials, and the public.

17 PUBLIC MEETINGS, PRESENTATIONS, AND CHARRETTES

KEY CONCEPTS AND TERMS IN THIS CHAPTER

- 360 Analysis Tab
- Analysis diagrams
- Keypads (clickers)
- Learning curves
- Presentation techniques and best practices
- Sample agendas for public meetings
- Saved Views
- Workgroups

CommunityViz enables planners and consultants to show their work in a format that their audience understands. The audience becomes interested, engaged, and excited because CommunityViz clearly frames the planning challenges and trade-offs. Questions are often richer, discussion is more informed, and people with opposing points of view move from confrontation to collaboration. One gets the sense that this is how citizen engagement in planning is supposed to work. Whether you are presenting to a large audience, sitting down with a workgroup for the first time, or are in the midst of a design session, CommunityViz can help you improve the group's understanding and help group members engage in productive planning work.

Planners who use CommunityViz in public meetings report four major benefits to the planning process:

1. The process moves along faster and requires fewer meetings.
2. There is broader and stronger public support for plans and decisions.
3. A large majority of participants say the resulting plan fairly represents the public input.
4. The chances increase that local officials will implement the plan.

All of these benefits are possible to achieve, and are indeed common, but they do not come without hard work and thoughtful preparation on the part of the CommunityViz analyst. This chapter offers our best advice on how a CommunityViz presentation can make public meetings live up to their potential.

WHY AND WHEN

Public engagement in a planning process can take many forms. Public meetings are common and usually required, and online forums, surveys, and creative exercises can also draw the public into the planning process. Public meetings that involve CommunityViz have several common themes:

- **Conveying information.** *Conveying* is a stronger term than *presenting*; it implies that you need to make sure the audience receives and understands the information you present.

- **Building a spirit of collaboration.** Collaboration does not necessarily mean the absence of disagreement or conflict; it means working toward shared goals. It also implies openness and trust.

- **Learning from everyone.** The audience needs to learn from planners and experts, and the reverse is also true. The most satisfying public meetings are those at which every participant feels like a contributor.

- **Guiding decisions.** Planners and elected officials must be willing to allow the meeting participants to help guide specific decisions about the community through the use of CommunityViz. Using CommunityViz is not always necessary when you are running a public meeting. Sometimes a public meeting is conducted as a formality and little public input is sought or expected, such as during the approval of a final subdivision plat. Other times, the topics of discussion do not touch on land use or design issues. But if your planning process is seeking thoughtful public input and discussion, CommunityViz can help.

PUBLIC MEETINGS

Public meetings may vary from a one- to one-and-a-half-hour presentation, to a half-day working session on a land use or design topic, to a large visioning or scenario-planning workshop that may last a half-day or longer. Figures 17.1, 17.2, and 17.3 provide a few sample agendas for meetings up to a half a day in length that feature CommunityViz.

CHARRETTES

A planning or design charrette is a collaborative working session in which planners, experts, stakeholders, and members of the public create plans or draft design guidelines. Almost any public meeting that combines sketching and discussion might be called a charrette. The structure of a charrette usually has the following features:

- A concentrated block of time, lasting between one day and a week of near-continuous work
- An outside team of experts from several disciplines working together in one place
- Close consultation with local stakeholders
- Opportunities for public comment and review
- A significant design component involving hand sketching and rendering, computer-generated design, and geodesign

CommunityViz can play a valuable role in charrettes. Geodesign supported by dynamic analysis provides a fast way to assess the impacts of different building designs, and 3-D modeling can place sketches into their geographic context. In addition, CommunityViz changeable assumptions provide an excellent tool for working with the public's subjective opinions and preferences.

Preparation is critical to a successful charrette. Set up as much of the analysis as you can before the start of the charrette, including data, existing conditions, impact models, indicators, value indexes, weighting assumptions, and categories. As specific building designs and development patterns begin to emerge from the rest of the charrette team, you can incorporate them into your scenarios. Your analysis will give you and the public immediate feedback on the effects of the design proposals.

The use of hand-drawn designs for geodesign in CommunityViz entails both engineering and some art. Hand sketches are usually either 2-D plan designs or 3-D architectural renderings and perspective drawings. For plan designs, the artist should start from paper maps of existing conditions that correspond to your GIS data and map projection. In most cases, you can provide the starting map by printing one from your GIS system. After the hand sketches are completed, scan them as digital images, and then add them to your map. You will need to use simple ArcGIS georeferencing tools to align the images properly.

In this form, the images provide a useful visual reference, and you can use ArcMap transparency and swiping tools to transition gracefully from a view of the hand sketch to a view of the corresponding GIS layers. If you want to do further analysis with the sketch, you will need to digitize it using hand sketching or digital image extraction software. Hand digitizing can be tedious, but for the purposes of geodesign in CommunityViz you do not need particularly high precision, so you can do it quickly. Once the sketch is in digital form, you can use it as the basis for a build-out analysis, impact analysis, the creation of 3-D scenes, and other useful functions.

Figure 17.1 Sample agenda for a public outreach meeting

PUBLIC OUTREACH MEETING (60–90 MINUTES)
INTRODUCTION TO THE PROJECT FOR LUNCHTIME OR EVENING GROUPS
ATTENDEES: 3–50

Duration	Topic	Action
10 min.	Welcome and Introductions *(remarks)*	Set an upbeat tone; acknowledge supporters; commit to closing the meeting on time (and do so!).
10 min.	Purpose and Context *(remarks with slides)*	Explain the purpose of the meeting; broadly describe the decisions to be made; describe how this meeting fits into the overall project and timeline; reinforce the value of public participation in the planning process and in addressing the decisions to be made; take questions.
10 min.	Existing Conditions *(remarks with CommunityViz)*	Introduce CommunityViz and acclimate the audience to the technology; establish a link between the computer model and the real world; establish expert credibility and openness to input; introduce the concept of indicators.
10 min.	Problems to Address and Forces of Change *(remarks with slides)*	Introduce key planning concepts and challenges; go to the next level of detail on decisions to be made; begin to establish a sense of urgency and need for action.
20–30 min.	Future Scenarios *(remarks with CommunityViz)*	Make the transition from realistic present-day to modeled future; reinforce the need for action; describe scenario planning concepts and compare scenarios; introduce the importance of changeable assumptions and uncertainties.
10 min.	How Public Can Engage in Next Steps *(remarks)*	Reinforce the value of public participation; establish specific follow-up dates and actions; take questions.

Figure 17.2 Sample agenda for a scenario planning workshop with a focus group

SCENARIO PLANNING WORKSHOP—FOCUS GROUP ON SPECIFIC TOPIC (HALF DAY)
WORKING SESSION ON A PARTICULAR TOPIC SUCH AS WATER OR TRAFFIC, USUALLY HELD PRIOR TO LARGER GROUP SESSIONS
ATTENDEES: 3–15

Duration	Topic	Action
15 min.	Welcome and Introductions *(remarks)*	Set an upbeat and constructive tone; acknowledge supporters; have attendees introduce themselves.
10 min.	Purpose and Context *(remarks with slides)*	Explain the purpose of the meeting; broadly describe the decisions to be made; describe how this meeting fits into the overall project and timeline; reinforce the value of public participation in the planning process; take questions.
20 min.	Educational Talk on Specific Topic *(remarks with slides)*	Ensure that participants understand key information, how the planning system works, trends, problems, and the planning and management tools available; take questions.
5 min.	Existing Conditions *(remarks with CommunityViz)*	Introduce CommunityViz and acclimate the audience to the technology; establish a link between the computer model and the real world; establish expert credibility and openness to input; introduce concept of indicators.
10 min.	Draft Future Scenarios *(remarks with CommunityViz)*	Make a transition from realistic present-day to modeled future; describe scenario planning concepts and compare scenarios; introduce variable assumptions and uncertainties.
20 min.	Identify Indicators *(facilitated discussion with CommunityViz for reference)*	Identify ways to quantify how well different scenarios perform on a particular objective; show existing draft indicators.
15 min.	Break	Refreshments and socializing.
30 min.	SWOT Analysis and Scenarios *(facilitated discussion)*	Consolidate and refine analysis goals; identify strengths, weaknesses, opportunities, and threats that need to be addressed by scenarios.
60 min.	Identify Drivers and Review Models *(facilitated discussion with CommunityViz for reference)*	Gather participants' insights about how the planning system works in this particular study area; demonstrate changeable assumptions and choose default values; describe and refine models.
20 min.	Goals and Targets *(facilitated discussion with CommunityViz for reference)*	If applicable, demonstrate CommunityViz alerts and thresholds; establish settings for future analysis.
20 min.	Review and Next Steps *(remarks with CommunityViz)*	Run through draft analysis, pointing out proposed changes and additions; consolidate learning and celebrate progress; reach agreement on how results will be shared and used; take questions.

Figure 17.3 Sample agenda for a hands-on visioning workshop

HANDS-ON VISIONING WORKSHOP (HALF DAY)
LARGE SESSION FOR THE GENERAL PUBLIC USING TABLE EXERCISES
ATTENDEES: 30–300

Duration	Topic	Action
10 min.	Welcome and Introductions *(remarks)*	Set an upbeat and constructive tone; acknowledge supporters; describe who is in attendance.
10 min.	Purpose and Context *(remarks with slides)*	Explain the purpose of the meeting; broadly describe the decisions to be made; describe how this meeting fits into the overall project and timeline; reinforce the value of public participation in the planning process; take questions.
15 min.	Existing Conditions *(remarks with CommunityViz)*	Introduce CommunityViz and acclimate the audience to the technology; establish a link between the computer model and the real world; establish both expert credibility and openness to input; introduce concept of indicators.
10 min.	Problems to Address and Forces of Change *(remarks with slides)*	Introduce key planning concepts and challenges; go to the next level of detail on decisions to be made; begin to establish a sense of urgency and need for action.
15 min.	Future Scenarios *(remarks with CommunityViz)*	Make a mental transition from realistic present-day to modeled future; reinforce the need for action; describe scenario planning concepts; introduce the importance of variable assumptions and uncertainties.
10 min.	Introduce Table Exercises *(remarks)*	Explain the goals and logistics; take questions.
45 min.	Table Exercises: First Round *(work sessions using CommunityViz and exercise guidelines or worksheet)*	Review and explore existing scenarios and indicators; understand trade-offs; discuss preferences.
20 min.	Break	Refreshments and socializing.
20 min.	First Round Report *(facilitated session with keypad polling or show of hands)*	Learn from everyone; build a sense of collaboration.
45 min.	Table Exercises: Second Round *(work sessions using CommunityViz and exercise guidelines or worksheet)*	Modify scenarios using sketching and variable assumptions; propose new solutions or explore new issues.
20 min.	Second Round Report *(facilitated session with keypad polling or show of hands)*	Learn from everyone; build a sense of collaboration.
15 min.	Review and Next Steps *(remarks)*	Report back to group; confirm how the results will be shared and used; take questions.

Designs for vertical elements such as buildings and signs may be harder to incorporate. If the designer used SketchUp or another 3-D sketching tool to create CommunityViz-compatible 3-D models, then you can add those models to your 3-D scene. Make new layers in your analysis to mark the locations of the objects, and then export those layers into your existing scene. When possible, create separate models for distinct elements such as individual buildings, rather than, say, a single SketchUp model for a downtown block. The smaller models will be easier for you to place correctly on the terrain, and they will enable the group to change small parts of the 3-D scene. The easiest way to show pencil and paper drawings in your analysis is to use hyperlinks instead of constructing a 3-D scene. Create new layers in the analysis to mark the locations, as described above, but instead of adding the layers' features to a 3-D scene, give them hyperlinks that point to digital images of the sketches. There are ways to use sketches in a 3-D scene, but they require more work. For details, see Chapter 6.

PRESENTATION TECHNIQUES AND BEST PRACTICES

During public meetings, you will need to give CommunityViz presentations that describe your analysis and one or more scenarios. Often, you will also need to help people work with the analysis, as they ask questions, suggest alternatives, and explore scenarios. This section describes presentations in which you are the only person interacting with the audience. Presentations to CommunityViz workgroups are covered later in this chapter.

DESIGNING THE ANALYSIS

The preparation for a successful public meeting with CommunityViz begins with designing your analysis for transparency. A clear analysis including an explanation of how you arrived at your results will be easier for you to present and easier for the audience to understand. Focus on the key components of your analysis in a step-by-step presentation. And be certain to use straightforward names for all the charts, indicators, and assumptions.

The rule of thumb for making a public presentation is that you should include no more than five scenarios in an analysis. Beyond that number, the audience becomes confused and finds it difficult to remember and distinguish important points.

Consider the processing times for any aspects of the analysis that you intend to update during the meeting. Figure 17.4 provides some suggested guidelines.

If a processing time appears to be a problem, look for ways to simplify the calculation, speed up processing, or precalculate the results and store them for quick retrieval. You can store results as screenshots or as separate layers in the analysis.

Figure 17.4 Processing time guidelines for public meetings

PROCESSING TIME	PUBLIC MEETING GUIDELINES
Less than 10 seconds	No restrictions
Less than 1 minute	Twice per meeting
1–2 minutes	Once per meeting
More than 2 minutes	Only during a break
More than 7 minutes	Do not attempt during a meeting

UNDERSTANDING THE AUDIENCE

A CommunityViz meeting is both a conversation and a presentation. As with any communication, the first rule is to understand your audience. Here is a checklist of information to consider gathering before or during the meeting:

- Names and contact information (including e-mail addresses) of participants
- Participants' roles in the planning process
- Participants' reasons for participating and personal goals for the session or the project
- Particular expertise or interests of participants
- Participants' familiarity with the project, planning, and CommunityViz
- Participants' preconceptions and expectations about the project
- Participants' particular points of view or stakes in the outcome
- Commonly used place-names and unusual local terms, and the audience's level of comfort with planning terms and acronyms
- Current or recent planning controversies in the community
- Formal and informal networks and organizations represented in the group
- Who is *not* attending and how they may influence the process outside the meeting

Think about the overall mix of attitudes and perspectives among the members of the audience. Judy Colby-George, a longtime CommunityViz practitioner and principal of Spatial Alternatives, Inc., has given us the playful terms lumpers and splitters to describe the two main types of participants you are likely to have in a public meeting. Lumpers prefer to see aggregate information, such as a single indicator or a representative example, and they are not as interested as others in the details of where it came from. Splitters are the opposite; they have trouble accepting a broad result until they have worked through the details and specifics, such as CommunityViz formulas and data. Most audiences contain both lumpers and splitters, and it's helpful to be aware of their separate interests.

To draw the attention of the lumpers, who tend to be in the majority, try to summarize your entire analysis in approximately five charts and five maps. Your goal is to express the primary messages of the analysis as succinctly as you can. These summaries do not replace the rest of the analysis; they simply serve as an overview that is clear and easy to remember.

Splitters are harder to satisfy within the time constraints of a public meeting, so for them it's helpful to have additional reports, diagrams, and data available outside of the meeting. Consider posting this kind of information on a project website or publishing it in a printed report, and if possible make it available before the meeting. You can also take a little time during the meeting to delve into detail on one or two points. For example, you might show the analysis diagram (see Figure 17.5) for one particular indicator, and then show its formula. In Figure 17.5, the best school locations were determined through an indicator based on the weighting of site factors, raw scores for each site, and minimum and maximum final scores of all sites. When showing an indicator and its formula, assure the lumpers that you are taking a temporary detour from the main story of the analysis and that they do not need to absorb all the detail you are showing. Also, assure the splitters that you are showing only one example of many.

DESIGNING THE DISPLAY

After working on a CommunityViz analysis for a few days, you may lose some perspective on how it appears to others. Before you present an analysis to the public, it's a good idea to tune it up for presentation. Imagine yourself as a member of the audience, and think about how to make the display communicate the information as clearly as possible. If you can, practice on a colleague or a test audience. Here are some suggestions:

■ Use Saved Views, because in our experience Saved Views mean rave reviews. You can use Saved Views (see Figure 17.6) almost like an

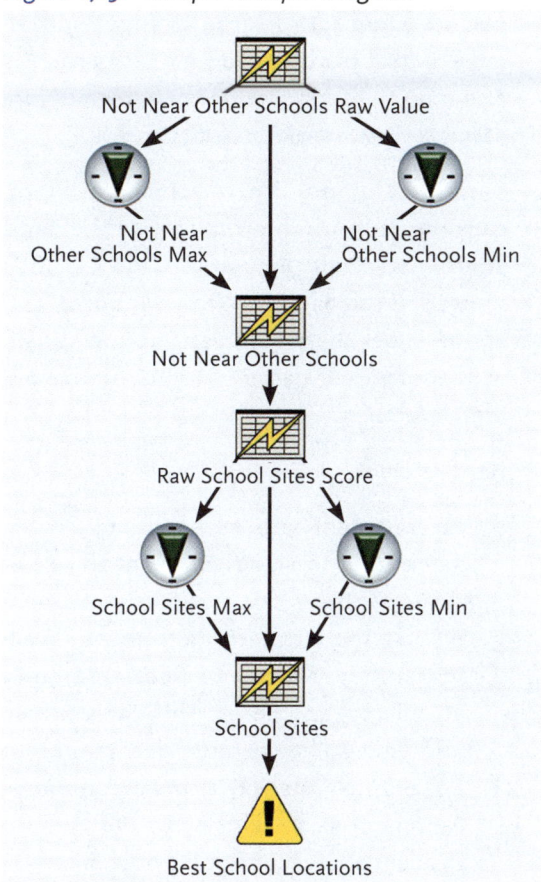

Figure 17.5 Sample analysis diagram

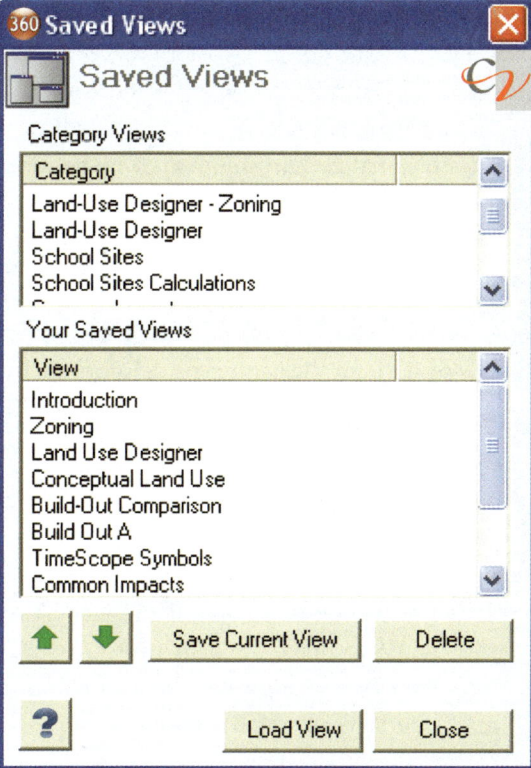

Figure 17.6 Saved Views screen

outline of your presentation, saving one view per new concept or idea. Arrange them in order so that you can follow the sequence. Pay attention to everything on the screen before saving a view to make sure it is accurate.

- Simplify. CommunityViz screens are typically packed with information, so the audience needs help focusing. Hide or close unneeded toolbars, legends, windows, and so on. Label charts and assumption sliders with short, clear names. Turn off unneeded map layers.

- Be consistent.

    a. Be consistent with terms. Do not use the same term to signify different things at different times. For example, some people use the term *density* to mean dwelling units per acre and floor area ratio, at different moments. This can confuse audiences new to land-use planning. For example, density is most commonly expressed as dwelling units per acre for residential development; floor area ratio is more common to describe the density of commercial development.

    b. Be consistent with colors. For example, you might adopt a rule that red always means commercial, whether it is on a land use map, a chart, or a 3-D object. If possible, match chart colors to corresponding map colors.

    c. Be consistent with layout. Do not move windows around the screen any more than you need to. Try to maintain a consistent location for the same type of information.

- Consider people with visual impairment. Imagine the audience member whose eyesight is not as good as it once was, sitting in a dimly lit room with a low-resolution, low-contrast projector casting a CommunityViz image on a screen far away. Is there anything you can do to make the display clearer? Use large charts and high-contrast labels, and read aloud any key information.

- Use additional media if needed. Sometimes the best way to illustrate a point is by using a photo, diagram, film clip, or some other medium that was not created by CommunityViz. You can easily include those alternatives in your presentation either by launching them with hyperlinks or buttons in CommunityViz, or simply by switching your computer display.

- "Dress in layers." That piece of advice is often given to travelers who don't know what weather to expect at their destination. In this case, you are the traveler, and the presentation is your destination. Dressing a CommunityViz display in layers means preparing additional views that you may not need. The views are there if you need them to answer a question or provide additional detail.

SPEAKING WITH COMMUNITYVIZ

A big part of presenting a CommunityViz analysis is teaching. You are conveying planning concepts, decisions that need to be made, and a great deal of information. Be organized, be clear, be interesting, and be brief. Here are some pointers to help you draft a script:

1. Start with a brief introduction to GIS technology. Two of the key concepts are the idea of a computerized map whose appearance varies in response to commands, and the idea that a GIS holds a lot of additional data that you cannot see on the map.

2. Display a map and a 3-D scene of existing conditions to orient the audience and establish connections with familiar places. Point out some landmarks on the map. Point out the study area boundaries and explain how you chose them. Acknowledge the sources of any unusual or valuable data.

3. Introduce CommunityViz, including its purpose, charts, and the term indicators. Show charts of some familiar data on existing conditions, such as current population and number of households. Then add less-familiar data, such as water and energy use, traffic counts,

auto emissions, and the jobs-to-housing ratio. You don't need to explain each one of these in detail, but do make the broader point that the study area contains a complex, connected set of economic, environmental, and social systems. Note that the CommunityViz analysis contains a lot of information about the systems and how they work, and that the information isn't all perfect or precise but gives you and the audience direction.

4. Talk about growth trends and the likelihood of change over time. Mention the time horizon you are using. Describe how planning choices made today can affect the future, and give an example from the past if you can. Reinforce the importance of choosing present-day actions wisely.

5. Introduce the idea of modeling the future. Acknowledge that models are imperfect, but also show confidence in their ability to inform. Show your Business as Usual future scenario. Talk about scenario planning concepts, and show one or two other scenarios, explaining the rationale for each one.

6. Focus on a chart that compares a single indicator across several scenarios, and remind the audience that its values are coming from a model. Depending on the audience, this may be a good time to display one or two formulas that affect the indicator. It may also be the right time to bring up the idea of variable assumptions and uncertainties, and to change an assumption to demonstrate its effects. Be cautious, however, because there is a risk that skeptical audiences will dismiss your entire approach at this early stage of their learning.

7. Turn to a particular topic area, such as the expansion of mass transit, and explain how the choices illustrated by your scenarios affect the outcomes for that topic. Repeat for one or two more topics.

8. If the audience will be interacting with the analysis, either on their own or with your help, demonstrate the tools you want them to use. These may include Sketch tools, variable assumptions, Saved Views, and 3-D features.

9. Close by returning to how CommunityViz tools and techniques support the purpose of the project.

When using CommunityViz in front of an audience, we recommend that you do the following:

- Use your mouse purposefully. *Do* use it to point out the part of the screen the audience should focus on. *Do not* let it wander aimlessly; it can be distracting.

- Explain what's happening. If the view on the screen changes for reasons that are not obvious, explain why. For example, "I am bringing up a new Saved View now," or "The analysis is now updating its calculations," or "These chart values changed because . . ." This practice is important for maintaining a sense of transparency about CommunityViz and your analysis.

- Introduce only one major new idea at a time. If the idea is complex, such as a multifactor suitability analysis, break it into pieces and gradually assemble the whole. The same advice applies to pieces of the CommunityViz display: The charts window, assumptions window, alerts, and so on each count as one "idea." Turn them on one at a time, explaining as you go.

VENUE AND LOGISTICS

CommunityViz requires you to pay more attention to the room setup and technology than if you were delivering a speech or PowerPoint presentation. Plan to spend some extra time on preparation to ensure that your tools perform at their best, and build in enough time for setup and equipment tests so that you can fix any glitches and are not pressured by attendees beginning to enter the room. Here are some points to consider:

- **Projection screen or screens.** Make sure everyone can easily see a screen and read small print such as assumption labels. Anticipate lighting conditions, such as daylight coming in through windows. Test your CommunityViz display with the projector and screen you will actually use, and set up Saved Views that fit the screen size. Check that the colors on your display show up well in projection.

- **Presenter's location.** It is best if you can see your computer screen and the faces of the audience at the same time. Make sure you have enough room for accessory equipment such as a mouse, a pointer, and a microphone.
- **Sound system.** If you will be using a sound system, test it ahead of time.
- **Power outlets and cords.** Make sure your cables and cords will reach wall sockets and that you can run them safely, without causing tripping hazards or electrical overloads.
- **Network connections.** If you plan to use an Internet connection, test it ahead of time.
- **Backups.** It never hurts to have a backup copy of your analysis on a portable drive, a backup slide show of screenshots, and a backup computer. It is also a good idea to find out in advance where you can get a backup projector on short notice. If you will be doing keypad polling, have a paper backup plan as well.

PRESENTING 3-D SCENES

Three-dimensional scenes are almost universally popular with audiences, whether they are created in Scenario 3D, Google Earth, ArcScene, or some other platform. If your presentation will include a 3-D scene, advertising that fact ahead of time will probably increase attendance at the public meeting and the likelihood that attendees will tell their friends about it afterward. If there is press coverage, the 3-D scene will probably receive the most attention in the newspapers the next day. Consider offering reporters screenshots in digital form for reproduction in their publications, or copies of the scene for posting on their websites. At the start of the meeting, attendees will focus on the 3-D parts of the agenda. A 3-D scene conveys a tremendous amount of information in a very accessible way. It transforms your numbers, charts, and maps into a visual form that people can easily absorb. If the 3-D scene is made well and presented well, it will be one of the most effective communication tools you have.

Be aware that everyone in the audience will be a critic. Human brains are adept at visual processing, and everyone who can see knows how the world is supposed to look. Small errors will be instantly evident, and your inevitable shortcuts and approximations will all be noticed. In addition, 3-D is an emotional medium. Viewers may have strong reactions to what they see; they may react with gasps, shouts, and shocked silence, as well as the expected oohs and aahs. Because of this strong connection between the audience and the scene, consider the following best practices:

- **Start slowly and simply.** Let the audience gradually become comfortable with the technology. Fly slowly through a scene at first.
- **Establish context.** Before showing any new development or planning proposal, spend some time showing the existing conditions. Display some familiar buildings and landmarks. The goal is to help viewers make a connection between the model and the real world so that when new proposals are shown, they can see them not only on the screen but also in their mind's eye.
- **Establish credibility.** Explain how the scene was made, where its data came from, and why the audience can believe the position and size of objects. If you are using Scenario 360, use the Identify tool to establish that the objects in the scene have a geodatabase attached to them.
- **Show humility.** Your scene can be credible, useful, and imperfect all at the same time, and you need the audience to forgive the imperfections while still trusting the important characteristics of the scene. Humility is a way of asking for that forgiveness. Point out, for example, some shortcuts you have taken or some elements that are missing, and invite suggestions for improvement. Your acknowledgment of these imperfections will make it easier for audience members to accept the scene as a tool that supports the decision-making process, instead of seeing it as a boast or stunt.
- **Follow the five-minute rule.** When people see a 3-D scene for the first time, there is a

period of five to 10 minutes during which they are distracted by the CommunityViz technology itself. If you want them to start responding to the *content*, such as whether they approve of the width of the road or whether they prefer one design over another, display and explore the scene for at least five minutes before attempting to engage them in a question-and-answer session. Five minutes is a surprisingly long time, but it pays to be patient. The five-minute rule does not apply to audiences that are already familiar with CommunityViz.

- **Match navigation to purpose.** For visioning exercises, use the thousand/thousand rule of thumb, which is to stay at least 1,000 feet above the ground and include no more than 1,000 features in your primary analysis layer. For more detailed plans or designs, spend at least some time navigating at the street level so that viewers experience the scene as they would from a car or on foot. Set your height at about 6 feet and look slightly upward as you move. In developed areas, walk or fly at speeds between 5 and 20 feet per second.

- **Plan your routes.** In order to navigate through a scene during a presentation, you don't have to memorize your routes, but you should have a good outline, and practice beforehand. (The same advice applies to what you say during the presentation: You don't have to memorize a script, but do have a good outline, and practice.) Make good use of bookmarks and paths, but do not rely on them entirely or the scene will seem prerecorded. Feel free to depart temporarily from your prepared presentation to respond to questions.

- **Look around.** One of the most helpful characteristics of a 3-D scene is that it enables you to go anywhere and look anywhere. When you are at a key location in the scene, take time to look in all directions and move up and down to give a full sense of the space. In Scenario 360, when you travel down a street, try looking to the side, as if you were looking out the side window of a car.

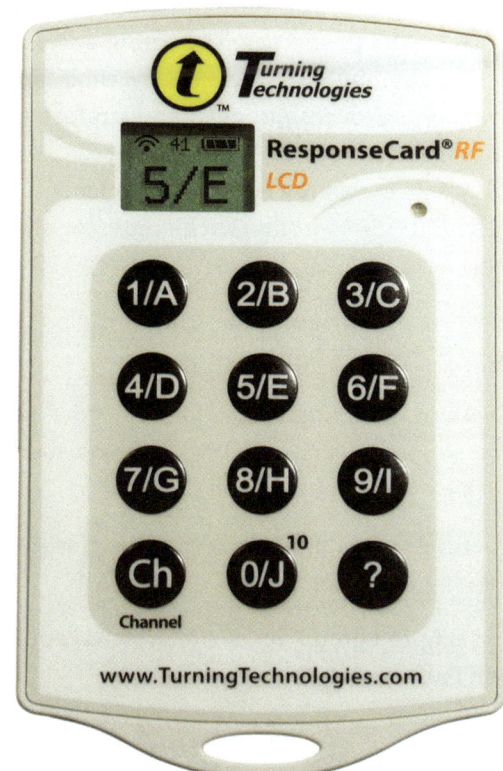

Figure 17.6 A wireless keypad

- **Adjust the field of view to the situation.** The standard field of view for most tools is 45 degrees, but people tend to focus more narrowly on objects that are close and more widely on objects that are far away. Field of view is particularly important in cases where distant views are important, such as in relation to wind turbines or ridgelines. In those cases, consider showing the audience several fields of view to help them establish a better mental picture.

KEYPADS AND ONLINE POLLING

Wireless keypads, or clickers, are popular and useful technology for public meetings. The keypad, about the size of a credit card, is marked with the digits 0 to 9, and sometimes other options (see Figure 17.6).

Each participant at the public meeting is given a keypad. When the facilitator asks for a vote on a particular question, participants register their opinions by pressing a number. The results are collected wirelessly by a base station, processed on the facilitator's computer, and then displayed through a projector onto a screen as charts that everyone can see. The voting is anonymous, so feedback is frank and fair. The voting also supports the CommunityViz tenet of "learning from everyone," not just those who are comfortable with speaking in public.

Keypads are a very effective complement to CommunityViz capabilities. The most common applications include:

- Setting assumption slider bars based on the group's preferences

- Setting weighting values for subjective factors in a suitability analysis, such as scenic value or land conservation priorities

- Setting weighting factors for value elements during value mapping

- Asking the group about preferred locations on the map.

In addition, keypads can be used to collect demographic information about the attendees and their evaluations of the meeting, and to decide on the best time for the next meeting.

If you have information about the participants, you can perform cross-correlation analysis about their votes, because the system tracks how each keypad voted on each vote. Cross-correlation can enable you to show the relationship between a particular group (by age, gender, or place of residence) and their votes for or against a certain issue. One real-world example is a project that was evaluating sites for a new superstore. The votes were about evenly split between two locations, one on the north side of town and one on the south, and the group discussion was not revealing any clear reasons for the split. But then the facilitator correlated the votes with the results of an earlier question about where each participant lived. This revealed that northerners preferred the southern location and southerners preferred the northern one. In other words, no one wanted the store in his or her neighborhood. This insight led to a more direct, honest discussion about participants' concerns.

You need to create keypad-polling questions that correspond to the information you want to input into CommunityViz. For example, you might include a weighting factor in a keypad question such as the one shown in Figure 17.7.

After the votes are cast, use the combined score to set the value of the corresponding changeable assumption in your analysis. If your keypad system provides an average or median score, median is preferable because it shows the mid-point value; half of the responses are above the median and half below. You can read the score and manually adjust the assumption to match. If the keypad system produces a tabular output such as an Excel spreadsheet or comma-separated values (CSV) file, you can link to those directly using Scenario 360 External Table Links. External Table Links will provide changeable inputs to your analysis in the form of indicators, not assumptions, so be sure to create a chart that displays the indicator values to provide visual verification that the analysis reflects the keypad results.

Online polling is similar to keypad polling except that it uses the Internet. You link the results to CommunityViz in the same ways. You can do an online poll simultaneously with a public meeting, or you can collect responses over time in a survey format. A major benefit of online polling is that you can reach a much larger audience, although you lose the personal touch of a live meeting.

Figure 17.7 Sample keypad polling question for a CommunityViz weighting factor

How important is this factor to you?	
0	Not at all important
1	...
2	Matters a little
3	...
4	...
5	Somewhat important
6	...
7	...
8	Matters a lot
9	...

COMMUNITYVIZ IN WORKGROUPS

A working session with a small number of people can be one of the most productive parts of any planning process. People with different fields of expertise, different roles in the project, and different stakes in the outcome can come together to reach consensus on a plan. CommunityViz supports the team effort by providing: a) a framework for the planning discussion, b) clear ways to communicate important information, c) ready access to data, and d) answers to "What if?" questions using geodesign.

When you use CommunityViz in a workgroup, combine both presentation and analysis. Start with a presentation, but then introduce the team to the interactive features of CommunityViz. Next, give the team some control over the questions asked and the answers displayed. Over time, the analysis will become a partner in the team discussion. Anyone around the table can consult the analysis, and everyone around the table can understand it.

This section describes how workgroups typically interact with CommunityViz and some best practices for introducing the tool into a small-group environment.

WORKGROUP LEARNING CURVES

If the people you are working with are unfamiliar with CommunityViz, introduce them to the basic principles just as you would introduce any new audience. Prepare your analysis ahead of time, and walk the group through the analysis, making sure that everyone understands the concepts of geodesign, scenario planning, indicators, and assumptions. Your analysis does not need to be complete before you show it to a workgroup; indeed, the purpose of the group is often to help you refine the analysis. But you do want to have enough structure in place so that others can understand the design of your analysis.

Workgroups usually go through a progression in learning to work with CommunityViz (see Figure 17.8).

At first, the group's attention will be focused on the computer technology. Over time, group members will grow accustomed to the capabilities of CommunityViz and turn more of their

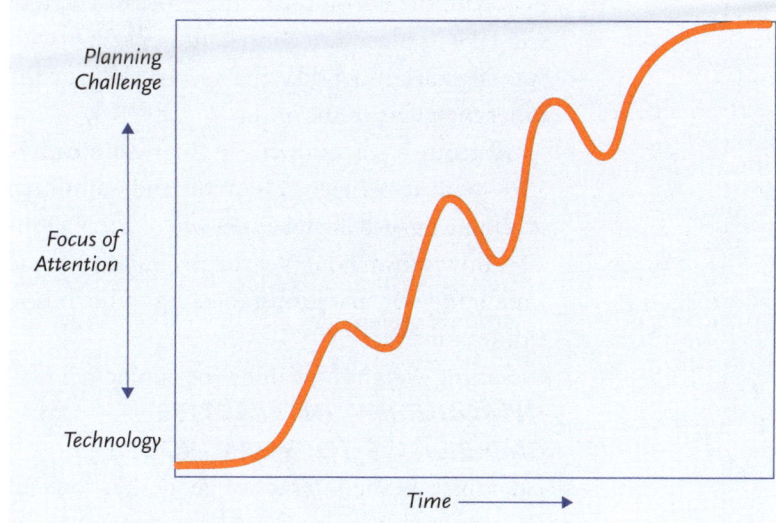

Figure 17.8 *How a CommunityViz workgroup's focus of attention progresses over time*

attention to the planning challenges at hand. This is the trend you want, and your goal is to move the group in that direction. Be aware, however, that the progression will take a little time and will be punctuated with occasional returns to a focus on the technology: "Wait, can CommunityViz do that?" or "That can't be right. It must be broken." As time goes by, questions and comments will become more planning oriented: "Would it help to move this transit stop farther south?" or "What if the price of gasoline goes up by 50 percent?"

At the beginning, some group members may be uncomfortable with a computer-based decision-support tool, and they may not want to use it. When you introduce CommunityViz, these group members will be quick to attack the validity of its results. Don't be alarmed or defensive about this reaction; it's part of the normal process of learning to work with any new tool. Emphasize that you intend to use CommunityViz only where it is helpful. As you continue to explain and demonstrate the analysis, group members will usually become more comfortable, and their reaction may even swing from an unreasonable distrust of the tool to an unreasonable awe of the tool. They may come to expect CommunityViz to do everything, including making decisions. Such unrealistic expectations will soon lead to frustration as people learn the limits of the tool's capabilities. And then, finally, the group will arrive at a balanced understanding of how CommunityViz and geodesign can help with the decision-making process. The tool will take its place as a contributing partner with special skills, much like the special skills of the other members of the group.

A group's learning curve for CommunityViz—both in terms of attention and emotional acceptance—usually takes anywhere from about 15 minutes to an hour. We suggest building some time into your first group meeting to introduce CommunityViz.

INTRODUCING INTERACTIVE CAPABILITIES TO WORKGROUPS

Demonstrate the interactive geodesign tools of CommunityViz in your initial presentation to the workgroup, and as you progress to teaching people how to use those tools, revisit them and provide more explanation. Eventually, you will want to introduce the group members to most or all of the Scenario 360 tools available from the Scenario 360 toolbar or Analysis tab (see Figure 17.9).

It is not necessary to introduce all of the CommunityViz tools at once. Start with the simplest tools and gradually move on to the others, talking about them only as the need arises. Here is a typical sequence:

1. Map display, including visible layers, pan, and zoom (ArcMap functions not displayed on the Scenario 360 Analysis tab)
2. Active scenario and the Scenario Comparison Window
3. Chart display, including chart display options
4. Indicators, including the indicator list that shows a table of indicator values
5. Dynamic analysis, including dynamic attributes and indicator formulas
6. Map symbols, emphasizing the idea that colors can represent attribute data (ArcMap functions that are not displayed on the Scenario 360 Analysis tab)
7. Variable assumptions, including a display of a chart's variable assumptions, being sure to introduce the idea of the linking and unlinking of assumptions across scenarios
8. Saved Views
9. Map editing, including the Scenario 360 sketch tools Painter and Clone if you are using them
10. Alerts, including the various ways of showing target lines on charts
11. Reports
12. Diagrams

If you are using 3-D, also introduce the team to the navigation and display features of the particular 3-D tool you are using.

BEST PRACTICES FOR USING COMMUNITYVIZ WITH WORKGROUPS

Here are some tips and best practices for using CommunityViz with small workgroups:

Figure 17.9 Scenario 360 Analysis tab

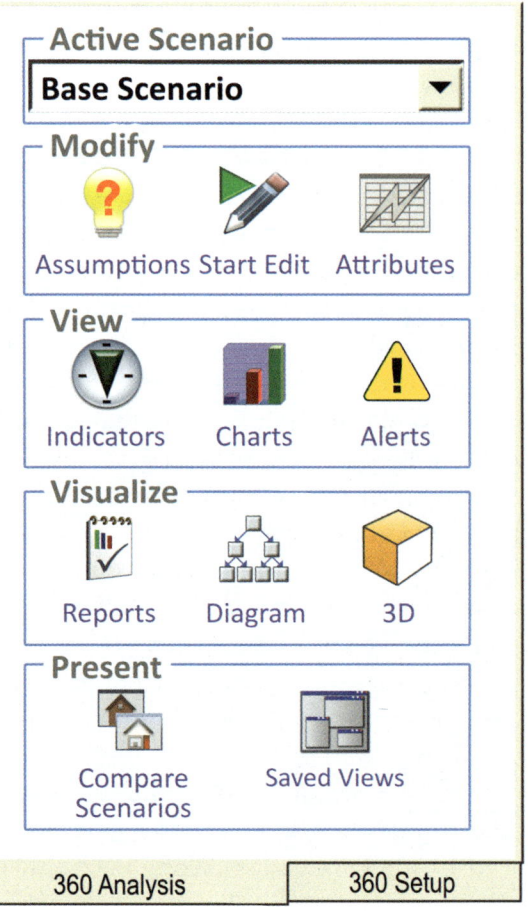

- Make a backup copy of your analysis before the meeting, and use a new version at the meeting. This will ensure that you do not lose any work during the meeting.

- Set up Saved Views beforehand so that team members do not become distracted while you search for information.

- Make sure everyone can see the screen. There is a risk that people who are sitting too far away will not be able to read the display and will therefore be less engaged in the results. If necessary, use a projector or a large monitor and ask attendees to move to the front rows.

- Explain the proper names of CommunityViz components—indicators, assumptions, attributes, and so on—so that everyone has a common language for reference.

- The first few times you use an interactive CommunityViz capability, be particularly careful to explain what you are doing and what is happening inside the analysis. By explaining your steps, you reinforce your instructions on how to use the tool, so that people can use it on their own later. By describing what is happening inside the analysis, you emphasize transparency and invite group members to suggest improvements to your analysis.

- Be aware of processing times. If certain changes to your analysis will take more than about seven minutes to run, try to avoid launching them during a workgroup meeting, because the analysis will be unavailable for other uses while it's being updated.

- Use the Symbol Saver feature or Saved Views to capture map symbols as you go. Changing map symbols provides an excellent way to explore data interactively and reveal patterns, but during the course of a discussion you will often find yourself returning to a previous view, so it's a good idea to save a copy of your work as you make changes.

- Create new scenarios to address or explore major new ideas as they arise. For minor ideas such as assumption changes or small map edits, work within existing scenarios.

- Keep a running list of ideas for improving the analysis after the presentation. Examples include ideas for new indicators, additional data needs, and suggested values for targets and assumption defaults. Do not slow down the discussion by making people wait while you try to improve the analysis. Show the list of ideas and proposed additional work on the analysis to the group to ensure agreement. This is a good way to generate interest in the next meeting.

CASE STUDY
CITY COMPREHENSIVE PLAN

Location: Fort Lupton, Colorado
Partners: City of Fort Lupton; Civil Resources, LLC; Foresee Consulting, Inc.

Context: Fort Lupton, which has a population of 7,500, is 25 miles from the cities of Denver, Boulder, and Greeley. Fort Lupton has ready access to major transportation routes and is within the rapidly growing urban corridor of Colorado's Front Range. In 2006, the city set out to update its 1997 comprehensive plan to make it "a statement of public policy and an expression of the community's vision for the future [that would] also represent the community's values for positive economic growth and development, as well as preserving the quality of life the residents enjoy."

The result, Fort Lupton's 2007 comprehensive plan, was notable for many reasons. It looked beyond the city boundaries to address lands in unincorporated areas of Weld County. In drafting the plan, the city made serious efforts to include county residents, the Hispanic population, the elderly, and students. Plan policies were implemented in numerous ways, such as through intergovernmental agreements (IGAs) with the surrounding communities and with Weld County. In 2008, the Colorado chapter of the American Planning Association gave the Fort Lupton plan its Community Engagement Award, because the awards committee "was impressed with the innovative ways of capturing public participation and the use of IGAs and other creative avenues. The Plan had great goals and is very realistic."

Project Description: The city engaged Civil Resources to lead a community-based, citizen-driven planning process. The consulting team worked closely with area youth and adults, elected and appointed officials, and staff. Early in the project, the city distributed surveys in both English and Spanish at City Hall, a chamber of commerce meeting, a workshop with area seniors, and the first of two communitywide meetings. The city also mailed the surveys with water bills and distributed them through the school district's English-as-a-second-language program and through local businesses. The consultants met with the middle school's student council to learn students' long-range hopes for their community.

The project team led three well-attended interactive community workshops, which formed the backbone of the project (see Figure 17.10). At the first workshop, participants used keypad polling to indicate how they wanted the city to grow, and to define criteria that would be used later to evaluate alternative land-use plans.

At the second workshop, participants were divided into six groups to play a growth challenge game—sometimes referred to as a chip game—in which each group placed chips representing homes, jobs, parks, trails, and public facilities on a detailed aerial photo of the planning area (see Figure 17.11). Most participants indicated support for the historic pattern of compact growth in and around existing neighborhoods. The consultants incorporated the citizen-developed plans into CommunityViz for comparison and analysis.

Figure 17.10 A public map exercise in Fort Lupton, Colorado

Images courtesy of Foresee Consulting

Figure 17.11 Fort Lupton's communitywide land-use concept plan

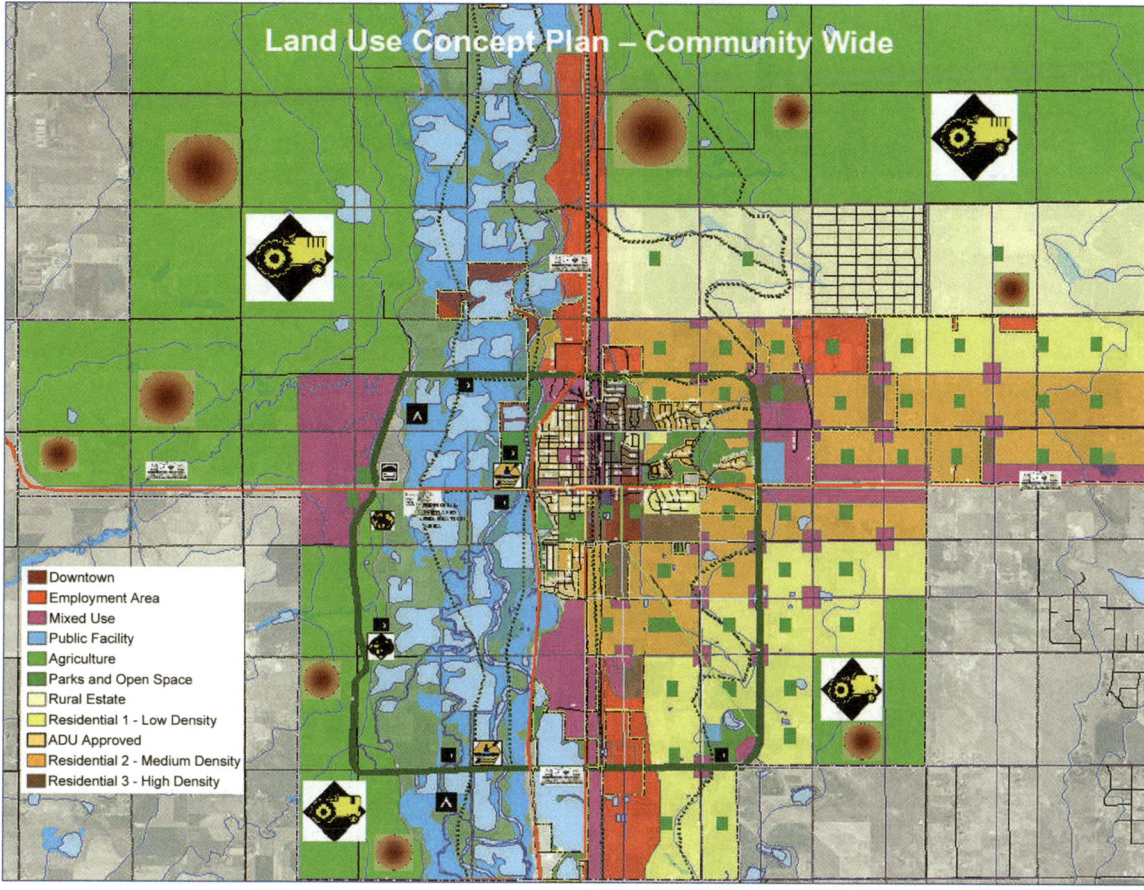

At the third workshop, the project team presented the results of the growth challenge game. They also used the criteria developed by residents in the first workshop to evaluate the alternatives with CommunityViz and to develop a synthesis plan. Keypad polling was used as a check to see whether citizens supported the plan. The results of the surveys and the workshops formed the basis of the final comprehensive plan.

Technology and Tools: Foresee Consulting used CommunityViz Scenario 360 to draft, evaluate, and illustrate the alternative plans and the synthesis plan. The community was engaged through widely distributed surveys in English and Spanish, and focused workshops with seniors, students, and the chamber of commerce. An interactive comprehensive plan website enabled people to complete an online survey, and provided them with project information and updates. In the workshops, CommunityViz, keypad polling and the growth challenge game were used to define residents' priorities; develop, analyze, and evaluate alternative land use plans; and confirm the synthesis plan that is the basis of the comprehensive plan.

Outcomes: The City of Fort Lupton adopted the comprehensive plan in early 2008. Since then, it has been used to craft a growing set of intergovernmental agreements, including ones that relate to growth boundaries and buffer areas, revenue sharing, cooperation on regional trails, and the efficient provision of public facilities. Two annexations, with related rezoning, have taken place, both in conformity with the plan. The city's planning director, Tom Parko, indicated that the annexations were facilitated by the fact that the citizen-developed plan had already identified the annexed areas for future development. The city is also using the design principles articulated in the plan in its review and evaluation of private and public development proposals.

CASE STUDY
LARGE-SCALE LAND CONSERVATION PLANNING

Location: Northern Rocky Mountains, in Idaho, Montana, Wyoming, and Alberta and British Columbia, Canada

Partners: Heart of the Rockies Initiative (a collaboration among 24 local, state, and national land trusts); Geodata Services, Inc.; major funding partners

Context: Land trusts along the Continental Divide came together in 2002 with a common objective: "to increase the pace of private land conservation in America's crown jewel, the Northern Rockies." The Heart of the Rockies Initiative (HOTR) was born. The collaboration focuses on three areas: the Greater Yellowstone Ecosystem (GYE), the Crown of the Continent and Idaho Panhandle (COC&IP), and the High Divide (see Figure 17.12).

These areas contain vast tracts of public and private lands, with spectacular landscapes (see Figure 17.13) and remarkable wildlife treasures.

Interspersed with public lands are private lands of working farms, ranches, and timber operations. Over time, development on these private lands could fragment wildlife habitats, reduce lands available for agriculture and forestry, and irretrievably alter communities. The Heart of the Rockies Initiative recognized that the voluntary conservation of strategic private lands is crucial to sustaining the wildlife heritage, ecological integrity, and agricultural and timber industries of the Northern Rockies. The group set out to identify the most important private lands and to establish land conservation goals for the next 10 years.

Since 2003, Geodata Services has been facilitating GIS mapping and analysis using CommunityViz. The company works with local stakeholders and area organizations to establish regionwide land conservation goals and local priorities.

Project Description: Early in the process, large group meetings, workshops, and small group meetings were held with area land trusts to develop criteria for the analysis. The land trusts agreed on three main criteria for land conservation: biological importance, strategic status

Figure 17.12 Heart of the Rockies, shown in the blue area

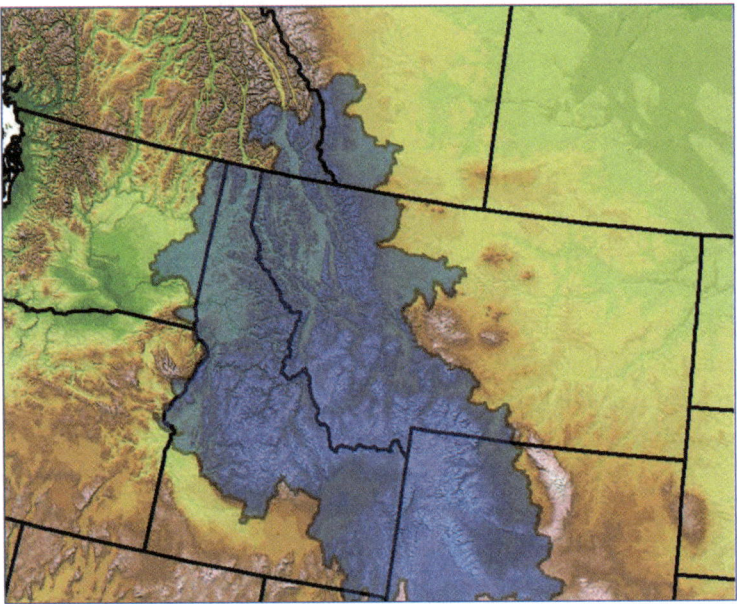

Courtesy of Geodata Services

Figure 17.13 A river valley in the Heart of the Rockies

of ranchland, and importance of land to local communities. In each of the three large regions, Geodata Services collected data on watersheds, wildlife species, strategic ranchlands, farmland soils, forest productivity, conservation easements, demographics, historic sites, and more.

The data were analyzed using CommunityViz. Landscape-scale analyses led to the identification of specific focus areas within each watershed. At this level, additional factors were added, including landownership characteristics and major threats. CommunityViz users were able to analyze land conservation priorities within each watershed based on ratings for biology, agriculture, and community values. State wildlife managers, federal land managers, and stakeholders from local communities, land trusts, watershed groups, and nongovernmental organizations cooperated to determine local conservation priorities and support implementation of the land conservation strategy.

Geodata Services used CommunityViz at meetings to help participants develop priorities. Changeable assumption slider bars tied to the weighting factors used in the Suitability Wizard provided graphical displays of biological, agricultural, and local community conservation values. This process took into account some 30 to 40 factors and showed the results in a single GIS layer on the study area map. Meeting participants could see a clear visual representation of their collaborative community values in one set of maps, and could employ this information to verify land conservation priorities (see, for example, Figure 17.14). The dark red areas were identified as high priority lands. The yellow dots are conservation easements acquired. The more conservation easements acquired in the high priority areas, the more successful the land conservation effort.

In the GYE and COC&IP, the land trusts used the results to develop conservation plans with 10-year goals for conserving high-value private lands, and strategies to achieve the 10-year goals, based on the estimated costs of conserving and stewarding these lands in perpetuity.

Technology and Tools: The project used CommunityViz components, including changeable assumptions and the Scenario 360 Suitability

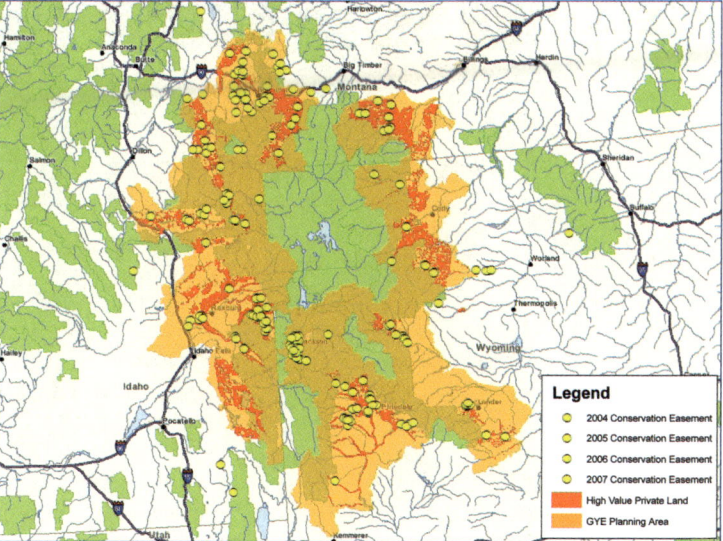

Figure 17.14 Map of high-value private land

Wizard, and large group meetings, small group meetings, stakeholder meetings, and workshops.

Outcomes: By early 2009, the HOTR collaboration had achieved several noteworthy accomplishments, including the creation of a $7 million revolving loan fund available to HOTR land trusts; matching capacity building grants for HOTR land trusts; new public funding programs in the United States and Canada; substantial private grants; and the creation of a state land trust association in Montana, with others under development in Idaho and Wyoming. Local land trusts have matured dramatically in capacity, vision, and credibility within their local communities. Many now have excellent GIS capacity, and more than half now use CommunityViz for detailed conservation analyses.

The funding efforts and strategic identification of private lands for conservation have contributed to impressive on-the-ground successes. From 2004 to 2007, HOTR land trusts completed 368 private land conservation projects and conserved 411,875 acres of private land in the GYE and COC&IP combined. Heart of the Rockies Initiative coordinator Michael Whitfield notes, "We can demonstrate that land trusts are conserving lands that have regional and landscape-scale conservation priority and that the rate of conservation is increasing as a result of HOTR collaboration."

18 REPORTS, DISPLAYS, AND WEBSITES

KEY CONCEPTS AND TERMS IN THIS CHAPTER

- Project websites
- Reporting and display best practices
- Reporting and display features
- Working with images of 3-D scenes
- Web-ready reports
- WebShots

Although CommunityViz is an interactive computer-based tool, on most projects you will also want to create and share printed reports, images, and snapshots of your work. This chapter highlights best practices for creating and sharing CommunityViz reports and displays.

REPORTING AND DISPLAY FEATURES

Chapter 17 described the capabilities of CommunityViz for engaging audiences at public meetings. Here is a summary of the major printed reports, online reporting, and display features available in CommunityViz. Technology is changing rapidly, so it's a good idea to check online for the latest CommunityViz capabilities.

- **Reports.** The Scenario 360 Reports tool provides an easy way to compile and share all kinds of information about your analysis. You can use Scenario 360 Reports to make tables containing information about scenarios, indicators, assumptions, dynamic attributes, alerts, component descriptions, Common Impacts Wizard data, and the details of a Build-Out Wizard analysis (see Figure 18.1). In addition, the Reports tool lets you include visual displays such as charts and maps. Scenario 360 creates the reports in a web-ready format so you can post them online. You can also open them, read them, and edit them in word-processing tools such as Microsoft Word.

- **Diagrams.** A Scenario 360 analysis diagram illustrates the logic of an analysis by showing all the analysis components and their relationships to one another. You can sort and organize the diagram to display subsets of information in many useful ways, such as all the components in one category or all the factors affecting one particular value.

- **Image capture.** Scenario 360 provides an easy way to capture image files of individual charts, which you can use in slides, documents, and other custom reports. Scenario 3D has a similar capability for capturing screenshots of 3-D scenes.

- **Exporting tables.** You can export tables of values for indicators and assumptions into Microsoft Excel–compatible files.

REPORTING AND DISPLAY BEST PRACTICES

When you create a report, keep in mind that you will probably not be present when it is being read. Therefore, the report needs to speak for itself as much as possible. Make sure you:

- Use clear names and labels for everything, including project names and scenario names.

- Include descriptions where possible, written in language that will make sense to your intended audience.

- Check the accuracy and clarity of measurement units.

- Clean up charts and maps.

- Simplify the report, omitting unnecessary details.

Figure 18.1 Part of a Build-Out Wizard report

DWELLING

Land-Use Designation	Numeric Build-Out	Spatial Build-Out	Difference	Existing Dwelling Units
Commercial	0	0	0	407
High Density Multifamily	10132	4400	5732	183
Med Density Multifamily	1509	156	1353	1
Park	0	0	0	10
Single Family	1802	1008	794	859
Total	13443	5564	7879	1460

COMMERCIAL FLOOR SPACE

Land-Use Designation	Numeric Build-Out Floor Area (sq. feet)	Spatial Build-Out Floor Area (sq. feet)	Difference	Existing Floor Area
Commercial	9096755.702	1380000	7716755.702	0
High Density Multifamily	0	0	0	0
Med Density Multifamily	0	0	0	0
Park	0	0	0	0
Single Family	0	0	0	0
Total	9096755.702	1380000	7716755.702	0

BUILDING QUANTITIES

Land-Use Designation	Numeric Build-Out Units	Spatial Build-Out Units	Difference	Existing Buildings
Commercial	305	46	259	407
High Density Multifamily	127	55	72	183
Med Density Multifamily	252	26	226	1
Park	0	0	0	10
Single Family	1802	1008	794	859
Total	2486	1135	1351	1460

BUILDABLE AREA

Land-Use Designation	Gross Area (sq feet)	Net Buildable Area (sq feet)	Difference (sq feet)
Commercial	18193511.405	18193511.405	0
High Density Multifamily	12871158.753	11234530.27	1636628.484
Med Density Multifamily	2192569.077	2192569.077	0
Park	10017127.948	9251742.52	765385.427
Single Family	29567427.405	28998355.333	569072.072
Total	72841794.588	69870708.605	2971085.983

EXCEPTIONS

Land-Use Designation	Number of dwelling units that couldn't be placed because of space constraints	Number of commerical buildings that couldn't be placed because of space constraints	Number of polygons where number of existing buildings exceeds build-out limit
Commercial	0	259	0
High Density Multifamily	5732	72	0
Med Density Multifamily	1353	226	0
Park	0	0	0
Single Family	794	794	0
Total	7879	1351	0

- Organize a large report into smaller sections so the report is easier to navigate.
- Include the date of the work.
- Use poster-size displays at public forums to make detailed CommunityViz information easier to view.

We encourage you to use CommunityViz reports and displays in conjunction with other good software tools, such as:

- ArcMap layout tools to create high-quality maps for printing
- Microsoft Excel for sophisticated charts of CommunityViz output data
- Photoshop or other image-editing software to create information-rich, easy-to-understand posters and slides
- Text and slide editors such as Microsoft Word and PowerPoint for creating complete reports and presentations.

IMAGES OF 3-D SCENES

The creation of a static image of a 3-D scene requires special attention. When people see an image of a scene in a report, their viewing experience is not the same as it is when they see a live computer application. The image may not compare favorably with a 2-D photo-simulation because the resolution will tend to be lower and more details will be missing. Here are some tips on how you can make a 2-D snapshot of a 3-D scene look its best and be most useful (see figures 18.2 and 18.3):

- Experiment to find the zoom level and field of view that best represents your scene.
- Turn off fog, and experiment with lighting.
- Try to reinforce the sense of depth of field by including in your snapshot foreground, middle-distance, and background objects.
- Capture an image from the largest screen size possible. You can shrink the image later if necessary, but enlarging an image will reduce its apparent resolution. Scenario 3D provides the ability to set very large image sizes, such as 4,096 x 2,304 pixels.
- Pay attention to aspect ratio. The wider an image is, the better it tends to capture the landscape—for example, moviemakers favor a 1.85:1 ratio of width to height, and high-definition television has a ratio of 16:9.
- Pay attention to the level of detail in the lower foreground. The part of the scene in front of you takes up a disproportionate amount of the 2-D space, so it's important that its level of detail is high.
- Include a caption explaining that the image is a snapshot or screenshot of an interactive 3-D scene.

PROJECT WEBSITE

A project website can stimulate outreach, communication, and interaction with broad audiences. We recommend using a website to show your work as it proceeds. CommunityViz provides a number of tools to help you share your work on a website.

WEB-READY REPORTS

Posting a Scenario 360 web-ready report is the easiest way to share your work on a website. You can display most of the same information you would present in a meeting, such as descriptions, scenarios, charts, indicators, and assumptions. In addition, you can capture and publish the details of your analysis, such as formulas, component descriptions, and references. By including "active" controls, you can enable website visitors to control how much or how little detail they see. Figure 18.4 shows a small part of a website report.

WEBSITE IMAGES AND DATA

If your website contains slide shows or custom webpages that describe the project and the CommunityViz analysis, you can illustrate them with CommunityViz charts, data, and 3-D models. Scenario 360 provides one-button tools for saving charts and images and for exporting assumption and indicator values to tables. Scenario 3D has a simple image-capture capability as well—for details, see the section 3-D Scenes on the Web, below.

Reports, Displays, and Websites 219

Figure 18.2 Screenshots from an interactive 3-D scene:

a) standard capture with a 45-degree field of view and time of day set to 2:00 p.m.

b) with fog

c) 21-degree field of view

d) 80-degree field of view

e) close-up view

f) with time of day set to 6:00 a.m.

Figure 18.3 An image of scene a), Figure 18.2 with a 16:9 aspect ratio

Figure 18.4 *Detail from a website report*

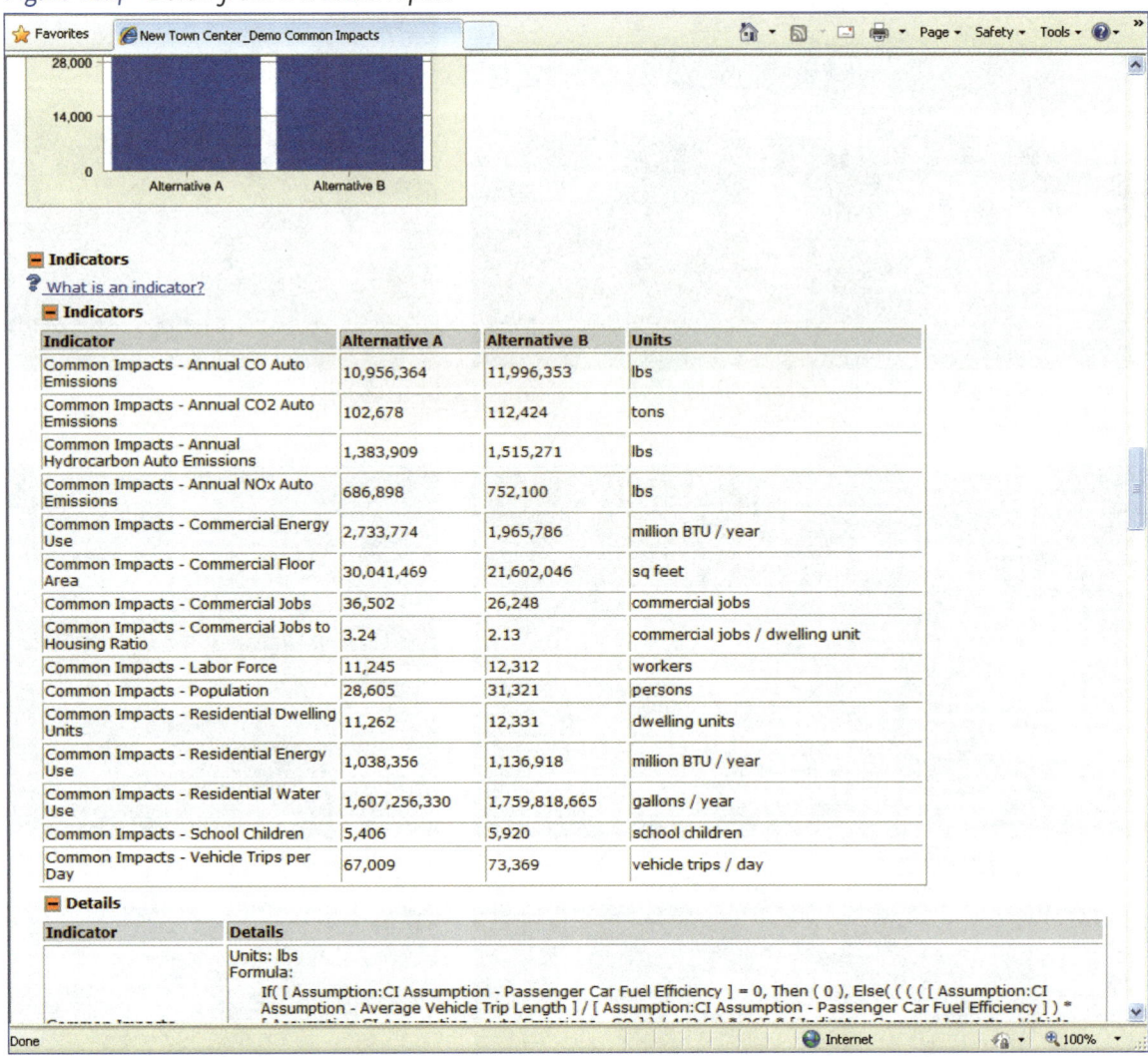

WEBSHOTS WIZARD

To create a more interactive, visual presentation of your analysis online, use the Scenario 360 WebShots Wizard (see Figure 18.5).

You can use the WebShots Wizard to produce partly interactive web pages that display maps, charts, indicators, and assumptions. In Slide Show mode in the WebShots Viewer on your website, visitors can step through a series of annotated WebShots displays that present the analysis in a logical sequence. In Explore for Yourself mode, visitors can change scenarios and vary assumption values on their own, receiving real-time updates as they work. These capabilities give visitors an online experience that is somewhat like taking part in a live Scenario 360 presentation. However, WebShots are not nearly as flexible as a live application, and they can only display limited amounts of data. Do not consider them a replacement for an in-depth CommunityViz analysis. Instead, use them as a form of online reporting or for giving website visitors a way to explore and react to the highlights of your analysis.

3-D SCENES ON THE WEB

Because they are immediately appealing and interesting, 3-D scenes are a good match with web-based communications. You can share material from your 3-D scenes on websites in several ways:

- **KMZ files.** The Scenario 360 Google Earth Exporter produces Google Earth–compatible

Figure 18.5   Sample WebShots Wizard screen

KMZ files. For a simple scene, post the file, along with a description of what it is and instructions on how to view it in Google Earth. Also provide directions for getting the free Google Earth viewer. For a scene that uses 3-D objects, make a compressed (zipped) folder that contains both the KMZ file and the 3-D models, with instructions to download the package, unzip it, and then launch the KMZ file. Keep in mind that if your scene contains more than one scenario or more than one chart, viewers will need to turn groups of layers on and off in the Google Earth viewer. You may also want to give special instructions for setting layer transparency, which can make a significant difference in the appearance of the scene.

■ **SCENE files.** Scenario 3D can create a self-contained SCENE file that includes all the 3-D content viewers will need. Post this SCENE file on your website, together with instructions for downloading the free Scenario 3D Viewer. Consider creating a short guide that provides a description and instructions for touring the scene using paths or bookmarks. Before saving the scene for posting, you should review it from a website visitor's perspective and make sure the scene uses clear names, includes useful bookmarks and paths, and has good-quality displays. Also check the size of the SCENE file to ensure that it is not too large to manage.

■ **Videos.** Most website visitors will watch a short video of your 3-D scene if you post one. Scenario 3D has built-in tools for creating videos, or you can use other video-capture technology with Scenario 3D or Google Earth scenes if you prefer. Try to keep the video shorter than one minute to reduce file size and hold the viewer's attention.

■ **Images.** You can take screenshots of 3-D scenes and post them on a website or include them in a slide show. Scenario 3D has built-in image-capture tools, or you can use your own. For more details, see the section Images of 3-D Scenes, above.

SHARING A COMPLETE ANALYSIS ON THE WEB

You can post an entire analysis on the web for other CommunityViz users to use. It is best to create a compressed (zipped) version of the entire analysis folder. Before posting, make sure that all the data in the analysis resides in the analysis folder. Scenario 360 provides a report that allows you to verify data sources used in the analysis. It is also a good idea to include careful descriptions in the Descriptions fields and to include the date in the name of the analysis.

MORE WEB OPTIONS

Web and network computing technology is advancing rapidly, and more options are becoming available for sharing and working with CommunityViz online. We encourage you to research and take advantage of the best available tools for your particular needs. Here are a few to watch:

- ArcGIS Explorer and the family of ArcGIS web services provide a growing library of data, tools, and information-sharing services.

- Multiplatform polling technology serves the same purpose as keypad polling but works from any handheld device.

- Mobile platforms such as phones, mobile GIS, and handheld devices can also work for keypad polling.

19 BEYOND PLANNING PROJECTS

KEY CONCEPTS AND TERMS IN THIS CHAPTER

- Coastal applications and ecosystem-based management (EBM) tools
- Federal lands applications
- Health and human services applications
- Military base planning
- Municipal budget priorities
- Parks and recreation applications
- Permitting
- Public safety and emergency response applications
- School planning applications
- Subsidy applications
- University campus planning

Planning work is not always confined to distinct projects; it often extends well beyond the planning department or a specific plan. Likewise, while the design and creation of a particular CommunityViz analysis or 3-D scene may be a distinct project, CommunityViz can assist with planning and decision making outside of traditional planning projects.

ANTICIPATING PLANNING PROBLEMS

Careful planners attempt to uncover problems before the general public does and address and solve those problems before they become more expensive or unmanageable. CommunityViz can help you do this in several ways:

- CommunityViz growth projections and future scenarios can identify risks such as the exhaustion of sewer service capacity or increased traffic congestion. If you come across this information while working on a growth-planning project, take a little extra time to isolate and describe the problem so you can share it with the people or organizations responsible. The water department, for example, may not need to understand your entire comprehensive planning project; the department just needs to know that one scenario being considered is expected to result in water supply problems within seven years. This information may lead to further study and proactive steps that avoid community water shortages.

- Indicator thresholds or alerts that you set up in a project will monitor future conditions and performance against a plan. If you use a good process for keeping the data current, these thresholds and alerts will notify you when limits are being reached. For example, you can set up indicators to monitor the mix of new housing being built. If the ratio of, say, multifamily units to single-family units falls too low, a CommunityViz alert will be triggered to bring the imbalance to light.

- CommunityViz analysis tends to be cross disciplinary, so the work on one project may uncover a potential risk or opportunity in a seemingly unrelated project. As you design any analysis, think broadly and be prepared to extend your work to include additional possibilities. We know of one project that began as a scenic assessment of a proposed new building development on a ridgeline. The assessment led to questions about septic systems, which raised questions about groundwater pollution, then sewers, then compact development, then private land ownership, then land conservation. In the end, the original ridgeline assessment produced a land conservation deal, a new wastewater infrastructure plan, and new zoning. This sequence of decisions may have arisen without CommunityViz, but *with* CommunityViz in the hands of a responsive analyst, the connections were more immediately evident and clearly understood by everyone involved.

CONNECTING PLANS TO DAY-TO-DAY PROCESSES

Plans are implemented through land-use regulations, design guidelines, and infrastructure standards and investment. These implementation tools and processes should be consistent with the plan, and they should guide everyday decisions about development proposals and public infrastructure. CommunityViz supports implementation and day-to-day decisions in many ways.

Chapter 3 introduced the concept of design for a living comprehensive plan. This means that the plan should prescribe immediate actions and long-term monitoring, follow-up, and adjustments to the plan. In future years, the CommunityViz indicators you built during an analysis can serve as a community's "dashboard," which they can monitor. For the monitoring process to work well, you need to establish a reliable method for updating the CommunityViz analysis or 3-D model with data about development changes as they occur. Ideally, you would set up real-time connections between your community's permitting system and the CommunityViz analysis so that updates appear automatically each time the CommunityViz analysis is opened. In practice, monthly, quarterly, or annual updates are more common. The updates—to the existing-conditions data used by CommunityViz—are done by entering data manually or by linking to automated data sets online. Although the manual updating method is less elegant than the fully automated one, it is easy to do and is sufficient for many planning needs. Manual updates are certainly better than the third alternative, which is a plan that becomes out of date, no longer providing an accurate assessment of the community's planning opportunities and challenges.

CommunityViz can be a useful part of a community's day-to-day development reviews, permitting operations, and evaluation of land-use regulations. In development review and permitting, CommunityViz is most commonly employed to carry out an evaluation that quickly assesses development and design proposals against a set of specific ordinance criteria using CommunityViz indicators. This system is particularly efficient if developers submit plans in a CommunityViz-compatible format, such as GIS data or Google SketchUp 3-D models, but it can also work with paper or CAD-format applications. Chapter 16 gives more details on using CommunityViz for design review.

CommunityViz projects often produce detailed parcel-by-parcel information that may be helpful for making decisions about land-use regulations and infrastructure investment. But you must treat this information with caution. If the original analysis was designed for a comprehensive plan, it may not be sufficiently detailed for making decisions about these other matters. Review the assumptions and approximations that were made in the original analysis, and do further work if necessary. On the other hand, comprehensive plan data are almost always useful as a starting point for land-use regulations, in part because the future land-use map in the comprehensive plan is the basis for the zoning map. Moreover, data in a comprehensive plan update may uncover problems or inconsistencies in your existing zoning and subdivision regulations (see Chapter 14).

The data analysis you do for any CommunityViz project adds to the database you or anyone else can use for future analyses and day-to-day work. After you have completed a particular planning project, you can help ensure your work will be reused by doing the following:

- Archive the original analysis, making sure it contains clear descriptions, Saved Views, reports, and other aids to help future users understand what you have done.

- Export data layers that contain new data that may be useful for future implementation, day-to-day operations, or other purposes. Save the data in a geodatabase with clear labels and metadata, and notify other potential users what the data contain and where to access them.

- Consider creating CommunityViz analysis templates that contain the formulas, indicators, assumptions, and other analysis components you created for the planning study. The templates can be used later for similar projects, turning a one-time project into a more easily repeatable process.

- If you created a 3-D scene, save a version of the analysis that contains only the components needed for that scene. You and others will be able to use it later as the starting point for new 3-D scenes with incremental additions.

SUPPORTING OTHER DEPARTMENTS

This book is about planning with CommunityViz, but the software works effectively in other disciplines as well. The following list describes a few ways in which planners can use CommunityViz for mutual benefit with government departments other than the planning department:

- **City managers and elected officials** often face problems that would not normally be classified as planning but that can be addressed by planners using CommunityViz. A frequent citizen complaint, for example, is that there are too many potholes in roads. The narrow response is to allocate funding to the street or public works department to fix potholes. A broader response is to identify the priority of road maintenance relative to other public service needs. Using CommunityViz, you could set up an analysis that models the impacts of different budget allocations among roads, utilities, parks, and other competing needs. The analysis could support a public discussion on overall budget priorities.

- **Public safety and emergency response** services, such as police, fire, and rescue, can benefit from the spatial analysis capabilities of CommunityViz. Administrators of these services make decisions that may influence other planning decisions. Here are two examples:

  a. Emergency responders need to be ready to reach people and buildings quickly. Plans that affect the future location of people and buildings therefore affect emergency responses. CommunityViz can help emergency services staff analyze travel distances and emergency response coverage areas for both existing and future conditions. A CommunityViz analysis can help them optimize the location of emergency facilities such as fire stations. Likewise, when a new emergency facility is proposed, CommunityViz analysis can inform which site or sites ensure the best response times to the greatest number of residents, in the present and in the future, based on growth area plans.

  b. In areas prone to wildfire, residents can invest in a number of changes to their homes that reduce the risk of fire damage. For example, they can use fire-resistant roofing and siding, clear defensible areas of trees and brush from near their homes, and design their driveways to allow easy access by fire trucks. At the neighborhood scale, they can invest in community fire ponds and additional fire access roads. CommunityViz makes an excellent platform for analyzing the costs and benefits of combinations of these options.

- **Health and human services** providers try to place clinics, offices, and other field resources in locations where they are most needed. CommunityViz site selection tools such as the Suitability Wizard (see Chapter 12) are designed to aid in making these decisions. Planners can work together with health and public safety professionals to identify areas of highest need based on factors such as housing type, income distribution, crime statistics, and transportation access.

- CommunityViz is a good fit with **school planning.** The software helps decision makers choose locations for new schools, plan for school capacity, analyze redistricting plans, select locations for bus stops, and identify safe routes to school. It is also useful for standard planning activities involving school buildings, such as visualization and conducting design review for new buildings, expansions, and renovations.

- **Parks and recreation planning** are very common uses of CommunityViz. The selection of park sites is a classic example, and trail planning is another popular application. In addition, CommunityViz can help to develop park management plans, plan new recreation facilities, visualize new landscapes or structures, and draft tree maintenance plans.

- **Economic development** departments often deal with applications for a variety of state and federal grants. You can set up a CommunityViz analysis to support programs in which certain projects, such as home weatherization, are eligible for government grants based on a scoring system. You create an analysis that has the scoring system built in, ready for plans to be added. Applicants can meet with an economic development grant administrator, input their proposal, and then work with the administrator to make adjustments in real time as required to qualify for the funds.

Sometimes, rather than other departments, you need to work with county, state, or federal agencies, tribal or First Nations governments, extension services, universities, the military, nonprofit organizations, or community groups. Here are some examples of projects that involve one or more of these groups:

- **Coastal communities** face unusual planning challenges, including sea-level rise, storms and storm surges, nonpoint-source water pollution, oil spills, unique coastal ecosystems, shipping lanes, and fisheries. In the United States, federal agencies such as the National Oceanic and Atmospheric Administration's Coastal Services Center assist coastal communities. CommunityViz can help communities and federal agencies tackle these complex problems because it has the flexibility to model unusual scenarios and impacts, and it works well with external models—in this case, the specialized scientific models often required for understanding the complex ecology of coastal areas. Two applications of particular note are: ecosystem-based management (EBM), which is a cross-disciplinary approach to environmental and land use planning;[1] and community vulnerability assessment, which overlays natural hazards such as risk of hurricanes and storm surges to community assets and fragile regions, especially parts of a city where people do not own cars and would have trouble evacuating in case of a hurricane.

- Communities adjacent to **federal lands,** such as those owned by the National Park Service, U.S. Forest Service, or the Bureau of Land Management, face changing conditions related to federal agency decisions about access, recreational uses, forestry, and land swaps or sales. Tribal government planners are also likely to have a stake in decisions about federal lands. CommunityViz can help federal agencies, tribal governments, and local communities work together to draft plans and design programs that take into account the widely diverse needs of the many stakeholders in those areas.

- **Military bases** can have a tremendous influence on their host communities because of their size, the number of jobs they provide, the number of families they house, and their tendency toward rapid population change. Some military bases use CommunityViz for internal planning purposes—they are their own communities, after all—and CommunityViz can also help the communities that host military

---

1. You can learn more at www.ebmtools.org.

bases. For example, a host community can create CommunityViz scenarios that model the potential effects of a large change in a base's population. The federal Department of Defense has recently drafted plans and purchased conservation easements on adjacent lands to maintain the military activities on bases to avoid encroachment from civilian development.

- **Universities** are also anchor institutions in their host communities. CommunityViz can be a particularly valuable tool for managing community and university relations when a university is contemplating expansions to its campus. University facilities personnel and community planners can use CommunityViz together to determine good locations for new facilities and to identify the potential impacts of any land-use changes. Another way universities and communities often work together is through students who gain valuable planning experience by doing volunteer work in the community. One popular example is 3-D modeling workshops in which students make SketchUp models of local buildings for use in CommunityViz 3-D scenes.

This list describes only some of the forms of cross-departmental and cross-organizational cooperation we have seen on CommunityViz projects. Many more opportunities exist for planners to work with others. CommunityViz is designed to help people work together to make informed decisions, and we encourage you to take advantage of its abilities to address not only your own planning needs but also those of other people and groups whose planning interests you share.

APPENDIX 1: WHEN AND HOW TO GET HELP

This appendix provides suggestions for the human resource aspects of using CommunityViz: a self-assessment of your readiness to use CommunityViz individually or within an organization; how to staff CommunityViz projects or work with consultants; and where to find resources and help as the work proceeds.

READINESS SELF-ASSESSMENT

Following are questions that will help you assess your readiness to use CommunityViz for a particular project, or to adopt CommunityViz as a tool in your department or consulting practice. The questions are intended only to raise considerations for you to think about: You certainly do not need to be able to answer "yes" to all, or even most, of the questions to be able to use CommunityViz. The questions that are worded *I* may apply just as well to your department, team, workgroup, or practice.

COMMUNITYVIZ SKILLS

- Have I used a CommunityViz analysis myself in the last two or three years?
- Have I set up a CommunityViz analysis myself, or with others?
- Do I have any formal or informal CommunityViz training?
- How advanced is my planning expertise, particularly with regard to planning analysis?
- Am I an analytical thinker, comfortable with creating my own spreadsheets, which is similar to creating CommunityViz analyses?
- Am I comfortable around computers?
- How advanced are my GIS skills?
- Have I ever worked with 3-D technology?
- Do I work with similar software tools?

TECHNICAL ENVIRONMENT

- Do I have the necessary up-to-date ArcGIS licenses?
- Do I have computers that meet or exceed the CommunityViz requirements specified on the CommunityViz website?
- Do I have access to baseline GIS data for the area I will be studying?
- Do I have access to the other technical resources I need for a particular project, as described in Chapter 2?

ORGANIZATIONAL READINESS

- Are others in my organization or team already using CommunityViz?
- Do our competitors use CommunityViz?
- Has previous CommunityViz work been done on this project or in our department?
- Will CommunityViz analysis and communications tools be useful to our work?
- What will happen to our project if we do not use CommunityViz?
- Do the people I will be working with—including coworkers, managers, partners, and customers—support the idea of using CommunityViz?
- Will I be able to spend at least 10 to 20 hours per week on CommunityViz during this project?
- Does my organization have the ability to train staff in how to use CommunityViz, so if I happen to leave there will be someone who can take over my CommunityViz work?

PARTNERS AND COLLABORATORS

- Are any of my partners or collaborators already using CommunityViz?

- Will I have access to at least one GIS professional who works on the physical location I will be studying?
- Will project partners be willing to share GIS data and models with me?

MODELING SKILLS AND RESOURCES

- Will this project require any specialized analytical models that are not built into CommunityViz?
- Do I have sufficient expertise in these models myself, or access to someone who does have sufficient expertise?
- Will I need to connect CommunityViz to external models or tools? Do I have access to those tools and the ability to make connections?

STAFFING FOR COMMUNITYVIZ

Using CommunityViz takes time and skill. To be successful, a planning department, planning firm, or other organization that plans to use CommunityViz needs sufficient staff resources. Our experience indicates that it takes one person at least 10 to 20 hours a week to make good progress on a project with CommunityViz, and allowing more time is better. It is best to keep current with technology, because the software is updated frequently and if you are away from it for a few years it will take a little time to adapt to the newest version.

Try to have more than one person on a team work with CommunityViz, because if there is only one, that person may quickly become swamped with requests for small projects that leave little time for other tasks. In addition, having only one person working with CommunityViz creates vulnerability for the organization, because if that person suddenly leaves, the team's expertise is lost.

CommunityViz is an excellent tool for small teams in which one person provides GIS expertise, another planning expertise, and others expertise on the project, models, 3-D, and public engagement. If each person is comfortable with CommunityViz, they can collaborate to produce highly effective results.

In many municipal governments, the GIS department and the planning department are separate. In this case, both departments should have access to CommunityViz licenses so that they can work together on projects. Usually the planners describe the questions that need to be answered and suggest ways to model impacts, and the GIS professionals set up the initial analysis. After that, the planners and GIS professionals work together to refine and improve the project.

There are no formal prerequisites for becoming a CommunityViz analyst. Basic to intermediate GIS skills are certainly helpful, and familiarity with fundamental planning concepts is very important. If you are going to be setting up your own analyses, you do not need to be a computer programmer or math whiz, but you do need to be comfortable with analytical thinking at about the level that is required for setting up a spreadsheet with formulas in it. Setting up 3-D scenes in CommunityViz requires no previous experience or skills, though practice with other 3-D tools certainly helps.

WORKING WITH CONSULTANTS

If you want to use CommunityViz for a project but you do not have the time or expertise in-house, professional CommunityViz consultants are available to help. Use certified consultants who work with CommunityViz regularly and are up to date on its latest capabilities. They will be able to show you how to use the software to its fullest potential. A list of certified CommunityViz consultants is provided on the CommunityViz website.[1]

Unlike some consulting work, a CommunityViz study is rarely a simple project that can be done solely on the basis of a work order and list of deliverables. As you have learned in this book, the design and implementation of a CommunityViz analysis is an iterative, adaptive process. It requires close communication between the analyst and other project participants. You should look at a CommunityViz consultant as more of a project partner than an outside worker. Try to include the consultant in project discussions throughout the life of the project, and plan for extra work sessions

---
1. The CommunityViz website is: http://placeways.com/communityviz.

and communications with the consultant during the height of the CommunityViz work.

Before the consultant leaves the project, be sure to obtain a well-documented copy of the consultant's analysis and data for your future use, even if you do not currently have any CommunityViz capabilities in house. You may be able to use the work later or at least provide it to future consultants for follow-up work. If appropriate, discuss the concept of designing for a living comprehensive plan (see Chapter 3) and how the consultant can help you use completed CommunityViz work going forward. Also review the many options for creating and sharing reports, displays, and 3-D scenes (see Chapters 17 and 18), and consider asking the consultant to provide results in formats that do not require you to have CommunityViz or ArcGIS software.

COMMUNITYVIZ RESOURCES

The single best place to find additional CommunityViz resources is the CommunityViz website, which contains documentation, guides, case studies, sample outputs, tutorials, sample data, instructional videos, slide shows, and many other materials that are free to use.

Training is available in many formats, ranging from free materials on the website to university classes and professional services provided by certified CommunityViz trainers. Certified trainers, listed on the CommunityViz website, provide a range of learning options, from web-based training and conference workshops to classroom training and customized in-person training sessions.

For assistance with the software, start with the built-in Help system, which provides complete information, instructions, and suggestions. The Help content is also available online. For support with suspected bugs or technical problems, consult the online user forums and knowledge database. And if you have purchased technical support, take advantage of the live e-mail, phone, and web support options.

APPENDIX 2: DATA MANAGEMENT

This appendix presents suggestions about data management techniques.

DATA MANAGEMENT BEST PRACTICES FOR ANALYSIS

The following are some best practices for managing data in a CommunityViz analysis.

1. Respect original sources. Document where the data came from, and do not disturb or change the original source. Maintain metadata describing your sources and any additional processing you have done to the data.

2. Separate reference data from analysis. When you begin collecting data, consider them to be reference data and treat them as you would any other GIS data. When you start creating a CommunityViz analysis, selectively make layers dynamic as required. Do not make any more layers dynamic than you need to. If you want to preserve a layer after you have done a dynamic analysis on it, use ArcMap Export tools to create a new reference layer outside your analysis geodatabase.

3. Back up your work. Make and maintain copies of your work as you progress with your analysis. The best way to back up an analysis is to use the Scenario 360 Save Analysis As command available from the ArcMap File menu. Give the backup analysis a helpful name, such as "AnalysisNameBackup-Date" so that you can find it later if needed. For further security, compress the backup analysis folder into a ZIP file and store it in a safe location.

4. Periodically compact your databases. A CommunityViz analysis makes frequent changes to the databases it is using, so you should perform the Compact Databases process provided in the ArcGIS toolbox.

5. Maintain data quality. Use ArcGIS data management tools to check the quality of your data and improve it if necessary. In particular, check for the following:

    a. **Topology,** including problems such as overlaps.

    b. **Vertex counts**. These may be excessively large if, for example, the features you are using were imported from a non-GIS source.

    c. **Projections.** Make sure that all layers used in your analysis are using the same projected coordinate system.

    d. **Size,** including excessively large images or rasters, or layers that extend far beyond your study area.

    e. **Null values** in attribute tables.

    f. **Outdated formats** such as coverages.

    g. **Names and naming conventions.** For example, make sure geodatabase folders have the required ".GDB" extension, and make sure that attribute fields have alias names that are easy to understand.

6. Organize source data carefully. Because CommunityViz analysis tends to be comprehensive, you will often be using data from many different sources. ArcMap will display all the data seamlessly on a single map, but if the data are disorganized you will find it harder to move, share, and update your work over time. If your analysis is large, consider creating a single geodatabase containing all your reference data, or at least a single data folder with clearly labeled subfolders.

7. Store working data locally. ArcGIS Desktop and CommunityViz usually work best using data that is stored on your local machine rather than accessed through a network. The CommunityViz analysis geodatabase must be on your local machine. Reference data may

be on your network, but if any part of your analysis uses a reference layer in a formula—for example, a formula using features in a layer to measure distances—create a copy of the reference layer on your computer.

8. Use clear names. Give layers, attributes, and other CommunityViz components clear names that anyone will be able to recognize. Avoid cryptic abbreviations that may be faster to type but will cause confusion later on.

9. Maintain data security if required. Some of the data you use may need to stay private for reasons of security, intellectual property, personal privacy, commercial propriety, or others. CommunityViz is built for transparency, so if you use private data in a public analysis you will need to build what is called a Chinese wall between the private source data and the public CommunityViz analysis. The most common technique is to run one CommunityViz analysis that uses the private data, export the results as a new reference layer, and then create a separate public CommunityViz analysis that relies only on the exported reference layer. Discuss the specifics of your strategy with the provider of the private data before proceeding.

DATA MANAGEMENT BEST PRACTICES FOR 3-D VISUALIZATION

Here are some best practices for handling and managing data used for 3-D visualization.

1. Respect original sources. As with 2-D data, document where the data, images, and models came from, and do not change the original sources. Maintain metadata describing your sources and any additional processing you have done. Do not use photos or 3-D models that you do not have permission to use. Display attribution information—that is, name and affiliation of the artist or author—if required.

2. Back up your work. Because 3-D models and 3-D scenes may require particular file structures to work properly, the best way to create a backup is to compress the entire folder into a ZIP file and save the result in a safe location.

3. Maintain file size discipline. Use the smallest 3-D models and textures you can while still maintaining the required resolution. You may find source models that meet your needs but have a very large file size. It is tempting to use them and hope for the best, but your scene will become sluggish. Either choose a different model or edit the original model so that it uses fewer triangles. If editing, pay particular attention to round edges that use far more segments than required. Refer to Chapter 6 for further suggestions.

4. Keep separate files for sharing and local use. When you create a scene on your local computer, the scene can use any 3-D resources on the computer without making copies of them. When you give the scene to someone else, however, you often need to include copies of the 3-D resources used. Including all those 3-D resources results in large file sizes, so it is best to create sharable files only when needed and to delete them afterward to remove duplicate information from your computer.

USING DATA FROM MULTIPLE SOURCES

The comprehensive nature of CommunityViz analysis often results in the use of data from many sources, including multiple jurisdictions, organizations, and even disciplines. This use of a combination of data can present both challenges and opportunities:

- **Conflicting data.** The common wisdom among GIS professionals is that "no map is perfect," and sometimes this reality becomes painfully evident when you overlay two layers that are supposed to represent the same features. A common example is roads, which are notorious for not aligning. Another glaring example is contour lines that cross lakes or ponds. When deciding on your response to these conflicts, think carefully about the purpose of your analysis and what you need from the data. Here are some choices:

    a. Find and fix errors. Ideally, the apparent differences came from a technical error that you can repair, such as an incorrect or missing projection, or an outdated source. If so, fixing the error will resolve the problem.

b. Do nothing. Simply work with one data source and ignore the other. If the difference between the sources is not significant at your scale of analysis, this may be the most reasonable course of action.

c. Determine the more accurate source. Research both sources to determine which one is more likely to be correct, and use that one.

d. Determine the more consistent source. Decide which data source matches better with the rest of your data, and use that one. For example, in the case of roads used for a 3-D visualization, you will want to use the source that aligns better with your aerial imagery. In the case of a floodplain map, you may decide to use the data source designated by the local land-use regulations even if a more recent data source is available.

e. Edit the data. Do this cautiously and carefully to maintain the original source. Work on a copy, document your actions, and be completely transparent in your editing process. Taking this course of action usually makes sense only when you want to make changes for cosmetic purposes, such as when you want the boundary of a pond that is not used in the analysis to match a contour line. It is also a reasonable choice in 3-D visualization, where the goal is aesthetic rather than analytical.

- **Missing data.** When you are combining data from multiple regions or jurisdictions, it is not uncommon to have more data for some regions than others. For example, detailed information on current land uses may be available for one region but not another. In this case, you need to decide whether to: a) design your analysis based on the lowest common denominator, b) fill in the missing data some way, or c) perform parts of your analysis only on the subareas for which data is available. All three can be viable options, so make your decision based on the overall goals of your analysis. Chapter 11 contains specific advice for combining data for regional plans.

- **Joining of tables.** If you have a GIS parcel map that includes an attribute called, for example, Parcel ID, and you also have a property tax table that includes a column called Parcel ID, you can combine the tax table with the attribute table to create a larger, more informative attribute table containing complete GIS and tax information for every parcel. The technical term for such a combination is a join. The same process can be undertaken for any table and layer that share at least one attribute or column in common. This process provides a way to combine data from many sources into a single, consolidated layer that may be easier to analyze. Sometimes you need to be creative to establish the join field, which is an attribute or column that the tables or layers have in common. Consider using *x,y* coordinates, street addresses, or even manually entered numbers. Scenario 360 also provides a number of text-editing functions that may make it easier to manipulate text codes and addresses to create matching fields. If the data types being joined are GIS layers, you can use ArcMap or Scenario 360 spatial join functions. In Scenario 360, these functions include GetFromClosest, GetWhereIntersects, GetWhereOverlaps, GetWhereContains, GetWhereIsContainedIn, and others.

APPENDIX 3: PERFORMANCE

This appendix provides suggestions and best practices for making CommunityViz analyses and 3-D scenes run as quickly as possible. In any analysis, there is a trade-off between processing speed and other needs, including the size of the study area, the spatial resolution of the analysis, the complexity of the analysis, and the level of detail of the 3-D scene. Fast performance is desirable, but it cannot be your only goal, and part of designing a good CommunityViz analysis is finding the right balance between speed and other goals.

Figure A3.1 Scenario 360 progress bar

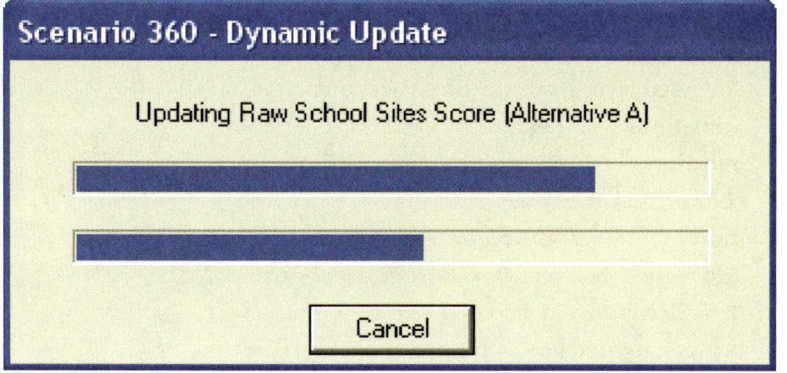

The performance considerations for analysis, which is done using Scenario 360, are different from those for the use of 3-D, so this appendix covers analysis and 3-D separately.

ANALYSIS PERFORMANCE

In a Scenario 360 analysis, performance is judged by the amount of time you wait for updates to occur after you change an assumption, edit a feature or feature attribute, or modify the analysis setup.

One of the strengths of Scenario 360 is that during your analysis of scenarios, you can make changes and *quickly* see their effects. This allows you to test your ideas as they arise. But as your analysis grows larger or more complicated, performance may require more of your attention. Update speed is particularly important in public settings. Before engaging a large audience, fine-tune your analysis so that any changes you expect to make will produce quick results. When you are working on your own or in small groups, longer processing times are acceptable; when you are setting up an analysis, you may find yourself running preprocessing calculations that take hours.

For any process that takes longer than approximately five seconds, a progress bar window is displayed while you wait. The window usually contains two horizontal bars that fill up, left to right, as processing proceeds. The lower bar tracks layers or indicators, and the upper bar tracks features within layers. Because there are numerous features within a layer, during an update, the upper bar moves back and forth much faster than the lower bar, which moves gradually from empty to full. Text above the bars tells you which component and which scenario is being processed (see Figure A3.1). Some processes that are not related directly to layers, indicators, or features show only a single progress bar.

The goal of performance management is to reduce the amount of time progress bars are showing yet still complete all of the calculations needed for the analysis of scenarios. If your analysis is taking longer to update than you want, watch the progress bars to see which components have the longest processing times, and begin looking there for opportunities to speed up performance.

Here is the approximate hierarchy of component processing during an analysis update:

Scenarios
  Indicators
    Layers
      Dynamic Attributes
        Features
          Where conditions
          Vertexes

Each scenario contains indicators and layers; each layer contains dynamic attributes; each dynamic attribute formula applies to each feature of a layer; and for each feature, you may have to calculate a Where condition and, in the case of lines and polygons, do separate calculations for each vertex.

For example, imagine that your analysis contains two scenarios and three dynamic layers, each containing four dynamic attributes and five features. If you change a single linked assumption that happens to be referenced in all of the dynamic attribute formulas, the computer will need to do at least

$2 \times 3 \times 4 \times 5 = 120$ *calculations.*

If each layer contains 5,000 features, there will be

$2 \times 3 \times 4 \times 5{,}000 = 120{,}000$ *calculations.*

And, if your dynamic attribute formulas all happen to contain a Where condition, that could mean 240,000 calculations in response to a single assumption change. Luckily, modern computers are extremely fast so a quarter of a million calculations will not take particularly long, but you should understand the pattern of exponentially increasing processing times.

Estimating the exact number of calculations and the total processing time required for any particular update is extremely complicated. For example, the Scenario 360 analysis engine is "smart" and performs calculations only on formulas that are affected by a change, not the entire analysis. Meanwhile, some calculations, such as spatial relationships, involve much more processing than others. The overall lesson is that simpler is faster. In particular, each new scenario substantially increases processing requirements, and the number of features your analysis needs to process is often the most important factor in determining performance.

Figure A3.2 provides recommendations for improving analysis performance in general, and Figure A3.3 provides additional details for dynamic attribute formulas.

3-D PERFORMANCE

The primary performance considerations in a CommunityViz 3D scene are how smoothly and quickly you can navigate through the scene. If performance is poor, motions may be jerky or slow; at worst, the scene may not respond at all to navigation commands. A large scene can also take a long time to export or to open.

A major factor determining 3-D performance is hardware. Most computers have one or more primary central processing units (CPUs), and a separate video processor that handles 3-D scenes. The video processor can be "virtual"—that is, built into the same physical chip as the CPU but logically separated. It can also be a dedicated video card, which is physically separate from the CPU. A higher-performance video processor generally means higher-performance scenes, and a dedicated video card is usually faster than a virtual video processor.

The video processor has its own memory; when using a dedicated video card, this is called on-board memory. The performance of a 3-D scene will be at its best if the video memory is large enough to hold the entire scene. If the scene is too large, parts of it must be shunted temporarily off to the computer's hard drive, then brought back in when you navigate around the scene and bring different portions into view. This process, known as paging, noticeably slows down performance. For maximum performance, then, you want a fast dedicated video card with as much on-board memory as possible.

The next most important factor in 3-D performance is the number of triangles in the scene. Chapter 6 described how triangles are used to create surfaces in a 3-D scene, and how several techniques, such as the use of x trees, transparent textures, and billboards can reduce the number of triangles required. Very large textures or images, such as high-resolution aerial photographs, also consume video memory and can slow down performance overall.

Once you have opened the scene, you can improve performance in several ways:

- Turn off layers that you are not using, especially large layers. In Google Earth, be sure to turn off other layers you are not using in

Figure A3.2 Performance recommendations for Scenario 360 analysis

ANALYSIS CHARACTERISTIC	RECOMMENDATIONS
Features	If you are working on a regional scale, you may need to use larger analysis polygons than if you are working on a smaller scale, where analysis polygons such as lots or parcels may work best. Chapter 11 describes some techniques. It is important to distinguish between the number of features in *dynamic* layers, which contain analysis formulas, and *nondynamic* layers, which do not. In most cases, the number of features in nondynamic layers makes no difference to performance. For example, there is no performance cost to include a regional-scale parcel map in your analysis as a nondynamic layer used only for display purposes. The exception is analysis formulas that point to nondynamic layers—or in Scenario 360 terms, use nondynamic layers as target layers—for a spatial calculation or look-up function, such as AngleTo or GetFromClosest. In those cases, the formula must evaluate every feature in the nondynamic layer, so the fewer features there are in the nondynamic layer, the faster the performance.
Dynamic attribute formulas	Each dynamic attribute formula you create must be evaluated at least once, so the greater the number of dynamic attributes, the longer the processing time. However, there is a great deal of variation in the processing times of different kinds of dynamic attributes. Table A3.2 provides details. Refer to Scenario 360 Help and technical documentation for additional suggestions and details about efficient formulas.
Subset layers	To speed up processing, consider creating new analysis layers that contain subsets of the features in the original layers. If you are working with a road network and studying regional transportation patterns, for example, you might create a subset layer that excludes local roads but keeps arterial highways and collector streets.
Selective updates	Scenario 360 gives you fine-grained control over the update process, so you can turn off updates to parts of your analysis as you work in other areas of it. This capability allows you to create complex, interrelated analysis models but still work quickly on small sections at a time.
File size	In Scenario 360, most analysis processing is performed within the analysis geodatabase, which contains the dynamic layers. In general, a smaller analysis geodatabase leads to faster processing because there are fewer data to process. This is a crude measure, however, because many other factors can come into play. It is more important to consider the size of particular layers within the analysis geodatabase. You can reduce the size of a layer by deleting unneeded features—such as those outside the study area—and unneeded attribute fields.
Feature complexity	In ArcGIS, a single polygon or line feature contains two or more vertexes. In some cases, particularly if the feature was imported from another source, such as a CAD drawing or hand drawing, there can be dozens or even hundreds of vertexes per feature. Any formula that includes spatial calculations such as distances will need to operate on each vertex, one by one. To reduce processing time, consider using the ArcGIS Generalize geoprocessing tool to reduce the number of vertexes.

Figure A3.3 Detailed performance recommendations for dynamic attribute formulas

DYNAMIC ATTRIBUTE FORMULA CHARACTERISTIC	RECOMMENDATIONS
Complexity	Keep individual dynamic attribute formulas simple. If your analysis logic is complicated, performance is usually faster if you make many simple formulas than if you make a few complicated formulas. This is because not all of the formulas will need to be calculated for all updates.
Precalculated values	Pre-calculate and store values that will not change during analysis. For example, you might create a new attribute in a Parcels layer that gives the average slope of that parcel. The formula may take a long time to run the first time, but it will only need to be run once. Other formulas in your analysis will then be able to use the result as a simple number, which makes for faster updates.
Where conditions	In Scenario 360 formula functions, a Where condition specifies that a calculation applies only to a subset of features that meet certain conditions. Where conditions are very useful, but each Where condition effectively doubles the number of calculations required for that formula. To improve performance, Scenario 360 provides automatic indexing of attributes whose formulas contain Where conditions. Still, be sure to monitor formulas with Where conditions. For instance, it often helps to avoid embedding a complex spatial function within an If or Where condition, such as Where (MaxDistance([Layer:TargetLayer]) < 500). Instead, calculate the condition separately so that the computer can evaluate the If or Where condition more quickly. In this example, you would make a separate attribute called, for example, Farthest Distance, and then change the Where condition to Where ([Attribute:Farthest Distance] < 500).
Cross-layer calculations	Reduce the number of cross-layer calculations, such as spatial functions and Get functions. In general, formulas that operate within a single layer run faster than formulas that operate in two or more layers. You can often precalculate the cross-layer information you need and store it as attributes in a single layer within which most of the analysis takes place.

My Places. (One way to identify which layers are using the most resources is to turn on one layer at a time and pay attention to performance. When a resource-intensive layer is on, you will find that navigation is sluggish and features take extra time to appear. When it is turned off, navigation will be smooth and fast, and features will appear almost instantaneously.) Zoom in and maintain a narrow field of view, so that the number of triangles appearing on the screen is as small as possible. You may need to wait a few moments after zooming in for the memory management process to finish before performance improves.

- In Scenario 3D, use the View Distance slider bar under Environment Controls to reduce the maximum distance of objects displayed in the scene. This will tend to eliminate ridgelines and other objects on the horizon, reducing the number of objects displayed.

- Navigate using bookmarks, Zoom-to-Feature, and other tools that do not require smooth flying or walking.

- Use a smaller view window on your computer.

- Close all other applications on your computer that may be using video-processing resources, such as movie players or webcams.

APPENDIX 4: DATA SOURCES

This appendix offers a list of data sources. Please refer to Chapter 2 for information about choosing data for your particular needs and about best practices for working with data.

Many of the data sources listed in this appendix are conveniently available and free in the United States. Our list is not comprehensive, and you should consult your own sources as well. If you are working outside the United States, you may need to find alternative sources. The sources in this appendix provide general-purpose data that apply to most CommunityViz planning analyses. Chapters in sections 2 to 5 describe data needed for specific types of planning projects.

Demographic information

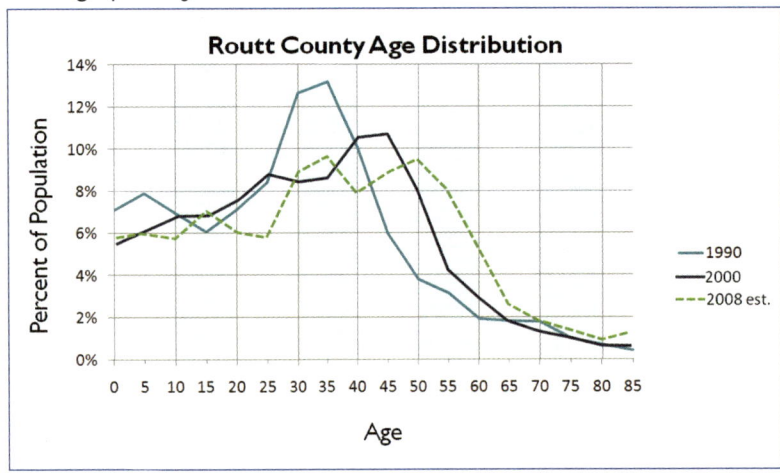

Figure A4.1 Popular sources of demographic information

DATA	SOURCES	SUGGESTIONS
Population growth over time	State demographer (preferred), U.S. Census Bureau, or commercial services	Try to go into the past as far as possible and into the future about 20 to 30 years. Decade-level census data is fine for past and future, but try to get annual-level data for the past several years and the present. The U.S. Census Bureau has Population Estimates data for years that fall between censuses. Commercial vendors such as Woods and Poole sell nicely aggregated county-scale data.
Persons per household	State demographer or U.S. Census Bureau	Present data and trend data are useful. Provide averages and distributions (e.g., single person, two people, three or more people per household).
Family data	State demographer or U.S. Census Bureau	The U.S. Census Bureau collects data on households with families and families with children. Present data and trend data are useful. Provide averages and distributions.
Age distribution	State demographer (preferred) or U.S. Census Bureau	The age categories used by the U.S. Census Bureau vary in the number of years they span. It is much easier for general audiences to understand age data if you break them into even-sized five-year categories, such as people aged 20–24, aged 25–29, and so on. Show trends.
Tenure	State demographer or U.S. Census Bureau	Tenure data show how long residents have lived in their current residences, who owns the land and buildings, and who rents.
Demographic rankings	State demographer or U.S. Census Bureau	Comparing key demographic indicators with those of other places that people are familiar with can help put population data in context.
Demographic profiles	Esri Business Analyst or Business Analyst Online	These sources are not free, but they compile large amounts of data and often contain information that is not available elsewhere.

Geographic information

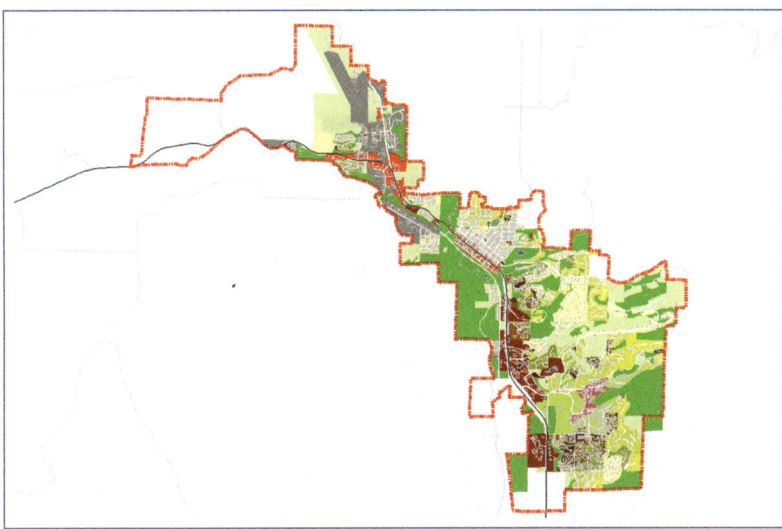

Figure A4.2 *Popular sources of geographic information*

DATA	SOURCES	SUGGESTIONS
Standard maps (base maps)	Local or regional government GIS office; online services such as ArcGIS Online or USGS, the National Map Seamless Server; or local tax assessor's office	If you can use a GIS system, do so; otherwise, ask for PDFs in the highest resolution available.
Housing density—existing	Local or regional government GIS office, tax assessor's office, or U.S. Census	Use the finest resolution available: house points if available, parcels, zoning, and land use. If existing house points are not available, try using assessed value of parcels as a way to estimate whether parcels have buildings on them.
Development patterns—historic	Tax assessor's office or historic maps	Ideally, a year-by-year animation can be shown using 3-D models.
Development patterns—future possibilities	Local or regional government planning office	Software such as CommunityViz can help you construct and illustrate these in 2-D or 3-D. Be careful not to over-specify future development patterns.
Special places—objective	Historic society, recreation office, parks department, local GIS office	Choose elements that relate to local heart-and-soul values, such as historic sites, farms, schools, trails, and waterways.
Special places—subjective	Google Maps, Community Almanac, other citizen-generated online sources	Examples might include sacred places, favorite gathering places for different age groups, favorite views, favorite fishing holes, and so on.
Land use and ownership	Local or regional government GIS office, or tax assessor's office	Particularly in the West, data on public versus private ownership are useful to have. The ratio of developed versus undeveloped land is also frequently of interest.

Photos, images, and 3-D models

Figure A4.3 *Popular sources of photos, images, and 3-D models*

DATA	SOURCES	SUGGESTIONS
Aerial photos	USDA Farm Service Agency Aerial Photography Field Office; USGS, The National Map Seamless Server; local sources	If possible, obtain historic as well as present-day images and compare them side by side.
Local people	Newspapers, amateur photographers	Use photos of local people liberally in project communications; they make a big difference.
Local places	Newspapers, amateur photographers, historic archives, libraries	Before-and-after photos can stimulate audience and reader responses.
Local events	Newspapers, amateur photographers	Examples might include photos of parades, fairs, and local traditions.
3-D models	CommunityViz model library; Google SketchUp 3D warehouse; your own 3-D models created with SketchUp; models exported from CAD tools	Refer to chapters 5 and 6 for tips. Pay attention to triangle count: An entire scene should usually contain fewer than 200,000 triangles. Google Earth uses only KMZ forms. Formats, in order of preference, for use in Scenario 3D are KMZ, COLLADA, and 3ds.

Economic and transportation data

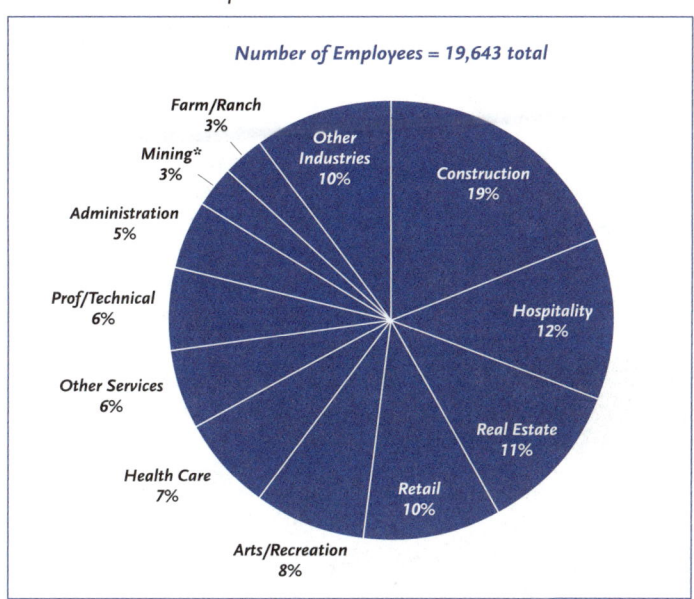

Figure A4.4 *Popular sources of economic and transportation data*

DATA	SOURCES	SUGGESTIONS
Household income	U.S. Census Bureau	Also compare with data from other cities, counties, the region, or the state.
Jobs and wages by industry	Bureau of Economic Analysis (BEA)	Include trends if possible, but note that because the BEA switched from Standard Industrial Classification (SIC) codes to North American Industry Classification System (NAICS) codes in 2001, categories, especially in service industries, may not line up well. Economic diversity—that is, variety of industries and income sources—may be particularly important to highlight.
Commuting times and distances	U.S. Census Bureau	Show trends if available.
Local property ownership	Tax assessor's office	Measure percentage of out-of-area property owners based on tax billing addresses.
Affordable housing data	U.S. Department of Housing and Urban Development (HUD)	Consider collecting your area median income (AMI), price distribution of recently sold homes by type, and a map of the prices of recently sold homes by location.
Economic profiles	Esri Business Analysis or Business Analyst Online	These sources are not free, but they compile large amounts of data and often contain information that is not available elsewhere.

Environmental data

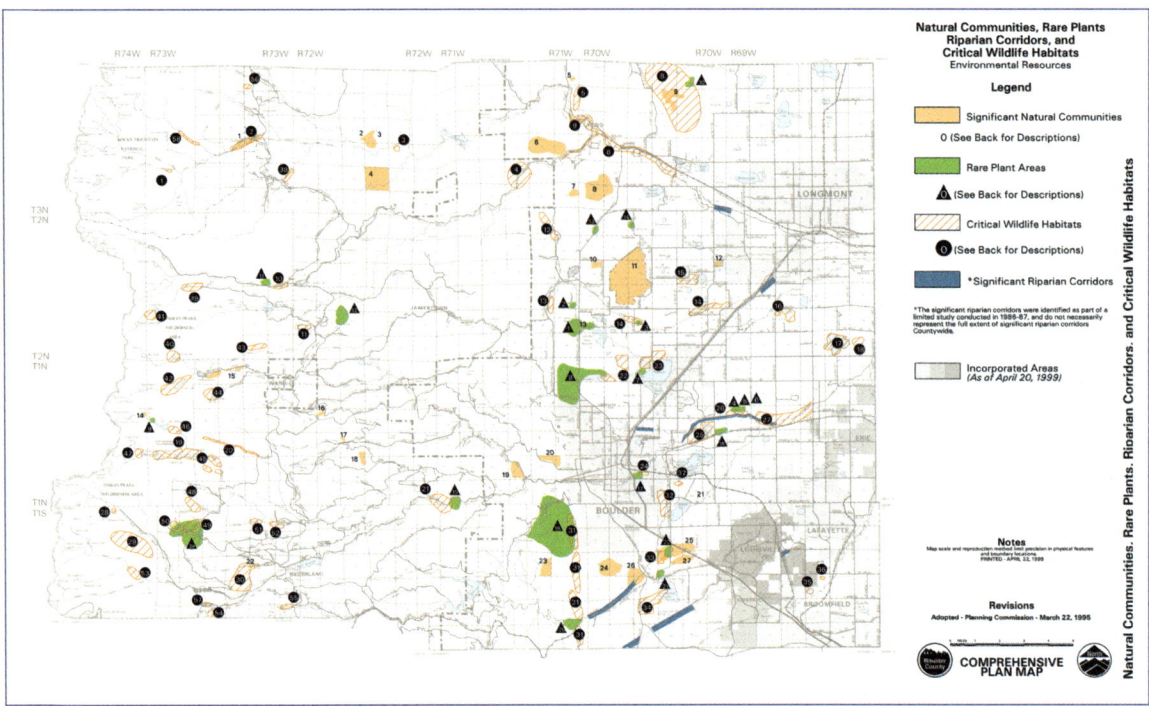

Figure A4.5 *Popular sources of environmental data*

DATA	SOURCES	SUGGESTIONS
Parks, trails, and conservation areas	USGS, The National Map Seamless Server; local or regional government GIS office; local or national nonprofits	Research in particular the legitimacy and accuracy of trail maps provided by nongovernmental organizations.
Local rare and endangered species	Local biologist, NatureServe, Conservation Biology Institute (CBI)	Sometimes the precise location of an endangered species is considered too sensitive to make public. If so, try to obtain generalized data that give approximate locations.
Local natural resources	USDA Natural Resource Conservation Service (NRCS); U.S. Forest Service	These sources have excellent information on soils data and soil capability for agricultural and forest production and the ability of different soils to support development.
Natural hazards	NOAA National Geophysical Data Center (NOAA-NGDC), NOAA's Digital Coast, Federal Emergency Management Agency (FEMA) flood maps, FEMA's HAZUS-MH tool	Be aware that there is controversy about the accuracy of some FEMA flood maps. In general, try to find the newest available information.

APPENDIX 5: COMMUNITYVIZ FEATURES

The introduction of this book gave you a brief tour of the features of CommunityViz Scenario 360 and Scenario 3D. Later chapters described particular tools and functions in more detail. This appendix provides summary descriptions of most of the key features for easy reference. The software is continually being updated, so for the latest version visit the CommunityViz website.[1]

SCENARIO 360 FEATURES

INTEGRATION WITH ARCGIS

Scenario 360 runs as an extension to ArcMap and integrates smoothly with the rest of ArcGIS Desktop. If you have the Network Analyst or Spatial Analyst extensions to ArcGIS, Scenario 360 can use them for network-based or raster-based formula functions. If you have the 3D Analyst extension, you can run Scenario 360 as an extension to ArcScene.

3-D VISUALIZATION

Scenario 360 allows you to connect to 3-D visualization tools, giving you new ways to see your community as it is and as it could be. As mentioned in the introduction:

- For viewing your analysis in its global 3-D context, Scenario 360 can export your scenarios, layers, charts, extruded buildings, and Google SketchUp objects into KMZ format for immediate viewing in Google Earth, ArcGIS Explorer, or other tools that can use KMZ format files.

- Scenario 360 also works within ArcScene, a component of the ArcGIS 3D Analyst extension. Used together, Scenario 360 and ArcScene provide an integrated 3-D environment for performing analyses and making geographic decisions.

- Scenario 3D, included as part of the CommunityViz package, enables you to create realistic, interactive 3-D scenes.

DYNAMIC CHARTS

Scenario 360 includes special charts that provide dynamically updated visual displays of information (see Figure A5.1).

You can set up a dynamic chart to display a single variable, multiple variables, and multiple scenarios. If you are curious about where the information is coming from, you can click directly on the chart to see the data and assumptions behind it. You can also embed charts in a map using the Chart Elements feature.

SCENARIOS

Scenario 360 allows you to create, analyze, and display multiple geographic alternatives—such as land use plans, growth patterns, or project sites—and compare them side by side.

One way to create scenarios is with Scenario Sketch tools. Once you have drawn the scenarios you want, you can compare how they look on a

Figure A5.1 An example of a dynamic chart

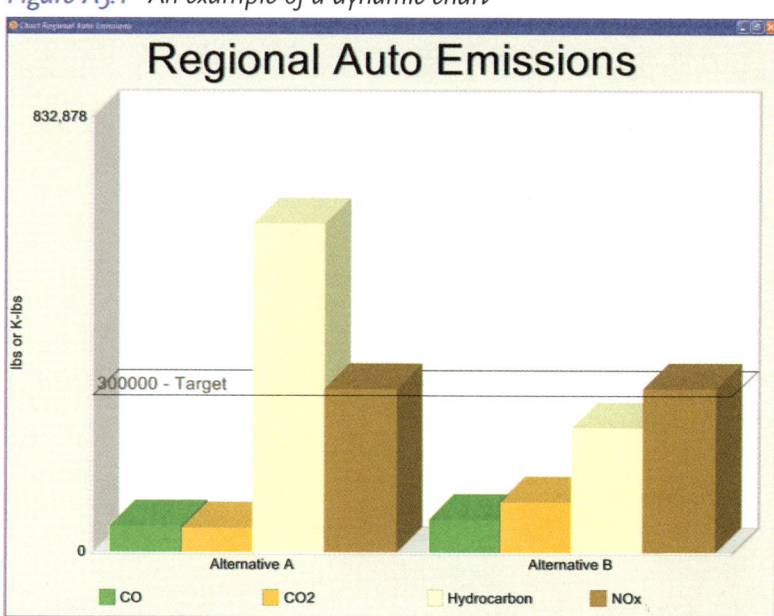

---

1. The CommunityViz website is: http://placeways.com/communityviz.

map, their quantitative effects such as public costs and revenues, and how each responds to changes in assumptions or external influences. And with the **Scenario Comparison** feature, you can display maps, charts, and images in a tiled display that makes it easy to compare, present, and review alternatives and their impacts (see Figure A5.2).

DECISION TOOLS

Scenario 360 decision tools help you accomplish common planning tasks such as build-out analyses and land suitability analyses. Some of the most popular decision tools are described below.

The **Common Impacts Wizard** automatically creates GIS-based impact analyses commonly associated with growth and development (see Figure A5.3). You can instantly start to see some of the most commonly used indicators of economic, environmental, and social outcomes for alternative growth scenarios. The Common Impacts Wizard will create everything you need—formulas, indicators, charts, reports, and variable assumptions with default values—to serve as a starting point for your analysis.

The wizard can calculate the following impacts, depending on the information you provide:

- Auto emissions
- Commercial energy use
- Commercial floor area
- Commercial jobs
- Commercial jobs-to-housing ratio
- Commercial tax revenue
- Distances to places of interest
- Residential water use
- Labor force
- Population
- Residential dwelling units
- Residential energy use
- Residential tax revenue
- Schoolchildren
- Sensitive lands impacts
- Vehicle trips per day.

The **Custom Impacts Wizard** sets up analysis models for impacts that are important to you but are not dealt with by the Common Impacts Wizard or other tools. You specify the type of analysis you want—counts, sums, classifications—and the parameters you want to use. The wizard sets up the formulas, attributes, indicators, assumptions,

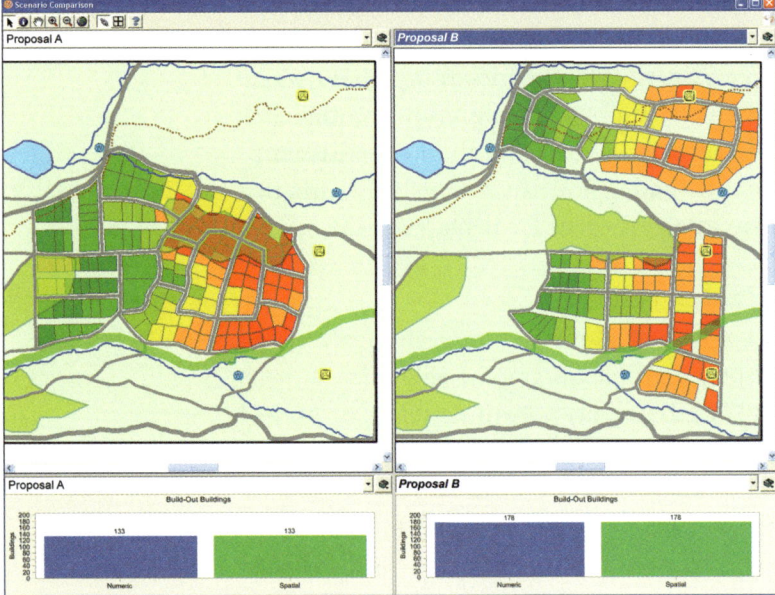

Figure A5.2 *Scenario Comparison*

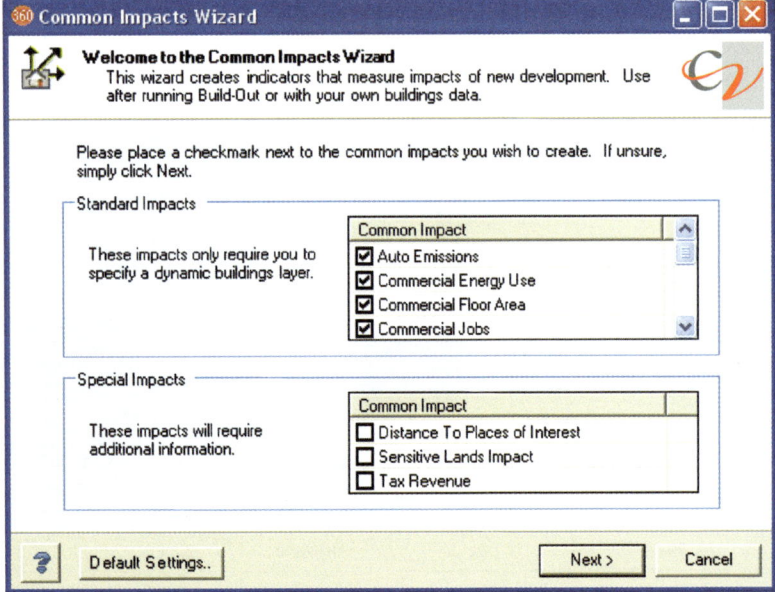

Figure A5.3 *Common Impacts Wizard*

and charts you can use to see the economic, environmental, and social impacts of alternative decisions that you might make. The impact models supported by the Custom Impacts Wizard work with some of the most commonly used simple features. For example, you can:

- Count features based on their location, such as all the trees in a park or all the septic tanks near a river

- Count items in features, such as all the chimneys in a group of houses

- Calculate amounts per feature attribute, such as the amount of water needed to irrigate a polygon layer representing farm fields

- Classify and count a feature based on one of its existing attribute values, such as how many roads are local, collector, or arterial

- Classify and count a feature based on its proximity to other features, such as how many septic tanks are near each of a number of rivers.

Land Use Designer (see Figure A5.4) allows you to study the economic, environmental, and social impacts of alternative land use plans with just a few clicks of the mouse. A special dialog box helps you choose predefined or custom land use models. Land use models provide an easy way to create land use scenarios and impact analyses simply by sketching on the map. Each model specifies the name and particular characteristics of a given land use, such as building density and resource utilization rates. When you apply a land use to a feature on the map, the feature takes on all the specified characteristics, and corresponding impacts are automatically calculated.

The **Suitability Wizard** is an easy-to-use, step-by-step tool that enables you to create site suitability or desirability analyses. You specify the factors you want to consider—such as proximity to roads and overlap with floodplains—and the wizard sets up a complete analysis for you. Once the analysis has been created, you can color code your map according to which sites are most suitable, and you can change the weighting of each factor and immediately see the results.

Allocator helps determine where growth is most likely to occur over time. It uses the classic supply-and-demand approach, allocating new growth to available building locations sequentially over time, using either strict-order or probability-based models.

The **Build-Out Wizard** performs all the work necessary for a build-out analysis, which shows the capacity of your land area to accommodate new development based on all the commercial or residential building allowed by current land use regulations. This popular CommunityViz feature supports numeric, spatial, and 3-D visual build-out analysis, and it works with everything from a simple land use map to a complex zoning code.

TimeScope lets you look at incremental changes in your area year by year. Buildings and roads appear on the landscape; infrastructure capacity fills up; land uses change; and economic, environmental, and social impacts are updated—all according to rules and assumptions you set. Results can be used with the Timeline in Google Earth.

INTERACTIVE ANALYSIS AND MODELING

Scenario 360 analysis capabilities go well beyond decision tools. Scenario 360 provides a complete environment for you to construct

Figure A5.4 Land Use Designer

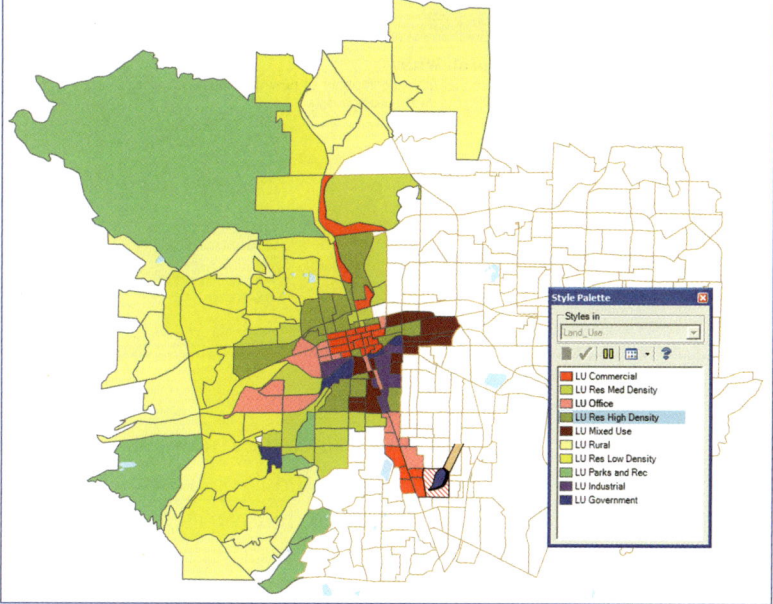

Figure A5.5 Creating dynamic formulas with the Formula Wizard

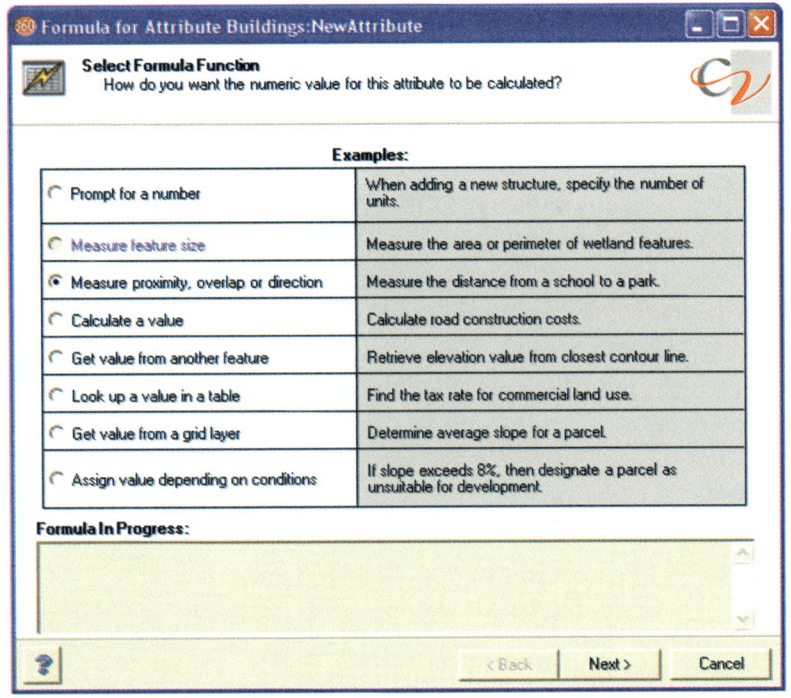

Figure A5.6 Formula Editor showing an example of a Scenario 360 formula

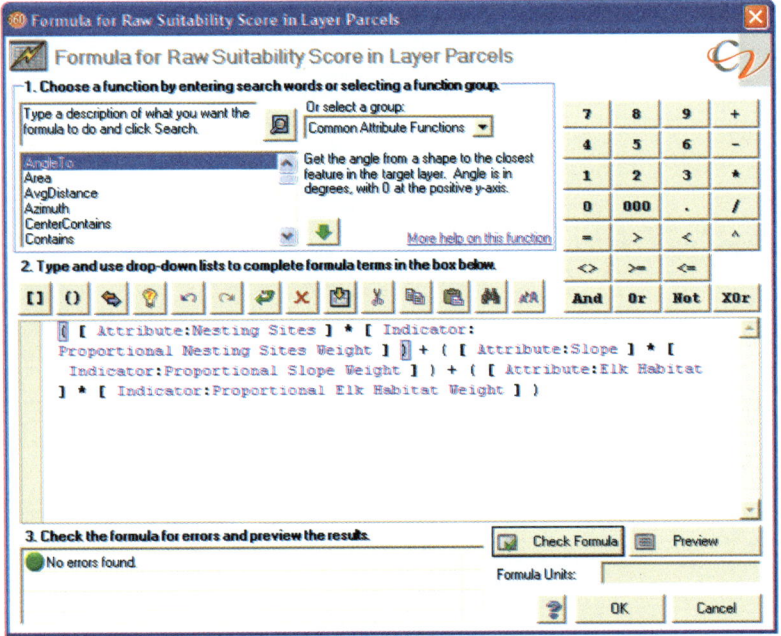

your own situation-specific analysis by writing formulas, creating models or calling on existing models, and setting up a variety of interactive analysis tools.

Dynamic Formulas: The way Scenario 360 handles spatial data is somewhat like the way a Microsoft Excel spreadsheet handles numbers (see Figure A5.5). To write formulas, you can use spatial information, tabular information, and changeable assumptions for variables such as unit costs or growth rates. The results from the formulas give you information you will need to make geographic decisions, such as how much an alternative development proposal will cost or which parcel of land is most suitable for a particular development project. Because the formulas are dynamic, the results are updated automatically as you make changes to the assumptions, edit the map, or experiment with other choices.

Scenario 360 enables you to write your own formulas and models without writing scripts or code (see Figure A5.6). Because you can write the formulas you will use, you have complete flexibility in what to study and how to model it. There are virtually no required data sets—you can use as much or as little data as you have, starting from an ArcMap base layer. Writing formulas requires no programming. You simply answer the step-by-step questions in the Formula Wizard, or if you are a more advanced user, customize your models with the powerful Formula Editor, which provides more than 70 building block functions.

Intuitive Controls: Scenario 360's intuitive, highly visual controls are designed to be easy to understand (see Figure A5.7). Slider bars encourage viewers to vary assumptions and change weighting factors to see the results. Large, colorful icons represent common functions. You can move, reorganize, and resize the toolbars, windows, charts, and other screen elements to suit your preferences. And built-in, context-sensitive help is always available.

Automated Alerts: In Scenario 360, you can create your own alerts that notify you when certain thresholds are crossed as you experiment with changes to your analysis. For example, you can set an alert that is triggered when a school runs out of capacity (see Figure A5.8) or an alert that highlights all the parcels that meet your criteria for a particular use.

Integration with External Models: If you are using specialized analysis models—such as for traffic or land conservation—you can often integrate the results into your Scenario 360 analysis using tables, databases, or XML. Scenario 360 becomes a framework for collecting and organizing all the information you have. For example, you can consider economic impacts side by side with environmental, social, and visual impacts, allowing for a more comprehensive decision-making process. You can even link to external tables and Excel spreadsheets so that as the external data changes, your analysis is automatically updated.

Templates: Once you create an analysis, you can save its formulas, charts, and other components and reuse them on other data sets. Scenario 360 template files are small, portable, and easily shared, so you can trade work with colleagues or develop standardized models to use within your practice.

COMMUNICATION AND ENGAGEMENT

CommunityViz can help people understand the sometimes complex economic, environmental, and social considerations that affect land use planning and development decisions.

Scenario 360 is carefully designed to be as easy on the outside as it is powerful on the inside. For example, Scenario 360 displays analysis functions separately from setup functions, making it easier for nontechnical audiences to focus on decision-making concepts without getting lost in details. Yet, the analysis is still transparent: It is simple to look up the formulas and assumptions behind any result and to change them if desired.

Web-Ready Reports and Presentations: The Reports Wizard helps you create clear, comprehensive reports that present data, images, and explanations about your analysis. Reports are in HTML format, so they are ready to be posted to a project website or viewed on your own computer. The CommunityViz WebShots Wizard enables you to create and post partly interactive web presentations that let your viewers explore your analysis or view it as a slide show (see Figure A5.9).

Figure A5.7 The task panel showing examples of intuitive controls

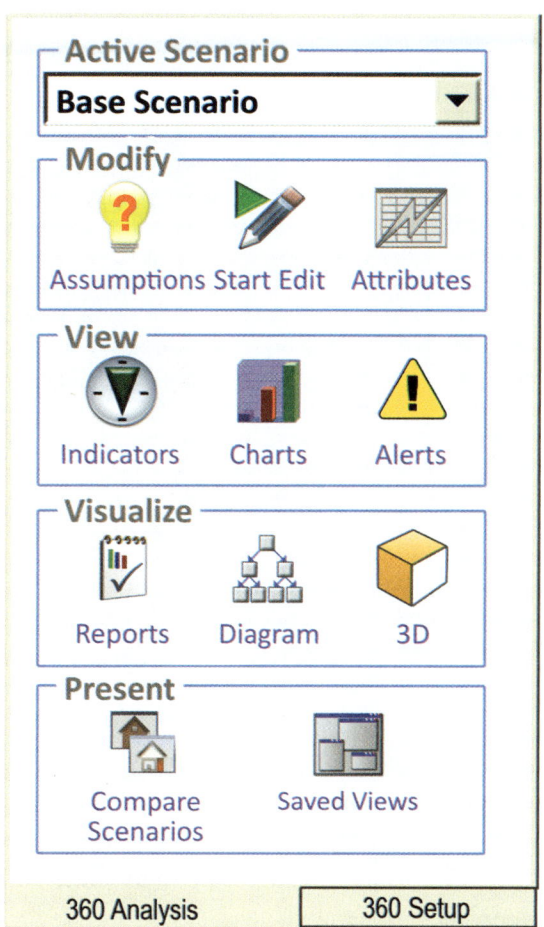

Figure A5.8 An alert on a chart shows that a threshold has been crossed

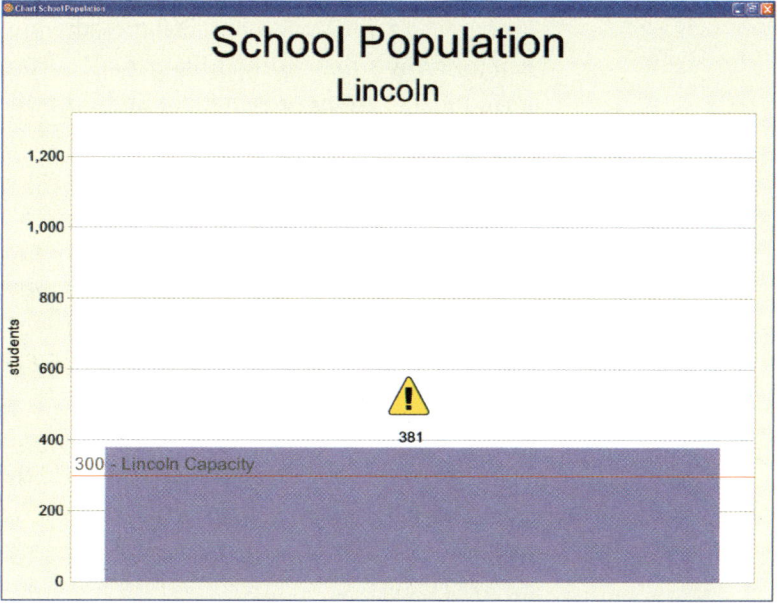

Figure A5.9 Example of a WebShots display

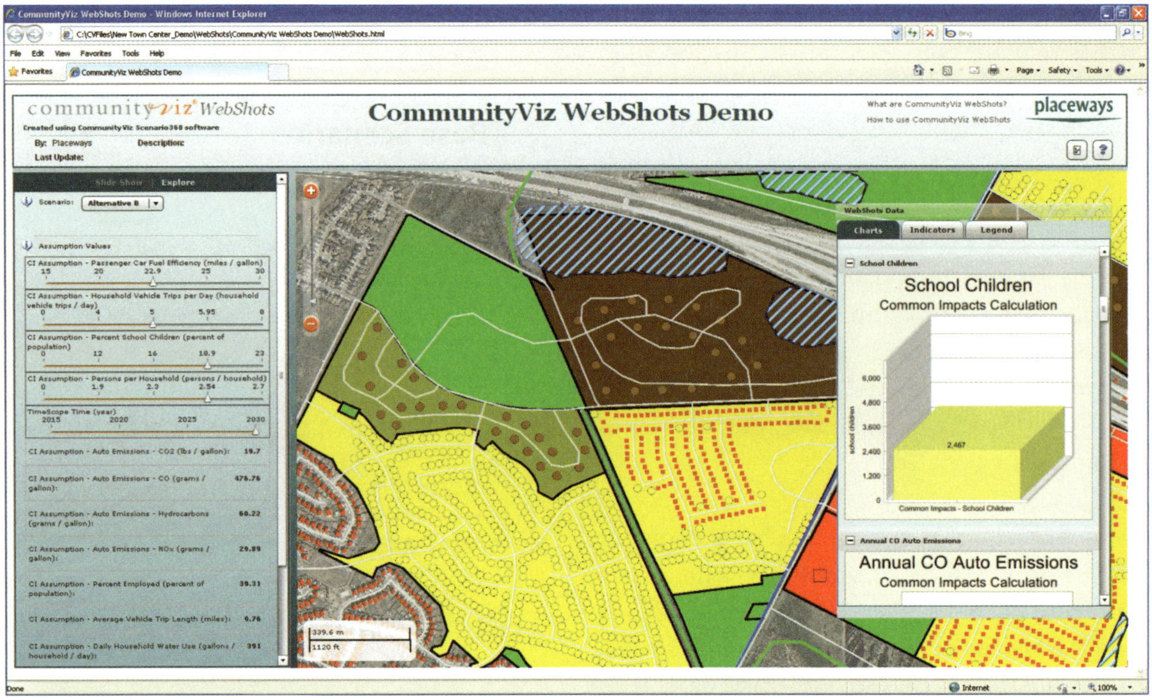

Analysis Diagrams: A Scenario 360 interactive analysis diagram (see Figure A5.10) provides a map of the logic of your analysis. An analysis diagram shows all of the analysis components and their relationships, using color-coded lines and icons. Such a diagram is an excellent tool for displaying, explaining, or identifying the interdependent economic, environmental, and social factors that are commonly involved in land use decisions.

Presentation Tools: Scenario 360 provides presentation tools that work at many scales, from small to large group presentations and distribution on the Internet. The clear, colorful visuals make excellent presentations. And tools such as the Saved Views feature, Symbology Saver, full-screen charts, and the Scenario Comparison window give a presenter extra speed and a presentation more visual clarity, both of which are helpful during a presentation to a large audience (see Figure A5.11).

SCENARIO 3D FEATURES

Scenario 3D is a companion to Scenario 360 in the CommunityViz suite and works as its own ArcGIS Desktop extension. Scenario 3D brings maps to life by helping you create realistic, interactive, and sharable 3-D scenes (see Figure A5.12). You make Scenario 3D scenes by starting with an ArcGIS map and then specifying how the 2-D features on the map will be represented in the 3-D scene. When viewing a scene, you can move through the scene as if you were there, walking, flying, and looking around. Buildings, trees, and roads all

Figure A5.10 Example of an analysis diagram

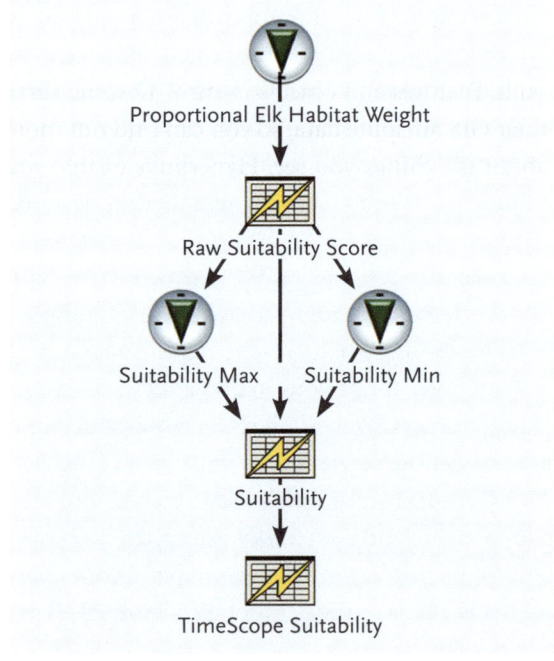

Appendix 5: CommunityViz Features 249

Figure A5.11 An example of a Scenario 360 display

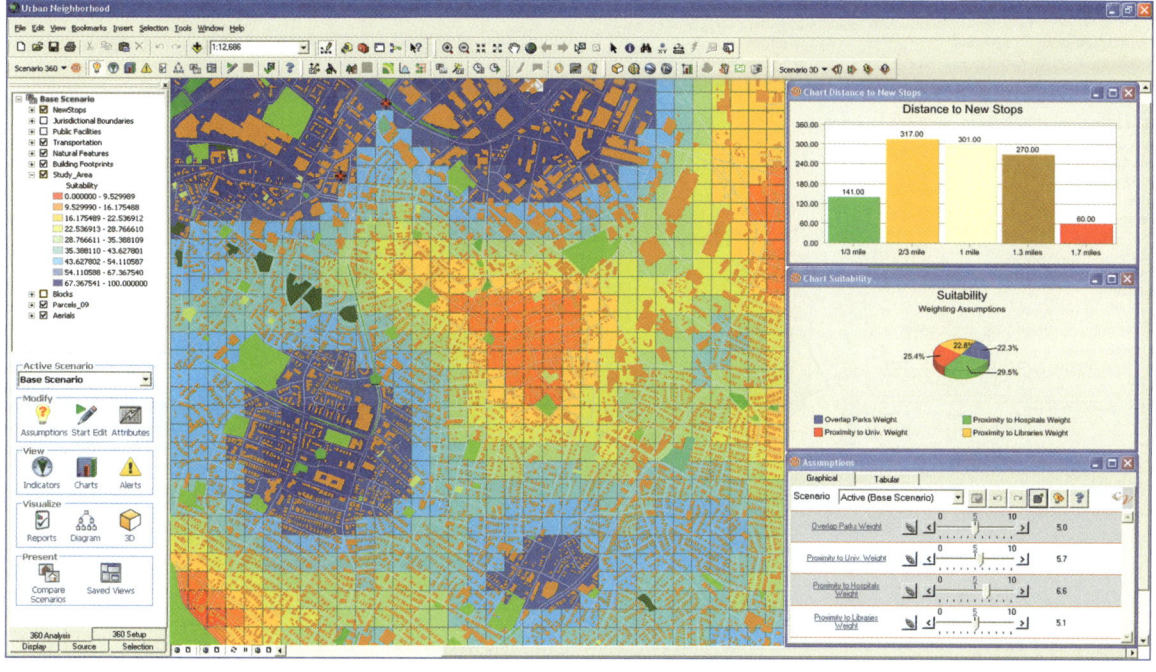

appear in realistic detail, and terrain rises and falls underfoot. Shadows, lighting, and fog effects lend a tangible sense of place. The idea is to help you get a feel for the place you are seeing.

Additional interactive features of Scenario 3D let you use transparency sliders to fade layers in and out, and you can change scenarios to see two or three different models of the same location. The Scenario 3D Viewer lets anyone view Scenario 3D scenes.

Scenario 3D scenes have all the geospatial accuracy of the ArcGIS map from which they are built. Features and objects in the 3-D scene carry their GIS attribute data, so you can find out more about the things you see. Hyperlinks enable you to launch websites, movies, or other multimedia content by clicking on objects in the scene. As Scenario 3D supports KMZ, 3ds, and DAE file formats, you can create scenes using the library of models provided or by using your own 3-D objects from Google SketchUp, CAD, 3ds Max, Maya, COLLADA, and other 3-D modeling tools.

SCENARIO 3D EXPORTER

Scenario 3D comes in two parts, the Scenario 3D Exporter and the Scenario 3D Viewer. The Scenario 3D Exporter (see Figure A5.13) is an ArcGIS extension for creating 3-D scenes.

Figure A5.12 An example of a Scenario 3D scene

Here are a few key points about the Exporter:

- It is a toolbar extension for ArcMap; no other software is required.

- It sets up scenes from ArcMap features, layers, and scenarios.

- A variety of methods to convert 2-D to 3-D are available, ranging from simple symbols to templates.

- Three-dimensional terrain can be created from contour lines or DEMs.

- Three-dimensional features can be created using geometry, extrusions, colors, textures,

Figure A5.13 Scenario 3D Exporter screen

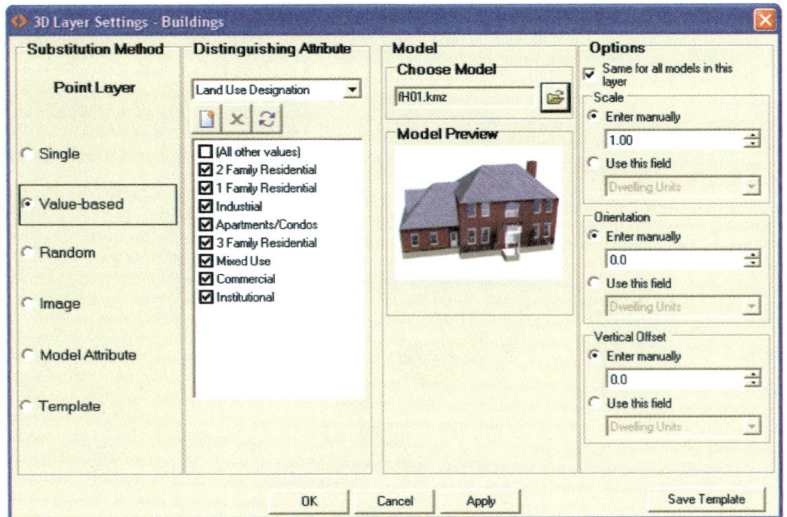

SCENARIO 3D VIEWER

The Scenario 3D Viewer (see Figure A5.14) is a stand-alone viewer that lets you explore scenes created by the Scenario 3D Exporter.

Here are a few key points about the viewer:

- There is a free download available, so anyone can view Scenario 3D scenes.[2]
- It has six modes of navigation, including flying, walking, and maneuvering.
- Environmental effects can be created, including fog, shadows, and lighting.
- Bookmarks, saved "fly-through paths," and built-in movie recording are provided.
- Multiple scenarios can be contained in one file.
- Features in the scene can be clicked to display attribute information and launch hyperlinks.
- There is an ArcMap-style layer list.
- Layers have variable transparency.

dynamic materials such as reflective water, 3-D models, orientation, scale, and more.

- The software includes a library of hundreds of 3-D models and textures, or you can add your own photos or 3-D models in SketchUp KMZ, 3ds, and COLLADA formats.
- There are time-saving features, such as templates and polygon-to-point conversion.

---

2. The download is available at http://placeways.com/communityviz.

Figure A5.14 A screenshot from the Scenario 3D Viewer.

CONTACTS

CommunityViz is a software product, not a company.

> CommunityViz
> Website: www.communityviz.com
> Product website:
> http://placeways.com/communityviz

Esri (founded in 1969 as **Environmental Systems Research Institute, Inc.**) is the world's largest GIS company and the maker of ArcGIS software, the platform for CommunityViz. Esri is a business partner of Placeways.

Esri
Redlands, California
Phone: (909) 793-2853
Website: www.esri.com

Google SketchUp is a product of Google, Inc., which also makes Google Earth.

> Google, Inc.
> Mountain View, California
> Phone: (650) 253-0000
> Website: www.google.com
> SketchUp website:
> http://sketchup.google.com
> 3D Warehouse website:
> http://sketchup.google.com/3dwarehouse

Orton Family Foundation, founded in 1995 by Lyman Orton and Noel Fritzinger, is an operating foundation that helps communities in the Northeast and Rocky Mountain West discover, describe, apply, and sustain their heart and soul.

> Orton Family Foundation
> Middlebury, Vermont
> Phone: (802) 388-6336
> Website: www.orton.org
> Send questions and comments to:
> info@orton.org

PlaceMatters is a nonprofit organization that provides a wide variety of informational resources on innovative planning decision-making tools and methods.

> PlaceMatters
> Denver, Colorado
> Phone: (303) 964-0903
> Website: www.placematters.org

Placeways, founded in 2005, is the home of CommunityViz. The company develops, supports, and distributes CommunityViz software, including Scenario 360 and Scenario 3D, in partnership with the Orton Family Foundation.

> Placeways LLC
> Boulder, Colorado
> Main Phone: (303) 442-8800
> Toll Free (U.S. only): (866) 953-1400
> Website: placeways.com
> Send questions and comments to:
> info@placeways.com

Smart Code Central is the source for SmartCode templates for form-based codes.

> Website: www.smartcodecentral.org

CASE STUDY AND TEACHING EXAMPLE CONTACTS

> Boston Metropolitan Area Planning Council
> Boston, Massachusetts
> Phone: (617) 451-2770
> Website: www.mapc.org
>
> Community Oriented Geography
> Burlington, Vermont
> Phone: (802) 598-8883
>
> Donley & Associates, Inc.
> Colorado Springs, Colorado
> Phone: (719) 471-9835
> Website: www.donleyassociates.com
>
> Foresee Consulting, Inc.
> Lyons, Colorado
> Phone: (303) 823-6219
> Website: www.foreseeconsulting.biz

Geodata Services, Inc.
Missoula, Montana
Phone: (406) 532-3239
Website: http://geodatawiki.com

Kimley-Horn and Associates, Inc.
Charlotte, North Carolina
Phone: (704) 333-5131
Website: www.kimley-horn.com

McCormick Taylor, Inc.
Pittsburgh, Pennsylvania
Phone: (412) 922-6880
Website: www.mccormicktaylor.com

Natural Resources Canada
Ottawa, Ontario, Canada
Phone: (613) 995-0947
Website: www.nrcan-rncan.gc.ca/com

Pikes Peak Area Council of Governments
Colorado Springs, Colorado
Phone: (719) 471-7080
Website: http://ppacg.org

Spatial Alternatives
Yarmouth, Maine
Phone: (207) 846-2355
Website: www.spatialalternatives.com

TerraCognito GIS
Eldora, Colorado
Phone: (303) 258-3515
Website: www.terracog.com

University of Wisconsin
Department of Urban and Regional Planning
Madison, Wisconsin
Phone: (608) 262-1004
Website: http://urpl.wisc.edu

University of Wyoming
Wyoming Geographic Information Science Center
Laramie, Wyoming
Phone: (307) 766-2532
Website: www.uwyo.edu/wygisc

Urban Systems
Kelowna, British Columbia, Canada
Phone: (250) 762-2517
Website: www.urban-systems.com

Winston Associates
Boulder, Colorado
Phone: (303) 440-9200
Website: www.winstonassociates.com

REFERENCES

Albers, Jan. *Hands on the Land: A History of the Vermont Landscape.* Cambridge, Mass.: MIT Press, 2000.

Brail, Richard K., ed. *Planning Support Systems for Cities and Regions.* Cambridge, Mass.: Lincoln Institute of Land Policy, 2008.

Daniels, Thomas L., John W. Keller, Mark B. Lapping, Katherine Daniels, and James Segedy. *The Small Town Planning Handbook.* 3rd ed. Chicago: APA Planners Press, 2007.

Knapp, Connie, and the Orton Family Foundation Community Mapping Program. *Making Community Connections.* Redlands, Calif.: Esri Press, 2003.

Kwartler, Michael, and Gianni Longo. *Visioning and Visualization: People, Pixels, and Plans.* Cambridge, Mass.: Lincoln Institute of Land Policy, 2008.

Orton, Lyman. "What's Your Community's Heart and Soul?" *Northwest Colorado Council of Governments Courier,* 2006, 4.

Roper, William, and Brian H. F. Muller. "Envisioning Rural Futures: Using Innovative Software for Community Planning." In *Conservation in the Internet Age: Threats and Opportunities,* edited by James N. Levitt, 218–42. Washington, D.C.: Island Press, 2002.

Sanborn, Rebecca, with Helen Whyte. *Planning for Community Heart & Soul: A Review of Processes & Practitioners.* Middlebury, Vt.: Orton Family Foundation, 2007. Published online at www.orton.org.

Snyder, Ken. "Putting Democracy Front and Center." *Planning* 72 (July 2006): 24–29.

Travis, William R. *New Geographies of the American West: Land Use and the Changing Patterns of Place.* Washington, D.C.: Island Press, 2007.

Walker, Doug. "Visualization as a Common Language for Planning: Good Practices, Caveats, and Areas for Research." *TR News* 252 (September–October 2007): 7–10.

GLOSSARY

360 Analysis tab: A Scenario 360 tool used for exploring an analysis after it has been set up. Novice users of CommunityViz should use the 360 Analysis tab features and avoid the 360 Setup tab features.

360 Setup tab: A Scenario 360 tool used for setting up, adding to, or changing an analysis. Novice users should use the 360 Analysis tab features and avoid the 360 Setup tab features.

alert: An alert monitors values during analysis and reports if specific conditions occur. Alerts may add special icons to charts and assumptions, change the color of charts, outline map features in a special color, or launch an external application such as an audio recording. An alert may be associated with an assumption, a dynamic attribute, or an indicator.

Allocator Wizard: The Allocator Wizard is a decision tool that performs the common planning function of allocating the demand for buildings across the available supply of potential building locations. Buildings are placed according to the desirability and capacity of each land use area. The wizard allows you to specify either strict ordering, in which the most desirable areas are always filled up first, or probability-based ordering, based on the probability that a location will be built upon because of its relative desirability.

analysis: In Scenario 360, analysis is both an object and an action. A Scenario 360 analysis (the object) is analogous to a Microsoft Word document, PowerPoint presentation, or Excel workbook. It is the overall framework for a decision-making process, and the analysis folder includes the map data, scenarios, calculations, and indicators for the work you are doing. The process of working with Scenario 360 to sketch scenarios, explore alternatives, change assumptions, and so on is also called analysis, which in this case refers to an action.

analysis diagram: An analysis diagram is a Scenario 360 feature that provides detailed information about analysis files and components, displaying connections and relationships between them. Using an analysis diagram to view interdependencies of components can be helpful when sharing an analysis, working with a shared analysis, or explaining an analysis to an audience.

analysis grid: An analysis grid is a polygon layer that you sometimes construct as a framework for aggregating or disaggregating data and conducting an analysis. The simplest analysis grid consists of uniform squares, but you can also make more-complex structures.

Analysis Publisher: The CommunityViz Analysis Publisher allows you to publish freely sharable, read-only versions of Scenario 360 analyses that anyone can view using the free CommunityViz Analysis Viewer together with Esri's free ArcReader software.

ArcGIS: This is a familiar suite of GIS software products made by Esri. CommunityViz works as an extension (plug-in or add-on) to ArcGIS Desktop products. CommunityViz requires ArcGIS ArcMap (available in all ArcGIS packages, including ArcView, ArcEditor, and ArcInfo), and it can also take advantage of ArcGIS 3D Analyst, ArcGlobe, ArcScene, ArcGIS Explorer, Network Analyst, and Spatial Analyst.

assumption: An assumption is a value that is an input to an analysis. You can easily change assumptions, which are often displayed as slider bars. Examples include water usage rates and land suitability weighting factors. Output values that depend on a particular assumption are automatically updated when that assumption is changed.

attribute: An attribute is a piece of information that describes a map feature. The attributes of a census tract, for example, might include its area in square miles, population, and average per capita income. In ArcGIS, attribute information is stored in an attribute table for each layer; each column in the table is an attribute. See also dynamic attribute.

base layer: In a GIS project, a base layer contains standard, commonly used information such as roads or transportation networks, cities or places, or water bodies.

base scenario: An analysis can contain one or more scenarios. The first scenario in your analysis is called the base scenario. It can represent existing conditions, a development proposal under evaluation, or the first of several alternatives you wish to compare in your analysis.

Boolean: *Boolean* describes a logical statement or condition that is either true or false. Boolean values are often represented as yes/no or 1/0.

Build-Out Wizard: A build-out analysis allows planners to estimate the amount and location of development allowed in an area according to current or proposed zoning regulations. It provides a convenient reference for future planning, because it represents a theoretical maximum. It does not imply or forecast how many buildings will actually be built. The Scenario 360 Build-Out Wizard automates the entire build-out process. It guides you through the choices and selections that will form the basis of a build-out analysis.

centroid: The point at the center of a polygon is called a centroid. In ArcGIS, the centroid is located at the center of the rectangle that contains the polygon, called its bounding box or extent.

change model: A change model is an algorithm or set of rules for estimating how a system will be affected by particular influences, such as population increases. Change models are a more general form of growth model.

charrette: A charrette is a structured, collaborative meeting or set of meetings held for the purpose of creating future visions, plans, or designs. The format varies, but typically there are subgroups that work on different aspects of the problem or plan and then share their proposals with the rest of the group. Revisions are made while the meeting is still in progress.

chart: A chart is a graphic display of the current values of your indicators and assumptions. As changes are made in the analysis, chart displays will be updated automatically to reflect analysis results.

Chart Elements: Chart Elements is a Scenario 360 feature that lets you embed small rectangles containing dynamic charts on a map. The rectangles are treated as graphic elements that do not resize when you zoom in or out but do display nicely on printed maps in layout view.

class: A class is a category or range of values used for classification. For example, if you classify county populations as small, medium, and large, you are using three classes. In ArcMap, classes correspond to legend entries in the table of contents.

Clone tool: In Scenario 360 Sketch tools, cloning allows you to save a particular feature, including its attribute values, and then reapply copies of it anywhere on the map by clicking with the Clone tool cursor.

Common Impacts Wizard: This is a Scenario 360 decision tool that lets you automatically create GIS-based impact analyses resulting from projected growth. With simple inputs, the Common Impacts Wizard creates charts, reports, formulas, indicators, attributes, and assumptions that help you analyze the economic, environmental, and social outcomes associated with alternative growth scenarios. This wizard is an excellent tool for starting all kinds of planning projects, as well as a powerful companion to the CommunityViz Build-Out Wizard and TimeScope.

CommunityViz: CommunityViz is a software tool for making informed, collaborative decisions about land-use planning. CommunityViz Version 4 includes both Scenario 360 and Scenario 3D. CommunityViz works as an extension to Esri's ArcGIS-brand GIS software.

computer-aided design (CAD): Also known as computer-aided design and development (CADD), this is sister technology to GIS. It is widely used by engineers and architects for creating 2-D and 3-D drawings. Compared to GIS, CAD tends to have finer control and precision, but less emphasis on geography and spatial relationships.

constraint: In planning, a constraint to development is a characteristic of the land or lot that makes building difficult or impossible. Examples include utility rights-of-way, rivers, and sometimes floodplains or steep slopes.

coordinate system: See **projection**.

Custom Impacts Wizard: The Scenario 360 Custom Impacts Wizard helps you set up simple analysis models for measuring impacts. Based on the specifications you provide, it automatically creates the dynamic attributes, indicators, or charts you need and lets you set up assumptions as well. You can do the same things manually using standard Scenario 360 Setup tools, but using the Custom Impacts Wizard will save you time and steps.

DAE: This is the filename extension used by the COLLADA Interchange Format, which is a standard format for 3-D objects and models.

decision tools: Scenario 360 decision tools allow you to set up analyses to make choices about scenarios. The tools are step-by-step wizards you can use to set up the rules and data you want to use. Examples include the Build-Out Wizard, Suitability Wizard, and TimeScope.

desirability surface: This is a map showing the relative attractiveness of each location for development. It is called a surface because you can think of it as a terrain of mountains and valleys, with the high points and low points corresponding to high and low desirability.

dwelling units (DU) per area: A dwelling unit (often abbreviated DU) is a house or apartment inhabited by a household of one or more people. Residential density is usually described in a site plan, comprehensive plan, or zoning ordinance by the number of dwelling units per acre or hectare.

dynamic: CommunityViz uses the term dynamic to mean changeable. When you work with a CommunityViz analysis, you can make changes to features on the map, assumptions, scenarios, and other elements. In response, CommunityViz updates its calculations and displays new results in the form of tables, charts, maps, colors, and other visuals. These are called *dynamic* changes. Also see dynamic attribute and dynamic data layer.

dynamic attribute: A dynamic attribute is an attribute that is automatically updated as changes are made in the analysis using Scenario 360 formulas. For example, a proposed Roads layer may contain dynamic attributes for length, pavement type, intersecting slopes, and construction costs. As each new road segment is added or changed, each of the dynamic attributes will be updated automatically or, if you choose, manually. A formula specifies how each dynamic attribute is calculated.

dynamic data layer: A dynamic data layer is a layer that is stored in the Scenario 360 analysis geodatabase. Only dynamic data layers can contain dynamic attributes. When you set up a Scenario 360 analysis, you often start with standard GIS layers (called nondynamic or reference layers) and make them dynamic so that you can add dynamic (formula-driven) attributes to them. When you make a dynamic layer, it is copied into the analysis geodatabase. The original reference layer remains intact.

efficiency factors: In build-out analysis, efficiency factors adjust building density values to reflect density losses at less than potential build-out. They are entered as a percentage where 100 percent means complete efficiency (no density lost), and 0 percent means no buildings will be estimated for that land use.

External Table Links: External Table Links enable you to link tables in your Scenario 360 analysis to external tables in such a way that when any changes are made in the external tables, your analysis is automatically updated. Typical applications include linking to Microsoft Excel spreadsheets, tables generated by keypad polling (clicker) systems, and tables generated by special-purpose external modeling tools.

feature: A feature on a map is an individual point, line, or polygon. A typical map layer contains multiple features that together illustrate geographic information. In the layer's attribute table, features are represented by rows in the table.

fishnet: A fishnet is a polygon layer of adjacent squares or rectangles, usually created to serve as an analysis grid.

floor area ratio: This is the ratio between the total floor space in a building (including all stories) and the buildable area of the lot it is built on. Floor area ratio is calculated by dividing the total floor area of all buildings or structures on a lot by the total buildable area of the lot. For instance, a floor area ratio of 4 with a bulk coverage limit of 50 percent means that a building 8 stories tall could be built on half of the lot. Also called floor space ratio.

form-based code: A form-based code is a method of regulating development that is based on physical form rather than land use. Form-based codes usually contain building form standards and public space standards that describe the shapes of buildings and their relationships to public areas. The standards are keyed to a regulating plan or map that indicates where each type of standard applies. Unlike design guidelines, form-based codes are regulatory.

Formula Editor: The Scenario 360 Formula Editor lets you set up or modify Scenario 360 formulas used for dynamic analysis. You can use the Formula Editor for both dynamic attribute formulas and indicator formulas. The Formula Editor gives you complete, direct access to formulas and functions, whereas the Formula Wizard creates formulas by asking you a series of questions.

Formula Wizard: The Scenario 360 Formula Wizard lets you create or modify Scenario 360 formulas used for dynamic analysis. You can use the Formula Wizard for both dynamic attribute formulas and indicator formulas. The Formula Wizard creates formulas by asking you a series of questions, whereas the Formula Editor gives you complete, direct access to formulas and functions.

function: In a Scenario 360 formula, a function performs a particular calculation. There are more than 70 functions available, and they include operations that do ordinary math, geospatial calculations, text functions, and more.

Gantt chart: This is a type of bar chart or table used to show project schedules. Project tasks are listed as rows in the table, and time is shown on the horizontal (left-to-right) axis. Horizontal bars show the start and end dates of each task.

geodatabase: In layman's terms, a geodatabase is the place where GIS data is stored. It is a database that "knows about" geographic shapes and rules. Technically, it is a database that provides services for managing geographic data. These services include validation rules, relationships, and topology. A geodatabase contains feature data sets and is located inside a relational database management system.

geodesign: This is the process of sketching plans or designs that incorporate geographic information, are informed by fast feedback about impacts and consequences, and can be easily changed and revised.

geographic information system (GIS): Informally, people sometimes use this term simply to mean a computerized map. More technically, to the CommunityViz user, GIS means a computer system that captures, stores, manages, analyzes, and displays information linked to location.

georeferencing: The process of matching an image or design to its correct place on a geographic map is called georeferencing. ArcMap provides georeferencing tools. In addition to placing the image so that it is in the right place, you may need to scale it, rotate it, and stretch it so that it matches the map at all points.

Google Earth Exporter: The Scenario 360 Google Earth Exporter lets you export layers and charts for viewing in Google Earth (or other tools, such as ArcGIS Explorer, that recognize KMZ format). After exporting, you can automatically launch Google Earth on your computer and have it zoom to the location, display your analysis layers overlaid on the terrain, and display your charts in an additional window. TimeScope features can also use the Google Earth Timeline. Multiple scenarios appear as separate folders in the Google Earth My Places list. Point layers, such as building points or trees, can be displayed using 3-D models in KMZ or DAE format.

Google SketchUp: This is a free, easy-to-use tool for creating 3D models of buildings or other objects. SketchUp models are suitable for use in Scenario 3D, Google Earth, ArcScene, and other 3-D viewing tools.

growth model: A growth model is an algorithm or set of rules for estimating how a community will change in size over time. Simple growth models might look at building permits for the last five years and extrapolate the same rate forward for five years. Complex growth models incorporate demographics, economics, historical statistics, and potentially many other factors. Also see **change model** and **impact model**.

Heart & Soul Community Planning: This is a term coined by the Orton Family Foundation to describe an approach that engages citizens in land-use planning as a pathway to vibrant, enduring communities. This approach helps diverse citizens identify and enhance a town's most valued attributes, or heart-and-soul resources: those special places, characteristics, and customs that residents treasure and that connect them to one another. If lost, these attributes would be widely missed and alter the character of the town.

hyperlink: In general, a hyperlink is a connection from one computer application, such as a text document, to another, such as a website. The most familiar example is underlined words in a document that lead you to a website when you click on them. In Scenario 3D, objects in the 3-D scene can have hyperlinks (also called links) that open websites, play audio files, or launch other computer applications.

impact model: An impact model is an algorithm or set of rules for estimating the consequences of an action, growth, or change. While growth models estimate how a community will change in size, an impact model estimates the consequences of that change.

indicator: An indicator is an impact or performance measure that applies to an entire scenario, such as total population or total water usage.

KMZ: This is the filename extension used by Google Earth. For example, a particular building model might be named MyHouse.kmz, or a Google Earth scene exported by the CommunityViz Google Earth Exporter might be MyAnalysis.kmz. A KMZ file is a compressed (zipped) version of a KML file.

Land Use Designer: The Scenario 360 Land Use Designer is a decision tool that helps you set up and manage land use models that you sketch onto a map. Once you have created them, land-use models provide an easy way to create land-use scenarios and impact analyses simply by sketching on the map. Each model specifies the name and particular characteristics of a given land use, such as building density and resource use rates. When you apply a land use to a feature on the map, the feature takes on all the specified characteristics, and corresponding impacts are automatically calculated.

LandFrag Wizard: The Scenario 360 LandFrag Wizard is a decision tool that helps you calculate and classify the fragmentation of an existing land-cover raster, based on the pattern of land cover in surrounding cells. A typical application is measuring forest fragmentation, but the model works on any land cover. The tool is useful for quantifying fragmentation in an objective, repeatable way. You can use it in the course of analysis to measure existing fragmentation and to measure the potential fragmentation effects of alternative land-use scenarios or growth over time.

layer: In ArcGIS, geographic information is displayed on a map as layers. Each layer represents a particular type of feature such as streams, lakes, or highways. All the features in a layer are the same type: points, lines, or polygons. Tables are also treated as layers, even though you cannot see them on the map. The technical term for a layer stored in a geodatabase is feature class.

Leadership in Energy and Environmental Design (LEED): This is a green building certification system from the U.S. Green Building Council. The first LEED systems focused on buildings, but newer standards are now available for sites and neighborhoods as well.

line feature: A line connects two or more *x,y* coordinate pairs. Often, a familiar object such as a road or river consists of a number of straight line segments.

Model Builder: This is an ArcGIS tool used for assembling sequences of geoprocessing functions. Model Builder models are sometimes compared to Scenario 360 formulas, but Model Builder uses geoprocessing tools and works primarily with raster layers, while Scenario 360 uses a variety of analysis functions and works primarily with vector feature attributes.

navigation mode: A navigation mode is one of a number of methods for moving through a 3-D scene. In Scenario 3D, you can maneuver about the scene, fly gracefully through the air, walk while maintaining a fixed height above the ground, zoom to move quickly to a particular feature or place, select features by clicking or dragging, or view the full extent of a scene. All of these are examples of navigation modes.

normalized suitability score: This is a suitability scale in which the smallest value in the analysis is 0 and the largest value is 100. For example, a suitability score based on proximity might range from 0 miles to 4.7 miles. The normalized version of the same factor would range from 0 (corresponding to 0 miles) to 100 (corresponding to 4.7 miles). The Scenario 360 Suitability Wizard normalizes suitability measures so that different types of suitability measures can be fairly compared.

Optimizer: The Scenario 360 Optimizer Wizard is a decision tool that assists you in choosing the best combination of features to satisfy certain goals, such as which parcels to conserve given a finite conservation budget. This advanced decision tool provides users a mathematical way to find near-optimal solutions to Scenario 360 analysis problems.

Orton Family Foundation: The Orton Family Foundation, based in Middlebury, Vermont, and Denver, Colorado, seeks to help small cities and towns discover and describe their heart and soul—the collective attributes that make communities unique—and build on those attributes in planning toward a vibrant, enduring future.

Painter tool: One of the Scenario 360 Sketch tools, Painter applies Sketch styles from the Sketch Palette to the map when you touch features with the special paintbrush-like cursor.

Palette tool: Part of the Scenario 360 Sketch tools collection, the Palette stores and displays all the Sketch styles you have created. You use it together with the Painter or Clone tool to specify which style or shape you want to apply to the map, just as if you were dipping a paintbrush into a painter's palette. You also use it to apply land-use styles created by Land Use Designer.

Photoshop: Photoshop is popular photo- and image-editing software from Adobe. The word has also become a verb describing the process of editing a photo or image.

point feature: A point feature is a single *x,y* coordinate representing a single geographic feature such as a tree or a house.

polygon feature: A polygon feature is an enclosed shape that may have any number of sides, such as a shape representing a parcel of land. A polygon layer is a collection of polygon features.

projection: Because the world is round and maps are flat, GIS uses rules to determine exactly how to display data on the map. The transformation from a curved surface to a flat surface is called a projection. A projected coordinate system is a standardized method for projecting the map and determining how to measure the location of any given point on the map (its coordinates). There are many standard projected coordinate systems, each optimized for use in particular parts of the globe. When using CommunityViz spatial formulas, all the layers must have the same projected coordinate system, including the same measurement units (for example, feet or meters), for the calculations to work correctly.

pull factor: Something that encourages or promotes growth or development is known as a pull factor. Classic examples are proximity to services and amenities.

raster: Raster is a GIS data format that manages information in the form of small, uniform pixels or cells covering an area. Rasters (or raster layers) are a little like digital photos except that what they store is not necessarily a picture. Raster format contrasts with vector format, which represents geographic information in the form of points, lines, and polygons combined with attribute tables.

Saved View: A Saved View is a configuration of your Scenario 360 display that you have saved in order to reload it at a later time. You can make Saved Views of settings such as map extent, layer symbols, visible windows, chart displays, and assumption displays. Ideal for use in presentations, Saved Views are also helpful when you share an analysis between multiple CommunityViz analysts.

scenario: In CommunityViz, a scenario is a model of a place under certain conditions. Usually, scenarios represent alternative future conditions that result from present-day choices, such as high growth or low growth. They are often hypothetical, and they are intended to help model and illustrate the complex interactions among many systems and variables. In Scenario 360, scenarios appear as separate versions of the map.

Scenario 3D: A component of CommunityViz, Scenario 3D provides one method for creating information-rich, interactive 3-D scenes built from your GIS map. It includes the Scenario 3D Exporter, which works as an extension to ArcMap and creates the scenes, and the Scenario 3D Viewer, which is a stand-alone application that allows you to view and explore the scenes.

Scenario 360: A key component of CommunityViz, Scenario 360 provides the framework for CommunityViz projects and most of the analysis capabilities.

Scenario Comparison Window: A feature of Scenario 360, the Scenario Comparison Window lets you look at multiple scenarios side by side in a single window. Resizable panes in the window can each show maps, charts, or images for any of the scenarios in your analysis.

scenario planning: Scenario planning is an approach to making informed decisions by considering alternatives (scenarios) and comparing measurements (indicators) of their outcomes.

SiteBuilder 3D: A component of older versions of CommunityViz, SiteBuilder 3D provided functions similar to Scenario 3D.

sketch: In scenario planning, geodesign, and CommunityViz, a sketch is a tentative plan or design that you create. Sketching often involves drawing on a paper map using pen or pencil, or onscreen using a mouse.

Sketch tools: Scenario 360 Sketch tools are a variety of methods for editing a map and its features by clicking with your mouse. See Clone tool, Painter tool, style, and Palette.

Slider bar: A slider bar is a Scenario 360 control used for changing variable assumptions. Slider bars appear in the Assumptions analysis window.

SmartCode: This is a widely used template for planning ordinances implementing the principles of a form-based code.

spatial: The term spatial pertains to space, a geographic area, or the relationships between geographic features, such as distance, slope, or density.

stakeholder: A stakeholder is a person or group that a) has a material interest (a stake) in a project and will be affected by any decisions that are made, or b) can influence the outcome of the decision-making process or project.

study area: The study area is the geographic location you are using for CommunityViz analysis. It is often a city or region, but it can range in size from a single building site to an entire country.

style: In Scenario Sketch tools, a style is a collection of predetermined values for particular attributes in a layer. When you use Sketch tools to apply a style to a feature in that layer, the feature takes on the attribute values specified in the style. Styles may also include feature shapes that are used during cloning.

suitability factor: A suitability factor is one of the considerations contributing to a suitability measure. Some examples include proximity to roads, overlap with sensitive lands, and property value.

suitability measure: This is a way of rating the suitability of features in a layer. For example, one measure could be suitability for building, and another measure could be suitability for farming.

suitability weighting factor: This is a number used to give greater or lesser importance to a suitability factor compared with other suitability factors. During an analysis, the Scenario 360 Suitability tool allows you to assign weighting factors between 0 and 10 using variable assumptions. A lower weighting makes a suitability factor less important in the overall measure, while a higher weighting makes a factor more important.

Symbol Saver: This is a Scenario 360 tool that memorizes ArcGIS symbology settings for one or more layers in your map so that you can reapply them at a later time.

target: Some Scenario 360 formula functions use inputs called "targets." There can be target layers, target features, or target attributes. Targets are appropriately named: they are the object the function "aims at," like an archer shooting an arrow at a straw target. For example, the MinDistance function measures the distance from each feature in the layer the formula is in, to the nearest features in some other target layer. Similarly, the AngleTo function measures the angle to features in a target layer.

template: A Scenario 360 template allows you to save parts or all of your analysis for reuse on other data sets. A template saves the properties of components (assumptions, indicators, charts, and so on), relationships between components, and formulas so they can be used with other data or shared with other users.

TimeScope: TimeScope is a Scenario 360 decision tool that enables you to see how a place will change over time, according to rules that you set, such as rate of growth and building sequence. You can change the future date you are viewing in the analysis, making features such as buildings and roads appear and disappear accordingly.

transect: The transect is a form-based code planning model that describes zones based on a gradual transition from city center to rural areas.

traffic analysis zones (TAZs): Transportation models use the aggregate travel demand of TAZs in a study area. Sizes vary, but a typical TAZ has a population of up to about 3,000 and can range in size from a city block to a large tract of rural land. A TAZ should share its outer boundaries with specific land parcels, rather than cut through parcels.

triangulated irregular network (TIN): A TIN is a set of nonoverlapping triangles that represent a surface, usually the terrain in a 3-D scene.

vector: In GIS, vector format is a method of storing geographic information using sets of points, lines, and polygons and associated attribute tables. It contrasts with raster format.

vertex: The endpoint of a line segment in a line or polygon feature is called a vertex. The term is also used in relation to a Scenario 3D view cone, in which the vertex is the point of the V and represents the observer's location.

WebShots Wizard: The Scenario 360 WebShots Wizard creates snapshots of your analysis that can be displayed on a website as a slide show or in a partly interactive format. Viewers of the free interactive WebShots Viewer on a website can change scenarios and have a limited ability to change assumptions and see the results.

weighting factor: A weighting factor is a number assigned to a factor in a computation to make the factor's effect on the computation reflect the level of its importance. Weighting factors are typically used in suitability analysis.

Where condition: You use a Where condition to specify one or more conditions for selecting which features to include in a calculation. For example, to count the number of buildings more than four stories tall, you would write a formula to count the number of buildings where the number of stories is greater than four.

wizard: A wizard is a tool within CommunityViz that makes certain tasks easier by taking you through a step-by-step process.

ACKNOWLEDGMENTS

We would like to thank several people for helping to make this book possible. The Orton Family Foundation provided crucial financial support and John Barstow, the foundation's communications director, helped us edit and organize the book. Helen Whyte made major contributions to documenting the case studies, which in turn tell about the remarkable work of the many CommunityViz practitioners involved. Aviva Johnson and Erin Joynt contributed many hours on improving the graphics. Professor Dana Tomlin offered important suggestions for strengthening the manuscript. Finally, we wish to thank Timothy Mennel of the American Planning Association for supporting the book idea and guiding us to its completion.

INDEX

accessibility, in regional planning, 121
accessory analysis, for changing scale, 124
accessory elements. *See also specific*
   in base models, 43
   caution in using, 52
   choosing, 54
   data sources, 42
   defined, 54
   in design review, 191
   example, 48
   in form-based code analysis, 191
   material forms vs., 50
   metro and regional models, 45
   in 3-D scenes, 50, 187
accessory land uses, 169
Accomack County (Va.), watershed plan in, 160–161
active materials, 39, 52
aerial imagery, 12, 41, 52–53, 240. *See also* photos; satellite imagery
age, data sources on, 238
agendas, for public meetings, 200, 201
Alberta (Canada), land conservation planning in, 214–215
alerts
   for anticipating problems, 223
   creating, 246, 247
   in natural resource planning, 152, 157
   in site selection and assessment, 138, 142
   in visioning process, 65
Allegheny County (Pa.), comprehensive plan for, 95–97
Allocator tool
   capabilities of, 245
   case study, 99
   for comprehensive plans, 110
   as data source, 83
   other tools vs., 76, 82
   overview, 81
   in regional growth projections, 129, 131–132
   teaching example, 85–86
   in transportation planning, 120
   in zoning analysis, 175
alpha channel, 38
alternative solutions, 2–3
American Rivers, 55
analysis. *See also specific types*
   cross-correlation, 208
   defined, xxiv, 21, 28
   design, 21–26, 202, 203–204 (*see also* setup)
   stakeholders and complexity of, 20–21
   study area size vs. scale of, 20–21
   SWOT, 2, 64–65
   in visioning process, 69–70
analysis diagrams, 203, 216, 248
analysis grids, 125–126, 140–141, 151. *See also* fishnet pattern; raster data
analysis layers, 41, 78, 81. *See also* layers
analysis process, 28
Analysis tab, 210
analysis templates, 123
aquifers, demand analysis for, 151–152. *See also* water
ArcGIS® Desktop, xxv, xxvii
ArcGIS Explorer, 36–37. *See also* 3-D project design
ArcGIS Model Builder, 111
ArcGIS Network Analyst, 111
ArcGIS systems. *See also* geographic information system (GIS)
   for agriculture planning, 148
   in analysis grid construction, 125
   CommunityViz integration with, 243
   external model compatibility with, 31n1
   Model Builder tool in, 99
   Spatial Analyst extension to, 150
   as web resource, 222
ArcGlobe, 116, 134
ArcMap Sketch tools, 125, 142, 199
ArcMap Statistics tool, 137
ArcScene, 37, 116, 134, 186. *See also* 3-D project design
ArcSketch, 125
area profiles, 5–6, 106
areas. *See* study areas
aspect ratios, 218, 219
aspirations, in value mapping, 92
assumptions. *See also* impact models
   in analysis design, 24
   in charrettes, 199
   in dynamic analysis, 34
   in natural resource planning, 156, 157
   in site selection and assessment, 138
   using multiple, 29–30
   in visioning process, 68
attribute tables, in geodatabases, 32–33
attributes, in geodatabases, 32–33

audiences, understanding, 202–203. *See also* presentations

base models, 42–44, 79
behaviors, in value mapping, 92
benchmarking, 27
Berra, Yogi, 63
best management practices (BMPs). *See also* ethics
   for creating 3-D scenes, 50
   for data handling, 231–232
   for giving presentations, 202–206
   in multimedia design, 25–26
   in natural resource planning, 153
   in reporting and display, 216, 218
   for visioning process, 67
   for workgroups, 210–211
billboards, for soft features, 52, 54
binary choice, for changing scale, 124
black box model, 2, 8, 10
blended choice, for changing scale, 124
blocks, comprehensive plan data on, 106
BMPs. *See* best management practices (BMPs)
Boston (Mass.), regional plan for, 72–74
Boulder (Colo.), rail service in, 194–195
British Columbia (Canada)
   comprehensive planning in, 109n1, 110
   hazard planning in, 144–146
   land conservation planning in, 214–215
   zoning development capacity analysis in, 171n2
British Columbia, University of, 144
Brown, Tim, 120
budget, staying within, 3, 19–20
Buildable Area layer, 46
building permits, 179, 180
build-out analysis, 115, 163–164
Build-Out Wizard
   capabilities of, 216, 217, 245
   case study, 87–89, 99
   for comprehensive plans, 107
   in creating 3-D scenes, 47
   for growth projections, 76–80, 82, 83, 84, 85
   in natural resources plans, 160, 161
   role of, xxvi
   in site selection and assessment, 141
   in zoning analysis, 166–169
built structures. *See also* housing
   comprehensive plan data on, 106

footprints of, 169, 170
in 3-D scenes, 41, 43, 44, 45, 47, 187
Bureau of Land Management, 226
buses. *See* regional land-use and transportation plans; transportation plans

CAD systems, 38, 42, 44
California, Klamath River dam removal in, 55–56
"calling" a script, 177n1
Calumet County (Wis.), agriculture planning in, 147–148
Canada
    comprehensive planning in, 109n1, 110
    hazard planning in, 144–146
    land conservation planning in, 214–215
    zoning development capacity analysis in, 171n2
capacities, operating, 177, 180
capacity utilization, estimating, 171
capital costs, in cost-of-services analysis, 177
capital improvements, 164
Capital Improvements Programs (CIPs), 164, 176
cars. *See also* roadways; traffic
    estimating emissions from, 111–112, 113
    in 3-D scenes, 37, 38
case studies. *See also* teaching examples
    city comprehensive plan, 115–117, 212–213
    comprehensive transportation plan, 118–120
    dam removal, 55–56
    hazard assessment and planning, 144–146
    land conservation planning, 214–215
    land use and transportation integration, 131–132
    natural areas plans, 158–161
    regional plans, 72–74, 95–97, 131–134
    transit-oriented development, 194–195
    visions and values, 98–99, 133–134
    wind farm, 57–59
categories, in site selection and assessment, 138
census data, sources of, 12. *See also* data; U.S. Census Bureau

change, forces of, 6–7
change models, in scenario planning, 16, 18
change projections, 75. *See also* growth projections
changes, including recent, 51. *See also* forces of change
charrettes, 61–62, 199, 201. *See also* focus groups; presentations; public involvement; public meetings
chip game, 66, 98, 99, 115, 133, 212. *See also* map exercises
CIPs (Capital Improvements Programs), 164, 176
citizens. *See* public involvement; public meetings
Civil Resources, LLC, 212
Clean Air Act Amendments of 1990, 102
clickers. *See* keypad polling
Clone tool, 66, 125, 153, 180
closed model. *See* black box model
CLUPs (comprehensive land-use plans), 118–120
coastal communities, CommunityViz application in, 226
coefficient-based impact models, 30, 177
coefficients, defined, 30
Colby-George, Judy, 202
collaboration, in public meetings, 198
Colorado
    comprehensive plans in, 115–117, 212–213
    transit-oriented development in, 194–195
commercial buildings
    comparing access to, 111, 112
    in growth projections, 79, 110–111
    site selection for, 141–143
Common Impacts Wizard. *See also* impact models
    capabilities of, 244
    for comprehensive plans, 107–108
    in growth analysis flowchart, 82
    rate-based impact models in, 29
    in regional plan case study, 96
communication design, 26, 68. *See also* presentations; public involvement; public meetings
Community Oriented Geography, 87
community planning. *See also* local comprehensive planning
    creating area profile in, 5–6

decision-making framework in, 8–10
describing goals in, 10
fundamental questions in, xvi
key people and organizations in, 7–8
overview, 1–2
problems and forces of change in, 6–7
vision statements in (*see* visioning)
community service costs, xiv, xv
community vulnerability assessments, 226
CommunityViz. *See also specific tools*
    consultants, 229–230
    defined, xiii
    introduction to, xvii–xviii
    overview, xxv–xxix
    performance best practices, 234–237
    readiness self-assessment, 228–229
    resources, 230
    roots and development of, xviii
    scope of, xviii–xix
    staffing for, 229
    uses outside planning departments, 223–227
commuting time, 85, 241. *See also* transportation plans
comparative community indicators, 189–190
comprehensive land-use plans (CLUPs), 118–120
comprehensive plans. *See also* local comprehensive planning
    documents supporting, 164
    land-use section of, 102 (*see also* land-use planning)
    living, 26–27, 68, 224
    role and timing of, 101–102
    shortcoming of traditional, 62
    support applications for, 122
comprehensive transportation plans (CTPs), 118–120
compromise techniques, 52–53. *See also* trade-offs
computers. *See also* technology
    community planning role of, xvi–xvii
    equipment checklist, 13
    required resources and staff, 11–12, 13, 229
conditions, in natural resource plans, 151–152
Congress for the New Urbanism, 118, 119
Connecticut, commercial development in, 190n1

Consensus Building Institute, 98
conservation, large-scale planning for, 214–215. *See also* environmental concerns
considerations, vs. requirements, 137
consistency, in presentations, 204
constraint areas, 105, 168–169, 170
context, in data presentation, 12
contour lines, in 3-D scenes, 41
conventional systems, modeling, 6
core value statements, 90, 91. *See also* value mapping
cost information, in regional plans, 122
cost-of-community-services studies, 164
cost-of-services analysis
    data needs and sources, 177
    defined, 164, 176
    pro forma analysis vs., 180
    setting up, 177–179
    subdivisions and land development in, 179–180
    teaching example, 180–184
    using, 179
cross-correlation analysis, 208
cross-departmental planning, 225–227
cross-organizational cooperation, 225–227
crowds, as knowledge source, 13. *See also* public involvement
CTPs (comprehensive transportation plans), 118–120
current conditions, in comprehensive plans, 106
custom analysis, of zoning development capacity, 170–171
custom impact models. *See also* dynamic analysis; impact models
    choosing correct, 31–32
    coefficient-based, 30
    in cost-of-services analysis, 177, 180
    creating, 28–32
    external, 31, 76, 81, 82
    rate-based, 29–30
    role and timing of, 28
    for site selection and assessment, 138
    spatially dependent, 31
    types of, 28–32, 177
Custom Impacts Wizard
    capabilities of, 244–245
    in cost-of-services analysis, 177
    in growth analysis flowchart, 82
    impact models vs., 28
custom scripts, for external models, 31n2, 177n1

dam removal case study, 55
dashboard format, 27, 224
data. *See also* information; *specific plans*
    in analysis design, 22
    for area profile, 5–6
    best practices and ethics, 12
    checklist, 13
    for comprehensive plans, 104–106, 109–110
    for cost-of-services analysis, 177, 179
    design review presentation of, 192–193
    in form-based code analysis, 192–193
    for growth projections, 82–83, 84
    management techniques, 224–225, 231–233
    missing, 233
    in project organization, 2
    regional land-use and transportation plans, 121–123, 131
    for resource plans, 149–151, 155
    sources of, 2, 12, 238–242
    for 3-D scenes, 41–42
    for zoning development capacity analysis, 133–134, 166, 167–169
decision making
    emotion vs. reason in, 24
    framework for, 8–10, 144–145, 146
    public meetings guiding, 199
    scenario planning in, 15 (*see also* scenario planning)
    tools for, xxv, 121, 244–245
decisions, vs. information, 10
Declaration of Community Heart & Soul Beliefs, xx
Delaware, watershed plan in, 160–161
demographic information data sources, 208, 238
DEMs (digital elevation models), 41, 191
density
    data sources, 239
    in growth projections, 78–79
    meaning of, 204
    as spatially dependent impact, 31
    in zoning analysis, 167–168, 170
Denver (Colo.), rail service in, 194–195
design. *See also* geodesign; Land Use Designer
    of communication, 26, 68

    multimedia, 24–26 (*see also* 3-D project design)
    as spatially dependent impact, 31
Design Centre for Sustainability, 144
design review boards, 165
design reviews
    guidelines for, 164–165
    indicators for, 189–190
    leaders of, 165
    role of, 185, 224
    teaching example, 190–193
    3-D modeling for, 185–188
design standards, xiv
desirability surfaces, 80–81, 85, 86
destinations, as spatially dependent impact, 31
developers, cost commitments by, 176. *See also* cost-of-services analysis
development. *See* planned developments; planned unit developments (PUDs)
development capacity, 164–169. *See also* zoning development capacity analysis
development patterns data sources, 239
digital elevation models (DEMs), 41, 191
digitizing, of hand sketches, 199
displays, best practices for, 216, 218. *See also* reports
diversity
    analysis complexity vs. stakeholders', 20–21
    as spatially dependent impact, 31
Dodson Associates, 98
Donley & Associates, Inc., 115, 160, 194–195
Doran, Leanne, 95
drafting, 3-D modeling for, 188–189. *See also* 3-D project design
driveways, in 3-D scenes, 47–48
Dunnington, Fred, 87
Durango (Colo.), comprehensive plan for, 115–117
dynamic analysis, 32–35, 236. *See also* impact models
dynamic attribute formulas, 33
dynamic attributes, 33
dynamic charts, 243
dynamic formulas, 246

EBM (ecosystem-based management), 226
economic activity, data source, 2, 241

economic development, CommunityViz application in, 226
ecosystem-based management (EBM), 226
efficiency factors, in zoning analysis, 169
electronic map tables, 66
emergency response, 108, 116, 225
endangered species, data sources, 242
Endless Energy Corporation, 59
engagement, in CommunityViz output, xxiv
environmental concerns
    data sources, 2, 242
    driving future planning, xv
    large-scale planning for, 214–215
    in visioning process, 134
Environmental Systems Research Institute, Inc. (Esri), xxv
Envision Utah, 133–134
Esri (Environmental Systems Research Institute, Inc.), xxv
ethics, 12, 23. See also best management practices (BMPs)
examples. See teaching examples
Excel, maintaining lookup tables in, 30
Exeter (R.I.)
    heart-and-soul places in, 150
    visioning and value mapping for, 98–99
experts, as knowledge source, 13
exporting tables, 216
external impact models
    in cost-of-services analysis, 177
    creating, 31
    for growth projections, 76, 81, 82
    integration with, 247
External Table Links
    for comprehensive plans, 110–111
    in cost-of-services analysis, 178, 182
    polling keypads used with, 208
    in regional planning, 125
    steps in using, 31
    in visioning process, 70

Faber, Brenda, 154
factor scores, 135, 136–137, 147–148
families, data sources on, 238
Federal Emergency Management Agency (FEMA), 144
Federal Energy Regulatory Commission (FERC), 55, 56

Federal Highway Administration, supporting scenario planning, 118
federal lands, CommunityViz application for, 226
FEMA (Federal Emergency Management Agency), 144
fences, as compromise technique, 53
FERC (Federal Energy Regulatory Commission), 55, 56
field of view, 207, 218, 219
file size management
    aerial imagery, 41
    best practices, 232
    large study areas, 53
    metro and regional models, 45
    soft or numerous features, 52–53
    terrain data, 41, 54
financial analysis. See cost-of-services analysis
fiscal impact analysis. See cost-of-services analysis
fishnet pattern, 69. See also analysis grids; raster data
five-minute rule, 206–207
focus groups, 62, 67–68, 200. See also charrettes
footprints, in zoning analysis, 169, 170. See also built structures
forces of change, 6–7
forecasts, vs. projections, 75. See also growth projections
Foresee Consulting, Inc., 98, 133–134, 212–213
formats, data management, 231
form-based codes. See also physical forms
    defined, 185
    indicators for, 189–190
    role of, 164–165
    teaching example, 190–193
    3-D modeling for, 185–187, 188–189
Formula Editor, 35
Formula Wizard, 35
formulas
    for changing scale, 123–124
    dynamic, 33, 246
    tools for creating, 35
Fort Lupton (Colo.), comprehensive plan in, 212–213
"4 Ds," spatially dependent impact based on, 31

fragmentation, in natural resource planning, 154
FreeMind software, 91n2

Gantt charts, for time management, 19
Geodata Services, Inc., 214, 215
geodatabase, dynamic analysis using, 32
geodesign, xvii, 28, 67, 176, 199
geographic areas. See study areas
geographic information, sources for, 239
geographic information system (GIS)
    baseline data from, 41 (see also 3-D project design)
    CAD systems vs., 38
    computer requirements for, 11–12
    defined, xvii
    hiring professional for, 11–12
    in land-use planning, 102
    natural resource data in, 103
    origin of, 135
    presentations including, 204
    terminology, 32
geospatial data sources, 12
GIS. See geographic information system (GIS)
goals
    choosing scenarios for, 18
    for creating area profiles, 5
    describing, 10
Google Earth
    active materials and, 39
    in comprehensive plan, 116
    creating scenes in, 40–45 (see also 3-D project design)
    for design reviews, 186
    for form-based codes, 186
    for hazard assessment, 145
    shadows and lighting in, 38
    timeline in, 80
    in visioning process, 134
Google Earth Exporter
    data for, 41
    for design reviews and form-based codes, 186
    for metro and regional models, 44
    other platforms vs., 36–37
    for 3-D website scenes, 220
government. See also legislation; political planning; specific organizations
    CommunityViz non-planning application in, 225

infrastructure funded by, xiv, 176 (*see also* cost-of-services analysis)
grids. *See* analysis grids
ground cover, in 3-D scenes, 46, 54. *See also* 3-D project design
growth allocation spreadsheets, 110
growth challenge game. *See* chip game
growth models, 16, 72–74
growth projections. *See also* population
  combining decision tools for, 82
  in comprehensive plans, 106–107, 110–111
  data needs and sources, 82–83
  defined, 75
  external models for, 76, 81, 82
  in regional planning, 128–130
  teaching example, 83–86, 128–132
  tools for, 75–82, 83, 84–86 (*see also* Allocator tool; Build-Out Wizard; Land Use Designer; TimeScope™)

hardscaping, 41, 187
hazard assessment and planning, 144–146, 242
HAZUS-MH, 144, 145, 146
health and human services, CommunityViz application in, 225–226
Heart & Soul Community Planning approach, xix, xxi
Heart of the Rockies Initiative (HOTR), 214–215
heart-and-soul resources. *See also* value mapping
  area profile data, 6
  comprehensive plans missing, 62
  defined, xvi, 90
  identifying, xv, 66, 191, 239
  in natural resource plans, 150
  in planning philosophy, xxi
  in project organization, 2
history
  in identifying trends, 5
  in project organization, 1–2
Hoch, Greg, 117
HOTR (Heart of the Rockies Initiative), 214–215
household income data source, 241
housing
  analyzing future demand for, 112, 113
  data sources, 2, 238, 239
  multifamily, 168

planning support applications for, 122
  in pro forma analysis, 180
  in 3-D scenes, 46
hub scenarios, 110, 111, 112, 113
HUD (U.S. Department of Housing and Urban Development), xiv

ICLEI Star Community Index, 139
iconic features, in 3-D scenes, 51. *See also* heart-and-soul resources; landmarks
Idaho, land conservation planning in, 214–215
illustrations
  in form-based codes, 185
  tools for, xxvi, 80
image captures, 216, 218, 221. *See also* photos; screenshots
image sizes, 218
IMPACS (Integrated Model for Planning and Cost Scenarios) tool, 134
Impact Analysis tools, 30, 99. *See also* Common Impacts Wizard; Custom Impacts Wizard
impact indicators. *See* indicators
impact models. *See also* Common Impacts Wizard; custom impact models; dynamic analysis
  in analysis design, 22
  for comprehensive plans, 107–108
  external, 31, 76, 81, 82, 177
  in scenario planning, 16, 18
  transit development case study, 194
impartiality of data, 12
implementation plan, in visioning process, 68
income data source, 241
indicators
  in analysis design, 22
  for anticipating problems, 223
  for design review, 189–190
  in dynamic analysis, 33
  examples of, 29
  for form-based codes, 189–190
  in natural resource planning, 152, 155, 156
  presenting detail on, 203
  in scenario planning, 16, 17, 18
  in value mapping, 93
infill development analysis, 115
information. *See also* data
  archiving, 224–225

conveying, 198 (*see also* presentations; public involvement; public meetings)
  decisions vs., 10
  for effective 3-D scenes, 50
  using enough good, 5–6, 124, 153
infrastructure, xiv, 176, 224. *See also* cost-of-community-services studies; *specific features*
input, assumptions as, 34
Integrated Model for Planning and Cost Scenarios (IMPACS) tool, 134
interaction. *See* presentations; public involvement
intermediate processing, for changing scale, 124
Intermodal Surface Transportation Efficiency Act (ISTEA) of 1991, 102
Internet. *See* technology; websites
intersections, in 3-D scenes, 46–47
intuitive controls, creating, 246, 247
inventory, requirements for, 2
ISTEA (Intermodal Surface Transportation Efficiency Act) of 1991, 102

jobs data
  in design review, 192, 193
  source of, 241

Kelowna (British Columbia, Canada), local comprehensive planning in, 109n1, 110
Keyhole Markup Language (KML) files, 36n1
keypad polling. *See also* surveys
  alternatives to, 222
  city comprehensive planning, 115, 116, 212, 213
  natural areas planning, 159
  need for, 11
  paper backup for, 206
  regional planning, 72, 134
  tips for using, 207–208
  in value mapping, 93
  in vision and values planning, 99
Killingly (Conn.), commercial development in, 190n1
Kimley-Horn and Associates, Inc., 118–120, 131–132
Klamath River, dam removal case study, 55

KML (Keyhole Markup Language) files, 36n1
KMZ files, 36, 36n1, 47, 221–222

LaCrosse County (Wis.), agriculture planning in, 147
land consumption, in comprehensive plans, 111
Land Evaluation and Site Assessment (LESA) system, 139, 147–148
land evaluation factors, 147
land trusts, 215
Land Use Designer. *See also* land-use planning; Sketch tools
    capabilities of, 84–85, 245
    for comprehensive plans, 107
    as data source, 83
    in growth analysis flowchart, 82
    lookup tables in, 30
    role and timing of, xxvi, 75–76, 77
    in visioning process, 66–67
land-development regulations, 164, 179, 224
LandFrag Wizard, 154
landmarks, 42, 43, 47, 51, 108. *See also* heart-and-soul resources
landowners, objections from, 108
landscape maps, 41
landscaping, in 3-D scenes, 44, 187
land-use data sources, 239
land-use overlay districts, 106
land-use planning. *See also* Land Use Designer
    comprehensive, 106, 115, 118–120 (*see also* comprehensive plans)
    defined, xviii
    natural resource inventory in, 103
    parts of, 102
    regional (*see* regional land-use and transportation plans)
    in zoning analysis, 167
Layer Transparency, 52
layers. *See also* analysis layers
    archiving, 225
    in GIS systems, 32
Leadership in Energy and Environmental Design (LEED) system, 139
learning, in public meetings, 198
learning curves, of workgroups, 209–210
Lee, Harley, 59
LEED (Leadership in Energy and Environmental Design) system, 139

LEED-Neighborhood Development, 139
LEED-Sustainable Sites, 139
legislation. *See also* government
    Clean Air Act Amendments of 1990, 102
    Intermodal Surface Transportation Efficiency Act of 1991, 102
    Safe, Accountable, Flexible, Efficient Transportation Equity Act: A Legacy for Users of 2005, 102
    Washington County Growth and Conservation Act, 133
LESA (Land Evaluation and Site Assessment) system, 139, 147–148
levels of service, 177
LIDAR imagery, 41, 54
Lieske, Scott, 180n2
lighting, in 3-D scenes, 38–39
limitations, in project planning, 20–21
live sketching, in visioning process, 66–67
living comprehensive plans, 26–27, 68, 224. *See also* comprehensive plans
local comprehensive planning. *See also* comprehensive plans
    case studies, 115–117, 212–213
    creating scenarios for, 106–107, 110–111
    current condition description in, 106
    data needs, 104–106, 109–110
    impact analysis in, 111–112
    impact modeling in, 107–108
    process steps, 105
    public participation in, 108–109
    role and timing of, 104
    teaching example, 109–114
    zoning ordinances linked to, 163 (*see also* zoning)
location factors, 143
logistics, for pubic meetings, 205–206
long-range transportation plans, 122
lookup tables, creating and maintaining, 29–30
lot coverage data, 192
Lowe's, 118
low-tech visioning, 65–66
lumpers, at public meetings, 202–203

Maine, natural areas plan in, 158–159
Manchester (Vt.), wind farm visualization in, 57–59
map exercises, 66, 68–71, 94. *See also* chip game

mapping special places, 90, 94. *See also* heart-and-soul resources; value mapping
maps
    in charrette preparation, 199
    conflicting data on, 232–233
    for cost-of-services analysis, 179, 180
    producing, 11
    smart location, 140, 141
    sources of, 2, 239
    in visioning process, 68–69 (*see also* visioning)
Mary Means and Associates, Inc., 118–120
Maryland, watershed plan in, 160–161
Massachusetts, regional plan in, 72–74
material forms, in creating 3-D scenes, 50
materials. *See* active materials
Matrix Analysis with All Values, 159
McHarg, Ian, 135
meetings. *See* public meetings
metro models, creating 3-D scenes for, 44–45
Metropolitan Planning Organizations (MPOs), 102
Middlebury (Vt.), build-out study, 87–89
military bases, planning for, 226–227
mixed uses, in zoning analysis, 168
mobile polling platforms, 222
ModelBuilder 3D, in transit-oriented development, 195
models
    black box and transparent, 2, 8–10
    choosing, 31–32
    in scenario planning, 16–17
Monopoly® buildings, as compromise technique, 46, 53
Montana, land conservation planning in, 214–215
Monte Carlo simulators, in growth projections, 81
Mooresville (N.C.), transportation plan for, 118–120
mosaic, in 3-D scenes, 45–46
MPOs (Metropolitan Planning Organizations), 102
multimedia design, 24–26. *See also* 3-D project design
multiple-attribute tracking, 124
municipal budget priorities planning, 225

naming conventions, in data management, 231, 232
Nashville (Tenn.), land-use and transportation plan for, 131–132
National Oceanic and Atmospheric Administration, 226
National Park Service, 226
natural resources, 151, 242. *See also* environmental concerns; resource plans
Natural Resources Canada, 144–146
Natural Resources Conservation Service, 2, 139
natural resources inventory, 103, 158
The Nature Conservancy, 98
navigational cues, in 3-D scenes, 51
neighborhood development plans, 122
neighborhoods
  in comprehensive plans, 106, 108
  development proposals for, 43–44
  study area for, 5
  suitability scoring systems for, 139–141
nested suitability, 138
network access points, 121. *See also* transportation networks
Network Analyst, 85, 111, 116, 123
New England Planning Concepts, 158
nontraditional indicators, in scenario planning, 16
Noonkester, Matt, 119
normalized scores, 137
North Carolina, transportation planning in, 118–120
Northampton County (Va.), watershed plan in, 160–161
null values, in data management, 231
numeric build-out, in growth projections, 78, 79

OCPs (official community plans), 109. *See also* comprehensive plans
online polling, 208. *See also* keypad polling
Onorato, Dan, 96, 97
open space planning. *See* parks and open space planning
operating capacities, in cost-of-services analysis, 177
operating costs, in cost-of-services analysis, 177
Optimizer Wizard, 96, 153–154
Oregon, Klamath River dam removal in, 55–56
organizations, identifying key, 2, 7–8. *See also* stakeholders
Orton Family Foundation, xviii, xxi, 98, 115
output, indicators and attribute values as, 34
overlay analysis, 135

PacifiCorp, 55–56
Painter tool, 66, 125, 153, 180
Palette tool, 125
parcels, 167. *See also* zoning development capacity analysis
Parko, Tom, 213
parks and open space planning, 122, 226, 242
Pathways-DM (Decision Making), 144–145
pedestrian networks, 121
Pennsylvania
  regional planning in, 95–97
  state funding for plans in, 102
people, key. *See* stakeholders
performance best practices, 234–237
permitting, CommunityViz application for, 224
photos. *See also* aerial imagery; image captures
  sources of, 240
  in 3-D scenes, 41, 43, 45–46 (*see also* 3-D project design)
Photoshop, for soft features, 52
physical forms, 91, 92, 93. *See also* form-based codes
physical metrics, in value mapping, 94
pie charts, 111, 138, 140
Pierce, Kay, 96
Pittsburgh, University of, 95
place. *See* study areas
Placeways LLC, xviii, 25, 57–59, 109n1, 171n2
planned developments, 43–44, 106
planned unit developments (PUDs), 81, 129–130
planner's judgments, in zoning analysis, 169
planning. *See also* project planning; *specific types*
  beliefs about, xiii
  connecting processes with, 224–225
  defined, xvi
  past, present, and future of, xiii–xiv, xv, xvii, xxi–xxii
  support for departments outside of, 225–227
  traditional process of, xix
  using this book for, xxii–xxiii
planning areas. *See* study areas
planning study design. *See* project planning; scenario planning
Planning Works, 115
political boundaries, defining study areas, 5
political planning, xiii–xiv, xvii. *See also* government; legislation
polling technology, 222. *See also* keypad polling
polygon features. *See also specific*
  analysis grids, 125–126, 140–141, 151
  changing size of (*see* scale)
  for comprehensive plans, 104, 109–110
  in creating 3-D scenes, 42, 45, 54
  for growth projections, 76, 78, 79, 83
population
  affecting future planning, xv
  data sources, 2, 238
  in old generation planning, xiv
  predicting increase in (*see* growth projections)
potential growth areas (PGAs), 109, 110
presentations. *See also* charrettes; public involvement; public meetings; reports
  aids for, 44, 248
  analysis design for, 21–22, 23
  best practices, 12, 188
  computing resources for, 11
  electronic polling in, 207–208, 222 (*see also* keypad polling)
  multimedia design benefits for, 24–25
  small-group, 209–211
  testing initial, 23, 48
  time spent preparing, 19
  using 3-D scenes in, 206–207 (*see also* 3-D project design)
  in visioning process, 67 (*see also* visioning)
pro forma analysis, 176, 180
probability-based allocation method, 131
problems
  anticipating, 223–224
  defining, 6–7

processes
  best practices in, 12
  connecting plans with, 224–225
  steps in, 1–2, 4–10 (*see also specific*)
processing time, 202, 211, 234–237. *See also* time schedules
project planning. *See also specific plan types*
  analysis design in, 21–24
  archiving work from, 224–225
  communication design in, 26
  comprehensive plan design in, 26–27
  multimedia design in, 24–26
  time and budget in, 19–20 (*see also* time schedules)
  trade-offs and limitations in, 20–21
projections
  data management, 231
  forecasts vs., 75 (*see also* growth projections)
projectors, for presentations, 11
projects
  defined, xxiv
  planning beyond, 223–227
  websites for (*see* websites)
property ownership data source, 241
public involvement. *See also* charrettes; presentations; public meetings
  in agriculture planning, 147, 148
  in build-out study, 87, 89
  in county-level comprehensive planning, 95–97
  in hazard assessment, 144
  in local comprehensive planning, 108–109, 112–114, 212–215
  in natural resource planning, 150, 158–159, 161
  in new generation planning, xxi–xxii
  in old generation planning, xiv
  as planning philosophy, xviii
  for successful planning, xiii
  in transit-oriented development, 194–195
  transparency for, 2 (*see also* transparency)
  in transportation planning, 115–117
  in visioning process, 66–67, 72–74, 98–99, 133–134
public meetings. *See also* charrettes; presentations; public involvement
  agendas for, 199, 200–201

role and timing of, 198–199
  techniques and best practices for, 202–206
  technology improving, 197, 198
  understanding audiences at, 202–203
public outreach meeting agenda, 200
public safety, CommunityViz application in, 225
PUDs. *See* planned unit developments (PUDs)
pull factors, 80–81
push factors, 80

quality of data, 12
questions, articulating, 8. *See also* decision making

rail transit, 194–195. *See also* regional land-use and transportation plans; transportation plans
raster data, 135, 150–151, 154. *See also* analysis grids; fishnet pattern
rate-based impact models, 29–30, 177
raw scores, 137
realism, in 3-D scenes, 50–51
recreation planning, 226
Regional Economic Models, Inc. (REMI), 81
regional land-use and transportation plans. *See also* land-use planning; transportation plans
  case study, 131–132
  data needs, 121–123
  role and timing of, 121
  teaching example, 127–130
  tools for, 123–126
regional planning
  case studies, 72–74, 95–97, 214–215
  comprehensive, 122 (*see also* comprehensive plans)
  creating 3-D scenes for, 44–45
  future of, xv
  legislation governing, 102
  study areas within, 5
  support applications for, 122
regional resource and watershed plans, 122
regional trails and pathways plans, 122
reports. *See also* presentations
  best practices for, 216, 218
  3-D scene images in, 218
  web-ready, 218, 220

Reports tool, 216, 217
requirements, vs. considerations, 137
resource plans. *See also* heart-and-soul resources
  case studies, 158–161
  conditions and targets, 151–152
  data needs and sources for, 149–151, 242
  teaching example, 154–157
  tools for, 152–154
  valuing resources in, 151
Rhode Island
  heart-and-soul places in, 150
  visioning and value mapping in, 98–99
roadways. *See also* cars; traffic; transportation plans
  comprehensive plan data on, 104
  cost-of-services analysis, 180, 184
  lane data, 122
  potholes in, 225
  in regional planning, 45, 121 (*see also* regional land-use and transportation plans)
  in 3-D scenes, 41, 43, 46–47, 189
Rothert, Steve, 55

Safe, Accountable, Flexible, Efficient Transportation Equity Act: A Legacy for Users (SAFETEA-LU) of 2005, 102
satellite imagery, 154. *See also* aerial imagery
Saved Views tool, 65, 203–204, 211
scale
  accessories showing, 54
  in analysis grids, 125–126
  in comprehensive plans, 109
  formulas for changing, 123–124
  in zoning analysis, 167
Scenario Comparison tool, 65, 67, 244
scenario planning
  case study, 118–120
  characteristics of, 16–17
  in decision-making process, 15
  defined, xvii, 15
  geodesign instead of, 18–19
  options available for, 3
  project design influenced by, 18
  steps in, 15–16
Scenario Sketch tools, 66, 141
Scenario 3D™, xxvii–xxix, 37, 248–250. *See also* 3-D project design

Scenario 3D Exporter, xxvii–xxix, 47, 249–250. *See also* 3-D project design
Scenario 3D Viewer, xxvii, xxix, 250. *See also* 3-D project design
Scenario 360™. *See also specific tools*
  for agriculture planning, 148
  capability overview, xxv–xxvi
  common applications of, xxvii
  component diagram, 29
  CustomScript functions, 177n1
  in design review, 189–190
  dynamic analysis in, 32–35 (*see also* dynamic analysis)
  features, xxvi, 243–248 (*see also specific features*)
  in form-based code analysis, 189–190
  Grid functions, 151
  for hazard assessment, 145
  in natural resource planning, 151
  performance recommendations, 236
  3-D visualization in, xxvii
  in transit-oriented development, 195
  in visioning process, 134
  workgroups learning to use, 210
scenarios
  in analysis design, 23
  for comprehensive plans, 106–107, 110–111
  public creating, 66–67
  single vs. multiple, 34–35
  tools for building, 243, 244
  viewing multiple, xxvi, 202, 205, 206–207
  in visioning process, 65–68
SCENE files, 221
schools. *See also* universities, planning for
  CommunityViz application for, 226
  in cost-of-services analysis, 180–182, 184
scientific modeling, 152–153
screenshots, 218, 219. *See also* image captures
set-asides, in zoning analysis, 170
setbacks, in zoning analysis, 168–169, 170
setup
  building, 32
  defined, 28
  tools for, 35
sewers, in cost-of-services analysis, 182–183, 184

shaders. *See* active materials
shadows, in 3-D scenes, 38–39
sidewalks. *See* roadways
simplification, of presentation data, 204
simulation method, 16n1
site assessment factors, 147
site selection and assessment. *See also* study areas
  LESA system, 139, 147–148
  role and timing of, 135–136
  scoring systems in, 139–141
  suitability concepts in, 136–137
  teaching example, 141–143
  tools for, 137–139
SiteBuilder 3D, 99, 116, 145, 195
sites, development proposals for, 43–44
site-specific indicators, 189
Sketch tools. *See also* Land Use Designer
  in form-based code modeling, 188–189
  in natural resource planning, 153
  in regional planning, 125
  in scenario planning, 16, 18
  in visioning process, 67
sketching, live, 66–67
SketchUp models
  for charrettes, 201
  in creating 3-D scenes, 38, 41, 42, 44, 47, 48
  in visioning process, 134
slider bars, 34, 68, 107, 136, 138. *See also* assumptions; *specific tools*
Smart Growth On the Ground, 144
smart location maps, 140, 141
SmartCode system, 185
soft features, in 3-D scenes, 52
software, specialized, 13–14. *See also* technology
soil map data source, 2
solutions, exploring. *See* alternative solutions
Spatial Alternatives, 158
spatial build-out, in growth projections, 78, 79
spatially dependent impact models, 31, 177
special places. *See* heart-and-soul resources; value mapping
splitters, at public meetings, 202–203
spoke scenarios, 110, 111, 112, 113
spreadsheet models, 177–179, 181, 182–183

spreadsheets
  external (*see* External Table Links)
  in local comprehensive plans, 110
  for rate-based impact models, 30
Squamish (British Columbia, Canada), hazard planning in, 144–146
St. Clair, Holly, 74
staff requirements, 11–12, 13, 229
stakeholders, 2, 7–8, 20–21
Star Community Index, 139
statutory factors, in zoning analysis, 169. *See also* government; legislation
streets. *See* roadways
strengths, weaknesses, opportunities, and threats (SWOT) analysis, 2, 64–65
study areas. *See also* site selection and assessment
  analysis scale and size of, 20–21
  for comprehensive plans, 106
  defining, 4–5
  file size for large, 53
  goals for, 10
  in growth projections, 78, 79, 83–84
  key people and organizations in, 7–8
  natural and man-made systems in, 5, 18
  problems and forces of change in, 6–7
  profile of, 5–6
  in project organization, 1
  questions about, 8 (*see also* decision making)
  size of, 5, 41
  in zoning analysis, 167
subdivision, 164, 179–180
subjective feel, in 3-D scenes, 51–52
sub-suitability analysis, 138
suburban scenarios, in comprehensive plan, 110, 111, 112, 113
suitability analysis. *See also* site selection and assessment
  case study, 115
  concepts, 135, 136–137
  defined, 135
  of natural resources, 151
  role and timing of, 135–136
  tools for, 137–139, 140
suitability score, 135, 136–137, 147–148
Suitability Wizard
  for agriculture planning, 148
  capabilities of, 245
  in growth projections, 80, 81, 82

in land conservation planning, 215
in regional plan case study, 96
role of, xxvi, 137
in site selection and assessment, 137–138, 142–143
in transportation planning, 120, 128–129
in zoning analysis, 173–174
support, for non-planning departments, 225–227
surveys, 115, 116, 134, 212. *See also* keypad polling; public involvement
Sussex County (Del.), watershed plan in, 160–161
SWOT (strengths, weaknesses, opportunities, and threats) analysis, 2, 64–65
Symbol Saver tool, 65, 211
symbology tools, 139, 140
system characteristics, in value mapping, 92
systems. *See also specific*
in analysis design, 21–22
natural and man-made, 5, 18 (*see also* study areas)

tables
exporting, 216
joining, 233
tangible forms, in value mapping, 92
targets
in comprehensive plans, 27
in natural resource planning, 151–152, 157
in scenario planning, 16
TAZS. *See* traffic analysis zones (TAZs)
teaching examples
cost-of-services analysis, 180–184
design reviews, 190–193
form-based codes, 190–193
growth projections, 83–86, 128–132
local comprehensive planning, 109–114
regional land-use and transportation plans, 127–130
resource plans, 154–157
site selection and assessment, 141–143
3-D project design, 45–49, 190–193
visioning, 68–71
zoning development capacity analysis, 171–175
technical planning, xiii, xvii, 11–12, 13

technology. *See also* computers
capacity limits, 20–21, 42
electronic map tables, 66
needs for multimedia design, 26
presentation tips, 205–206 (*see also* presentations; public involvement; public meetings)
specialized software, 13–14
in visioning process, 73–74 (*see also* visioning)
web resource options, 222
templates, analysis, 123, 225, 247
Tennessee, land-use and transportation plan in, 131–132
tenure, data sources on, 238
TerraCognito GIS, 55–56, 144
terrain, in 3-D scenes, 39–40, 41, 54
textures, in 3-D scenes, 38, 39, 46, 52
thousand/thousand rule of thumb, 67, 207
3-D models, sources of, 240
3-D project design. *See also* multimedia design
archiving work from, 225
art of making effective, 50–52
charrettes benefiting from, 199
choosing platform for, 36–37
creating scenes in, 40–45
data management best practices for, 232
for design review, 185–188
explained, 37–40
for form-based codes, 185–187, 188–189
making static images from, 218, 219
performance best practices, 235–237
project design, 24–25
role and timing of, 36
solutions to challenges in, 52–54
teaching examples, 45–49, 190–193
on websites, 220–221
3-D visualization, 36, 243
360 Analysis tab, 210
tiles, in 3-D scenes, 45
time schedules
in comprehensive plans, 27
in creating 3-D scenes, 48–49
processing time guidelines, 202, 211, 234–237
for public meetings, 200, 201, 206–207
tasks completed with, 19–20
for workgroup meetings, 209–210
working within, 3, 4

TimeScope™
capabilities of, 245
for comprehensive plans, 107
for growth projections, 76, 80–81, 82, 83
in pro forma analysis, 180
role of, xxvi
TimeScope Animator, 107
TINs (triangulated irregular networks), 41
topology data management, 231
Topsham (Maine), natural areas plan in, 158–159
trade-offs, 20–21, 27, 41. *See also* compromise techniques
traditional indicators, in scenario planning, 16
traffic, 111–112, 113, 116, 192. *See also* cars; roadways; transportation plans
traffic analysis zones (TAZs)
in land-use and transportation planning, 132
in regional planning, 74, 121, 124, 127, 130
trains, 194–195. *See also* regional land-use and transportation plans; transportation plans
TransCAD, 116, 132
transects, 185
transit stops, 106, 121, 125, 126
transit-oriented development, 194–195. *See also* regional land-use and transportation plans; transportation plans
transparency
in analysis design, 23–24, 35
black box models vs., 8–10
in cost-of-services analysis, 179
as planning philosophy, xv, xviii
for public involvement, 2
for successful planning, xiii
in 3-D scenes, 38, 39, 52
in value mapping, 94
transportation data source, 241
transportation networks, 121, 122, 126. *See also* regional land-use and transportation plans; transportation plans
transportation plans. *See also* cars; roadways; traffic
case study, 118–120, 194–195
legislation on, 102
regional (*see* regional land-use and transportation plans)

in site selection and assessment, 141–143
transit-oriented development, 194–195
trees
   compromise technique for, 53
   in 3-D scenes, 38, 39, 42, 48, 54
trends, for area profiles, 5
triangulated irregular networks (TINs), 41
tribal government planners, 226

ultra compact scenarios, 110, 111, 112, 113
unconventional systems modeling, 6
undeveloped land, study area for, 5
universities, planning for, 227. *See also* schools; *specific universities*
urban centre scenarios, 110, 111, 112, 113
Urban Systems, Ltd., 109n1, 171n2
U.S. Census Bureau
   as data source, 2
   in population projections, xv, 81, 82, 85
   web address, 82n2
U.S. Department of Agriculture, 139, 147–148
U.S. Department of Housing and Urban Development (HUD), xiv
U.S. Environmental Protection Agency, 2
U.S. Forest Service, 56, 226
U.S. Geological Survey, 2, 41, 56, 146, 191
U.S. Green Building Council, 139
Utah, regional visioning in, 133–134
utility service areas, data on, 106

value, of natural resources, 151
value drivers, 91–93
value elements, 91, 92
value indexes, 93–94
value mapping. *See also* heart-and-soul resources
   case study, 98–99
   core value statement in, 90
   mapping special places vs., 94
   in natural resources planning, 158
   physical form in, 93
   role and timing of, 90, 94
   steps in, 90–91
   value drivers in, 92–93
   value element categories in, 92
   value indexes in, 93–94
value trees, 91–92

value voting, in natural resources planning, 158
Van Meter Williams Pollack, LLP, 194–195
venue, for pubic meetings, 205–206
Vermont
   build-out study in, 87–89
   wind farm visualization in, 57–59
vertex counts, in data management, 231
Victoria (British Columbia, Canada), zoning development capacity analysis in, 171n2
Virginia, watershed plan in, 160–161
vision statements, role of, 62
visioning
   beginning process of, 61–62, 64
   best practices for, 67
   case study, 98–99, 133–134
   in comprehensive plans, 26–27, 62, 106
   current situation assessment, 64–65
   defined, 63
   implementation plan for, 68
   meeting agenda, 201
   process steps, 63
   in regional plans, 133–134
   role and timing of, 63–64
   scenario building in, 65–67
   scenario selection in, 67–68
   teaching example, 68–71
   value mapping in, 90
visual build-out, 78, 79
visualization, 3, 115
Vizhen tool, 134

Washington County (Utah), regional visioning in, 133–134
Washington County Growth and Conservation Act, 133
water
   anticipating problems with, 223
   assessing supply of, 151–152, 180
   coastal community planning, 226
   in cost-of-services analysis, 182–183, 184
   evaluating quality of, 152
   presenting runoff data, 192
   in 3-D scenes, 39, 187
watershed plans, 122
watersheds, 5, 160–161, 215
web-ready reports, 218, 220, 247, 248
WebShots Wizard, 220, 221, 247, 248

websites
   creating and maintaining, 11, 218, 220–222
   data available to public on, 203
   interactive, 134
   for online polling, 208
weighting factors
   in agriculture planning, 148
   with polling keypad data, 208
   in site selection and assessment, 135, 136–137
   in value mapping, 93–94
Westminster (Colo.), transit-oriented development in, 194–195
What If? multivariate allocator, 81
Where conditions, 142
Whitfield, Michael, 215
wind farm case study, 57–59
Winston Associates, 133–134
wireframes, in 3-D scenes, 37–38
wireless keypads. *See* keypad polling
Wisconsin, agriculture planning in, 147–148
Wisconsin, University of, 147, 148
Worcester County (Md.), watershed plan in, 160–161
work plan, step-by-step, 4. *See also* time schedules
workgroups, 209–211
workshops. *See* charrettes; presentations; public meetings
Wyoming, land conservation planning in, 214–215

"you've got to be kidding" test, 79

zoning
   alternative to (*see* form-based codes)
   evaluating future effects of, 76, 77, 79
   in old generation planning, xiv
   purposes of, 163
zoning development capacity analysis
   build-out analysis of, 166–169
   capacity utilization estimates, 171
   custom analysis of, 170–171
   data needed for, 133–134, 166, 167–169
   role and timing of, 166
   teaching example, 171–175
zoning districts, 163
zoning ordinances, 163